THE EUROPEAN UNION SERIES

General Editors: Neill Nugent, William E. Paterson, Vincent Wright

The European Union series is designed to provide an authoritative library
on the European Union ranging from general introductory texts to
definitive assessments of key institutions and actors, policies and policy
processes, and the role of member states.

Books in the series are written by leading scholars in their fields and reflect
the most up-to-date research and debate. Particular attention is paid to
accessibility and clear presentation for a wide audience of students,
practitioners and interested general readers.

The series consists of four major strands:

- general textbooks
- the major institutions and actors
- the main areas of policy
- the member states and the Union.

Launch titles

Desmond Dinan
**Ever Closer Union? An Introduction
to the European Community**

Neill Nugent
**The Government and Politics of the
European Union (Third Edition)**

Forthcoming

Simon Bulmer and Drew Scott
European Union: Economics, Policy and Politics

John Peterson and Elizabeth Bomberg
Decision-making in the European Union

•   •   •   •

David Bell and Chris Lord
Political Parties in the European Union

Simon Bulmer and Wolfgang Wessels
The European Commission (Second Edition)

David Earnshaw and David Judge
The European Parliament

Stephen George and Neill Nugent
The European Commission

Justin Greenwood and Andrew McLoughlin
Representing Interests in the European Union

Fiona Hayes-Renshaw and Helen Wallace
The Council of Ministers

Hjalte Rasmussen
The Court of Justice

Anne Stevens
The Administration of the European Community

•   •   •   •

Michelle Cini
Competition Policy in the European Union

Wyn Grant
The Common Agricultural Policy

Bridid Laffan
The Finances of the European Union

Janne Haaland Matláry
Energy Policy in the European Union

Anand Menon
Defence Policy and the European Union

James Mitchell and Paul McAleavey
Regionalism and Regional Policy in the European Union

John Redmond, René Schwok and Lee Miles
Enlarging the European Union

Hazel Smith
The Foreign Policy of the European Union

•   •   •   •

Simon Bulmer and William E. Paterson
Germany and the European Union

Phil Daniels and Ella Ritchie
Britain and the European Union

Alain Guyomarch, Howard Machin and Ella Ritchie
France in the European Union

Other titles planned include

European Union: A Brief Introduction
The History of the European Union
The European Union Source Book
The European Union Reader
Theories of European Integration
The Political Economy of the European Union

•   •   •   •

The European Union after Maastricht
Social Policy
Environmental Policy
High Technology Policy
External Economic Relations
The European Union and the Third World
Monetary Union
Political Union
The USA and the European Union

•   •   •   •

The European Union and its Member States
Reshaping the States of the Union
Italy and the European Union
Spain and the European Union

The Government and Politics of the European Union

Third Edition

Neill Nugent

MACMILLAN

First edition (*The Government and Politics of the European Community*) 1989
Reprinted 1990 (twice), 1991
Second edition 1991
Reprinted 1991, 1992 (with new postscript)
Third edition (*The Government and Politics of the European Union*) 1994

Published by
THE MACMILLAN PRESS LTD
Houndmills, Basingstoke, Hampshire RG21 2XS
and London
Companies and representatives
throughout the world

ISBN 0–333–61444–5 hardcover
ISBN 0–333–61445–3 paperback

A catalogue record for this book is available
from the British Library.

Copy-edited and typeset by Povey–Edmondson
Okehampton and Rochdale, England

Printed in Great Britain by The Bath Press, Avon

10   9   8   7   6   5   4   3   2
03   02   01   00   99   98   97   96   95

Series Standing Order (The European Union Series)

If you would like to receive future titles in this series as they are published, you can
make use of our standing order facility. To place a standing order please contact
your bookseller or, in case of difficulty, write to us at the address below with your
name and address and the name of the series. Please state with which title you wish
to begin your standing order. (If you live outside the UK we may not have the rights
for your area, in which case we will forward your order to the publisher concerned.)

Standing Order Service, Macmillan Distribution Ltd,
Houndmills, Basingstoke, Hampshire, RG21 2XS, England

Summary of Contents

Contents

List of Tables, Figures, Exhibits and Documents

■ Tables

■ Figures

■ Exhibits

■ Documents

Preface to the Third Edition

So much has happened to Europe since this book appeared in its second edition in 1991 that, as with the first edition, I have felt obliged to undertake a revision much earlier than ideally I would have liked. Again, this edition does not just consist of updating, although there is a great deal of that, but also includes a substantial amount of new material. Included amongst this new material are two new chapters: one on the much discussed and extremely important Treaty on European Union (TEU), and one on the increasingly significant area of external relations.

A major problem in writing this third edition has concerned usage of the terms 'European Community' and 'European Union'. As is explained in Chapter 3, the Treaty on European Union (the so-called Maastricht Treaty), which came into effect in November 1993, created a highly confusing situation in this regard. It did so by incorporating what had come to be commonly known as the European Community into a broader European Union, and by renaming the European Economic Community – which was the most important of the *three* Communities which made up the European Community – the European Community! In other words, under the Treaty on European Union, the European Community is one of three European Communities, and these three Communities are component parts of the European Union. So as to try and keep confusion to a minimum, and so as to avoid repeated explanations in the text of my usage of terms, I have used the term European Union, and its acronym EU, wherever possible. Where, however, it would have been factually inaccurate to use EU, then EC or EC/EU are used as appropriate.

As before, there are people whom I would like to thank for the assistance they have given me. Simon Bulmer, John Gibbons, Gary Titley MEP, and Vincent Wright all kindly read parts of the manuscript and made valuable observations on it. Steven Kennedy of Macmillan provided, with his customary deftness of touch, the necessary badgering until the book was completed. My wife Maureen produced a marvellous typescript whilst working to tight deadlines. Last, but not least, I must thank my daughters, Helen and Rachael, for being extremely tolerant when – all too frequently – the pressures of writing meant they were not given the attention they deserved.

June 1994   NEILL NUGENT

List of Abbreviations

ACEA	Association of European Automobile Constructors
ACP	African, Caribbean, and Pacific Countries
APPE	Association of Petrochemical Producers in Europe
ASEAN	Association of South-East Asian Nations
BEUC	European Bureau of Consumers' Associations
BRITE	Basic Research in Industrial Technologies for Europe
CAP	Common Agricultural Policy
CCEE	Countries of Central and Eastern Europe
CCP	Common Commercial Policy
CCT	Common Customs Tariff
CDU/CSU	German Christian Democratic Union/Christian Social Union
CEA	European Insurance Committee
CEEP	European Centre of Enterprises with State Holdings
CEFIC	European Chemical Industry Federation
CEN	European Committee for Standardisation
CENELEC	European Committee for Electrotechnical Standardisation
CET	Common External Tariff
CFP	Common Fisheries Policy
CFSP	Common Foreign and Security Policy
COPA	Committee of Professional Agricultural Organisations of the European Community
COR	Committee of the Regions
COREPER	Committee of Permanent Representatives
CSF	Community Support Framework
CSCE	Conference on Security and Cooperation in Europe
DC	Italian Christian Democratic Party
DG	Directorate General
DRIVE	Dedicated Road Infrastructure for Vehicle Safety in Europe
EAGGF	European Agricultural Guidance and Guarantee Fund
EBRD	European Bank for Reconstruction and Development
EC	European Community
ECB	European Central Bank
ECMM	European Community Monitoring Mission
ECOFIN	Council of Economic and Finance Ministers
ECSC	European Coal and Steel Community
Ecu	European Currency Unit
ED	European Democratic Group

EDA	Group of the European Democratic Alliance
EDC	European Defence Community; also European Documentation Centre
EDF	European Development Fund
EEA	European Economic Area
EEB	European Environmental Bureau
EEC	European Economic Community
EFTA	European Free Trade Association
EIB	European Investment Bank
EIF	European Investment Fund
ELDR	Federation of European Liberal, Democratic and Reform Parties
EMI	European Monetary Institute
EMS	European Monetary System
EMU	Economic and Monetary Union
EP	European Parliament
EPC	European Political Cooperation
EPP	European People's Party
ER	Technical Group of the European Right
ERDF	European Regional Development Fund
ERM	Exchange Rate Mechanism
ESC	Economic and Social Committee
ESCB	European System of Central Banks
ESF	European Social Fund
ESPRIT	European Strategic Programme for Research and Development in Information Technology
ETUC	European Trade Union Confederation
EU	European Union
EUCOFIL	European Union of Fruit and Vegetable Wholesalers, Shippers, Importers and Exporters
EUL	European United Left
Euratom	European Atomic Energy Community
EUREKA	European Programme for High Technology Research and Development
EUROBIT	European Association of Manufacturers of Business Machines and Data Processing Equipment
EUROFER	European Confederation of Iron and Steel Industries
FCO	Foreign and Commonwealth Office
FDP	German Free Democratic Party
FEEM	Federation of European Explosives Manufacturers
FN	French National Front
FRG	Federal Republic of Germany
G7	Group of Seven

GATT	General Agreement on Tariffs and Trade
GCECEE	Savings Bank Group of the EEC
GDP	Gross Domestic Product
GDR	German Democratic Republic
GNP	Gross National Product
IEA	International Energy Agency
IGC	Intergovernmental Conference
IMF	International Monetary Fund
IMP	Integrated Mediterranean Programme
IUR	International Union of Railways
JET	Joint European Torus
JHA	Justice and Home Affairs
JRC	Joint Research Centre
LDR	Liberal Democratic and Reformist Group
LU	Left Unity
MCA	Monetary Compensation Amount
MEP	Member of the European Parliament
MSI	Italian Social Movement
NATO	North Atlantic Treaty Organisation
NCI	New Community Instrument
NTB	Non-Tariff Barrier (to trade)
OECD	Organisation for Economic Cooperation and Development
OEEC	Organisation for European Economic Cooperation
OJ	Official Journal of the European Communities
PASOK	Greek Socialist Party
PCF	French Communist Party
PCI	Italian Communist Party
PDB	Preliminary Draft Budget
PES	Party of European Socialists
PHARE	Poland and Hungary: Aid for the Restructuring of Economies
PLO	Palestine Liberation Organisation
RACE	Research and Development in Advanced Communications Technologies for Europe
RBW	Rainbow Group
R & TD	Research and Technological Development
SCA	Special Committee on Agriculture
SEA	Single European Act
SEM	Single European Market
SME	Small and Medium-Sized Enterprise
TAC	Total Allowable Catch (fish stocks)
TEU	Treaty on European Union
UK	United Kingdom

UKREP	United Kingdom Permanent Representation to the European Communities
UN	United Nations
UNCTAD	United Nations Conference on Trade and Development
UNICE	Union of Industrial and Employers' Confederations of Europe
USA	United States of America
VAT	Value Added Tax
WEU	Western European Union

Founding members (1952 ECSC; 1958 EEC and Euratom)

First enlargement (1973)

Second enlargement (1981)

Third enlargement (1986)

Incorporation of the territory of the German Democratic Republic into a united Germany (1990)

Countries which agreed accession terms in 1994

■ PART 1 ■

THE HISTORICAL EVOLUTION

■ Introduction

No political system or organisation can properly be understood unless it is set in its historical and operational contexts. The structure and functioning of government institutions, the nature and dynamics of political forces, and the concerns and conduct of those who exercise power do not happen as a matter of chance. They are shaped, and are constantly being remoulded, by evolving forces and events.

Though a relatively new organisation, the European Union is no less subject to these dictates than are long established nation-states and, like them, its nature cannot be appreciated without reference to its historical sources or to the world in which it functions. (See the Preface for an explanation of the usage of the terms European Union (EU) and European Community (EC) in this book.) Thus, the EU is often criticised for being weak in structure and quarrelsome in nature, with far too much bickering over matters such as the price of butter and not enough visionary thinking and united action to tackle unemployment, regional imbalances, and other major problems. Unquestionably there is much in these criticisms, but that the EU should find harmonious collective policy-making difficult is not surprising to anyone with a historical perspective. For before they joined the EC/EU the member states made decisions for themselves on most matters. It is not easy, especially for those states which, until relatively recently, have been great powers or which believe themselves to be different or to have special interests, to have to cede sovereignty by transferring decision-making responsibilities to a multinational organisation in which other voices may prevail. Any explanation and understanding of what the EU is, and what it has and has not achieved, must recognise this. The EU must, in other words, be seen in the context of the forces that have made it, and are still making it. Some of these forces, notably ones of increasing economic interdependence, have served to push the states together. Others – and long established assumptions regarding the importance of national independence and sovereignty are very much amongst these – have resulted in progress towards cooperation and integration being slow, difficult, and far from continuous.

1

The sovereignty issue may also be used to give another, rather different, example of the importance of both historical background and contemporary operational context in explaining and evaluating the European Union. Many of the EU's opponents and critics subscribe to the view that the nation state, not an international organisation, is the 'natural' supreme political unit. They argue that insofar as transferences of power to Brussels, Luxembourg and Strasbourg – the three main seats of the EU's institutions – undermine national sovereignty, they should be resisted. But what proponents of this view all too often fail to recognise is that the member states of the EU were seeing their sovereignties being steadily eroded long before the EC/EU was established, and since it was established they have seen their sovereignties further eroded by forces that are not a consequence of EU membership. Whether it is because of movements in financial markets, transfers of capital within multinational corporations, changing trade patterns, or United States military dominance, virtually all West European states have become increasingly affected by, and at the mercy of, international developments they cannot control. This loss of power may not have involved legal transfers of sovereignty as has been the case within the EU, but it has had a very similar effect. The fact is that in an ever expanding range of policy- and decision-making sectors, states have not been able to act in isolation but have had to adjust and adapt so as to fit in with an array of external influences. The EU should not, therefore, be viewed as constituting a unique threat to the sovereignties of its member states. On the contrary, it is in some ways an attempt to meet this threat by providing a means by which the member states, if not able to regain their sovereignty, can at least reassert control over aspects of decision-making by cooperating together at levels and in ways which match post-war internationalism.

The purpose of Part 1 is thus to provide a base for an understanding of the EU by tracing its evolution and placing it in its historical and operational settings.

In Chapter 1 the sharp divide between pre-war and post-war West European inter-state relations is examined. The factors which explain what amounted to a post-war transformation in those relations are analysed, and the early organisational responses to that transformation are described.

Chapter 2 analyses the creation and development of the three European Communities: the European Coal and Steel Community (ECSC) which was founded by the Treaty of Paris in 1951, and the European Atomic Energy Community (Euratom) and the European Economic Community (EEC) which were both established in March 1957 with the signing of the Treaties of Rome.

Chapter 3 looks at the evolution of the European Community into a broader European Union. Central to the concerns of this chapter is the Treaty on European Union which was agreed at Maastricht in December 1991, which was formally signed by national representatives in February 1992, and which came into effect in November 1993.

■ *Chapter 1* ■

The Transformation of Western Europe

■ Historical divisions

It has become common today, with Western European integration proceeding apace and with democratic and market-based systems being established throughout Eastern and Central Europe, for commentators and observers on European affairs to emphasise the increasing unity and identity of the Continent.

It is well to remember, however, that such unity and identity as there can be said to exist – and, in truth, there is not very much if Western and Eastern Europe are lumped together – is of very recent vintage. For the fact is that throughout its history Europe has been characterised much more by divisions, tensions, and conflicts than it has by any common purpose or harmony of spirit. Even if attention is just restricted to that part of Europe which is of most interest to us in this book, which is also the part of Europe where unity has been most developed – Western Europe – the peoples and nation-states have long differed and been divided from one another in many ways.

Language has been perhaps the obvious divisive force. Linguists may identify structural similarities between European languages, but the fact is that most peoples have not been able to, and still cannot, directly converse with one another. (Today, 23 per cent of the citizens of the European Union speak German as their first language, 18 per cent English, 18 per cent French, and 17 per cent Italian; see Table 1.2, p. 21.) Religion has been another source of division, with the northern countries (except Ireland) being mainly Protestant, and the southern countries (including France but excluding Orthodox Greece) being predominantly Catholic. Contrasting cultural traditions and historical experiences have further served to develop distinct identifications – and feelings of 'us' and 'them' – across the map of Europe.

4

Such differences have helped to bind some peoples together, but they have also served to separate others from one another. Along with the legacies of power struggles and wars they help to explain why Western Europe has been divided into so many states, each with its own identity and loyalties. Some of these states – France, Spain and the United Kingdom for example – have existed in much their present geographical form for centuries. Others – including Germany, Italy and Ireland – were constituted only comparatively recently, mostly in the nineteenth and early twentieth centuries as nationalism flourished and as force was used to bring nation and state into closer alignment.

Until at least the Second World War, and in some cases well beyond, linguistic, religious and cultural divisions between the West European states were exacerbated by political and economic divisions.

The political divisions took the form of varying systems of government and competing ideological orientations. In the nineteenth and early twentieth centuries autocracies contrasted with emerging, and more liberal, parliamentary democracies. Between the two world wars parliamentary democracy found itself under attack and in some cases was overthrown: in Italy in 1922 by Fascism, in Germany in 1933 by Nazism, and in Spain after the 1936–9 civil war by conservative authoritarianism. It was not until the mid-1970s – following the collapse of the dictatorships of the Iberian peninsula and the overthrow of the military regime in Greece – that parliamentary democracy finally became general throughout Western Europe.

The economic divisions were no less marked. From the beginnings of the Industrial Revolution until the middle of the nineteenth century Britain was industrially and commercially dominant. Gradually it was challenged – particularly by Germany, but also by Belgium, France and others – so that by the early years of the twentieth century competition between these countries for overseas markets was fierce. At the same time, the economies of the northern countries were increasingly differentiated from those of the south, in that the former mostly had substantial industrial bases while the latter remained predominantly agricultural and underdeveloped.

Western Europe was thus long divided and many of these divisions provided sources for tensions, hostilities and wars. Finding their expression in economic and ideological competition, in drives for national power and prestige, and in territorial disputes, and compounded by dangerous mixtures of assertive/weak/incompetent leaderships, the divisions ensured that until after the Second World War rivalry and distrust governed the relationships between most of the states most of the time.

In the twentieth century alone two devastatingly destructive world wars, both of which began as European wars, have been fought. The First (1914–

18) saw the countries of the Triple Entente – Britain, France and Russia – plus Italy from 1915, fighting against Germany and Austria-Hungary. The Second (1939–45) saw Germany, assisted from 1940 by Italy, attempting to impose itself by force on virtually the whole of Europe outside the Iberian peninsula.

The background to the Second World War is worth outlining briefly because it puts in perspective how dramatically different, and how suddenly found, were the more cooperative relationships between the West European states in the post-1945 era. In short, the period between the wars was characterised by particularly sharp and fluid inter-state relations. There was no stable alliance system and no clear balance of power. For the most part, European states, including West European states, regarded one another with, at best, suspicion. Though multi-lateral and bi-lateral treaties, agreements, and pacts abounded, there was little overall pattern to them and few had any lasting effect. States came together in varying combinations on different issues in a manner which, far from indicating mutual confidence, was increasingly suggestive of fear.

From time to time in the inter-war period proposals for greater cooperation between European states were advanced but little came of them. The international climate – characterised by national rivalries and clashing interests – was not favourable, and most of the leading advocates of closer linkages were seen as having, as indeed they did have, specific national purposes in mind. Aristide Briand, for example, who was French Foreign Minister from 1925 to 1932, supported European cooperation but clearly had as his prime aim a stable European political system which would preserve the peace settlement that had been imposed on Germany in the 1919 Versailles Treaty. Gustav Stresemann, by contrast, who was the German Foreign Minister from 1923 to 1929, saw European cooperation as a way in which Germany could loosen the grip of Versailles and regain its position as a major power.

The lack of any real interest in European cooperation before the Second World War is revealed in the functioning of the League of Nations. Established in 1919 to provide for international collective security it was, in practice, dominated by the Europeans and had some potential as a forum for developing understandings and improving relationships between the European states. It failed, and did so for three main reasons. First, its aims were rather vague and were interpreted in different ways. Second, it was intergovernmental in its structure and therefore dependent on the agreement of all member states before any action could be taken. Third, and most importantly, the states wanted different things from it: some – notably France, most of the medium-sized central European countries which had been constituted in 1918–19 out of the collapsed Austria–Hungarian Empire, and to some extent Britain – saw it as a means of preserving the Versailles *status quo*; others – particularly Germany and Italy – wanted to use it to change the 1919 settlement and were prepared to leave or ignore it if it did not serve that purpose.

Inter-war Europe thus experienced rising tensions as national rivalries remained unharnessed and, above all, as German territorial and power ambitions could not be satisfied. When war did finally break out, the Axis Powers (Germany and Italy) gained control for a while over virtually the whole of the Continent from the Atlantic to deep inside the Soviet Union. In Western Europe only Britain and those countries which remained neutral (Ireland, Portugal, Spain, Sweden and Switzerland) were not occupied. By May 1945, when German government representatives agreed to unconditional surrender, Nazism and Fascism had been defeated, but economies and political systems throughout Europe had been severely shaken, cities and towns had been destroyed, and millions had been killed.

■ The post-war transformation

Since the Second World War the relations between the Western European states have been transformed. There are three principal aspects to this:

□ A half-century of peace

The states have lived peacefully with one another since 1945 and armed confrontation between any two does not now appear to be even remotely possible. As Altiero Spinelli, one of the great advocates and architects of European integration, observed in 1985 shortly before his death:

> [a] major transformation . . . has occurred in the political consciousness of Europeans, something which is completely new in their history. For centuries, neighbouring countries were seen as potential enemies against whom it was necessary to be on one's guard and ready to fight. Now, after the end of the most terrible of wars in Europe, these neighbours are perceived as friendly nations sharing a common destiny.

The belief in a common destiny is perhaps questionable, but the reality and importance of the transformation from hostile to friendly relations is not. Certainly the states have continued to compete against one another in many areas, and this has sometimes led to strains and tensions, but these disagreements have been mostly on issues where military conflict has not been relevant to the resolution of differences.

Indeed, not only has military conflict been irrelevant to the resolution of differences, but such friction as has occurred has been within a context in which West European states have usually shared similar views as to who are basically their friends and who are real or potential enemies. Until the revolutions and upheavals in Eastern Europe and the Soviet Union in the late 1980s/early 1990s, communism was the most obvious common threat and this led most significant Western European states to be full or part members of the same military alliance: the North Atlantic Treaty Organisation (NATO, see Table 1.1, on pp. 10–11). With the communist danger now seemingly removed, Western security arrangements are being revamped to adjust to a situation in which the countries of Eastern and Central Europe are seen as potential partners rather than as foes, and in which the main potential security concerns for Western Europe are seen as lying in bubbling national and ethnic tensions in parts of the former Soviet Empire – not least in Russia – and in the unrest and turbulence of the Middle East. As part of this revamping, security linkages are being developed with Eastern and Central European states – notably via the Conference on Security and Cooperation in Europe (CSCE) – and in Western Europe itself stronger Western European-based security arrangements are being established via the linked processes of reconstructing the Western European Union (see below) and developing within the European Union a Common Foreign and Security Policy (CFSP).

□   *A transformed agenda*

Throughout the international system the subject matter of discussions and negotiations between states has become more varied. Whilst, as regional conflicts show, the case should not be overstated, international agendas have undoubtedly become less centred upon traditional or 'high policy' issues and have increasingly focused on 'low policy' issues. That is to say, policies concerned with the existence and preservation of the state (such as defence policy and balance of power manoeuvrings) have been joined by policies concerned more with the wealth and welfare of populations (such as policies on trade, monetary stability, environmental protection, and airline safety).

This change in the content of agendas has been particularly marked throughout the Western industrialised world, and above all in Western Europe where a transformation can be said to have occurred. Classic 'power politics' have not, of course, disappeared, but they are just not as dominating or as prominent as they were formerly. When representatives of the twelve EU states meet it is normally to consider topics which a generation or two ago would not even have been regarded as proper subjects for international negotiations. For instance: what constitutes 'fair' economic competition, how might research information be pooled to the general advantage, should farmers be given a 5 or 7 per cent increase in their incomes, and what should be the maximum weight of lorries permitted on roads?

□ New channels and processes

Paralleling, and partly occasioned by, the increasingly diverse international agenda, there has been a transformation in the ways in which states interrelate with one another. The traditional diplomatic means of inter-state communications via Ministries of Foreign Affairs and embassies have declined in importance as new channels and processes have become established.

As with changing agendas, changing forms of inter-state communications have been taken further in the Western industrialised world, and particularly in the EU, than anywhere else. There are now few significant parts of any Western state's machinery that do not have some involvement in managing external relations. Written communications, telephone conversations, facsimile messages, and bilateral and multilateral meetings between states increase by the year. Contacts range from the *ad hoc* and informal to the regularised and highly structured.

In the EU, governmental representatives of different sorts meet with one another every working day. They may have as their purpose the taking of binding decisions (decisions which in many circumstances may be taken by majority vote), the exploration of possible advantageous policy coordination, or merely the exchanging of views and information. At the lower end of the seniority scale junior and middle-ranking officials, working often from tightly drawn negotiating briefs and with their actions subject to later approval from national capitals, convene in committees to try and hammer out detailed agreements on proposed legislation. At the other end of the scale Heads of Government regularly meet, for what are often wide-ranging and relatively unstructured discussions, in a number of forums: in the twice yearly European Councils where all twelve EU states are represented; in bilateral meetings, which in the case of the British Prime Minister, the French President, the German Chancellor, and the Italian Prime Minister, are fixed on an at least annual basis; and in the broader setting of the annual Western Economic Summits which bring together the political leaders of Britain, France, Germany, Italy, Canada, Japan and the United States, plus the President of the European Commission and the

Table 1.1 Membership of Western and Western European organisations

	Western Organisations		Western European Organisations				
	NATO	OECD	Council of Europe	European Union	EFTA	WEU	Nordic Council
Australia		✓(1971)					
Austria		✓(F)	✓(1956)		✓(F)		
Belgium	✓(F)	✓(F)	✓(F)	✓(F)		✓(F)	
Bulgaria			✓(1992)				
Canada	✓(F)	✓(F)					
Cyprus			✓(1961)				
Czech. Republic			✓(1993)				
Denmark	✓(F)	✓(F)	✓(F)	✓(1973)	Withdrew in 1972 on joining EC		✓(F)
Estonia			✓(1993)				
Finland		✓(1969)	✓(1989)		✓(1961)		✓(F)
France	S(Since 1966)(F)	✓(F)	✓(F)	✓(F)		✓(F)	
Germany	✓(1955)	✓(F)	✓(1951)	✓(F)		✓(F)	
Greece	✓(1952)	✓(F)	✓(1949)	✓(1981)		✓(1992)	
Hungary			✓(1990)				
Iceland	✓(F)	✓(F)	✓(1950)		✓(1970)		✓(F)
Ireland		✓(F)	✓(F)	✓(1973)			
Italy	✓(F)	✓(F)	✓(F)	✓(F)		✓(F)	
Japan		✓(1964)					
Liechtenstein			✓(1978)		✓(1991)		
Lithuania	✓(F)		✓(1993)				
Luxembourg	✓(F)	✓(F)	✓(F)	✓(F)		✓(F)	
Malta			✓(1965)				
Netherlands	✓(F)	✓(F)	✓(F)	✓(F)		✓(F)	
New Zealand	✓(F)	✓(1973)					

| | Western Organisations | | | Western European Organisations | | | |
	NATO	OECD	Council of Europe	European Union	EFTA	WEU	Nordic Council
Norway	✓(F)	✓(F)	✓(F)		✓(F)		✓(F)
Poland			✓(1991)				
Portugal	✓(F)	✓(F)	✓(1976)	✓(1986)	Withdrew in 1985 on joining EC	✓(1988)	
Romania			✓(1993)				
San Marino			✓(1988)				
Slovakia			✓(1993)				
Slovenia			✓(1993)				
Spain	✓(1982)		✓(1977)	✓(1986)		✓(1988)	
Sweden		✓(F)	✓(F)		✓(F)		✓(F)
Switzerland		✓(F)	✓(1962)		✓(F)		
Turkey	✓(1952)	✓(F)	✓(1949)				
United Kingdom	✓(F)	✓(F)	✓(F)	✓(1973)	Withdrew in 1972 on joining EC	✓(F)	
United States	✓(F)	✓(F)					

Note:
Dates in brackets refer to when membership of post-foundation members came into effect.
Situation in January 1994.

KEY ✓ Full member.
   S Special status or associate member.
   (F) Founding member.

head of government of the member state which is currently chairing the EU's Council of Ministers if he is not already present.

■ Explanations of the transformation

In seeking to explain post-war cooperation and integration in Western Europe – which includes locating the foundations of, and reasons for the development of, the European Union – observers have often highlighted different factors, and sometimes indeed have looked in rather different directions. Amongst the questions that have caused difficulties are these: to what extent do the developments have deep historical roots and to what extent have they been a reaction to specifically post-1945 circumstances; what has been the balance between political and economic factors; what has been the role of general international influences as opposed to more narrowly based West European ones; and has there been a constant underlying movement in an integrationist direction or just a series of specific, and not very well coordinated, responses to specific problems?

In looking at the ways in which questions of this sort have been answered, four broad explanatory themes can be found in the literature. For analytical purposes they will be considered here separately, but it should be recognised that, in practice, they are by no means mutually exclusive but rather complement, overlap and reinforce one another. It should be recognised, too, that their usefulness as explanations is not constant, but varies over time. So, for example, whilst political ideals and utopian visions of a united Europe may have had a least some part to play in the early post-war years, more recently they have counted for little, and it has been hard-headed national calculations of economic and political advantages and disadvantages that have been the principal determinants of progress.

☐ *The deep roots of integration?*

Some have found the roots of post-war developments in the distant past. Supporters and advocates of European integration have been especially prominent in this regard. They have suggested that Europe is, and has long been, a unique and identifiable entity. As evidence of this it is often argued that Europe was the cradle of modern civilisation and from this developed European values and a European culture, art and literature. Walter Hallstein, the first President of the Commission of the EEC, typifies this sort of view:

Europe is no creation. It is a rediscovery. The main difference between the formation of the United States of Europe and that of the United States of America is not that America did not have to merge a number of firmly established nation-states, but that for more than a thousand years the idea of a unified Europe was never quite forgotten . . . [The advocates of a European federation] know that Europe shares a sense of values: of what is good and bad; of what a man's rights should be and what are his duties; of how society should be ordered; of what is happiness and what disaster. Europe shares many things: its memories that we call history; achievements it can take pride in and events that are shameful; its joys and its sufferings; and not least its tomorrows (Hallstein, 1972).

Clearly there is much idealism in this. People such as Hallstein are suggesting that transcending the differences, divergences and conflicts between peoples and states there has long been a certain commonality and identity of interest in Europe based on interrelationships between geography and historical, political, economic, social and cultural developments. It is a contentious view and certainly not one to which many historians would attach much importance. Divisions and dissension, they would contend, have been more prominent than identity of interest or shared values and experiences. Such limited commonality as has existed has largely been a consequence of geographical proximity.

But if the 'idealistic' interpretation does not now find much favour, there are still those who would wish to stress the importance of the historical dimension of Western European integration. Inter-state relations in the nineteenth century are sometimes seen as foreshadowing post-1945 developments insofar as peace endured for much of the century and did so, in part at least, as a result of understandings and agreements between the major powers. The problem with this view, however, is that it rather overstates the extent to which the nineteenth century was a century of peace, and it exaggerates too the extent to which the states did cooperate. Arguably, the so-called Concert of Nations represented an embryonic attempt to exercise strategic control through diplomacy and summitry, but that was at a time when conservative autocracies ruled much of Europe and when many of today's states did not even exist in their present forms. And in any event, the system lasted at best only from 1815 to the Crimean War. It then gave way to the wars of the mid-century and later to the balance of power – which was hardly based on European trust and cooperation – as the means of seeking to preserve the peace.

It is perhaps in the field of economic history that the most fertile ground for identifying long-term influences and explanations is to be found. From about the late eighteenth century *national* economic integration began to occur, as barriers to economic activity *within* states were dismantled. This helped to promote, and in turn was encouraged by, national political integration which manifested itself in nationalism and in the elevation of the sovereign state to the status of the supreme collective unit. From about the middle of the century the achievement and successes of this internal economic and political integration, allied with an increasing interconnectedness in Europe which followed from technological changes and economic advance, resulted in increasing inter-state cooperation to promote trade, competition and growth. For some economic historians an embryonic European economy was being established. Pollard, for example, has written of the mid-nineteenth century:

> Europe's industrialisation proceeded relatively smoothly among other reasons precisely because it took place within what was in many essentials a single integrated economy, with a fair amount of movement for labour, a greater amount of freedom for the movement of goods, and the greatest freedom of all for the movement of technology, know-how and capital (Pollard, 1981).

But, unlike the customary pattern within nation-states, there was nothing inevitable about European economic integration. Nor was there a clear and developing relationship between it and political integration. On the contrary, from the last quarter of the nineteenth century, states, for a variety of reasons, moved increasingly in the direction of economic protectionism and at the same time developed national identities and consciousness such as had not been seen before. In the first part of the twentieth century, and especially between the wars, the European free trading system virtually disappeared, as states sought to protect themselves at the expense of others and as national economies were increasingly reshaped along autarkic lines. Alongside these increasingly closed economic systems developed the ever sharper political tensions and rivalries between the states that were noted earlier.

The European historical experience thus emphasises the extremely important, but often overlooked, fact that although industrialisation and economic liberalisation provide potential bases for the furtherance of interconnections, agreements, and harmonious relations between states, they do not ensure or guarantee them. The powers of Europe went to war with their principal trading partners in 1914. Furthermore, between the wars, economic linkages did little to bring the nations together or to act as a restraint on governments when divergences developed in their aims and strategies. This must be borne in mind when, later in this chapter, attention is turned to modernisation and interdependence as explanations for post-war political and economic integration. Doubtless they have both been extremely important but, as pre-1939 European history shows, they do not have an inevitable integrationist logic attached to them. Much depends on their relationship to the circumstances of the time and, as will now be shown, these were very different in the post-1945 world from what they had been before the war.

☐ The impact of the Second World War

The Second World War unquestionably marks a turning point in the West European state system. Within a few years of the war ending states were cooperating, and in some instances and in some respects were even integrating, in a manner that would have been inconceivable before the war. Fundamental to this transformation were a number of factors resultant upon the war that combined to bring about radical changes in both the climate of opinion and the perceptions of requirements. They can be grouped under two broad headings:

☐ *Political factors*. These may be subdivided into four key areas.

(1) The Second World War produced a greater realisation than had existed ever before that unfettered and uninhibited nationalism was a recipe for war, which in the post-1945 world was increasingly seen as meaning mass destruction. At the international level this thinking was reflected in calls for a larger and more powerful body than the pre-war League of Nations, and it played an important part in the establishment of the United Nations in 1944. But the fact that the two world wars had begun as European wars, and that Germany was generally seen as having been the prime cause of those wars, also brought forth demands and moves for specifically European arrangements. Amongst the strongest advocates of this view were many of those who had been associated with the Resistance movements of Continental Europe which, from 1943 onwards, had come to be linked via liaising networks and from which ideas and proposals had been generated looking forward to a post-war world that would be based more on cooperation and less on confrontation.

There was thus a widely shared optimism that if the states could work together in joint schemes and organisations barriers of mistrust could be broken down. On this basis, over 750 prominent Europeans came together at the Hague in May 1948 and from their Congress issued a call to the nations of Europe to create a political and economic union. This stimulated discussions at governmental levels, and in May 1949 the Statute of the Council of Europe was signed by representatives of ten states. Article 1 of the Statute states:

The aim of the Council of Europe is to achieve a greater unity between its Members for the purpose of safeguarding and realising the ideals and principles which are their common heritage and facilitating their economic and social progress.

This aim shall be pursued through the organs of the Council by discussions of questions of common concern and by agreements and common action in economic, social, cultural, scientific, legal and administrative matters and in the maintenance and further realisation of human rights and fundamental freedoms.

Despite these grandiose ambitions, however, the Council of Europe was to be a disappointment to those who hoped that it might serve as the basis for a new West European state system. In part, the problem was that its aims were too vague; in part, that its decision-making structure was essentially intergovernmental and therefore weak; but mainly that some of its members, notably the UK, were not much interested in anything that went beyond limited and voluntary cooperation. (Ernest Bevin, British Foreign Secretary, commented on proposals for a really effective Council of Europe thus: 'Once you open that Pandora's box, you'll find it full of Trojan horses.') That all said, the weaknesses of the Council should not be overstated. It was to perform, and continues to perform, certain useful functions – notably in the human rights field through its European Convention of Human Rights, and as a forum for the discussion of matters of common interest to its member states. (The value of this latter function long lay in the fact that, unlike other Western European regional groups, virtually all Western European states were members of the Council. More recently, as East European countries have become members, an additional value has been as a forum for establishing links and building understanding between Western and Eastern Europe.)

(2) Although it was not immediately apparent when hostilities ceased in 1945, the Second World War was to result in a fundamental redrawing of the political map of Europe. Most obviously, by the late 1940s it was clear that the legacy of war had left the Continent, and with it Germany, divided in two. In Winston Churchill's phrase an 'Iron Curtain' divided East from West.

In the West there was no question of the victorious powers – Britain and the United States – seeking or being able to impose anything like a Soviet-style straitjacket on the liberated countries. Nonetheless, if Western Europe did not quite take on the form of a bloc, liberal democratic systems were soon established, and not wholly dissimilar political ideas were soon prevailing, in most of the states. Inevitably this facilitated intergovernmental relations.

Perhaps the most important idea shared by the governments was one which stemmed directly from the East-West division: a determination to preserve Western Europe from communism. Not only had the Soviet Union extended its influence far into the European heartland, but in France and Italy domestic communist parties were commanding considerable support and from 1947 were engaging in what looked to many like revolutionary activities. The United States shared this anti-communist concern, and the encouragement and assistance which it gave to the West European states after the war to cooperate was partly driven by a belief that such cooperation could play a major part in helping to halt the communist advance. In March 1947 President Truman, concerned with the events in Greece (where the communists were trying to overthrow the government), outlined what became known as the Truman doctrine which amounted to a political guarantee of support to 'free peoples who are resisting attempted subjugation by armed minorities or by outside pressures'. This political commitment was quickly followed up in 1948 by economic assistance in the form of Marshall Aid, and in 1949 by military protection with the foundation of NATO and a guarantee to the then ten West European member states (Canada and the US brought the founding membership to twelve) of US military protection against a Soviet attack.

A role for the United States in Western Europe at this time should not be seen as having been unwelcome, for, contrary to the impression that is sometimes given, American aid was not unwillingly or insidiously imposed on the states but, rather, was actively sought. At the same time, the extent of US influence should not be exaggerated. By its political, economic, and military interventions and assistance the United States did exert integrationist pressures and did help to make a number of developments possible, but the US government wanted much more West European inter-state integration than was to be achieved.

(3) With the post-war division of Europe, with the moving of the international power balance from European state relations to United States–Soviet relations, and with the onset of the Cold War from 1947–8 producing the possibility of Europe being the battleground between East and West, there was a sense from the late 1940s of Western Europe beginning to look like an identifiable political entity in a way in which it had not done so before. Not all states or politicians shared this perspective, but amongst many of those who did it produced a desire that the voice of Western Europe should be heard on the world stage and a belief that this could be achieved only through unity and by speaking with one voice. For some of the smaller European states, which had rarely exercised much international influence and whose very existence had periodically been threatened by larger neighbours, the prospects of such cooperation were particularly attractive.

(4) The future of Germany naturally loomed large in the minds of those who had to deal with post-war reconstruction. Three times in seventy

years, and twice in the twentieth century, Germany had occupied much of Europe. Rightly or wrongly it had come to be seen as innately aggressive. As a consequence, the initial inclination of most governments after the war was to try and contain it in some way. Just how this should be done, however, divided the wartime allies, with the consequence that matters drifted until what was initially intended as an interim division of Germany into zones gave way, as the Cold War developed, into a *de jure* division: the Federal Republic of Germany (West Germany) and the German Democratic Republic (East Germany) were both formally constituted in 1949.

By this time the Soviet Union was replacing Germany as the perceived principal threat to democracy and stability in Western Europe. As this occurred those who were already arguing that a conciliatory approach towards Germany ought to be tried (since a policy of punitive containment had demonstrably failed between the wars), saw their hands strengthened by a growing feeling that attempts must be made to avoid the development of a political vacuum in West Germany which the communists might attempt to exploit. Furthermore, and the US government played an important role in pressing this view from the early 1950s, use of West Germany's power and wealth could help to reduce the contributions that other countries were making to the defence of Europe. The perceived need to incorporate the Federal Republic into the Western European main-stream, which had a number of political aspects to it, thus further stimulated pressures for inter-state cooperation and integration.

☐ *Economic factors.* Just as pre-war and wartime experiences helped to produce the United Nations, so did they stimulate an interest in the creation of new international economic and financial arrangements. The first fruits of this were realised at the Bretton Woods Conference in 1944 where the representatives of forty-four countries, with the United Kingdom and the United States playing the leading roles, agreed to the establishment of two new bodies. The first was the International Monetary Fund (IMF), which was to alleviate problems of currency instability by creating facilities for countries with temporary balance of payments difficulties to have access to short-term credit facilities. The second was the International Bank for Reconstruction and Development (the 'World Bank'), which was to provide long-term loans for schemes which necessitated a major investment. In 1947, at much the same time as the IMF and the World Bank became operative, international economic cooperation was taken a stage further when twenty-three countries negotiated the General Agreement on Tariffs and Trade (GATT) which had as its purpose the facilitating of trade through the lowering of international trade barriers.

Although West European governments (or, more usually, national representatives, since governments on the Continent were not properly restored until 1945–6) played their part in helping to create the new international economic arrangements, it was felt in many quarters that there should also be specifically West European-based economic initiatives and organisations. In 1947–8 these feelings were given a focus, an impetus, and an urgency when the rapid post-war economic recovery that most states were able to engineer by the adoption of expansionist policies created massive balance of payments deficits and dollar shortages in particular. Governments were faced with major currency problems, with not being able to pay for their imports, and with the prospect of their economic recoveries coming to a sudden and premature end. In these circumstances, and for reasons that were not altogether altruistic – a strong Western Europe was in its political, security and economic interests too – the United States stepped in with the offer of Marshall Aid. But it was an offer that had attached to it the condition that the recipient states must endeavour to seek greater economic cooperation between themselves. As a result, the first major post-war Western European organisation, the Organisation for European Economic Cooperation (OEEC), was established, with sixteen founding member states in April 1948. Its task, in the short term, was to manage the aid, encourage joint economic policies, and discourage barriers to trade; in the longer term, its stated aim was to build 'a sound European economy through the cooperation of its members'. In the event, though the OEEC did some valuable work, the most notable perhaps being in establishing payments schemes which in the 1940s and 1950s did much to further trade between member countries, it never made much progress with its grander ambitions. Rather like the Council of Europe, its large and somewhat heterogeneous membership, coupled with the strictly intergovernmental nature of its decision-making structure, meant that ambitious proposals were always successfully opposed. Partly as a result of this, and partly in recognition of growing interdependence between all industrialised countries, the OEEC gave way, in 1961, to the Organisation for Economic Cooperation and Development (OECD) whose membership was to be open to non-European countries and which was to have broader objectives reflecting wider and changing interests.

The OEEC thus stemmed from post-war circumstances that mixed the general with the particular. That is to say, attitudes coming out of the war that favoured economic cooperation between West European states were given a direction by particular requirements that were related to the war and its immediate aftermath. Only three years later, in a way that is described in Chapter 2, a similar mixture of general underlying and specific triggering factors combined to produce the first of the European Communities: the European Coal and Steel Community (ECSC).

It is, of course, true that the effects of some of the political and economic factors that have just been considered, such as the existence of Resistance leaders in governments, were essentially short-term. It might also be argued that some of the factors, such as the increased need and willingness of the states to cooperate with one another to promote economic growth, were not so much caused by the war as given a push by it. But what can hardly be disputed is that the factors taken together produced a set of circumstances associated with the war that enabled Western European cooperation and integration to get off the ground in the 1940s and 1950s.

States naturally differed in the particulars and the perceptions of their post-war situations. As a result, there was no general agreement as to just exactly what the new spirit of cooperation should attempt to achieve. Many different schemes were advanced and many different organisations were established to tackle particular issues, problems and requirements. The war did not thus produce anything remotely like a united West European movement between the states. But it did produce new realities and changed attitudes which enabled, or forced, virtually all the states to recognise at least some commonalities and shared interests. As a consequence, it became possible for new inter-state European organisations to be established. Of these organisations, those that were able to offer clear advantages and benefits to members were able to act as a base for further developments. As the ECSC in particular was quickly to demonstrate, cooperation and integration can breed more of the same.

☐ *Interdependence*

It has become customary to suggest that whilst both political and economic factors were crucial to Western European cooperation and integration in the formative post-war years, the former have now declined in relation to the latter. The impact of modernisation is generally agreed to be a key reason for this. It has broadened the international agenda from its traditional power and security concerns to embrace a range of economic and social issues, and at the same time it has produced an interconnectedness and interrelatedness between states, especially in the economic and monetary spheres, that amounts to an interdependence.

Economic interdependence arises particularly from three features of the post-1945 world: the enormously increased volume of world trade; the

Table 1.2 *Key information on the member states and prospective member states of the European Union*

	Population (million)*	Main language	Currency	GDP (Ecu, bn 1991)	Exports to EC (% total 1991)*
Austria	7.8	German	Schilling	132	66
Belgium	9.8	Flemish/French	Belgian Franc	160	75
Denmark	5.1	Danish	Krona	105	54
Finland	5.0	Finnish	Markka	101	50
France	57.0	French	French Franc	967	63
Germany	79.3	German	Deutschmark	1269	54
Greece	10.0	Greek	Drachma	57	63
Ireland	3.5	English	Punt	35	74
Italy	57.0	Italian	Lira	926	59
Luxembourg	0.4	French	Lux/Belgian Franc	7	included in Belgian exports
Netherlands	15.0	Dutch	Guilder	231	77
Norway	4.3	Norwegian	Krona	86	66
Portugal	10.6	Portuguese	Escudo	55	75
Spain	39.0	Spanish	Peseta	425	71
Sweden	8.6	Swedish	Krona	190	55
United Kingdom	57.4	English	Pound	819	57

*Source: Financial Times, 4 January 1993.

internationalisation of production – in which multinational corporations have played a prominent part; and – especially since the early 1970s – the fluctuations and uncertainties associated with currency exchange rates and international monetary arrangements. Within Western Europe there have been many regional dimensions to this development of interdependence, two of which have been especially important. First, all significant Western European countries have, since the Second World War, seen their external trade become increasingly West European focused. The EC/EU has played an important – although by no means a sole – role in encouraging this trend: a trend which, as Table 1.2 indicates, has produced a situation today whereby all EU member states and potential member states conduct at least 50 per cent of their trade inside the EU. Second, monetary power within Western Europe has increasingly come to be centred in the hands of those who make the monetary decisions for the strongest economy: Germany. Changes in German interest rates or exchange rates can have immense, and potentially very destabilising, implications elsewhere in Western Europe.

As a result of interdependence a wide variety of economic and financial issues can thus no longer be limited to, and indeed in some respects do not even bear much relationship to, national boundaries. States are increasingly vulnerable to outside events and are increasingly unable to act in isolation. They must consult, cooperate and, some would argue, integrate with one another in the interests of international and national economic stability and growth. When the nature of the problem has been seen to require a truly international economic effort most West European states have been prepared to try solutions at this level: in the IMF, in the Bank for International Settlements, in Western Economic Summits, and elsewhere. Where a regional response has seemed to be more appropriate or more practical, West European-based arrangements have been sought. The most obvious examples of such arrangements are those associated with the EU. For instance: the creation of the Single European Market (SEM) is rooted in the belief that the dismantlement of trade barriers will further economic efficiency and prosperity in the participating states; the movement towards Economic and Monetary Union (EMU) is based on the assumption that the coordination and the convergence of national economic and monetary policies is necessary for the full completion of the SEM programme and will also provide a further major stimulus to trade and prosperity; and the development at EU level of advanced research programmes is a response to an increasing belief that Western European states must show a greater willingness to pool their scientific and technological resources and knowledge if they are to compete successfully in world markets against the Americans, the Japanese, and other competitors.

Economic interdependence is not the only feature of modern interdependence. Advances in communications and travel have necessarily placed on the international and European agendas issues which a generation or two ago either did not exist or were seen as being of purely domestic concern. Now it is commonly accepted that if they are to be tackled with any prospect of success they must be dealt with at an inter-state level. Governments thus discuss, and in Western Europe have adopted understandings and made decisions on, matters as diverse as transfrontier television arrangements, data protection, action against drug traffickers, and football hooliganism.

But despite all the attention that is now given to modern interdependence as the motor of West European integration, and despite too the associated assertion that economic factors now far outweigh political factors in shaping the relations between the West European – and particularly the EU – states, the case should not be overstated. One reason why it should not be is that modern interdependence does not necessarily produce an inescapable and wholly unavoidable set of integrationist processes and developments: there is certainly an integrationist logic attached to modern interdependence, but for much of integration to actually proceed political choices and decisions have to be made. As the history of West European integrationist negotiations since the Second World War demonstrate – from the negotiations in the late 1940s to establish the Council of Europe to the negotiations in the early 1990s on the Treaty on European Union – politicians, and indeed publics, are capable of adopting an array of often sharply conflicting views of what is necessary and what is desirable when they are faced with these choices and decisions. A second reason for exercising some caution in evaluating the impact on integration of economic interdependence is that *political* factors continue to be important in shaping the nature and pace of integration processes. This was clearly illustrated in the wake of the 1990 re-unification of Germany, when a powerful stimulus to initiating a new round of integrationist negotiations was emerging concern amongst decision-making elites, most particularly in France, that if Germany was to be prevented from dominating the Continent it must be tied in more tightly to its neighbours. And a third reason for not over-emphasising the importance of modern interdependence to the neglect of other factors, is that interdependence of a quite different kind – different in that it does not arise from modernisation but rather from the relatively diminished significance of the West European states in the post-1945 period – continues to play a part in encouraging cooperation and integration between states. So, for example, in respect of the external political role of the EU, the relatively limited power and weight of the West European states acting individually provides a powerful inducement for them to try and speak as one if they wish to exert a significant influence on world political events. Most of the EU states do wish to exert such an influence and consequently, since the early 1970s, they have gradually strengthened their mechanisms for inter-state foreign policy cooperation so as to enable them to engage in extensive consultations, and increasingly to adopt joint positions, on foreign policy issues. Similar processes have been under way in respect of security considerations, with the perception, until recently, of the Soviet Union as Western Europe's main political enemy, allied with the inability of any single Western Europe state to offer by itself a wholly credible defence capability, encouraging close military cooperation between the states in the context of both the Western alliance and associated Western Europe defence groupings. The Soviet threat has now disappeared, but potential security dangers of many kinds still abound – be they in the newly independent former Soviet states, in South-East Europe, in the Middle East, or elsewhere – and these have played an important part in ensuring that not only security in a general sense, but defence in a more specific sense, is now on the EU's agenda.

☐ *National considerations*

Whilst most Western European states since 1945 have paid at least lip service to the idea of a united Western Europe, there has never been any consensus between them on what this is to mean in practice. The rhetoric has often been grand, but discussions on specific proposals have usually revealed considerable variations in ambitions, motives, intentions and perceptions. Most crucially of all, states have differed in their assessments of the consequences for them, in terms of gains and losses, of forging closer relations with their neighbours. As a result, some states have been prepared, and have been able, to go further than others, or have been prepared to do so at an earlier time. There has not, therefore, been a coherent and ordered movement towards West European unity. In the late 1940s and during the 1950s most states were willing to be associated with intergovernmental organisations that made few demands on them – and hence joined the OEEC and the Council of Europe – but there was no similar breadth of support when organisations were proposed that went beyond intergovernmental cooperation into supranational integration. Consequently, the more ambitious post-war schemes – for the ECSC, for a European Defence Community (EDC – which in the event was never established), and for the EEC and Euratom – initially involved only a restricted membership. It was not until circumstances and attitudes in other states changed, and until an obstacle that emerged amongst the founding states themselves – in the form of President de Gaulle's opposition to UK membership – was removed, that the EC's membership opened out in the 1970s and 1980s to include eventually most, though not all, of Western Europe's larger and medium-sized states.

So although all states have long been touched by at least some of the factors that have been examined on the last few pages, the differences between the states have been such that their interest in, and enthusiasm for, cooperation and integration processes has varied, both with regard to nature and timing. Four broad categories of states can be identified:

☐ *The six founding members of the European Community*. Belgium, France, West Germany, Italy, Luxembourg and the Netherlands – the six states which, in 1951, signed the Treaty of Paris to found the ECSC and in 1957 signed the Treaties of Rome to found the EEC and Euratom – were the first to show a willingness to go beyond the essentially intergovernmental organisations which were established in Western Europe in the late 1940s. Cautiously, tentatively, and not without reservations, each took the view that the benefits of integration, as opposed to just cooperation, would outweigh what appeared to be the major disadvantage – some loss of sovereignty. Some of the perceptions of the advantages of creating organisations with supranational characteristics were shared by all of the six. But there were also more nationally-based hopes and ambitions:

● For the three Benelux countries the experience of the war had re-emphasised their vulnerability to hostile and more powerful neighbours and the particular desirability of being on good terms with West Germany and France. Related to this, their size – Belgium and the Netherlands were only middle-ranking European powers whilst Luxembourg was an almost insignificant one – meant that their only real prospect of being able to exercise any sort of influence in Europe, let alone the world, was through a more unified inter-state system. As for economic considerations, the idea of integration was perhaps more acceptable to them than it was to most other states since their own Benelux economic agreements and arrangements pre-dated the war, and negotiations to re-launch and deepen these were under way well before the war ended. Finally, there was the simple fact that none of the Benelux states was in a strong enough position to ignore Franco–German-led initiatives for economic integration.

● Italy, too, had a number of particular reasons for welcoming close relations with other West European states. First, after over twenty years of Fascist rule followed by military defeat, European integration offered the opportunity of a new start, and from a basis of respectability. Second, in May 1947, as also occurred in France, the Communist Party left government and for some years thereafter seemed to be intent on fermenting internal revolution. The clear anti-communist tenor of other West European governments looked comforting, and a possible basis of assistance, to Italy's nervous Christian Democratic-led governments. Third, Italy faced economic difficulties on all fronts: with unemployment, inflation, balance of payments, currency stability, and – especially in the south – poverty. Almost any scheme which offered the possibility of finding new markets and generating economic growth was to be welcomed.

● Integration helped French governments to deal with two of their key post-war policy goals: the containment of Germany, and economic growth. The ECSC was especially important in this regard in the early 1950s, offering the opportunity to break down age-old barriers and hostilities on the one hand, and giving France access to vital German raw materials and markets on the other. Later in the 1950s, when 'the German problem' was seen to be no longer so pressing, but when German economic competition seemed to be an increasing threat, France took steps to ensure that as part of the price of continued integration certain French interests would be given special treatment (see below).

● For Konrad Adenauer, the West German Chancellor from 1949 to 1963, it was to be primarily in and through West European unification that the Federal Republic would establish itself in the international mainstream and German self-respect would be regained. Western Europe would also, along with the Atlantic Alliance, provide a much-needed buttress against the perceived threat from the East. At more specific levels the ECSC was a means by which West Germany could rid itself of Allied restrictions and interference, whilst the more open markets of the EEC offered immense opportunities for what, in the 1950s, quickly became the fastest growing economy in Western Europe.

Since helping to create the EC in the 1950s, four of the founding states – Belgium, Luxembourg, the Netherlands, and Italy – have remained firm and consistent supporters of the integration process. They have almost invariably backed, and sometimes have been prominent in the initiation of, the many proposals that have been put forward over the years for further integrationist advance. Insofar as they have voiced reservations about the course of integration it has usually been to express concern that it is not proceeding sufficiently quickly.

Germany – or to be strictly accurate West Germany up to 1990 and united Germany since – has also been a fairly dependable member of the integrationist camp. However, since EMU assumed a central position on the EC policy agenda in the late 1980s, and since too the unification of Germany has led to great strains on the German economy, a more cautious attitude has emerged towards certain aspects of the integration process. Political union is still generally supported, but concerns have arisen over whether EMU – and especially the projected single European currency – could threaten what have been central bulwarks of post-war German economic policy: low inflation and a strong currency.

In the early years of the EC France assumed a very wary attitude towards the integration process. This was a consequence of President de Gaulle's hostility to any international organisation which assumed supranational characteristics and, thereby, undermined French national sovereignty. The economic benefits which the Community was bringing to France were recognised and welcomed, but they were not to be paid for with transfers of national sovereignty to the likes of the Commission, the European Parliament, or a Council of Ministers taking its decisions by majority votes. Since de Gaulle's resignation in 1969, French concerns about losses of sovereignty have been less to the fore and this has enabled France to link with Germany on many issues and provide much of the drive of integrationist development. However, concerns with the sovereignty issue have never quite disappeared and this is why today France, although a strong supporter of monetary integration and defence cooperation (objectives which sit well with the traditional French aim of containing Germany), still tends towards a more intergovernmentalist stance than the other five founding states in respect of the powers of the EU's institutions.

☐ *The six post-foundation members of the European Community.* Although all were to make approaches to the European Community between 1961 and 1963 for either full or associated membership, and although all were to become full members by 1986, Denmark, Greece, Ireland, Portugal, Spain and the United Kingdom kept and/or were kept to the fringes of the development of Western European integration in integrative developments in the 1950s and 1960s and did not become Community members at that time. There were a number of reasons for this:

● In the case of Spain and Portugal, political and economic circumstances were unfavourable. The political circumstances were that both countries were authoritarian dictatorships to which the democratic governments of the founding six did not wish to be too closely attached. The economic circumstances were that both were predominantly agricultural and underdeveloped, and both were pursuing essentially autarkic economic policies until the end of the 1950s: factors which hardly made them suitable candidates for the ECSC, and which had the knock-on effect of excluding them from the EEC negotiations which the founding six opened up only to the UK.

• The Greek economy was similarly unsuitable for ECSC or EEC membership, being predominantly peasant-based. Additionally, Greece's history, culture and geographical position all rather put it outside the West European mainstream.

• Ireland and Denmark were also heavily dependent on agriculture and thus had little interest in the ECSC. As for the EEC, there were several reasons to doubt that it would be to their benefit, the most important of which was that both countries had strong economic and historical links elsewhere: in Denmark's case with the other Scandinavian countries and with the UK; in Ireland's case with the United Kingdom.

• Three factors were especially important in governing the United Kingdom's attitude. First, Britain saw itself as operating within what Churchill described as three overlapping and interlocking relationships: the Empire and Commonwealth; the Atlantic Alliance and the 'special relationship' with the United States; and Western Europe. Until the early 1960s Western Europe was seen as being the least important of these. Second, British governments were not prepared to accept the loss of sovereignty that integration implied. There were several reasons for this, in particular: Britain's long established parliamentary tradition; the record, in which there was considerable pride, of not having been invaded or controlled by foreign powers in modern times; a generally held view that cessation of sovereignty was neither desirable nor necessary, since Britain was still a world power of the first rank; and a certain distaste with the idea of being dependent on the not altogether highly regarded governments and countries of 'the Continent'. Third, Britain's circumstances were such that three of the four main integrationist organisations to be proposed in the 1950s had few attractions in terms of their specific areas of concern: the restrictions on national decision–making powers entailed in the ECSC looked very unappealing to a country whose coal and steel capacity far exceeded that of any of the six; the EDC would have limited governmental manoeuvrability and options at a time when Britain's defences were already stretched by the attempt to maintain a world role; and Euratom looked as though it would involve sharing secrets with less advanced nuclear powers. Only the EEC seemed to have much to offer, but amongst the problems it carried with it was its proposed supranationalism. From 1955 to 1958 attempts were made to persuade the six not to be so ambitious and to direct their attention to the construction of a West European free trade area, but with no success. As a result, and with a view also to increasing its bargaining power with the six, Britain looked elsewhere: to other non-signatories of the Treaty of Rome. This led, in January 1960, to the Stockholm Convention which established the European Free Trade Association (EFTA). Its founding members were Austria, Denmark, Norway, Portugal, Sweden, Switzerland and the United Kingdom.

❊   ❊   ❊   ❊

Two to three years after the EEC began functioning in 1958 the attitude of the UK Government began to change and membership came to be sought. The first enlargement of the Community could, in fact, have occurred much earlier than it did had President de Gaulle not opposed UK applications which were made in 1961 and 1967 – applications to which separate applications from Denmark, Ireland and Norway were, in practice, attached. There has been much speculation about the reasons for the General's veto: he feared that the United Kingdom would rival and would attempt to thwart his desire to place France at the centre of the European stage; he believed UK membership would unsettle the developing Franco-German alliance – an alliance that was given symbolic force with the signing in 1963 of a Friendship Treaty between the two countries; he was suspicious of the United Kingdom's close links with the United States and thought they would pave the way for American penetration and domination of Europe if the United Kingdom joined the Community. Whatever the explanation, the fact is the United Kingdom was barred from membership until after the resignation of de Gaulle and the election as President of Georges Pompidou. A different view was then taken in Paris: the United Kingdom might serve as a useful counterweight to the increasingly strong and self-confident Germany; UK governments would lend support to the French opposition to pressures within the Community for increased supranationalism; and France would probably gain economically by virtue of having better access to UK markets and as a result of the United Kingdom being a net contributor to the Community budget.

The reasons for the United Kingdom's changed position on Europe were a mixture of the political and the economic. Politically, it was increasingly clear that the United Kingdom was no longer a world power of the first rank. The Suez debâcle underlined the decline, and the increasing tendency from 1960 for key world issues to be discussed between the United States and the USSR on a purely bilateral basis further confirmed it. Paralleling this decline the nature and status of the 'special relationship' with the United States weakened and became increasingly questionable. Further to all this the Empire was giving way to the Commonwealth, a very loose organisation and not one that was capable of providing the United Kingdom with much international political support.

On all the usual economic indicators, such as growth in trade, in investment, in gross national product, and in income, the member states of the EC were outperforming the United Kingdom. For example, between 1958 and 1969 real earnings in Britain increased by about 38 per cent, whereas in the EC they increased on average by about 75 per cent. Quite simply the figures appeared to show that the Community was a success; all this at a time when the United Kingdom's pattern of trade, even when not a Community member, was turning away from the Commonwealth and towards Europe. Moreover, the growing economic strength of the EC seemed to be linked with a growing political status.

When Pompidou opened the door the Heath Government thus willingly took the United Kingdom in. It was joined by Denmark and Ireland, both of which had traditional economic and cultural links with the United Kingdom and which had consciously tied their applications to the Community with those from the United Kingdom since the early 1960s.

Since joining the Community Britain has been something of an awkward partner. This is because British Governments, especially since the Conservative Party assumed office in 1979, have taken a largely minimalist view as to what the Community should be doing and what organisational shape it should take. The strong preference has been for a Community that is primarily concerned with market-related matters: more particularly, for a Community that directs most of its efforts at creating a fully integrated and largely de-regulated common market. In order for this market to function properly and efficiently it has not been seen as being necessary for it to be associated with a raft of common economic, financial, and social policies, let alone for it to have a common currency. As for the political dimensions of Community membership, Britain has been willing to support the development of intergovernmental cooperation when that has seemed to be useful – as, for example, in the fields of foreign policy and aspects of internal security policy – but it has almost invariably sought to resist supranational developments and losses of national sovereignty.

Denmark's record since joining the Community has been not wholly dissimilar to that of the United Kingdom. Danish Governments have not been as obstructionist as their UK counterparts to integrationist developments but, aware of domestic scepticism on the supposed benefits of EC membership, they have preferred to swim in a slow integration stream. The most dramatic manifestation of Danish concern with the integration process occurred in 1992 when, in a national referendum, the Danish people rejected ratification of the Maastricht Treaty. This rejection, which was reversed in a second referendum in 1993, upset the schedule for applying the Treaty, took much wind out of the sails of those who wished to press ahead quickly with further integration, and saw Denmark distance itself from certain future integrationist projects (see Chapter 3 for further details on the Danish referendum).

As for the third country to join the Community in 1973 – Ireland – it has created no particular difficulties for the integration process since its accession. From time to time Irish Governments have intimated that their support for further integration is conditional on Ireland continuing to be generously treated by the Common Agricultural Policy (CAP) and the

Community's Structural Funds, but there has been no significant resistance to pro-integrationist winds.

Just as the countries which joined the Community in 1973 would have liked to have been members earlier, so was the accession of Greece delayed longer than Greek governments would have liked. The initial problem, recognised on both sides when Greece made its first approaches to Brussels soon after the EEC came into being, was the underdeveloped nature of the Greek economy. A transition period prior to membership was deemed to be necessary and this was negotiated in the form of an Association Agreement that came into force in 1962. The object of the Association was the 'continuous and balanced strengthening of trade and economic relations between the contracting parties, having particular regard to the need to secure an accelerated development of the Greek economy'. Full incorporation into the Community would, it was understood, follow when the Greek economy was capable of sustaining the obligations imposed by membership. However, from April 1967, when there was a military coup in Greece, until June 1974, when civilian government was re-established, the Association Agreement was virtually suspended. It might be thought that the effect of this would have been to further delay full membership. In fact, it had the opposite effect. After elections in Greece in November 1974 the new Government immediately made clear its wish to become a full member of the Community. The Commission issued a formal opinion that Greece was still not economically ready and proposed a pre-accession period of unlimited duration during which economic reforms could be implemented. In response, the Greek Government restated its wish for full membership and, in so doing, particularly emphasised how Community membership could help both to underpin Greek democracy and to consolidate Greece's West European and Western Alliance bonds. The Council of Ministers was sympathetic to these arguments, rejected the Commission's opinion, membership negotiations were opened in July 1976, and Greece entered the Community in 1981.

Since becoming a member of the Community, Greece has generally supported the advancement of the integration process. That said, particular Greek policies, concerns, and special needs have sometimes created considerable difficulties: sovereignty reservations have raised their head from time to time, especially when the Socialist Party (PASOK) has been in power; the deep-rooted Greek hostility towards Turkey and the complicated web of friendships and hostilities with parts of the former Yugoslavia have been major obstacles in the way of Community attempts to develop united and effective policies in South-East Europe; Greece's poverty (it is the poorest member state) has contributed to pressures on the

Community's redistributive policies and funds; and the highly unstable nature of the Greek economy has meant that it has had to seek special economic assistance from its partners and also that it has not been a very attractive or realistic participant in talks on EMU.

As with Greece, political considerations were also extremely important in influencing the relations between the two Iberian states and the Community prior to their accession. Initially the influence was a negative one: had not both Spain and Portugal been governed by dictatorial political systems until the mid-1970s they would in all probability have been members of the Community long before they were. Not that there was anything in the Treaties specifying that Community members must be liberal democracies: Article 237 of the EEC Treaty simply stated 'Any European State may apply to become a member of the Community'. The assumption was, however – as it is today in regard to applications to join the EU – that a democratic political system was a necessary qualification for entry. (Quite what the EU would do should democracy be overthrown in a member state is uncertain.)

So, although both Spain and Portugal requested negotiations on an association with the Community as early as 1962, and Spain made it quite clear that its request was with a view to full membership at some future date, both countries were treated with caution by the Community. Eventually they were granted preferential trade agreements – that for Spain coming into force in 1970, and for Portugal in 1973 as part of an agreement between the Community and all EFTA countries – but it was only with the overthrow of the Caetano regime in Portugal in 1974 and the death of General Franco in 1975 that full membership became a real possibility. Portugal applied in March 1977 and Spain in July 1977. The negotiations were protracted and difficult covering, amongst many problems, the threat posed to other Mediterranean countries by Spanish agriculture, the size of the Spanish fishing fleet, and the implications of cheap Spanish and Portuguese labour moving north. As in the Greek negotiations political factors helped to overcome difficulties: member states wished to encourage political stability in southern Europe; there was the opportunity to widen and strengthen the political and economic base of the Community; and, by helping to link southern Europe to the north, there were seen to be strategic advantages for both Western Europe and NATO.

Since their accession both Spain and Portugal have broadly gone along with integrationist developments, with the former perhaps being a little more integrationist than the latter. Fears which were expressed in some quarters before their accession that they would come to constitute a disruptive Iberian bloc have not been realised. To be sure, and as was to be expected, they usually adopt similar positions on issues of common concern – issues which in many instances are a consequence of them being southern, poorer, and neighbouring countries – but, as with other member states, their preferences on specific policy matters often diverge.

□ *Prospective members of the European Union.* In 1992 the EC formally opened accession negotiations with Austria, Finland and Sweden, and in 1993 it opened negotiations with Norway. These negotiations were successfully concluded in March 1994, with a view to each of the countries becoming members of the EU in 1995.

Two sets of factors stimulated these four countries (and Switzerland too – of which more below) to seek membership of the EU. First, what were previously regarded as virtually insuperable obstacles came, in the late 1980s/early 1990s, to be seen as less of a problem. So, for Austria and Sweden (and Switzerland too) the end of the Cold War diminished the importance of their traditional attachment to neutrality. For Finland, the difficulties posed by the country's relative geographical isolation, the close links with other Scandinavian countries, and the special position in relation to the Soviet Union, either withered or disappeared. And in Norway – which could hardly stand aside from the applications of its neighbours for membership – there were grounds (although by no means overwhelming grounds) for believing that the long-standing public opposition to EC membership was not as strong as formerly it had been. (Norway applied for EC membership on three occasions in the 1960s, linking its applications to those of the United Kingdom. On the third occasion terms of entry were agreed by the Norwegian Government, but were rejected by the Norwegian people in a referendum following a campaign in which suspicions about the implications for Norwegian agriculture, fishing, and national sovereignty figured prominently.)

The second set of factors stimulating the accession applications stemmed from the relationships of these countries to the EC. Austria, Finland, Sweden and Norway, plus Switzerland, Iceland, and the micro-state of Liechtenstein, make up the membership of EFTA. When it was constituted in 1960 with, as noted above, Denmark, Portugal and the United Kingdom then also as members, but not, at that stage, Finland or Iceland, EFTA had two principal objectives: the establishment of a free trade area in industrial products between the member countries, and eventually making Western Europe as a whole a free trade area for industrial goods. The first of these objectives was established in 1966 with the removal of virtually all customs duties and quantitative restrictions on trade in industrial products between EFTA countries, and the second was achieved in 1977 with the creation of an industrial free trade area between the EC and EFTA. Over time, however, despite relations between 'the twelve' and 'the six' being essentially friendly, and being indeed further developed via cooperation in such areas as environmental protection, scientific and technical research, and transport policy, EFTA states increasingly came to view key aspects of the EC–EFTA relationship as unsatisfactory. One reason for their dissatisfaction was that the EC was collectively much stronger than EFTA. A second, and related reason, was that the EC was prone to present EFTA with *de facto* situations to which EFTA countries had little option but to adjust – as, for example, when the Community laid down product specifications. This latter problem, of having to accept trading rules which they had played no part in helping to formulate, became of increasing concern to EFTA countries as the EC's programme to complete the internal market by 1992 – the SEM programme – gathered pace in the late 1980s/early 1990s. This concern played an important part in encouraging EFTA countries to reconsider the attractions of EC membership. It also led the EC – concerned that a widening of its membership might threaten its own deepening – to suggest that EC–EFTA relations be strengthened by the creation of a European Economic Area (EEA) which would, in effect, extend the SEM programme to the EFTA states but which would stop short of EC membership. The EEA was duly negotiated, and after a series of delays during the ratification process – which resulted in Switzerland withdrawing from the agreement – came into effect in January 1994. However, by this stage it had come to be accepted by most interested parties – including the governments of the EC which had in the interim succeeded in moving Community deepening forward via the Maastricht Treaty – that the ambitions of the governments of Austria, Finland, Sweden, and Norway would be satisfied only by full EU membership.

☐   *Other West European countries.* Leaving aside the assorted collection of micro-states which are scattered around Western Europe – such as Liechtenstein, Monaco, and San Marino – there are now only four significant Western European countries which are not members of, or which are not in the foreseeable future prospective members of, the EU.

The most prominent of these four countries is Switzerland. Until December 1992 Switzerland was in much the same position as Austria and Sweden. That is to say, it had long been a member of EFTA, the end of the Cold War had removed the main obstacle to it becoming a member of the EC/EU, an application for accession had been made, and it anticipated entry some time in the mid-1990s. However, in December 1992, in a referendum on whether to ratify the EEA, the Swiss people voted by 50.3 per cent to 49.7 per cent, not to ratify. As a consequence, the timetable for bringing the EEA into effect was delayed, and the Swiss application to join the EU, though left on the table, necessarily had to be put aside. In all probability it will be picked up again when political circumstances appear more favourable.

Cyprus and Malta both applied for EC membership in July 1990 but saw their applications received with less than enthusiasm – partly because of a reluctance on the Community's part to tackle the institutional questions which would be raised by the accession of very small states and, in the case of Cyprus, because it has long been the view in Community circles that the problem of the Turkish occupation of Northern Cyprus must be resolved before the accession of Cyprus can be contemplated. However, the prospects for both countries did improve in June 1993 when the Commission issued its official opinion on the two applications: whilst recognising that there were many difficulties ahead, the Commission generally supported the applications and, in a significant break with the past, indicated that it did not favour allowing the partition of Cyprus to be a reason for permanently excluding the accession of Greek Cyprus.

The fourth country, Iceland, did consider the possibility of EC membership at the time of the 1973 enlargement but concluded that there were too many policy difficulties in the way, especially in regard to fishing. This continues to be the case and explains why Iceland has not joined other EFTA states and sought EU accession.

▍ Concluding remarks: the ragged nature of the integration process

Since the Second World War the way in which West European governments relate and communicate with one another has been transformed. As part of this transformation a key role has been played by new international governmental organisations. Some of these are world-wide in their composition, others are regionally based; some have sweeping but vaguely defined responsibilities, others have specific sectoral briefs; some are purely intergovernmental in structure, others are overlain with supranational powers. At a minimum all provide frameworks in which national representatives meet with one another to discuss matters of mutual interest.

The best known, the most developed, and the most important West European-wide organisation is the EC which, since November 1993, has been part of the broader EU. But the EC has never been the only significant West European-wide organisation, and it was not the first organisation to be established. On the contrary, indeed, over the half century since the end of the Second World War, numerous proposals have been advanced, and many arrangements have been set in place, involving organised cooperation and integration between the states. The more ambitious of these have sought to bring the whole of Western Europe together in some sort of federal union. The more cautious and, it may be thought, the more realistic, have limited themselves to the pursuit of restricted aims for only some of the states.

So, although the logic of circumstances and of political and economic changes have brought the states much more closely together, there can hardly be said to have been a common and coherent integrationist force at work in Western Europe in the post-war years. Far from the states being bound together in the pursuit of a shared visionary mission, relations between them have frequently been extremely uncomfortable and uneasy, based as they have been on a host of different needs and of different perceptions of what is possible and necessary. In consequence, the processes of cooperation and of integration have operated in many different forums, at many different levels, in many different ways, and at many different speeds. Even in the EC, which has been at the integrationist core, the course of the integration process has varied considerably, with the mid-1970s until the early 1980s being the years of slowest integrationist advance, and the mid-1980s until the early 1990s being the fastest.

It is, of course, the conflicting nature of many of the factors which affect the integrationist process which has led to that process being so rocky, uncertain and unpredictable. Moreover, the factors themselves have been subject to considerable and unforeseeable change, as has been no more clearly demonstrated than since the late 1980s with the context in which the pressures which affect the furtherance of integration being transformed with the ending of the Cold War and the break-up of the Soviet Union. After four decades of Europe having been politically divided in two, decades in which Western Europe tended to think of itself as *being* Europe, fundamental issues concerning the nature of the Continent as a whole are now on the agenda. In these circumstances, new links, contacts and forms of cooperation are being established between the countries of Western and Eastern Europe. They are being established in ways and via means which are not wholly dissimilar to the processes which brought the nations of Western Europe themselves closer together in the early post-war years: tentatively, gradually, and via an array of functional, mixed-membership, and largely intergovernmental, groupings and institutions. The openly expressed hope of most East European countries is that as these East–West contacts become increasingly close, and as liberal democratic and market-based systems become more firmly established throughout Eastern and Central Europe, the way will be opened for their accession to the EU some time towards the end of the 1990s.

This wish on the part of East European states for close association with, and rapid accession to, the EU is illustrative of just how important the Union now is, most obviously in Europe itself but on the world stage too. Attention is, therefore, now turned, from what has been in this chapter a rather general review of the integration process, to a more specific examination of the creation and development of the EC (Chapter 2) and of the establishment of the EU (Chapter 3).

■ *Chapter 2* ■

The Creation and Development of the European Community

■ The European Coal and Steel Community

Much of the early impetus behind the first of the European Communities, the ECSC, emanated from two Frenchmen. Jean Monnet, who had pioneered France's successful post-war experiment with indicative economic planning, provided much of the technical and administrative initiative and behind-the-scenes drive. Robert Schuman, the French Foreign Minister from 1948 to early 1953, acted as the political advocate. Both were ardent supporters of European unity; both believed that the OEEC and the Council of Europe – where anyone could be exempted from a decision – could not provide the impetus that was required; and both came to the conclusion that, in Monnet's words, 'A start would have to be made by doing something both more practical and more ambitious. National sovereignty would have to be tackled more boldly and on a narrower front'.

Many of those who were attracted to the ECSC saw it in very restrictive terms: as an organisation that might further certain limited and carefully defined purposes. Certainly it would not have been established had it not offered to potential member states, and in particular to its two main pillars, France and West Germany, the possibility that it might act as a means of satisfying specific and pressing national interests and needs (see Chapter 1). But for some, not least Monnet and Schuman, the interest was much more ambitious and long-term. When announcing the plan in May 1950, Schuman – in what subsequently became known as the Schuman Declaration – was quite explicit that the proposals were intended to be but the first step in the realisation of a vision; a vision of a united Europe which would have Franco-German reconciliation at its heart. But, he warned, 'Europe will not be made all at once or according to a single general plan. It will be built through concrete achievements, which first create a *de facto* solidarity'. In similar vein, Monnet informed governments during the negotiations:

> The Schuman proposals provide a basis for the building of a new Europe through the concrete achievement of a supranational regime within a limited but controlling area of economic effort . . . The indispensable first principle of these proposals is the abnegation of sovereignty in a limited but decisive field.

Konrad Adenauer agreed with this. Addressing the Bundestag in June 1950 he stated:

> Let me make a point of declaring in so many words and in full agreement, not only with the French Government but also with M. Jean Monnet, that the importance of this project is above all political and not economic.

Schuman made it clear in his Declaration that whilst he hoped other countries would also participate, France and West Germany were going to proceed with the plan in any event (West Germany having already agreed privately in principle). Italy, Belgium, Luxembourg and the Netherlands took up the invitation, and in April 1951 the six countries signed the Treaty of Paris which established the ECSC. It came into operation in July 1952.

The Treaty broke new ground in two principal ways. First, its policy aims were extremely ambitious, entailing not just the creation of a free trade area, but also the laying of the foundations of a common market in some of the basic materials of any industrialised society: coal, coke, iron ore, steel and scrap. This, it was hoped, would ensure orderly supplies to all member states, would produce a rational expansion and modernisation of production, and would improve the conditions and lifestyles of those working in the industries. Second, it was the first of the European inter-state organisations to display significant supranational characteristics. These were found in the new central institutions that were established with powers, amongst other things, to: see to the abolition and prohibition of internal tariff barriers, state subsidies and special charges, and restrictive practices; fix prices under certain conditions; harmonise external commercial policy by, for example, setting minimum and maximum rates of customs duties on coal and steel imports from third countries; and impose levies on coal and steel production to finance the ECSC's activities. Four main institutions were created:

The High Authority was charged 'To ensure that the objectives set out in this Treaty are attained in accordance with the provisions thereof

(Article 8, ECSC Treaty). To enable it to perform its task the High Authority could issue, either on its own initiative or after receiving the assent of the Council of Ministers: decisions (which were to be binding in all respects in the member states); recommendations (which were to be binding in their objectives); and opinions (which were not to have binding force). Matters on which the High Authority was granted decision-making autonomy included the prohibition of subsidies and aids, decisions on whether agreements between undertakings were permissible or not, action against restrictive practices, the promotion of research, and the control of prices under certain conditions. It could impose fines on those who disregarded its decisions.

The High Authority thus had a formidable array of powers at its disposal and this, when taken in conjunction with its membership, gave it a clear supranational character. There were to be nine members, including at least one from each member state, and, crucially, all were to be 'completely independent in the performance of their duties'. In other words, none was to be, or to regard himself as being, a national delegate or representative.

In a number of respects the High Authority's powers were stronger than those which were to be given to the High Authority's equivalent, the Commission, under the Treaties of Rome. This has meant that since the institutions of the three Communities were merged in 1967, the Commission – which assumed the High Authority's powers – has had rather more room for independent manoeuvre when acting under the Treaty of Paris than it has when acting under the Treaties of Rome. In practice, however, it has not always been possible for these greater powers to be used to the full: from the earliest days of the ECSC, political realities have dictated that the High Authority/Commission be sensitive to governmental opinions and policies.

The Council of Ministers was set up mainly as a result of Benelux concern that if the High Authority had too much power, and there was no forum through which the states could exercise some control, the ECSC might be too Franco–German dominated. Ministers from the national governments were to constitute the membership of the Council, with each state having one representative.

'The Council shall exercise its powers in the cases provided for and in the manner set out in this Treaty, in particular in order to harmonise the actions of the High Authority and that of the Governments, which are responsible for the general economic policies of their countries' (Article 26, ECSC Treaty). More specifically, the Treaty gave the Council formal control over some, but very far from all, of the High Authority's actions: the Council had, for instance, to give its assent to the declaration of a manifest crisis which opened the door to production quotas. Decision-making procedures in the Council were to depend on the matter under consideration: sometimes a unanimous vote would be required, sometimes a qualified majority, sometimes a simple majority.

Practice has shown the Council to be not altogether consistent in the manner in which it has exercised its role under the ECSC Treaty. On the one hand, a general reluctance of the states to lose too much power over their domestic industries has normally resulted in the Council seeking to take most major decisions itself. Since decision-making in the Council has customarily proceeded on the basis of consensus, and since the states have often been unable to agree when difficult decisions have been called for, this has frequently led to very weak, or indeed even to an absence of, decision-making. On the other hand, when practicalities and political convenience have combined to suggest a less Council-centred decision-making approach, as they did with steel from the late 1970s, then the Council has been prepared to allow the High Authority/Commission a considerable measure of independence.

The Common Assembly's role was to provide a democratic input into ECSC decision-making. In practice it can hardly be said to have done so in the early years: members were not elected but were chosen by national parliaments, and the Assembly's powers – notwithstanding an ability to pass a motion of censure on the High Authority – were essentially only advisory. However, the expansion of the remit of the Assembly under the Rome Treaties to cover all three Communities, plus developments since the 1970s such as the introduction of direct elections and more streamlined procedures, have increasingly made for a more effective Assembly (or European Parliament as it is now called).

The Court of Justice was created to settle conflicts between the states, between the organs of the Community, and between the states and the organs. Its judgements were to be enforceable within the territory of the member states. In similar fashion to the Assembly, but not the High Authority or Council of Ministers which remained separate until 1967, the Court assumed responsibility for all three Communities when the EEC and Euratom Treaties entered into force in 1958.

In addition to these four main institutions a Consultative Committee, made up of producers, workers and other interested parties, was also created by the ECSC Treaty. The role of the Committee was to be purely advisory.

In its early years the ECSC was judged to be an economic success. Customs tariffs and quotas were abolished, progress was made in removing non-tariff barriers to trade, the restructuring of the industries was assisted, politicians and civil servants from the member states developed the practice of working with one another and, above all, output and inter-state trade rapidly increased (although many economists would now query whether the increases were *because* of the ECSC). As a result the ECSC helped to pave the way for further integration.

However, the success of the early years was soon checked. In 1958–9, when cheap oil imports and a fall in energy consumption combined to produce an overcapacity in coal production, the ECSC was faced with its first major crisis – and failed the test. The member states rejected the High Authority's proposals for a Community solution and sought their own, uncoordinated, protective measures. The coal crisis thus revealed that the High Authority was not as powerful as many had believed and that it was not in a position to impose a general policy on the states if they were resolved to resist.

This relative weakness of the High Authority/Commission to press policies right through is one of the principal reasons why truly integrated West European coal and steel industries, in which prices and distributive decisions are a consequence of an open and free market, have not emerged. Many barriers to trade still remain. Some of these, such as restrictive practices and national subsidies, the High Authority/Commission has tried to remove, but with only limited success. Others, particularly in the steel sector, have been formulated and utilised by the Commission itself as its task has switched from encouraging expansion to managing contraction.

But arguably the major problem with the ECSC has been that as coal and steel have declined in importance in relation to other energy sources, what has increasingly been required is not so much policies for coal and steel in isolation, but a coordinated and effective Community energy policy. National differences have prevented any such policy being possible.

■ From the ECSC to the EEC

In addition to the impetus that came from the ECSC there was another institutional development in the 1950s which played a particularly important role in paving the way for the creation of the two further European Communities that were to be created in 1957. This was the projected European Defence Community (EDC).

In the early 1950s, to the background of the Cold War and the outbreak of the Korean War, many Western politicians and military strategists took the view that there was a need for greater Western European cooperation in the field of defence. As part of this there was seen to be a pressing need to integrate West Germany – which was not a member of NATO – into the Western Alliance. The problem was that some European countries, especially France, were not yet ready for German rearmament, whilst West

Germany itself, though willing to rearm, was not willing to do so on the basis of the tightly controlled and restricted conditions that other countries appeared to have in mind for it. In these circumstances the French Prime Minister, René Pleven, launched proposals in October 1950 which offered a possible way forward. In announcing his plan to the National Assembly he stated that the French government 'proposes the creation, for common defence, of a European Army under the authority of the political institutions of a united Europe'. By the end of 1951 the same six governments which were in the process of establishing the ECSC had agreed to establish an EDC. Its institutional structure was to be similar to the ECSC: a Joint Defence Commission, a Council of Ministers, an advisory Assembly and a Court of Justice. In May 1952 a draft EDC Treaty was signed.

But, in the event, the EDC, and the European Political Community which increasingly came to be associated with it, were not established. Ratification problems arose in France and in Italy, and in August 1954 the French National Assembly rejected the EDC by 319 votes to 264 with 43 abstentions. There were a number of reasons why it did so: continuing unease at the thought of rearming Germany; concern that French governments would not have sole control of their military forces; doubts about the efficiency of an integrated force; disquiet that the strongest European military power (the United Kingdom) was not participating; and a feeling that, with the end of the Korean War and the death of Stalin, the EDC was not as necessary as it had seemed when it was initially proposed.

Following the collapse of the EDC, an alternative, and altogether less demanding, approach was taken to the still outstanding question of West Germany's contribution to the defence of the West. This took the form of a revival and extension of the Brussels Treaty 'for collaboration in economic, social and cultural matters and for collective defence' that had been signed in 1948 by the three Benelux countries, France and the United Kingdom. At a conference in London in the autumn of 1954 West Germany and Italy agreed to accede to the Brussels Treaty, and all seven countries agreed that the new arrangements should be incorporated into a Western European Union (WEU). The WEU came into effect in May 1955 as a loosely structured, essentially consultative, primarily defence-orientated, organisation that, amongst other things, permitted West German rearmament subject to various constraints. It also enabled West Germany to become a member of NATO.

The failure of the EDC, especially when set alongside the 'success' of the WEU, highlighted the difficulties involved in pressing ahead too quickly with integrationist proposals. In particular, it showed that quasi-federalist approaches in politically sensitive areas would meet with resistance. But, at the same time, the fact that such an ambitious scheme had come so close to adoption demonstrated that alternative initiatives, especially perhaps if they were based on the original Schuman view that political union was best achieved through economic integration, might well be successful. It was partly with this in mind that the Foreign Ministers of the ECSC six met at Messina in June 1955 to discuss proposals which had been made by the three Benelux countries for further economic integration. At their Conference the Ministers agreed on a resolution which included the following:

> The governments of Belgium, France, the Federal Republic of Germany, Italy, Luxembourg and the Netherlands consider that the moment has arrived to initiate a new phase on the path of constructing Europe. They believe that this has to be done principally in the economic sphere, and regard it as necessary to continue the creation of a united Europe through an expansion of joint institutions, the gradual fusion of national economies, the creation of a common market, and the gradual coordination of social policies. Such a policy seems to them indispensable if Europe is to maintain her position in the world, regain her influence, and achieve a steady increase in the living standards of her population.

To give effect to the Messina Resolution, a committee of governmental representatives and experts was established under the chairmanship of the Belgian Foreign Minister, Paul-Henri Spaak. The United Kingdom was invited to participate and did so until November 1955, but then withdrew when it became apparent that UK hopes of limiting developments to the establishment of a loose free trade area were not acceptable to the six. In April 1956 the Foreign Ministers accepted the report of the Spaak Committee and used it as the basis for negotiations which, in 1957, produced the two Treaties of Rome: the more important of these Treaties established the European Economic Community (EEC), the other created the European Atomic Energy Community (Euratom).

Both before and after April 1956 negotiations between the six governments were extensive and intense. In very broad terms it can be said that clear provisions were made in the Treaties for those areas on which the governments were able to reach agreement, whilst where there were divisions matters were largely left aside for further negotiations and were either omitted from the Treaties altogether or were referred to only in a general way. So, in the EEC Treaty, the future rules on trade were set out fairly clearly, but only guiding principles were laid down for social policy and for agricultural policy.

The inclusion in the EEC Treaty of topics such as social policy and agricultural policy highlights the fact that the content of the Treaties reflected a series of compromises between the six, especially between the two strongest countries – France and West Germany. France feared that Germany was likely to be the main beneficiary of the more open markets of the proposed customs union and so looked for compensation elsewhere. This took a number of forms. For instance: insisting on special protection for agriculture – the French farmer had historically been well protected from foreign competition and around one-fifth of the French population still earned their living from the land; pressing the case of an atomic energy Community, which would help guarantee France greater independence in energy through joint use of resources; and seeking privileged relations with the six for France's overseas dependencies.

Eventually the negotiations were completed, and, on 25 March 1957, the two Treaties were signed. Only in France and Italy were there any problems with ratification: the French Chamber of Deputies voted 342 for and 239 against, and the Italian Chamber of Deputies voted 311 for and 144 against. In both countries the largest bloc opposition came from the communists. The Treaties came into effect on 1 January 1958.

■ The EEC and Euratom Treaties

Of the two Rome Treaties the EEC Treaty was by far the most important. Article 2 of the Treaty laid down the following broad objectives:

> The Community shall have as its task, by establishing a common market and progressively approximating the economic policies of Member States, to promote throughout the Community a harmonious development of economic activities, a continuous and balanced expansion, an increase in stability, an accelerated raising of the standard of living and closer relations between the states belonging to it.

Many of the subsequent Treaty articles were concerned with following up these broad objectives with fuller, though still often rather general, guidelines for policy development. These policy guidelines can be grouped under two broad headings:

□ *Policy guidelines concerned with the establishment of a common market.* The common market was to be based on:

(1) The removal of all tariffs and quantitative restrictions on internal trade. This would make the Community a free trade area.

(2) The erection of a Common External Tariff (CET). This would mean that goods entering the Community would do so on the same basis no matter what their point of entry. No member state would therefore be in a position to gain a competitive advantage by, say, reducing the external tariffs on vital raw materials. The CET would take the Community

beyond being a mere free trade area and would make it a customs union. It would also serve as the base for the development of a Common Commercial Policy (CCP).

(3)   The prohibition of a range of practices having as their effect the distortion or prevention of competition between the member states.

(4)   Measures to allow not only for the free movement of goods between the member states but also the free movement of persons, services and capital.

☐   *Policy guidelines concerned with making the Community more than just a common market.* Making it exactly what, however, was left unclear, as it had to be, given the uncertainties, disagreements and compromises which formed the background to the signing of the Treaty. There was certainly the implication of a movement towards some sort of general economic integration, and references were made to the 'coordination' of economic and monetary policies, but they were vague and implicitly long-term. Such references as there were to specific sectoral policies – as, for example, the provisions for 'the adoption of a common policy in the sphere of agriculture', and the statement that the objectives of the Treaty 'shall . . . be pursued by Member States within the framework of a common transport policy' – were couched in fairly general terms.

The EEC Treaty was thus very different in character from the constitutions of nation-states. Whereas the latter have little, if anything, to say about policy, the EEC Treaty had policy as its main concern. The nature of that concern was such that many have suggested that the policy framework indicated and outlined in the Treaty was guided by a clear philosophy or ideology: that of free market, liberal, non-interventionist capitalism. Unquestionably there is much in this view: on the one hand, the market mechanism and the need to prevent abuses to competition were accorded a high priority; on the other hand, there were few references to ways in which joint activities and interventions should be promoted for non-market-based purposes. But the case should not be overstated. First, because competition itself was seen as requiring considerable intervention and management from the centre. Second, because there were some provisions for non-market policies: in the proposed common policy for agriculture, for example, which was given a special place in the Treaty precisely because of (mainly French) fears of what would happen should agriculture be exposed to a totally free market; in the proposed social policy which was intended to help soften unacceptable market consequences; and in the proposed common transport policy where specific allowance was to be made for aids 'if they meet the needs of coordination of transport or if they represent reimbursement for the discharge of certain obligations inherent in the concept of a public service'. Third, because much of the Treaty was so vague, so general, and so dependent on the future cooperation of the states for successful policy development, there was never any question (let alone preference given the christian democratic and social democratic principles of most of the founders) of an immediate abandonment of national economic controls and a remorseless and inevitable drive towards uninhibited free market capitalism.

The policy concerns of the Euratom Treaty were naturally confined to the atomic energy field. Chapters of the Treaty covered many vitally important areas of activity – promotion of research, dissemination of information, health and safety, supplies, a nuclear common market, etc. However, and probably even more than with the EEC Treaty, differences between the states on key points resulted in the apparent force of many of the provisions of these chapters being watered down by exceptions and loopholes. For example, under Article 52 an Agency was established with 'exclusive right to conclude contracts relating to the supply of ores, scarce materials and special fissile materials coming from inside the Community or from outside'. Article 66, however, set out circumstances in which states could buy on the world markets provided Commission approval was obtained. Similarly, Treaty provisions aimed at a pooling and sharing of technical information and knowledge were greatly weakened – and were so largely at French insistence – by provisions allowing for secrecy where national security was involved.

Where the EEC and Euratom Treaties were most similar to national constitutions was in those articles which identified the main institutions of the Communities and those articles which specified the powers and some of the procedures of the institutions. The ECSC served as the institutional model, but with certain modifications which had as their effect a tilting away from supranationalism towards intergovernmentalism. As with the ECSC, both the EEC and Euratom were to have four principal institutions:

(1)   An appointed Commission would assume the role exercised by the High Authority under the ECSC. That is to say, it would be the principal policy initiator, it would have some decision-making powers of its own, and it would carry certain responsibilities for policy implementation. But it would have less power than the High Authority to impose decisions on member states.

(2)   A Council of Ministers, with greater powers than its equivalent under the ECSC, would be the principal decision-making body. Circumstances in which it must take its decisions unanimously, and circumstances in which majority and qualified majority votes were permissible, were specified.

(3)   An Assembly would exercise advisory and (limited) supervisory powers. In the first instance it would be composed of delegates from national parliaments but after appropriate arrangements were made it was to be elected 'by direct universal suffrage in accordance with a uniform procedure in all Member States'.

(4)   A Court of Justice was charged with the duty of ensuring that 'in the interpretation and application of this Treaty the law is observed'.

A Convention, which was also signed on 25 March 1957, specified that the Assembly and the Court of Justice should be common to all three Communities.

These institutional arrangements were rather more intergovernmental in character than those who dreamed of political integration would have liked. In particular, the Council of Ministers was judged to have been given too much power and there was also disappointment that most of the key decisions in the Council would have to be made unanimously. However, there was hope for the future in that there were grounds for believing that the system could, and probably would, serve as a launching pad for a developing, a creeping, supranationalism. One of these grounds was provision in the EEC Treaty for increased use of majority voting in the Council as the Community became established. Another was the expectation that the Assembly would soon be elected by direct suffrage and that its power would thereby be increased. And a third was the seemingly reasonable assumption that if the Community proved to be a success the member states would become less concerned about their national rights and would increasingly cede greater powers to the central institutions.

■ Supplements and amendments to the Treaties

The Treaty of Paris and the two Treaties of Rome thus constitute the Founding Treaties of the three European Communities. Each of the three treaties is still of very great importance today since each – especially the EEC (now called EC) Treaty – constitute, albeit in considerably amended form, core elements of the Treaty on European Union.

Over the years, in response to pressures for the constitutional framework of the EC to be simplified, to be clarified, to be extended, to be made more democratic, and generally to be strengthened, the Founding Treaties have been supplemented and amended in various ways. Up to the supplements and amendments introduced by the Treaty on European Union – which constitute the principal focus of Chapter 3 – the most important supplements and amendments were brought about via the following Treaties and Acts:

☐ *The Treaty Establishing a Single Council and a Single Commission of the European Communities.* Signed in 1965, coming into force in 1967, and generally known as the Merger Treaty, this established a single Council of Ministers for all three Communities (though different individuals would attend different meetings), and also merged the High Authority of the ECSC, the Commission of Euratom, and the EEC Commission with one Commission. The powers exercised by these merged bodies were still to be based on the Founding Treaties: in other words, the Treaties and the Communities themselves were not merged.

☐ *The Treaty Amending Certain Budgetary Provisions of the Treaties* (signed in 1970) and the *Treaty Amending Certain Financial Provisions of the Treaties* (signed in 1975). Together, these two Treaties laid down a budgetary procedure and allocated budgetary powers between the Community institutions. Of particular importance, given its relative weakness in most policy areas, were the powers allocated to the Parliament. The 1975 Treaty also established a Court of Auditors to examine the accounts of all revenue and expenditure of the Community.

☐ *The Act Concerning the Election of the Representatives of the Assembly by Direct Universal Suffrage.* Signed in 1976, but not finally ratified by all the member states until 1978, this Act provided the legal base for direct elections to the European Parliament, laid down certain rules for their conduct, but did not in any direct way increase the powers of the Parliament.

☐ *The Treaties of Accession.* These provided for the enlargement of the Community to include Denmark, Ireland and the United Kingdom (signed in 1972 and taking effect on 1 January 1973), Greece (signed in 1979 and taking effect on 1 January 1981), and Spain and Portugal (signed in 1985 and taking effect on 1 January 1986).

☐ *The Single European Act (SEA).* Signed in February 1986, but not coming into force until mid-1987 because of ratification difficulties in Ireland, the SEA was something of a mixed bag, containing tidying up constitutional provisions, provisions designed to give the Community a new impetus, and provisions which altered aspects of the Community's decision-making system. The most important measures of the SEA were:

(1)   A number of new policy areas were formally incorporated into the EEC Treaty, and the capacity for decision-making in these areas was thereby increased. The policy areas included environment, research and technological development, and 'economic and social cohesion' (basically regional policy).

(2)   The completion of the internal market by 1992 was identified as a specific goal and was incorporated into the EEC Treaty via a new Article 8A.

(3)   For ten EEC Treaty articles a new legislative procedure was established – the cooperation procedure. The purpose of the new procedure was to improve the efficiency of decision-making in the Council of Ministers, and to increase, though not by too much, the powers of the European Parliament. Key features of the cooperation procedure were to be: the single reading of legislative proposals by the European Parliament and the Council of Ministers under the traditional consultation procedure was replaced by two readings; the Council could, subject to certain restrictions, take its decisions at both first and second readings by a qualified majority vote – this amounted to a significant increase in the Treaty base for majority voting; the European Parliament's ability to influence the content of Community legislation was increased, though it still did not enjoy full legislative powers; a strict timetable was established for the later stages of the legislative process. Legislative areas covered by the cooperation procedure included some social policy matters, implementing decisions in connection with the regional fund and research and technological development programmes, and, most crucially of all – under a new EEC Article 100A – most of the measures 'which have as their object the establishment and functioning of the internal market'.

(4)   The European Parliament's role and potential influence in the Community was also increased via the establishment of a new 'assent procedure'. Under the procedure, the European Parliament's assent, by an absolute majority of members, became necessary both for the accession of new members to the Community (under Article 237, EEC) and for association agreements between the Community and third countries (under Article 238, EEC).

(5)   European Political Cooperation (EPC) (the official Community term for foreign policy cooperation), which had increasingly been practised since the early 1970s, but outside the Treaty framework, was put on a legal basis. (But not by Treaty incorporation.)

(6)   Meetings of the twelve Heads of Government in the framework of the European Council, which had been taking place since 1975 were, for the first time, given legal recognition. (But not by Treaty incorporation.)

(7)   The capacity of the Court of Justice, which had been becoming very overstretched, was extended by the provision for the establishment of a new Court of First Instance.

In addition to its 'constitutional evolution', the Community has developed in many other ways too since it began functioning in 1958. The most important of these ways can be grouped under the three headings which now follow.

■ Enlargement

The most obvious change since the Community's foundation has been the doubling of the size of its membership from six states to twelve. As was explained in Chapter 1, this enlargement has taken place in three waves: in 1973 (when Denmark, Ireland and the United Kingdom joined), in 1981 (when Greece joined), and in 1986 (when Portugal and Spain joined).

All three enlargements have inevitably affected and changed the Community in important ways. First, and most obviously, the Community has, simply by becoming bigger, become a more important international organisation. It now contains a population of over 340 million; its membership includes all the larger, and traditionally more influential, West European states; and it is the world's principal commercial power, accounting for around one-fifth of world imports and world exports (not counting commerce between the member states themselves).

Second, internal decision-making has become more complex, with twelve representatives sitting around the Council of Ministers' table rather than six, and with a much wider range of national and political interests wishing to be satisfied.

Third, and this is linked to the previous point, the Franco–German axis, which did so much to set the pace in the 1960s and early 1970s, has become less central and less dominating. More generally, as the number of smaller states has increased, it has not been quite so easy for the larger states to push their preferences through.

Fourth, the policy debates, concerns, and priorities of the EC/EU have been affected as the new members have brought with them their own requirements and problems. So, for example, and of considerable importance for the future development of the EU, the growing influence, as a result of the second and third enlargements, of southern, less industrialised and poorer countries has produced pressures both for a reorientation of the Common Agricultural Policy (CAP) away from northern temperate products towards Mediterranean products, and also for more redistributive policies which will directly assist economic development in the south. (The North–South divide does not, of course, coincide completely with industrial/non-industrial or rich/poor divides: much of northern Spain is industrialised, most of Ireland is not; most of the UK outside southern England is relatively poor, much of northern Italy is relatively rich.)

On the subject of Community enlargement, it is worth making the point, because there has been some misunderstanding on the matter, that the incorporation of the territory of the former German Democratic Republic (GDR) into the Community in 1990 did not constitute an enlargement. German unification took the form of the GDR integrating into the Federal Republic of Germany, so there was no question of a new state joining the Community, nor, therefore, any need for an Accession Treaty.

The full implications of German unification for the EU are not yet clear. Much will depend on how quickly the territory of the former GDR adjusts to the full rigours of Community laws and policies in spheres such as the internal market and environmental protection. What is clear, however, is that in the medium to long term the position of Germany as the strongest and most influential Union state is likely to be enhanced.

As for the prospective enlargement of the EU to EFTA states (see Chapters 1 and 16), the transition should be relatively smooth since the countries concerned are all affluent, are all well established liberal democracies, and are all already well adjusted to many EU rules as a result of EU–EFTA arrangements and the EEA. Each country will, of course, bring with it particular concerns – about, for example, agriculture in the far north and about security on Finland's 700 mile border with Russia – but no fundamental disruption should be occasioned.

■ Developments in policy processes

In general terms, it may be said that the Rome Treaties indicated a pattern of policy-making and decision-making in which the Commission would propose, the Parliament would advise, the Council would decide, and – where law was made – the Court would interpret. In many respects this is indeed how relationships and processes have worked in practice. But there have also been important additions and amendments to the projected pattern. The nature of these additions and amendments is examined in some detail in later chapters, but three are particularly worth noting at this stage.

First, the relationships between the four institutions themselves have altered in a number of ways. As integration has evolved, all of the institutions have extended their interests and as this has happened they have increasingly become less compartmentalised and less self-contained within the Community system. This has led not only to a certain blurring of responsibilities, as lines of division over who does what have become less clear, but also to changes in the power balance and indeed to a more general sharing of powers. So, for example, the Council of Ministers has usurped some of the Commission's proposing responsibilities by becoming progressively more involved in helping to initiate and set the policy agenda; the Court has significantly affected the direction and pace of the integration process by issuing many judgements which have had considerable policy and institutional implications; and the European Parliament, greatly assisted by Treaty changes, has increasingly extended its legislative influence.

Second, an increasing range of participants not associated with the four main institutions have become involved in policy-making and decision-making. The most important of these participants are the Heads of Government who, in regular summits – known as European Council meetings – have come to assume key agenda setting responsibilities which have had the effect of reducing the power and manoeuvrability of both the Council of Ministers and the Commission. Prominent amongst other actors who have inserted, or have attempted to insert, themselves into decision-making processes are the many national and transnational sectoral interests and pressures that have come to cluster around the main institutions in order to monitor developments and, where possible, to advise or pressurise decision-makers.

Third, policy-making and decision-making processes have simply become more varied and more complex over the years as they have come to function in many different ways at many different levels. In addition to what occurs in the structured settings of Council and Commission meetings, Parliamentary plenaries and committees, and Court sittings, there is a mosaic of less formal channels in which representatives of the institutions, the states, and interests, meet and interact to discuss and produce policies and decisions. Which processes and channels operate in particular cases, and what types of interactions occur therein, varies considerably from sector to sector, and can even do so from decision to decision.

■ Development of policies

Along with its institutional structure and its policy-making and decision-making processes the EU is most distinguished from other international organisations by the range and weight of its policy responsibilities and commitments. These have expanded steadily over the years, stimulated and encouraged by factors such as the provisions of the Treaties, the increasing internationalisation of economic forces, stiffening international economic competition, a growing recognition of the benefits of working together, integrationist pressures emanating from central institutions (notably the Commission and the European Parliament), and the stimulus that policy development in one sphere often gives to developments in others.

Most of the EU's policies are firmly placed within the context of the EC. The best known of these policies is the Common Agricultural Policy (CAP). Consuming around half of the annual budget, the CAP has been the focus of frequent disagreements, most of which have centred on whether, and how, to deal with the closely related problems of guaranteed prices and overproduction. Since the early 1980s a series of measures have been adopted which have had the effect of bringing at least some aspects of the CAP's problems under control.

Though not, until recently at least, receiving as much publicity as the CAP, the policies which lie closest to the heart of the EC's policy framework are those which are aimed at creating what used to be called 'the Common Market' and which is now known as 'the internal market' or 'the Single European Market' (SEM). In essence, these are policies which are designed, on the one hand, to promote the free movement of goods, services, capital and people between the member states and, on the other hand, are designed to enable the EC to act jointly and present a common front in its economic and trading relations with third countries. Since the mid-1980s the SEM programme (or '1992 initiative' as it is still frequently called) has resulted in a considerable development of these market-based policies and in so doing, it has produced a great increase in the range and extent of the EC's regulatory presence. This is somewhat ironic since a key aim of the SEM programme is to liberalise and de-regulate the functioning of the market, but it is generally recognised and conceded (by some more readily than by others) that the market can operate on a truly fair and open basis only if key features of it are properly managed and controlled from the centre.

The EC has thus developed many policies which have direct implications for the operation of the market. So, for example, Community decision-makers have been, and still are, much concerned with the following:

establishing essential conditions for product standards and for their testing and certification (the details are usually worked out later by European standards organisations); opening up national monopolies and public procurement to competition; laying down criteria which companies must satisfy if they wish to trade in the market (this has been especially important in the sphere of financial services); and controlling the circumstances in which governments can and cannot subsidise domestic industries. In addition, however, to these 'pure' market policies, several policy areas in the social realm which have market implications have also become increasingly subject to EC regulatory control – usually as a consequence of some mix of genuine social concern on the one hand and appreciation on the other hand that divergences of national approaches and standards, whatever their intended purpose, create trade barriers. Examples of policy areas which have become subject to such social regulations include the environment, consumer protection, and working conditions.

The SEM momentum has had other policy consequences too. It has, for example, greatly boosted sectoral policies, with transport, telecommunications and energy amongst the policy spheres which have been the subject of considerable attention in recent years. Perhaps most dramatically, the SEM has stimulated the movement towards Economic and Monetary Union (EMU). Having long been identified as a Community goal, real progress towards EMU only began to be made in the late 1980s when most of the member states – strongly encouraged by the President of the Commission, Jacques Delors – came to the view that harmonised macroeconomic and financial policies, and perhaps also a single currency, would be required before the SEM could realise its full potential benefits. Accordingly, a strategy for creating EMU was gradually developed and this was specified in procedures and a timetable which were set out in the Maastricht Treaty.

In addition to the increasing involvement in market and market-related policies, the Community has, over the years, moved into other policy areas too. The most significant instances of this – significant in that they involve highly sensitive policy areas which are far removed from the original EEC policy focus of constructing a common market – are the Community's increasing responsibilities from the 1970s in respect of foreign policy and aspects of internal security policy. So extensive was the Community's foreign policy role by the 1980s that it was given legal recognition in the SEA, whilst both foreign policy and internal security policy were important components of the Maastricht Treaty (though, as will be shown in Chapter 3, as pillars of the EU rather than integral parts of the EC). Other non-market-based policies which illustrate the extent of the Community's net include the involvement – though not usually on mainstream policy matters – in various, educational, health, and cultural programmes.

■ *Chapter 3* ■

From European Community to European Union

■ The origins of the Treaty on European Union

Many of the Community's decision-making elites – both in Community institutions and in member states – were disappointed with the 1986 Single European Act (SEA). It did not, they believed, sufficiently advance the process of integration. In consequence, even before the SEA was ratified, the view was being expressed in many influential quarters that further integration would soon be necessary.

In the second half of the 1980s a number of factors combined to give weight and force to this body of opinion. These factors were both internal and external in kind.

The internal factors were mostly associated with the stimulus to further integration which stemmed from the 're-launching' of the Community in the mid-1980s. This re-launching, which was embodied in the Single European Market (SEM) programme and in the SEA, contained its own integrationist logic in that it gave a greater urgency to some long-standing but unresolved issues facing the Community and it also served to bring new issues onto the Community's agenda. Of particular importance in this context were four factors. First, many member states increasingly came to the view that the full benefits of the SEM could be realised only if action was taken to give effect to the commitment which was made in the SEA to move towards Economic and Monetary Union (EMU). More particularly, a single currency was increasingly seen as being desirable so as to eliminate the distortions to trade occasioned by changes in the value of currencies, so as to provide more stable conditions for business planning, and so as to remove the costs of currency conversions. Secondly, there was a growing acceptance of the need for a Community 'social dimension' which would soften and offset some of the liberal market/de-regulatory implications of the SEM. In addition to the social equity arguments for a social dimension, member states with high levels of social provision were anxious that there should not be 'social dumping' in the form of businesses being attracted to countries where levels of social provision were low and where, in consequence, business overheads were also likely to be low. Thirdly, the dismantling of border controls in the internal market created pressures for new and much improved mechanisms at Community level to deal with such problems as cross-border crime, drug trafficking, international terrorism, and the movement of peoples (the latter issue came to be seen as a cause of rising concern with the 'threat' of mass migration from Eastern Europe and North Africa to Western Europe). Fourthly, the long existing problem of a 'democratic deficit', which had not been properly addressed in the SEA, was increasingly seen as needing attention as the Community exercised ever more powers across a broad range of policy areas, but in a political context in which its decision-makers were not democratically accountable.

The external factors arose largely from the break-up of both the Soviet bloc and the Soviet Union. There were four main aspects to this. First, the collapse of communism in Central and Eastern Europe from the autumn of 1989, and the emergence in its place of would-be liberal democratic states with market-based economies, produced the likelihood that the Community would increasingly be dealing not only with West European, but with European-wide, issues and problems. In such circumstances – and with EFTA countries also contributing to the emergence of a wider Europe via the projected EEA and the reality or prospect of EC membership applications – it seemed to many that the Community should consolidate and strengthen itself so as to be better able to meet the challenges of the rapidly transforming Europe. Secondly, the unification of Germany, which formally occurred in October 1990, increased the potential for German domination of the Community and led many to conclude that it was necessary to advance the integration process so as to try and ensure that the future would see a European Germany rather than a German Europe. Advancing integration would also, it was argued, ensure that the new Germany would not be tempted to start detaching itself from aspects of Community affairs so as to enable it to be in a better position to take advantage of the new opportunities to its east. Thirdly, the break-up of the Soviet Union in 1991 greatly contributed to feelings of uncertainty about the future nature and stability of the European continent. More broadly, the break-up also raised questions about the shape and direction of the international system. In this situation the already existing pressures for a strengthening of the Community's policy and institutional capacities were inevitably strengthened. Fourthly, the implications of the ending of the Cold War had to be addressed since they heralded the disappearance of the framework which had provided much of the rationale, focus and setting for the foreign and defence policies of most West European countries for over forty years. Questions now inevitably arose about the suitability of existing arrangements in the post-Cold War era. Was it not time for the Community to be seeking to develop and strengthen its foreign and security policy roles and mechanisms? The belief of many that indeed it was time was reinforced by what was seen to be an inadequate Community response to the 1990–1 Gulf crisis and war: during the conflict the twelve member states were able to act in a reasonably united way at the declaratory level, but they could not agree on all aspects of policy action and they adopted very different positions in regard to making contributions to the Task Force of Operation Desert Storm.

From the mid-1980s several factors thus combined to build up a head of steam for another round of Community deepening: that is to say, for the further development of integration between the member states. There were, of course, those who sought to resist the rising pressures – notably the UK Government which had little desire to go much beyond a Community which was essentially a common market with various forms of intergovernmental cooperation tacked on – but most of the Community's key decision-making elites accepted the need for further integration. Their motives varied considerably: for some, long-held adherences to the federalist cause were a source of inspiration; for many, there was a fear that if deepening was not advanced the Community could be seriously threatened by dilution when the anticipated widening of the Community in the form of accessions by EFTA states occurred in the mid-1990s; and, for virtually all, there was a perceived need to press ahead with, and enhance the Community's competence and authority in regard to, at least some of the issues and matters which had become problematical since the mid-1980s – EMU, the social dimension, foreign and security policy, and the efficiency and accountability of the Community's institutions. As the 1980s gave way to the 1990s there was, therefore, a widely held belief in most Community circles that further fundamental reforms were necessary.

■ The making of the Treaty on European Union

There were three main stages involved in the making of the Treaty on European Union: the convening of the Intergovernmental Conferences, the work of the Intergovernmental Conferences and the Maastricht summit, and the ratification of the Treaty.

☐ *The convening of the Intergovernmental Conferences*

A series of European Council meetings between 1988 and 1990 saw steps taken which led to the convening of Intergovernmental Conferences (IGCs) on Political Union and on Economic and Monetary Union:

(1) At the June 1988 Hanover summit it was recalled that the SEA had confirmed the objective of progressive realisation of EMU and it was decided to entrust to a committee chaired by the President of the Commission, Jacques Delors, the task of studying and proposing concrete stages which could lead to EMU.

(2) The June 1989 Madrid summit agreed that the 'Delors Report' (which had been presented in April 1989) represented a basis for further work, agreed that stage one of EMU would begin on 1 July 1990, and also agreed that an IGC would be needed to lay down developments beyond stage one.

(3) The December 1989 Strasbourg summit formally agreed – against the wishes of the UK Government – to the convening of the IGC on EMU.

(4) The special April 1990 Dublin summit (Dublin I), which had initially been called to discuss German unification, responded to a Franco–German initiative to broaden out the impending IGC on EMU. The European Council 'confirmed its commitment to Political Union' and instructed the Foreign Ministers to carry out a quick and detached study of the need for possible Treaty changes with a view to the convening of an IGC on the matter.

(5) The June 1990 Dublin summit (Dublin II) agreed that IGCs on Political Union and on EMU would be opened in December at the Rome summit.

(6) The special October 1990 Rome summit (Rome I) accepted preparatory work which had been undertaken by officials on EMU and set out a framework for the IGC on EMU.

(7) The December 1990 Rome summit (Rome II) gave a broad remit to the IGC on Political Union and presided over the ceremonial opening of both IGCs.

At the procedural level the convening of the IGCs was thus very much the consequence of an incremental process. The need to make specific arrangements for EMU came increasingly to be accepted, and as this occurred the need to have a parallel examination of Political Union was increasingly recognised.

☐ The Intergovernmental Conferences and the Maastricht Summit

The IGCs met throughout 1991. They each operated at three levels. At the most senior level were national ministers – Foreign Ministers in the IGC on Political Union and Finance Ministers in the IGC on EMU. Both sets of ministers met once a month for most of the year. At the second level were very senior national officials – in the IGC on Political Union these were usually the Permanent Representatives to the Community (see Chapter 5), whilst in the IGC on EMU they were drawn from Ministries of Finance and Central Banks. The officials in the IGC on Political Union usually met weekly and those in the IGC on EMU met bi-monthly. The third level consisted of working parties of national experts which were established and convened as and when they were deemed to be necessary. Coordination of the work of the two IGCs was the responsibility of the Foreign Ministers.

As their title makes clear the Conferences were intergovernmental in character, so the two main non-governmental Community institutions – the Commission and the European Parliament (EP) – were always likely to have to struggle to exert an influence. The Commission was, in fact, a participant in the discussions at all levels and did its utmost – not least via the submission of numerous position papers – to influence outcomes. However, because it did not enjoy the same negotiating status as the member states, and was certainly in no position to attempt to veto agreements, its negotiating hand was weak. Partly in consequence of this, but partly in consequence too of it adopting an advanced integrationist position on many issues, the eventual outcome of the IGCs, especially that on Political Union, was a disappointment to the Commission.

The EP was even more disadvantaged than the Commission in that it was not a participant in the discussions, though it was given some opportunities to make an input: there were monthly inter-institutional conferences between ministers and a delegation of twelve MEPs (alternating between the two IGCs); the President of the EP was invited to address the opening of ministerial level meetings; the chairmen of the IGCs attended relevant EP debates and appeared, once during each presidency, before the appropriate EP committee; and the Presidents of the Council, the Commission and the EP met from time to time. On these and other occasions the EP did what it could to press its hopes for significant integrationist advance – hopes which were expressed in the Martin Reports (named after the *rapporteur* of the Committee on Institutional Affairs). The EP also sought to take advantage of resolutions adopted by the Italian and Belgian parliaments which stated that they would only ratify the

Treaty amendments if the EP (which had no formal veto powers) gave its approval. Despite its best efforts, however, the IGC negotiators did not concern themselves too much with the EP's views – not least because it was known that in the last analysis MEPs would be extremely unlikely to reject reforms which advanced the cause of integration, even if they did not advance it as much as the EP wanted. In consequence, the EP – rather like the Commission, and for much the same reasons – was disappointed with the eventual outcome.

As to the positions adopted by the key participants in the IGCs – the representatives of the member states – certain generalisations can be made: the Netherlands, Luxembourg, Belgium and Italy were the most consistent in taking a highly integrationist – federalist, some would call it – outlook; Spain, Ireland, Portugal, Greece and, to a lesser extent, Denmark were willing to support significant integrationist advances but had reservations on a mixture of specific issues; Spain, Ireland, Portugal and Greece also made it clear that – as the least prosperous member states of the Community – they wished to see a considerable strengthening of policies dealing with economic and social cohesion included in any final agreement; France was very supportive of EMU but tended towards an intergovernmental stance in the Political Union IGC – by arguing, for example, for a stronger European Council and only very limited increases in the powers of the EP; Germany, by contrast with France, was a firm advocate of further political integration, and especially of greater powers for the EP, but was very cautious on EMU; finally, the United Kingdom adopted a minimalist position on virtually all proposals which implied integration with supranational implications.

But generalisations tell only part of the story, for on particular subjects in the IGCs a complex mosaic of views, reflecting different national interests, often existed. This may be illustrated by reference to the reactions to a proposal put forward by the Dutch Presidency in early November to apply the proposed new co-decision-making procedure (which would greatly enhance the powers of the EP) to a wide span of Community policies: Spain and Portugal opposed the application of the procedure to the research framework programme and to the environment; Luxembourg, with some support from the Commission, opposed its application to internal market harmonisation; France and Spain opposed its application to the objectives of the Community's structural funds, and France also opposed its application to development cooperation programmes; and the United Kingdom opposed its application to anything.

Despite, however, all the differences of view and of interest, progress was gradually made and, as scheduled, both IGCs presented their reports to the December 1991 meeting of the European Council at Maastricht. The IGC on EMU was able to reach agreement on virtually all issues within its remit and to present clear recommendations on Treaty reform to the summit. The IGC on Political Union – which had had to deal with a much wider range of institutional and policy issues – was not quite so successful, in that a number of particularly contentious matters had to be referred to the summit for final resolution.

At Maastricht, the matters which it had not been possible to resolve in the IGCs were tackled. The most difficult of these issues were the United Kingdom's opposition to any significant extension of the Community's social dimension and its opposition also to being committed to participating in the projected single currency. After extremely difficult, tense, and exhausting negotiations all the outstanding issues were resolved. Concessions were made on all sides and a new treaty – the Treaty on European Union – was agreed.

After being carefully examined by a working party of legal and linguistic experts the Treaty on European Union (TEU) was formally signed by Foreign and Finance Ministers at Maastricht in February 1992.

☐ *The ratification of the Treaty*

In accordance with established procedures for Community Treaties and Treaty amendments, Article R of the TEU states that ratification by the member states should be 'in accordance with their respective constitutional requirements'. In ten of the member states this meant that ratification would be by parliamentary approval whilst in two – Ireland and Denmark – it meant that in addition to parliamentary approval it would also be necessary for the citizenry to give their approval in national referenda.

It was hoped that all ratifications could proceed relatively smoothly and quickly so as to enable the Treaty to enter into force on 1 January 1993. In eight member states – including Ireland – these hopes were realised, but in four they were not:

• In Denmark, in June 1992, the Danish people voted, by 50.7 per cent to 49.3 per cent, not to approve ratification. Naturally, this threw the ratification schedule off course, but more importantly it was also to have considerable implications for the interpretation of the Treaty because it was subsequently decided at European Council meetings that a twin track approach would be needed to persuade the Danes to give their approval in a second referendum: at the general level, integrationist rhetoric would be toned down and the decentralising subsidiarity principle, which (as will be shown below) had been only briefly referred to in the Treaty, would be given greater precision and a greatly enhanced status; at the level of dealing with specific Danish concerns, Denmark would be given special guarantees

– notably in the form of clear opt-outs from the Treaty provisions for a single currency and for a possible future Union defence policy. These 'concessions' to the Danes produced approval of the Treaty, by 56.8 per cent to 43.2 per cent, when the second referendum was held in May 1993.

● Shortly after the Danish vote was announced, President Mitterrand decided that France too would hold a referendum on the Treaty. The main reason for his decision was that he anticipated that the Treaty would be comfortably endorsed and that this would act as a boost to his domestic authority. In the event, however, the referendum campaign was bitterly and closely fought and ratification was approved in September 1992 by only 51.05 per cent to 48.95 per cent.

● In the United Kingdom, a combination of several factors – notably the Government's narrow majority in the House of Commons, considerable Parliamentary scepticism on the claimed beneficial consequences of the Treaty, and opposition by the Labour Party to the opt-out which had been granted to the United Kingdom from the Treaty's Social Chapter – combined to create a protracted ratification process in Parliament which was not completed until July 1993.

● Problems in Germany arose not from the people (there was no referendum) nor from the politicians (both the Bundestag and the Bundesrat ratified the Treaty with huge majorities in December 1992), but rather from claims that ratification would infringe the country's constitution. It was not until October 1993 that the German Constitutional Court ruled that there was no infringement, though it laid down conditions which would have to be met if there were to be significant changes or additions to the Treaty in the future.

German ratification cleared the way for the implementation of the Treaty and this took effect, ten months later than had originally been intended, on 1 November 1993.

■ The contents of the Treaty

The structure of the Treaty on European Union can be seen from its contents which are set out in Document 3.1.

In essence, the Treaty creates a new organisation, the European Union, which is based on three pillars: the European Communities; a Common Foreign and Security Policy; and Cooperation in the Fields of Justice and Home Affairs. The general objectives and overall structure of the European Union are set out in the Common Provisions of the Treaty (see Document 3.2).

Document 3.1 Treaty on European Union: contents		
Preamble		Articles
Title I	Common Provisions	A–F
Title II	Provisions amending the Treaty establishing the European Economic Community with a view to establishing the European Community	G–G86
Title III	Provisions amending the Treaty establishing the European Coal and Steel Community	H–H21
Title IV	Provisions amending the Treaty establishing the European Atomic Energy Committee	I–I29
Title V	Provisions on cooperation in the fields of justice and home affairs	J–J11
Title VII	Final provisions	L–S
Protocols (17)		
Declarations (33)		

Much time and effort was expended in the IGC on Political Union haggling over how the Treaty should describe the European Union, both in terms of its current character and the stage of its evolutionary progress. Most states wanted the word 'federal' included, and would have settled for a phrase which appeared in drafts where the Treaty was described as marking 'a new stage in the process leading gradually to a Union with a federal goal'. The UK government, however, was completely unwilling to see 'the F word' appear in any form at all and in the political trading which occurred at the Maastricht summit this point was conceded to the United Kingdom and the reference to federalism was replaced by 'This Treaty marks a new stage in the process of creating an ever closer union among the peoples of Europe, in which decisions are taken as closely as possible to the citizen'. To most Continental Europeans the phrase 'ever closer union' sounds more centralist than the word 'federal', but the UK delegation was satisfied.

As can be seen from the Common Provisions of the Treaty, the Union has a range of objectives (set out in Article B), it is based on a set of guiding principles (including subsidiarity and respect for democracy and fundamental human rights), and it is governed by an institutional structure which is presided over by the European Council. The Common Provisions are, however, relatively brief and general in character and it is with the more detailed provisions for the three pillars that the Treaty is mostly concerned. The principal features set out for the three pillars will now be examined.

Document 3.2   Common Provisions of the Treaty on European Union

Title I
COMMON PROVISIONS

Article A
By this Treaty, the High Contracting Parties establish among themselves a European Union, hereinafter called 'the Union'.

This Treaty marks a new stage in the process of creating an ever closer union among the peoples of Europe, in which decisions are taken as closely as possible to the citizen.

The Union shall be founded on the European Communities, supplemented by the policies and forms of cooperating established by this Treaty. Its task shall be to organize, in a manner demonstrating consistency and solidarity, relations between the Member States and between their peoples.

Article B
The Union shall set itself the following objectives:

– to promote economic and social progress which is balanced and sustainable, in particular through the creation of an area without internal frontiers, through the strengthening of economic and social cohesion and through the establishment of economic and monetary union, ultimately including a single currency in accordance with the provisions of this Treaty;

– to assert its identity on the international scene, in particular through the implementation of a common foreign and security policy including the eventual framing of a common defence policy, which might in time lead to a common defence;

– to strengthen the protection of the rights and interests of the nationals of its Member States through the introduction of a citizenship of the Union;

– to develop close cooperation on justice and home affairs;

– to maintain in full the '*acquis communautaire*' and build on it with a view to considering, through the procedure referred to in Article N(2), to what extent the policies and forms of cooperation introduced by this Treaty may need to be revised with the aim of ensuring the effectiveness of the mechanisms and the institutions of the Community.

The objectives of the Union shall be achieved as provided in this Treaty and in accordance with the conditions and the timetable set out therein while respecting the principle of subsidiarity as defined in Article 3b of the Treaty establishing the European Community.

Article C
The Union shall be served by a single institutional framework which shall ensure the consistency and the continuity of the activities carried out in order to attain its objectives while respecting and building upon the '*acquis communautaire*'.

The Union shall in particular ensure the consistency of its external activities as a whole in the context of its external relations, security, economic and development policies. The Council and the Commission shall be responsible for ensuring such consistency. They shall ensure the implementation of these policies, each in accordance with its respective powers.

Article D

The European Council shall provide the Union with the necessary impetus for its development and shall define the general political guidelines thereof.

The European Council shall bring together the Heads of State or of Government of the Member States and the President of the Commission. They shall be assisted by the Ministers for Foreign Affairs of the Member States and by a Member of the Commission. The European Council shall meet at least twice a year, under the chairmanship of the Head of State or of Government of the Member State which holds the Presidency of the Council.

The European Council shall submit to the European Parliament a report after each of its meetings and a yearly written report on the progress achieved by the Union.

Article E

The European Parliament, the Council, the Commission and the Court of Justice shall exercise their powers under the conditions and for the purposes provided for, on the one hand, by the provisions of the Treaties establishing the European Communities and of the subsequent Treaties and Acts modifying and supplementing them and, on the other hand, by the other provisions of this Treaty.

Article F

1. The Union shall respect the national identities of its Member States, whose systems of government are founded on the principles of democracy.
2. The Union shall respect fundamental rights, as guaranteed by the European Convention for the Protection of Human Rights and Fundamental Freedoms signed in Rome on 4 November 1950 and as they result from the constitutional traditions common to the Member States, as general principles of Community law.
3. The Union shall provide itself with the means necessary to attain its objectives and carry through its policies.

☐ *The European Communities*

This is by far the most important pillar since it incorporates most of the EU's policy responsibilities. Under the Treaty, the *acquis* of the existing three Communities is preserved and in several important respects is extended and strengthened by revisions of the EEC, ECSC, and Euratom Treaties. The revisions of the EEC Treaty are naturally the most significant and it is on these that attention will be focused here (see Document 3.3 for the contents of the Treaty in its revised form).

Article 1 of the revised EEC Treaty states 'By this Treaty, the High Contracting Parties establish among themselves a European Community'. This means that the European Economic Community – the EEC – is renamed the European Community. A rather confusing situation is thereby

Document 3.3 Treaty Establishing the European Community: contents

produced, in which the European Community is now part of the European Communities, which in turn are part of the European Union. Doubtless, in practice, all three names will be used virtually as synonyms for many years to come.

Two important new principles are introduced into the EC Treaty. First, the much discussed principle of subsidiarity is formally incorporated by a new Article 3b:

ARTICLE 3b

The Community shall act within the limits of the powers conferred upon it by this Treaty and of the objectives assigned to it therein.

In areas which do not fall within its exclusive competence, the Community shall take action, in accordance with the principle of subsidiarity, only if and in so far as the objectives of the proposed action cannot be sufficiently achieved by the Member States and can therefore, by reason of the scale or effects of the proposed action, be better achieved by the Community.

Any action by the Community shall not go beyond what is necessary to achieve the objectives of this Treaty.

Clearly Article 3b is very vague and much remains to be worked out in practice. In general, however, subsidiarity is taken to mean that policies should be decided at national, and perhaps even regional or local levels, whenever possible. Since the Treaty was negotiated, European Council meetings – notably the December 1992 Edinburgh summit – have developed guidelines designed to assist with the application of the subsidiarity principle.

Second, Part Two of the EC Treaty establishes Union citizenship, with every national of a member state becoming a citizen of the Union. Though symbolically significant, the practical effect of this is limited since citizens of the Union only 'enjoy the rights conferred by this Treaty'. One of these rights is the right to live and work anywhere in the territory of the member states, subject to certain limitations. Union citizens are also given the right to vote and stand as candidates in EP and local elections, subject again to certain limitations.

Because the principles of subsidiarity and Union citizenship are incorporated into the EC Treaty, and are not just confined to the Common Provisions of the EU Treaty, they are subject to the jurisdiction of the Court of Justice.

Other revisions to the EEC Treaty can be grouped under two broad headings:

(1)   *Institutional changes.* The revisions which fall under this heading are mostly designed to improve the efficiency and democratic nature of the Community's institutional structures and decision-making processes. Overall, the greatest impact is on the Council of Ministers, which becomes empowered to take a greater range of decisions on the basis of qualified majority votes, and on the EP, which is given increased powers and influence in several respects – notably regarding legislation.

The following list indicates the most significant institutional changes.

● A new legislative procedure – the co-decision procedure – is established. In effect the co-decision procedure builds on the cooperation procedure which was established by the SEA, by allowing – if the Council and the EP cannot agree at second reading – for the convening of a Conciliation Committee and for a third reading of legislation by both the Council and the EP. Unlike the cooperation procedure, however, which enables a determined Council to ignore the EP's expressed views, the co-decision procedure gives the EP, for the first time, a veto over legislative proposals it does not wish to accept.

● The policy areas subject to the cooperation procedure are revised, with some areas previously covered by the procedure being 'transferred out' to the co-decision procedure, and some new policy areas previously subject to the consultation procedure (which only allows for one reading of legislation) being 'transferred in'.

● The scope of the assent procedure, by which EP approval is necessary for certain EC actions, is extended.

● From January 1995 the term of office of Commissioners is extended from four to five years so as to bring the lifespan of a Commission closely into line with the lifespan of a Parliament. The national governments are to nominate by common accord, after consulting the EP, the person they intend to appoint as the President of the Commission. Other members of the Commission are to be nominated by the national governments in the established manner, but now in consultation with the nominee for Commission President. The entire prospective Commission is to be subject to a vote of approval by the EP before being formally appointed by common accord of the national governments.

● A Committee of the Regions is established for the purpose of providing the Council and the Commission with advice on matters of major importance for the regions. The Committee is of the same size (189) and to have the same distribution of national representatives as the Economic and Social Committee, but its members are to be representatives of regional and local authorities.

● The Court of Justice is given the power to impose fines on member states not complying with its judgements or failing to implement Community law.

● The EP is to appoint an Ombudsman to receive complaints from citizens 'covering instances of maladministration in the activities of the Community institutions or bodies, with the exception of the Court of Justice and the Court of First Instance acting in their judicial role'.

(2) *Policy changes*. The Community's policy competence is extended and strengthened. It is so in three main ways.

● The main features of Economic and Monetary Union are defined and a timetable for establishing EMU is specified.

With respect to the features, EMU is to include the irrevocable fixing of exchange rates leading to the introduction of a single currency and to the establishment of a European Central Bank (ECB) which will operate within the framework of a European System of Central Banks (ESCB). The main objectives of the ESCB will be to maintain price stability. In so doing it shall support the general economic aims and policies of the Community. The basic tasks to be carried out through the ESCB shall be: to define and implement the monetary policy of the Community; to conduct foreign exchange operations; to hold and manage the official foreign reserves of the member states; and to promote the smooth operation of payment systems. Under EMU, member states are to regard their economic policies as a matter of common concern and are to coordinate them within the Council.

With respect to the timetable, EMU is to be established in three stages. Stages one and two are transitional stages and are essentially concerned with promoting economic and monetary cooperation, coordination, and convergence between the member states. Stage one began in 1990 and stage two began on 1 January 1994. By the end of 1996 the Council, acting by qualified majority, shall decide: (1) whether a majority of the member states meet the convergence criteria for the adoption of a single currency (the criteria involve low rates of inflation, low government deficits, currency stability, and low interest rates); (2) whether a majority of the member states wish to enter stage three. If a date for the beginning of stage three has not been set by the end of 1997, the third stage will start automatically on 1 January 1999 for those states which meet the convergence criteria. In a protocol attached to the Treaty it was recognised that the United Kingdom 'shall not be obliged or committed to move to the third stage of Economic and Monetary Union without a separate decision to do so by its government and Parliament'. In another protocol the Danish Government reserved the right to hold a national referendum before participating in the third stage of EMU. (See below for accounts of both a subsequent 'hardening' of the Danish position on EMU, and also of the more general doubts about the prospects for EMU which arose in 1992–3.)

● Some policy areas in which the Community has not been previously involved, or in which its involvement has not had an explicit Treaty base, are brought into the EC Treaty for the first time. For example, a new chapter of the Treaty confirms the Community's commitment to help developing countries and to do so by providing multi-annual programmes. Beyond development policy, most of the other policy areas newly introduced into the EC Treaty are brought in only in a rather tentative manner, in the sense that the Community's responsibilities are carefully restricted. Policy areas thus identified include education, public health, consumer protection, trans-European networks, and competitiveness of industry.

● Community responsibilities in some policy areas which were first given Treaty recognition by the SEA are further developed. This applies particularly to research and technological development, the environment, and economic and social cohesion. As part of the strengthening of economic and social cohesion, a new fund – the Cohesion Fund – is established to provide financial assistance in the fields of environment and trans-European transport infrastructures.

● A policy area which created particular difficulties in the negotiations both before and at Maastricht was social policy. Eleven member states wished to build on and give a firm Treaty base to the Social Charter which had been adopted (by eleven votes to one) by the European Council in 1989, whilst the UK government wished to see no extension to the Community's existing responsibilities in this area – either by way of itemising specific social policies which the Community would develop, or by relaxing unanimity requirements and increasing the circumstances in which decisions could be taken by a qualified majority vote. After almost bringing the Maastricht summit to the point of collapse, the impasse was resolved by the eleven contracting a separate protocol and agreement on social policy. Precisely how this will operate in practice remains to be seen, but in broad terms it implies that many, probably most, social policy proposals will continue, in the first instance at least, to be brought forward in the traditional manner of trying to get full agreement by all twelve member states. If it then becomes apparent that the United Kingdom cannot accept a proposal, it will opt out of the deliberations and the eleven member states – using the Community's institutions, procedures, and mechanisms – will proceed on the basis of the protocol and agreement.

☐ *A common foreign and security policy*

The SEA stated that the member states 'shall endeavour jointly to formulate and implement a European foreign policy'. The TEU greatly stiffens this aim by specifying that the Union and its member states 'shall define and implement a common foreign and security policy . . . covering all areas of foreign and security policy', and by further specifying that the common policy 'shall include all questions related to the security of the Union, including the eventual framing of a common defence policy, which might in time lead to a common defence'.

The objectives of the Common Foreign and Security Policy (CFSP) are defined only in general terms: for example, 'to safeguard the common values, fundamental interests and independence of the Union', and 'to develop and consolidate democracy and the rule of law, and respect for human rights and fundamental freedoms'. More specific definition and elaboration of the principles and general guidelines of the CFSP are to be the responsibility of the European Council.

There are to be three principal ways in which the objectives of the CFSP are to be pursued:

• Systematic cooperation is to be established between the member states on any matter of foreign and security policy that is of general interest. Whenever it deems it necessary the Council shall, on the basis of unanimity, define common positions. Member states shall ensure that their national policies conform to such common positions.

- On the basis of general guidelines from the European Council, the Council may decide that a matter is to be the subject of joint action. In deciding on joint action, or at any stage during the development of a joint action, the Council may determine that implementation decisions should be taken by qualified majority vote.
- Under Article J.4 'The common foreign and security policy shall include all questions related to the security of the Union, including the eventual framing of a common defence policy, which might in time lead to a common defence'. The Western European Union, which 'is an integral part of the development of the Union', is requested 'to elaborate and implement decisions and actions of the Union which have defence implications. The Council shall, in agreement with the institutions of the WEU, adopt the necessary practical arrangements'. There is no provision for qualified majority voting on issues which have defence implications. In a Declaration annexed to the Treaty the Community members of the WEU (nine at the time of the Maastricht summit, ten since Greece joined in 1992) stated that the WEU 'will be developed as the defence component of the European Union and as the means to strengthen the European pillar of the Atlantic Alliance'.

This second pillar of the TEU thus puts European Political Cooperation (EPC), which has been well established for some time, within the broader framework of a Common Foreign and Security Policy. The pillar is also extremely significant in that it introduces two important new elements into the West European integration process. First, although foreign policy remains essentially intergovernmental in character, it does nonetheless become potentially subject to some qualified majority voting, if only for 'second-order' decisions. Second, defence makes its first formal appearance on the policy agenda, albeit somewhat tentatively.

☐   *Cooperation in the spheres of justice and home affairs*

The member states are to regard the following areas as matters of common interest:

(1) asylum policy;
(2) rules governing, and controls on, the crossing by persons of the external borders of the member states;
(3) immigration policy and residence rights of third-country nationals;
(4) combatting drug addiction;
(5) combatting international fraud;
(6) judicial cooperation in civil matters;
(7) judicial cooperation in criminal matters;
(8) customs cooperation;

(9) police cooperation to combat terrorism, drug trafficking and other serious crime through an EU-wide police intelligence office (Europol).

Any measures taken in regard to these matters must be in compliance with the European Convention on Human Rights.

In the nine areas of 'common interest' the Council may:

(1) Adopt joint positions and promote any suitable form of cooperation. Decisions are to be by unanimity.
(2) Adopt joint actions. It may decide, by unanimity, that measures implementing joint action are to be adopted by a qualified majority.
(3) Draw up conventions which it shall recommend to the member states for adoption in accordance with their respective constitutional requirements. Unless otherwise provided by such conventions, implementing measures shall be adopted within the Council by a majority of two-thirds of the member states.

To bring about cooperation in the areas of 'common interest' the member states are obliged by the Treaty to establish (and indeed have established) coordinating mechanisms between the relevant departments of their administrations. At the political level these mechanisms are headed by the Council of Ministers meeting in the form of Justice and Home Affairs ministers, and at the administrative level are headed by the Article K.4 Coordinating Committee. (The Committee was established under Article K.4 of the TEU.)

As with the CFSP pillar of the TEU, the significance of this Justice and Home Affairs (JHA) pillar lies not only in the substantive content of its provisions but also in the broader contribution which it makes to the integration process in Europe. There are, as there are with the CFSP pillar, policy and institutional aspects to this. Regarding the policy aspects, a legal base is given to cooperation in areas of activity which in the past have either been dealt with purely on a national basis or have been the subject of only rather loose and informal cooperation between the member states. Regarding the institutional aspects, whilst intergovernmentalism continues to prevail, a small hole in the dyke has appeared with the possibility of qualified majority decisions on certain aspects of policy implementation, and a rather big hole with provision for visa policy to be determined by qualified majority voting from 1996.

■ The Treaty and the integration process

Clearly the TEU significantly enhances the deepening of the integration process in Western Europe. As a result of the Treaty more policy competencies are passed from the member states to the European level, the powers of the institutions at the European level are strengthened, and supranationalism is given a further boost (see Table 3.1).

Whether, however, as many have claimed, the Treaty has created a federal system in all but name must be doubted. Or at least it must be doubted if the term federal is taken to denote a political system in which there is a reasonably clear and balanced division of policy responsibilities between central and regional levels, and in which too there is a reasonably coherent institutional framework in which the allocation of powers between the central and regional levels is set out. Certainly the EU displays federal characteristics, of which the most obvious are: (1) important policy

Table 3.1   *The Treaty on European Union and the deepening of the integration process: key points*

Institutional deepening	(a)	Provisions for greater efficiency
	•	more qualified majority voting in the Council of Ministers
	•	the European Council identified as the body which defines 'the general political guidelines' of the EU
	•	Court of Justice given the power to fine member states
	(b)	Provisions for greater democracy
	•	greater powers for the European Parliament, notably via the new co-decision procedure and the extension of the cooperation and assent procedures to more policy areas
Policy deepening		Extensions and consolidations of the EU's policy agenda, notably via:
	(1)	nature of, and timetable for, EMU specified
	(2)	CFSP provisions
	(3)	JHA provisions
	(4)	some policy areas explicitly brought into EC Treaty for the first time (including industrial competitiveness, consumer protection, and culture) and EC remit in some other policy areas extended (including environment, research and technological development, and economic and social cohesion)

responsibilities are exercised at both the central (EU) and the regional (member state) levels; (2) well developed institutional structures exist at both levels; (3) a central judicial body (the Court of Justice) has the authority to rule on 'who does what' disputes between the two levels in the EC pillar; and (4) there is common citizenship. However, several features normally found in federal systems are not present in the European Union, most notably: (1) although the centre's policy responsibilities are now considerable, the power balance between the centre and the regional units is still tipped very much towards the latter; (2) the control of financial resources is overwhelmingly in favour of the regional units, with the EU budget accounting for only around 3 per cent of the total of the national budgets; (3) the political structure of the EU can hardly be said to be well ordered or to be based on established and shared principles such as accountability, democracy, or the separation of powers; and (4) the rights embraced by the notion of Union citizenship are extremely limited in scope.

But, however the European Union's political nature is to be described – as federal, quasi-federal, confederal, or something else altogether which is perhaps unique to the EU – the fact is that a highly developed system of governance does exist. It is a system, moreover, which is still very much evolving. After all, the Maastricht Treaty does not, in any sense, mark the end of the integration process or even identify where that end may be. The discussions and negotiations which took place before and at Maastricht were characterised – as have been all such post-war discussions and negotiations – by considerable differences between the participants on the nature and pace of integration. What emerged from the process of negotiating the Maastricht Treaty was a compromise: a compromise which included aspects of different visions of the future of Europe, and a compromise which though it did not advance integration as much as most governments (notably the German, Italian and Benelux had hoped), did advance it further than at least one government (the UK) would have liked.

From the viewpoint of understanding the foundations, the development, and the essential nature of the European Community – now European Union – the Maastricht 'story' is extremely revealing. It is so because it highlights and confirms long-established characteristics and features of the integration process:

- *Economics before politics.* The major 'history-making' advances in integration have taken the form of agreeing to integrate aspects of economic activity and then, at times almost seemingly as an afterthought, realising that this requires political integration too if there is to be political direction and control. In practice there has, naturally, been considerable overlap and blurring between the economic and the political, but, from 1950–1, when the ECSC was created, to the Maastricht Treaty, the economic has usually preceded the political. So, for example, the strengthening of Community institutions that was provided for in the SEA was largely a consequence of this being seen to be necessary if the SEM programme was ever to be achieved. Similarly, the decision in 1991 to establish the IGC on Political Union was in considerable measure a follow-on from the earlier decision to establish the IGC on EMU.

• *Flexibility*. When, in the past, the member states, or a sufficient number of them, have wished to act together in a policy area and the established mechanisms have been judged to be not suitable for the purpose, then alternative ways of proceeding have been found. This was, for example, the case with the establishment and development of EPC from the early 1970s. The TEU continues with this tradition of adaptability and innovation, most notably in regard to: (1) the framework set out for the two non-Community pillars (some states regarded it as premature to bring the policy areas covered by the pillars into the EC); (2) the virtual opt-outs given to Denmark and the UK on EMU; and (3) the protocol and agreement on social policy. In one key respect, indeed, the Treaty even advanced the tradition of furthering integration by 'using what works', for though it is true that prior to Maastricht the Community did not always proceed twelve abreast – witness, for example the Exchange Rate Mechanism (ERM) of the European Monetary System (EMS) and the Schengen Agreement (which is concerned with free movement of persons) – the non-inclusion of member states in a policy area had never been provided for in treaty form before.

• *Incrementalism*. The integration process has been characterised by an almost constant edging forward, with 'advances' followed by pressures for more 'advances'. The TEU continues in this tradition with, for example, EMU very much a consequence of the unfolding of the SEM programme, and the increased powers of the EP resulting in large part from the long process of policy transfers to the Community. The Maastricht process reveals, not for the first time, phases and forms of integration inevitably and logically following from earlier – perhaps less significant – phases and forms.

• *Variable pace*. The pace of the integration process has varied considerably since the Community was founded in the 1950s with, in very general terms, the early 1960s, and the mid-1980s to 1991–2, being periods of rapid integration, and the late 1960s to the early 1980s being much more sluggish. A series of events and circumstances which have occurred since the TEU was signed in February 1992 have combined to, in some respects, raise doubts as to whether rapid integration can be maintained at the pace that was set in the years leading up to the Treaty. The most prominent of these events and circumstances have been: (1) the Danish and French referenda of 1992 have required the supporters of integration to become more cautious, whilst Denmark itself has been obliged to distance itself from some projected future integrationist developments – notably EMU and defence policy; (2) the prospects for EMU have been severely damaged by instability in the ERM and the EMS – an instability which became so acute in July/August 1993 that the ERM, one of the key mechanisms in the anticipated movement to EMU, was virtually suspended; (3) the inability of the EU states to act (as opposed to speak) in a united manner on the crisis in the former Yugoslavia, has raised serious doubts about the prospects for the CFSP pillar of the Maastricht Treaty.

• *Interplay between central and national actors.* Many theorists of Western European integration, most notably those who are sympathetic to what is known as neo-functionalism, are prone to make much of the role played in the integration process by central/supranational/transnational/ EU-wide actors of various kinds. The influence of the Commission, the EP, the Court of Justice, business elites, and an array of economic interests are cited most frequently in this regard. Unquestionably such actors have played a key role. For example, the Commission has been crucial in pressing the case for three of the major policy initiatives of recent years: the SEM, the social dimension, and EMU. However, it has been *national* decision-makers, in the collective forums of the European Council and the Council of Ministers, who have taken the final policy decisions, and these have been decisions of which the 'supranational' actors have frequently not approved, as in the case of the Political Union elements of the TEU which were extremely modest compared to what the Commission and the EP had been pressing for. Moreover, the role of national decision-makers has not been limited to responding to what is presented to them from 'central' actors, for they have frequently been in the forefront of setting the integrationist agenda themselves: the UK Government, for example, has been a strong advocate of the SEM; the French Government has been prominent in pressing for EMU; and several governments, not least those of the Benelux states, have sought to press forward whenever possible with further political integration. In addition to the key roles played by governments, other recent important national inputs into the integration process have included: the wishes of electorates (the 1992 Danish and French referenda); the views of a bank (*Bundesbank* reluctance to cut German interest rates is widely believed to have played a major part in precipitating the ERM crises of 1992–3); and the deliberations of a court (the delay in ratifying the Maastricht Treaty which was occasioned by the deliberations of the German Constitutional Court).

● *Interplay between intergovernmentalism and supranationalism.* A constant tension in the Western European integration process since the days of the 1948 Hague Congress has been the balance to be struck between intergovernmentalism and supranationalism. Some states – notably France under de Gaulle but still to some extent today, Denmark, and above all the UK – have wished to preserve as much national sovereignty as possible and thus have usually preferred loose, intergovernmental, forms of cooperation. Other states – notably Italy and the Benelux countries – have not worried too much about sovereignty issues and so have usually been in the fast, supranational, integrationist stream. These differing views have provided much of the focus for, and difficulties in, integrationist negotiations with, in recent years, most states wanting supranational progress to be made on many fronts and a minority of states (sometimes just one) wanting to hold the line. The line has not been held, but intergovernmentalism is still very important, and the TEU makes provision for it to be the operating principle in respect of many important matters: further Treaty revisions, new accessions, policy-making (as opposed to policy application) decisions under the CFSP and JHA pillars, and several policy spheres falling under the EC Treaty including fiscal and citizenship issues.

● *Prizes for everybody.* The big 'constitutional' integrationist advances of 1951 (the Treaty of Paris), 1957 (the EEC and Euratom Treaties), 1986 (the SEA), and 1992 (the Treaty on European Union) have been possible because member states have judged it to be in their interests to promote integration. Certainly there have been strong disagreements between the states as to just how much, and what kind of, integration they want, but it has been generally accepted that there are prizes for all to be gained from the integration process – with economic growth and prosperity being the most obvious prizes. However, because of their own particular needs and preferences, states have frequently argued that in addition to taking a share of general prizes they should also be awarded special prizes and they have sometimes insisted that such prizes be component parts of general agreements on integrationist advance. Notable instances of special prizes include: the provisions made in the SEA, largely at the behest of the poorer states, for the development of redistributive policies, and the provisions in the TEU on subsidiarity (mainly to satisfy the United Kingdom), on the possibility of opt-outs (for Denmark and the United Kingdom), and on strengthened redistributive policies including the creation of a new Cohesion Fund (at the insistence of the four poorer states – Greece, Ireland, Portugal and Spain).

● *An elite driven process.* Insofar as political and administrative elites tend to set the policy agenda, and in so far too as they take decisions without constant references back to electorates, political activity in all nation-states – in Europe and beyond – may be said to be elite driven. But it is so particularly in the EU because there are no direct lines of accountability between decision-makers and the citizenry. There is no opportunity to elect a European Government or to elect a European Parliament which commands full decision-making powers. Rather are the key EU decision-makers – in the European Council, the Council of Ministers, and the Commission – largely insulated from the normal democratic requirements of responsibility and accountability. Arguably this would not matter too much if there were strong grounds for believing that the citizenry were supportive of the integration process, or were happy to leave decisions about integration to the appropriate elites, but public opinion polls have suggested that in some states considerable reservations and doubts have existed at various times. The extent to which the integration process is elite driven, and the extent to which elites are not always fully in accord with popular concerns, was clearly demonstrated during the ratification process of the TEU when not only did the Danes vote 'No' in their first referendum and the French almost vote 'No', but opinion polls indicated that German and UK voters might also have rejected the Treaty had they been given the opportunity to do so.

The traits and features of the integration process which have just been identified can be expected to recur in the years ahead. For there is no final goal in the process; no point at which integration can be said to have reached its optimum point or to have been completed. Indeed, with aspects of the TEU hotly contested, with another IGC scheduled for 1996, with the EU committed to moving beyond the deepening questions which were the focus of the Maastricht Treaty to widening questions, it can confidently be anticipated that the 1990s will see continuing discussions and negotiations on the course of European integration.

■ *PART 2* ■

THE INSTITUTIONS AND POLITICAL ACTORS OF THE EUROPEAN UNION

■ Introduction

There are five main European Union institutions: the Commission, the Council of Ministers, the European Council, the European Parliament, and the Court of Justice. Chapters 4–8 consider each of these institutions and the political actors that are associated with them. Chapter 8 has also been taken as the most appropriate place to examine the nature and status of European Union law.

Chapter 9 looks at those institutions and actors which, though not given a chapter in their own right because of pressures of space, nonetheless also exercise an important influence in the EU: the Economic and Social Committee, the Committee of the Regions, the European Investment Bank, the Court of Auditors, and Interests.

■ *Chapter 4* ■

The Commission

Frequently portrayed as the civil service of the EU, the Commission is in reality both rather more, and rather less, than that: rather more in the sense that the Treaties, and political practice, have assigned to it much greater policy initiating and decision-making powers than national civil services, in theory at least, enjoy; rather less in that its role regarding policy implementation is greatly limited by virtue of the fact that it is agencies in the member states which are charged with most of the EU's day-to-day administrative responsibilities.

The Commission is centrally involved in EU decision-making at all levels and on all fronts. With an array of power resources and policy instruments at its disposal – and strengthened by the frequent unwillingness or inability of other EU institutions to provide clear leadership – the Commission is at the very heart of the EU system.

■ Appointment and composition

☐ *The College of Commissioners*

Seated at the summit of the Commission are the individual Commissioners who are each in charge of particular policy areas and who meet collectively as the College of Commissioners. Originally, they numbered nine, but with enlargements their size has grown: to thirteen, to fourteen, and now to seventeen. Each of the five larger countries has two Commissioners (France, Germany, Italy, Spain, and the United Kingdom), and the remaining seven smaller countries each has one. (See Appendix for the size of the Commission in the event of enlargement.)

Prior to the Commission which took up office in January 1993, Commissions were appointed every four years 'by common accord of the governments of the Member States'. Under TEU this procedure was changed to the following:

1. The members of the Commission shall be appointed, in accordance with the procedure referred to in paragraph 2, for a period of five years. . .

Their term of office shall be renewable.

2. The governments of the Member States shall nominate by common accord, after consulting the European Parliament, the person they intend to appoint as President of the Commission.

The governments of the Member States shall, in consultation with the nominee for President, nominate the other persons whom they intend to appoint as members of the Commission.

The President and the other members of the Commission thus nominated shall be subject as a body to a vote of approval by the European Parliament. After approval by the European Parliament, the President and the other members of the Commission shall be appointed by common accord of the governments of the Member States . . . (Article 158, EC Treaty).

The main effect of this new appointment procedure is to strengthen links between the Commission and the EP. This is done in two ways. First, by formalising, and stiffening a little, practices which developed in the 1980s regarding the appointment of the Commission and its President: member states are now obliged to consult the EP on who should be President (this will probably amount in practice to the EP having the right of confirmation since it is unlikely that a candidate who does not receive its approval will wish to proceed); the Commission is now obliged to present itself before the EP for a vote of confidence. Second, by bringing the terms of office of the EP and the Commission into close alignment: since 1979 the EP has been elected on a fixed five yearly basis in the June of years ending in four and nine (e.g. 1989 and 1994), and from January 1995 Commissions will take up office for periods of five years. (The transition gap was covered by appointing the Commission which took up office in January 1993 for only two years.)

The emphasis in the appointment procedure that the governments of the member states are to act by 'common accord' is to emphasise the collective, as opposed to the national, base of the Commission: Commissioners are not supposed to be national representatives but should 'in the general interests of the Community, be completely independent in the performance of their duties' (Article 157, EC). Much the same sentiments require Commissioners, on taking up their appointment, to give a 'solemn undertaking' that they will 'neither seek nor take instructions from any government or any other body'.

In practice, a full impartiality is neither achieved nor attempted. Although in theory the Commissioners are collectively appointed they are, in fact, national nominees. It would, therefore, be quite unrealistic to expect them, on assuming office, suddenly to detach themselves from previous loyalties and develop a concern solely for 'the wider European interest' – not least since a factor in their appointment is likely to have been an expectation that they would keep an eye on the national interest. (A particularly graphic illustration of this latter point was seen in the way that a UK Commissioner, Lord Cockfield, was not reappointed by Mrs Thatcher to the Commission which took up office in January 1989. She believed he had been over-zealous in his support for aspects of the internal market programme for which he was responsible, and rather than looking to British interests had 'gone native'.)

The Treaty insistence on complete independence of Commissioners is therefore interpreted flexibly. Indeed, total neutrality is not even desirable since the work of the Commission is likely to be facilitated by Commissioners maintaining links with sources of influence throughout the EU and this they can most easily do in their own member states. But the requirements of the system and the necessities of the EU's institutional make-up are such that real problems arise if Commissioners try and force their own states' interests too hard. It is both legitimate and helpful to bring favoured national interests onto the agenda, to help clear national obstacles from the path, to explain to other Commissioners what is likely to be acceptable in 'my' national capital. But to go further and act consistently and blatantly as a national spokesman is to risk losing credibility with other Commissioners. It also makes it difficult for the Commission to function properly since clearly it cannot fulfil its set tasks if its divisions match those of the Council of Ministers. The Commission which was appointed to office in January 1985 under the Presidency of Jacques Delors soon ran into difficulties of this kind: the chauvinism of some of its members played an important part in limiting the ability of the Commission to act efficiently as a coherent team. Open criticisms by members of the German Government of its two Commissioners for allegedly failing to defend their country's interests in Brussels created further problems.

There are no rules or understandings as to what sort of people, with what sort of experience and background, member governments should nominate. In general, it would be fair to say that Commissioners tend to be former national politicians just short of the top rank. However, there are many who do not fully fit such a description. So a significant – and increasing – number have held senior ministerial posts in their own countries, whilst others – now constituting a declining number – are best described as 'experts', 'technicians', or 'prominent national figures' of one kind or another.

Given the diverse political compositions of the EU's national governments there is naturally a range of political opinion represented in the Commission. The smaller countries tend to put forward somebody from, or associated with, their largest party. The five larger countries vary in what they do, but 'split representations' are common practice. Crucially, all governments have made it their custom to nominate people who are broadly pro-European and who have not been associated with any extremist party or any extreme of a mainstream party. So whilst Commissions have certainly contained party political differences, these have usually been within a range that has permitted at least reasonable working relationships.

The most prestigious and potentially influential Commission post is that of the Presidency. Although most important Commission decisions must be taken collectively by the seventeen Commissioners, the President is very much *primus inter pares*: he is the most prominent, and usually best known, of the Commissioners; he is the principal representative of the Commission in its dealings with other EU institutions and with outside bodies; he must try to provide forward movement for the EU and to give a sense of direction to his fellow Commissioners and, more broadly, to the Commission as a whole; he is directly responsible for overseeing some of the Commission's most important administrative services – notably the Secretariat General (which, amongst other functions, is responsible for the coordination of Commission activities and for relations with the Council and the EP) and the Legal Service; and he may take on specific policy portfolios of his own if he chooses. Inevitably, therefore, given the importance of the office, the European Council – which, notwithstanding the EP's increased powers, will continue to take the lead role in making the nomination for the post – takes great care as to who is chosen. In the past, appointees have tended to be people with senior ministerial experience and considerable political weight in their own country: Jacques Delors, for example (President for the unprecedentedly long period of ten years from January 1985) was a former French Minister of Finance. The dynamic interpretation which Delors gave to the role of the Presidency, and the expectations which have now come to be attached to the office, are likely to mean that in the future only the most prominent of national politicians are likely to be considered for the Presidency.

The distribution of the policy portfolios between the Commissioners is largely a matter of negotiation and political balance. The President's will is the most important single factor, but he cannot allocate posts simply in accordance with his own preferences. He is intensively lobbied – by the incoming Commissioners themselves, and sometimes too by governments trying to get 'their' Commissioners into positions which are especially important from the national point of view. Furthermore, the President is made aware that re-nominated Commissioners – of which there are usually nine or ten – may well be looking for advancement to more important portfolios, and that the five states which have two Commissioners expect at least one of 'their' nominees to be allocated a senior post. Bearing in mind all of these difficulties it is not surprising that unless a resignation, a death, or an enlargement enforces it, reshuffles do not usually occur during the lifetime of a Commission.

To assist them in the performance of their duties Commissioners have personal *cabinets*. These consist of small teams of officials, normally numbering six or seven except for the President's *cabinet* which is larger and numbers around twelve. Members of *cabinets* are mostly fellow nationals of the Commissioner, although at least one is supposed to be drawn from another member state. Typically, a *cabinet* member is a dynamic, extremely hard-working, 30–40 year old, who has been seconded or recruited from some part of the EU's administration, from the civil service of the Commissioner's own state, or from a political party or a sectional interest with which the Commissioner has links. *Cabinets* undertake a number of tasks: they generate information and seek to keep their Commissioner informed of developments within and outside his allocated policy areas; they liaise with other parts of the Commission, including other *cabinets*, for purposes such as clearing routine matters, building support for their Commissioner's policy priorities, and generally trying to shape policy proposals as they come up the Commission system; and they act as a sort of unofficial advocate/protector in the Commission of the interests of their Commissioner's country. Over and above these tasks, the President's *cabinet* is centrally involved in brokering the many different views and interests which exist amongst Commissioners and in the Commission as a whole, so as to ensure that as an institution the Commission is clear, coherent, cohesive, and efficient (see below for further discussion of the roles of Commissioners' *cabinets*).

☐ The Commission bureaucracy

Below the Commissioners lies the Commission bureaucracy. This constitutes by far the biggest element of the whole EU administrative framework, though it is tiny compared with the size of administrations in the member states. Of a total EU staff in 1993 of 26,4000, almost 18,000 were employed by the Commission – less than many national ministries and, indeed, many large city councils. (EU member states average 322 civil servants per 10,000 inhabitants, as against 0.8 per 10,000 for all EU institutions.) Of these 18,000, around 12,000 were employed in administration – including just over 4000 at the policy-making 'A' grades – 3400 were engaged in research and technological development, and 1650 were engaged in the translation and interpretation work which arises from the EU's nine working languages. (There are 72 possible language combinations, although most of the Commission's internal business is conducted in French or English.) The majority of the Commission's non-research staff are based in Brussels.

The Commission makes use of temporary employees of various kinds, many of whom do not have official contracts and who are not therefore included in official staffing figures. Most employees, however, are engaged on a permanent basis following open examinations, which, for the 'A' grades in particular, are highly competitive. (The 'A' grade has an eight point scale, with A1 at the top for Directors-General and A8 at the bottom for new entrants who have little or no working experience.) An internal career structure exists and most of the top jobs are filled by internal promotion. However, pure meritocratic principles are disturbed by a policy that tries to provide for a reasonable national balance amongst staff. All governments have watched this closely and have sought to ensure that their own nationals are well represented throughout the EU's adminis-trative framework, especially in the 'A' grades. For the most senior posts something akin to an informal national quota system operates, though this is now coming under threat following a ruling in March 1993 by the Court of First Instance annulling the appointments of two Directors – at A2 grade – in DGXIV (Fisheries) on the grounds that the successful applicants were chosen not because of their qualifications but because the countries from which they came – Italy and Spain – were 'owed' the jobs.

This multi-national staffing policy of the Commission, and indeed of the other EU institutions, has both advantages and disadvantages. The main advantages are:

(1)   Staff have a wide range of experience and knowledge drawn from across all the member states.

(2)   The confidence of national governments and administrations in EU decision-making is helped by the knowledge that compatriots are involved in policy preparation and administration.

(3)   Those who have to deal with the EU, whether they be senior national civil servants or paid lobbyists, can often more easily do so by using their fellow nationals as access points. A two way flow of information between the EU and the member states is thus facilitated.

The main disadvantages are:

(1)   Insofar as some senior personnel decisions are not made on the basis of objective organisational needs but result from national claims to posts and from the lobbying activities which often become associated with

this, staff morale and commitment is damaged. The parachuting of outsiders into key jobs is less easy than it was – partly because staff and staff associations have pressed for a better internal career structure – but in the Commission's upper reaches promotion is still not based on pure meritocratic principles.

(2) Senior officials can sometimes be less than wholly and completely EU-minded. For however impartial and even-handed they are supposed to be, they cannot, and usually do not wish to, completely divest themselves of their national identifications and loyalties.

(3) There are differing policy styles in the Commission, reflecting different national policy styles. These differences are gradually being flattened out as the Commission matures as a bureaucracy and develops its own norms and procedures, but the differences can still create difficulties, both within DGs – where officials from different nationalities may be used to working in different ways – and between DGs where there are concentrations of officials from one country: French officials, for example, have traditionally been over-represented in DGVI (Agriculture).

■ Organisation

☐ *The Directorates General*

The work of the Commission is divided into separate policy areas in much the same way as at national level governmental responsibilities are divided between ministries. Apart from specialised agencies and services – such as the Statistical Office and the Joint Research Centre – the Commission's basic units of organisation are its Directorates General. Somewhat confusingly for those who do not know their way around the system, these are customarily referred to by their number rather than by their policy responsibility. So, for example, Competition is DGIV, Agriculture is DGVI, and Energy is DGXVII (see Table 4.1).

The size and internal organisation of DGs varies. Most commonly, a DG has a staff of between 150 and 450, divided into between four and six directorates, which in turn are each divided into three or four divisions. However, policy importance, workloads, and specialisations within DGs, produce many departures from this norm. Thus, to take size, DGs range from DGIX (Personnel and Administration) which employs just over 2500 people and DGVI which employs around 850, to DGXVIII (Credit and Investments) and DGXXIII (Enterprise Policy) which each employ around 80. As for organisational structure, DGVI has eight directorates (two of which are themselves subdivided) and thirty-six divisions, whilst DGXV

Table 4.1 *Directorates General and Special Units of the Commission*

Directorates General

DGI	External Economic Relations
DGIA	External Political Relations
DGII	Economic and Financial Affairs
DGIII	Internal Market and Industrial Affairs
DGIV	Competition
DGV	Employment, Industrial Relations and Social Affairs
DGVI	Agriculture
DGVII	Transport
DGVIII	Development
DGIX	Personnel and Administration
DGX	Audiovisual, Information, Communication and Culture
DGXI	Environment, Nuclear Safety and Civil Protection
DGXII	Science, Research and Development
DGXIII	Telecommunications, Information Technologies and Industries
DGXIV	Fisheries
DGXV	Financial Institutions and Company Law
DGXVI	Regional Policy
DGXVII	Energy
DGXVIII	Credit and Investments
DGXIX	Budgets
DGXX	Financial Control
DGXXI	Customs and Indirect Taxation
DGXXII	(Formerly coordination of structural policies. Now disbanded).
DGXXIII	Enterprise Policy, Distributive Trades, Tourism and Cooperatives

Main Special Units and Services

Secretariat General of the Commission
Forward Studies Unit
Legal Service
Spokesman's Service
Translation Service
Joint Interpretation and Conference Service
Statistical Office
Consumer Policy Service
Joint Research Centre
Task Force 'Human Resources, Education, Training and Youth'
European Office for Emergency Aid
Euratom Supply Agency
Security Office
Office for Official Publications of the European Communities

(Financial Institutions and Company Law) has only two directorates and seven divisions and DGXXII has but one directorate and five divisions.

To meet new requirements and to improve efficiency, the organisational structure of the DGs is changed relatively frequently. So, for example, to enable the Commission to adapt to the Common Foreign and Security Policy (CFSP) requirements of the TEU, DGI (External Relations) was split in 1993 into two separate entities: a DGI for External Economic Relations and a DGIA for External Political Relations. DGI more or less corresponded to the former DGI, but DGIA was quite new and much of it was put together from staff who moved across from the Secretariat General – where they had been dealing with foreign policy in the context of European Political Cooperation or had been in the Legal Service – and from DGIX – those responsible for managing EC delegations in non-EC countries. (Further information on DGI and DGIA is provided in Chapter 14).

☐ *The hierarchical structure*

The hierarchical structure within the Commission is as follows:

- All important matters are channelled through the weekly meetings of the College of Commissioners. At these meetings decisions are taken unanimously if possible, but by majority vote if need be.
- In particular policy areas the Commissioner who is assigned the portfolio carries the main leadership responsibility.
- DGs are formally headed by Directors General who are responsible to the appropriate Commissioner or Commissioners.
- Directorates are headed by Directors who report to the Director General or, in the case of large DGs, to a Deputy Director General.
- Divisions are headed by Heads of Division who report to the Director responsible.

The structure thus appears to be quite clear. In practice, it is not completely so. At the topmost echelons, in particular, lines of authority and accountability are sometimes blurred. One reason for this is that a poor match often exists between Commissioners' portfolios and the policy responsibilities of the DGs. Community enlargements and the consequent increasing size of the Commission over the years have allowed for greater policy specialisation on the part of individual Commissioners, and a better alignment with the responsibilities of individual DGs but, even now, most Commissioners carry several portfolios, each of which may touch on the work of a number of DGs. Moreover, the content of portfolio responsibilities is changed from Commission to Commission. Some, such as Budget, Agriculture, or Regional Policy, are more or less fixed, but others, of a broader and less specific kind, can be varied, or even created, depending on how a new President sees the role and tasks of the Commission and what pressures the Commissioners themselves exert.

Another structural problem that arises in relation to Commissioners is the curious halfway position in which they are placed. To use the British parallel, they are more than permanent secretaries but less than ministers. For whilst they are, on the one hand, the principal Commission spokesmen in their assigned policy areas, they are not members of the Council of Ministers – the body which takes the final policy decisions on important matters.

These structural arrangements mean that any notion of individual responsibility, such as exists in most member states in relation to ministers – albeit usually only weakly and subject to the prevailing political currents – is difficult to apply to Commissioners. It might even be questioned whether it is reasonable that the Commission should be subject to collective responsibility – as it is by virtue of Article 144 of the EC Treaty which obliges it to resign if a motion of censure on its activities is passed in the EP by a two-thirds majority of the votes cast, representing a majority of all members. (No motion of censure has ever been passed.) Collective responsibility may be thought to be fair insofar as all Commission proposals and decisions are made collectively and not in the name of individual Commissioners but, at the same time, it may be thought to be unfair insofar as much of the Commission's activity and the fortunes of its attempts to develop policy are dependent on the Council. Indeed, the Commission is at a theoretical risk of being dismissed by a Parliament frustrated by its inability to censure the Council.

□ *Decision-making mechanisms*

The hierarchical structure that has just been described produces a 'model' route via which proposals for decisions make their way through the Commission machinery:

● An initial draft is drawn up at middle-ranking 'A' grade level in the appropriate DG. Outside assistance – from consultants, academics, national officials and experts, and sectional interests – is sought, and if necessary contracted, as appropriate. The parameters of the draft are likely to be determined by existing EU policy, or by guidelines that have been laid down at senior Commission and/or Council levels.

- The draft is passed upwards through superiors and through the *cabinets* of Commissioners and through the weekly meeting of the *chefs de cabinet*, until the College of Commissioners is reached. During its passage the draft may be extensively revised.
- The College of Commissioners can do virtually what it likes with the proposal. It may accept it, reject it, refer it back to the DG for re-drafting, or defer taking a decision.

From this 'model' route all sorts of variations are possible, and in practice are commonplace. For example, where draft proposals are relatively uncontroversial, or where there is some urgency involved, procedures and devices can be employed which have as their purpose the prevention of logjams at the top and the expediting of business. One such procedure enables the College of Commissioners to authorise the most appropriate amongst their number to take decisions on their behalf. Another procedure is the so-called 'written procedure' by which proposals which seem to be straightforward are circulated amongst all Commissioners and are officially adopted if no objection is lodged within a specified time, usually a week. Urgent proposals can be adopted even more quickly by 'accelerated written procedure'.

Another set of circumstances producing departures from the 'model' route is where policy issues cut across the Commission's administrative divisions – a common occurrence given the sectoral specialisations of the DGs. For example, a draft directive aimed at providing a framework in which alternative sources of energy might be researched and developed, would probably originate in DGXVII (Energy), but would have direct implications too for DGXII (Science, Research and Development), DGXIX (Budgets), and perhaps DGIII (Internal Market and Industrial Affairs). Sometimes policy and legislative proposals do not just touch on the work of other DGs, but give rise to sharp conflicts, the sources of which may be traced back to conflicting 'missions' of DGs: there have, for example, been several disputes between DGIII and DGIV (Competition), with the former tending to be much less concerned than the latter about rigidly applying EU competition rules if European industry is thereby assisted and advantaged. Provision for liaison and coordination is thus essential if the Commission is to be effective and efficient. There are various procedures and mechanisms which attempt to provide this necessary coordination. Four of these are particularly worth noting.

First, the President of the Commission has an ill-defined, but generally expected, coordinating responsibility. A forceful personality may be able to achieve a great deal in forging a measure of collective identity out of the varied collection of people, from quite different national and political backgrounds, who sit around the Commission table. But it can only be done tactfully and with adroit use of social skills. Jacques Delors, who presided over three Commissions – 1985–9, 1989–93, 1993–4 – unquestionably had the requirement of a forceful personality, but he also displayed traits and acted in ways which, many observers have suggested, had the effect of undermining team spirit amongst his colleagues: he indicated clear policy preferences and interests of his own; he occasionally made important policy pronouncements before fully consulting the other Commissioners; he criticised Commissioners in Commission meetings and sometimes, usually by implication rather than directly, did so in public too; and he frequently appeared to give more weight to the counsel of personal advisers and to people who reported directly to him – drawn principally from his *cabinet* and from the Commission's Forward Studies Unit – than to that of Commissioners.

Second, the College of Commissioners is, in theory at least, in a strong position to coordinate activity and take a broad view of Commission affairs. Everything of importance is referred to the Commissioners' weekly meeting and at that meeting the whole sweep of Commission interests is represented by the portfolios of those gathered around the table.

Commissioners' meetings are always preceded by other meetings designed to ease the way to decision-making:

• Informal and *ad hoc* consultations may occur between those Commissioners particularly affected by a proposal.
• The Commissioners' agenda is always considered at a weekly meeting of the heads of the Commissioners' *cabinets*. These *chefs de cabinet* meetings are chaired by the Commission's Secretary General and are usually held two days before the meetings of the Commission itself. Their main purpose is to reduce the agenda for Commission meetings by reaching agreements on as many items as possible and referring only controversial/difficult/major/politically sensitive matters to the Commissioners.
• Feeding into *chefs de cabinet* meetings are the outcomes of the six or seven meetings which are held each week of the *cabinet* members responsible for particular policy areas. These meetings are chaired by the relevant policy specialist in the President's *cabinet* and they have two main purposes: to enable DGs other than the sponsoring DG to make observations on policy and legislative proposals – in other words, they assist in the task of horizontal coordination; and to allow proposals to be evaluated in the context of the Commission's overall policy priorities.
• Officials from the different *cabinets*, who are generally well known to one another, often exchange views on an informal basis if a proposal which looks as though it may create difficulties comes forward. (Officially *cabinets* do not become involved until a proposal has been formally

launched by a DG, but earlier consultation sometimes occurs. Where this consultation is seen by DGs to amount to interference, tensions and hostilities can arise – not least because *cabinet* officials are usually junior in career terms to officials in the upper reaches of DGs.)

Third, at the level of the DGs, various management practices and devices have been developed to try and rectify the increasingly recognised problem of horizontal coordination. In many policy areas this results in important coordinating functions being performed by a host of standing and *ad hoc* committees – normally referred to as inter-service meetings – task forces and project groups, and informal and one-off exchanges from Director General level downwards.

Fourth, the main institutional agency for promoting coordination is the Secretariat General of the Commission, which is specifically charged with ensuring that proper coordination and communication takes place across the Commission. In exercising this duty the Secretariat satisfies itself that all Commission interests have been consulted before a proposal is submitted to the College of Commissioners.

However, despite these various coordinating arrangements a feeling persists in many quarters that the Commission continues to function in too compartmentalised a manner, with insufficient attention paid to overall EU policy coherence. Amongst the problems are these:

(1)   The Commission has a rather rigid organisational framework. Despite the development of horizontal links of the kind that have just been noted, structural relationships, both between and within DGs, remain too vertical. Although encouragement has been given, principally via the President's office, to the creation of agencies and teams which can plan on a broad front, these are not sufficiently developed, and in any event they have had difficulties in asserting their authority in relation to the DGs – especially the larger and traditionally more independent ones. As for the President himself, he has no formal powers to direct the actions of DGs, let alone the authority to dismiss or reassign the duties of those in the DGs whom he judges to be incompetent or uncooperative.

(2)   Departmental and policy loyalties sometimes tend to discourage new and integrated approaches to problems and the pooling of ideas. Demarcation lines between spheres of responsibility are too tightly drawn, and policy competences are too jealously guarded.

(3)   Sheer workload has made it difficult for many Commissioners and senior officials to look much beyond their own immediate tasks. One of the duties of a Commissioner's *cabinet* is supposedly to keep him abreast of general policy developments, but it remains the case that the Commissioner holding the portfolio on, say, energy, can hardly be

blamed if he has little to contribute to a Commission discussion on the milk market regime.

■ Responsibilities and powers

Some of the Commission's responsibilities and powers are prescribed in the Treaties and in Community legislation. Others have not been formally laid down but have developed from practical necessities and the requirements of the EU system.

Whilst recognising that there is, in practice, some overlap between the categories, the responsibilities and associated powers of the Commission may be grouped under six major headings: proposer and developer of policies and of legislation, executive functions, guardian of the legal framework, external representative and negotiator, mediator and conciliator, and the conscience of the Union.

□ *Proposer and developer of policies and of legislation*

Article 155 of the EC Treaty states that the Commission 'shall formulate recommendations or deliver opinions on matters dealt with in this Treaty, if it expressly so provides or if the Commission considers it necessary'.

What this means in practice is that under the EC Treaty, and indeed under the ECSC and Euratom Treaties too, the Commission is charged with the responsibility of proposing measures which are likely to advance the development of the EU. Under the CFSP and JHA pillars of the TEU such a role is not allocated, since the relevant Treaty provisions merely state that the Commission 'shall be fully associated with the work' in these areas.

In addition to its formal Treaty powers, political realities arising from the institutional structure of the EU also dictate that the Commission should be centrally involved in formulating and developing policy. The most important of these realities is that there is nothing like an EU Prime Minister, an EU Cabinet, or EU ministers capable of providing the Commission with clear and consistent policy direction, let alone a coherent legislative programme. Senior Commission officials who have transferred from national civil services are often greatly surprised at the lack of political direction from above and at the amount of room for policy and legislative initiation that is available to them. Their duties are often only broadly defined and there can be considerable potential, especially for the more senior 'A' grade officials, to stimulate development in specific and, if they wish, new and innovative policy areas. An indication of the scale of this activity is seen in the fact that in an average year the Commission is likely to send the Council 600–800 proposals, recommendations, and drafts, and over 300 communications, memoranda and reports.

Although in practice they greatly overlap, it will be useful here, for analytical purposes, to look at policy initiation and development, and legislative initiation and development, separately.

Policy initiation and development takes place at several levels in that it ranges from sweeping 'macro' policies to detailed policies for particular sectors. Whatever the level, however, the Commission – important though it is – does not have a totally free hand in what it does. As is shown at various points elsewhere in this book, all sorts of other actors – including the Council of Ministers, the EP, the member states, sectional groups, regional and local authorities, and private firms – also attempt to play a part in the policy process. In so doing they exert pressure directly on the Commission wherever and whenever that is possible. From its earliest deliberations on a possible policy initiation the Commission is obliged to take note of many of these outside voices if its proposals are to find broad support and if they are to be effective in the sectors to which they are directed. The Commission must concern itself not only with what it believes to be desirable but also with what is possible. The policy preferences of others must be recognised and, where necessary and appropriate, be accommodated.

Of the many pressures and influences to which the Commission is subject in the exercise of its policy initiation functions, the most important are those which emanate from the Council of Ministers. When the Council indicates that it wishes to see certain sorts of proposals laid before it, the Commission is obliged to respond. However, important though the Council has become as a policy initiating body (see Chapter 5), the extent to which this has produced a decline in the initiating responsibilities and powers of the Commission ought not to be exaggerated. For the Council often finds it difficult to be bold and imaginative, and tends to be better at responding than at originating and proposing. Further to this, there has been an increasing tendency since the early 1980s for major policy initiatives to be sanctioned at European Council rather than Council of Ministers level, and the Commission has adjusted itself quite well to this shift by not only taking instructions from the European Council but using it to legitimise its own policy preferences. Four examples, covering issues of great importance, illustrate the increasing mutual interdependence of the Commission and the European Council as regards policy initiation and development. First, the Commission's 1985 White Paper *Completing the Internal Market*, which spelt out a rationale, a programme, and a timetable for completing the internal market by 1992, was approved at the June 1985 Milan summit. Six months later, at the Luxembourg summit, it was agreed that this policy objective would be incorporated into the EEC Treaty via the SEA and that the institutional reforms which would be necessary if the 1992 objective was to be achieved would also be given Treaty status. Second, from shortly after the SEA came into operation in 1987, the Commission, and more especially Jacques Delors, began pressing the case for Economic and Monetary Union (EMU). The Commission played a major part in helping to set and shape the EMU policy agenda, with the consequence that the EMU provisions of the TEU largely reflected the Commission's preferences. Third, at the Strasbourg European Council in December 1989, the Commission's *Community Charter of the Fundamental Social Rights of Workers* (commonly referred to as 'the Social Charter') was adopted. The Charter did not contain specific legislative proposals for the application of the Charter – they were left to an accompanying action programme – but the adoption of the Charter has since acted as an important reference point for the development of an EU social dimension. Fourth, the important agreement reached at the 1992 Edinburgh summit for the EU's future spending plans for the rest of the decade was based to a considerable extent on the proposals which had been made earlier in the year by the Commission in its document *From the Single Act to Maastricht and Beyond: The Means to Match our Ambitions*. (The totals proposed by the Commission were scaled down, but the distributional pattern was, for the most part, accepted.)

The Commission's policy initiating activities are not, of course, restricted just to major, cross-sectional, innovatory policies and policy programmes of the kind which have just been cited. They can take many different forms. For example: attempting to generate a more integrated approach to a policy sector – as with the 1992 White Paper *Communication on the Future Development of the Common Transport Policy*; attempting to strengthen existing policy frameworks – as with the 1993 Communication *Reinforcing the Effectiveness of the Internal Market* and the working document *Towards a Strategic Programme for the Internal Market*; and attempting to promote ideas, discussion and interest as a possible preliminary to getting a new policy area off the ground – as with the 1992 Green Paper on the *Development of the Single Market for Postal Services* or the 1993 Green Paper on *The European Dimension of Education*. Whatever their particular focus, however, most – though not all – policy initiatives need to be followed up with legislation if they are to have bite and be effective.

❈   ❈   ❈   ❈

The Commission alone has the powers to initiate and draft legislation. The other two main institutions which are involved in the legislative process, the Council and the EP, can request the Commission to produce proposals (the Council under Article 152, EC and the EP under Article 138b, EC) but they cannot do the initiating or the drafting themselves. Moreover, after a legislative proposal has been formally tabled the Commission still retains a considerable measure of control, for though the proposal may fail to find sufficient support to enable it to be passed (in practice increasingly unlikely, except for controversial matters), it is extremely difficult for the Council or the EP to amend it without the Commission's agreement: the Council can only do so by acting unanimously, and the EP can only do so in limited circumstances and then only with the support of an absolute majority of its component members.

As with its drafting of policy proposals, in drafting its legislative proposals the Commission makes considerable use of outside sources, and is often subject to considerable outside pressures. An important part in these sounding and listening processes, especially at the pre-proposal stage (that is, before the Commission has formally presented a legislative proposal to the Council and the EP) is played by a vast network of advisory committees that have been established over the years.

☐ *The Commission's advisory committee network.* The committees are of two main types.

(1) *The expert committees.* These consist of national officials, experts and specialists of various sorts. Although nominated by national governments the members are not normally viewed as official governmental spokesmen – in the way that members of Council working parties are (see Chapter 5) – so it is usually possible for the committees to conduct their affairs on a very informal basis. Many of these committees are well established, meet on a fairly regular basis, and have a more or less fixed membership; others are *ad hoc* – set up, very frequently, to discuss an early draft of a Commission legislative proposal – and can hardly be even described as committees in that they may only ever meet once or twice. As for their interests and concerns, some of the committees are broad and wide-ranging, such as the Advisory Committee on Restrictive Practices and Dominant Positions and the Advisory Committee on Community Actions for the Elderly, while others are more specialised and technical, such as the Advisory Committee on Unfair Pricing Practices in Maritime Transport and the Committee of Experts on International Road Tariffs.

(2) *The consultative committees.* These are composed of representatives of sectional interests and are organised and funded by the Commission

without reference to the national governments. Members are normally appointed by the Commission from nominations made by representative EU level organisations: either umbrella groups such as the Union of Industrial and Employers' Confederations of Europe (UNICE), the European Trade Union Confederation (ETUC), and the Committee of Professional Agricultural Organisations of the European Community (COPA), or more specialised sectoral organisations and liaison groups such as the Common Market Group of the International Union of Railways (IUR), or the Committee of Transport Unions in the Community (ITF–ICFTU). The effect of this appointments policy is that the consultative committees are made up overwhelmingly of full-time employees of associations and groups. The largest number of consultative committees are to be found in the agriculture sector, where there are over twenty committees for products covered by a market regime, plus half a dozen or so more general committees. Most of the agricultural advisory committees have a membership of between thirty and fifty, but there are a few exceptions: the largest are those on cereals (54), milk and dairy products (52), and sugar (52); the smallest are the veterinary committee and the committee on hops, each of which have fourteen members.

In addition to these two types of committees there are many hybrids with mixed forms of membership.

Most of the advisory committees are chaired and serviced by the Commission. A few are serviced by the Council and are, technically, Council committees, but the Commission is entitled to observer status on these so the distinction between the two types of committees is of little significance in terms of their ability to advise the Commission.

The extent to which policy sectors are covered by advisory committees varies. One factor making for variation is the importance of the policy within the EU's policy framework – it is hardly surprising, for example, that there should be many more agricultural advisory committees than there are educational advisory committees. Another factor is the dependence of the Commission in particular policy areas on outside expertise and technical knowledge. And a third factor is the preferences of DGs – some incline towards the establishment of committees to provide them with advice, others prefer to do their listening in less structured ways.

The influence exercised by the advisory committees varies enormously. In general, the committees of national experts are better placed than the consultative committees. There are a number of reasons for this. First, Commission consultation with the expert committees is usually compulsory in the procedure for drafting legislation, whereas – despite their name – it is usually optional with the consultative committees. Secondly, the expert committees can often go beyond offering the Commission technical advice, to alerting it to probable governmental reactions to a proposal and, therefore, to possible problems that may arise at a future decision-making stage if certain views are not incorporated. Thirdly, expert committees also have the advantage over consultative committees of tending to meet more regularly – often convening as necessary when something important is in the offing – whereas consultative committees tend to gather on average no more than two or three times a year. Usually, consultative committees are at their most influential when they have high-ranking figures amongst their membership, when they are given the opportunity to discuss policy at an early stage of development, when the timetable for the enactment of a proposal is flexible, and when the matter under consideration is not too constrained by existing legislation.

☐ *Executive functions*

The Commission exercises wide executive responsibilities. That is to say, it is closely involved in the management, supervision and implementation of EU policies. Just how involved varies considerably across the policy spectrum but, as a general rule, it can be said that the Commission's executive functions tend to be more concerned with monitoring and coordinating developments, laying down the ground rules, carrying out investigations and giving rulings on significant matters (such as proposed company mergers, state aids, and applications for derogations from EU law) than they are with detailed 'ground level' policy implementation.

Three aspects of the Commission's executive functions are worth special emphasis.

(1) *Rule-making powers*. It is not possible for the Treaties, or for legislation which is made in the name of the Council or the European Parliament and the Council, to cover every possible area and eventuality in which a rule may be required. In circumstances and under conditions that are defined by the Treaties and/or EU legislation the Commission is, therefore, delegated rule-making powers. This puts the Commission in a similar position to national executives: because of the frequent need for quick decisions in that grey area where policy overlaps with administration, and because too of the need to relieve the normal legislative process of over-involvement with highly detailed and specialised matters, it is desirable to have truncated and special rule-making arrangements for 'administrative' and 'technical' law.

The Commission normally issues between 6000 and 7000 legislative instruments per year. These are in the form of directives, regulations, and decisions. (The Commission also issues a large number of other instruments – in particular recommendations and opinions – but these do not usually have legislative force.) Most of this Commission legislation is confined to the filling in of details, or the taking of decisions, that follow automatically from Council, or European Parliament and Council, legislation. So the greatest proportion of Commission legislation is made up of regulations dealing with price adjustments and market support measures under the Common Agricultural Policy. Exhibit 8.1 (p. 212) provides an example of such legislation. (See Chapter 8 for an examination of the differing types of EU legislative instruments.)

But although most of the Commission's rule-making powers are confined to the routine and the straightforward, not quite all are. In at least three areas opportunities exist to make not just 'administrative' law, but what verges on 'policy' law. First, under the ECSC Treaty, the Commission is granted extensive rule-making powers subject, in many instances, only to 'consultations' with the Consultative Committee of the ECSC and with the Council of Ministers. Article 60, for example, gives the Commission powers to define what constitutes 'unfair competitive practices' and 'discrimination practices', and under Article 61 it may set maximum prices. If a state of 'manifest crisis' is declared, as it was in October 1980 because of the Community's chronic over-production of steel, the Commission's powers are increased further: it may then set minimum prices (Article 61) and also, with the 'assent' of the Council of Ministers, establish a system of production quotas (Article 58). Second, the management of the EU's Common External Tariff gives the Commission considerable manoeuvrability. It is, for example, empowered to introduce preventive measures for a limited period in order to protect the EU market from dumping by third countries. Third, in furtherance of the EU's .competition policy, the Commission, supported by decisions of the Court of Justice, has taken advantage of the rather generally phrased Article 85 of the EC Treaty to clarify and develop the position on restrictive practices through the issuing of regulations and decisions.

(2)   *Management of EU finances.* On the revenue side of the budget, EU income is subject to tight constraints determined by the Council (see Chapter 12 for an explanation of budgetary revenue). In overseeing the collection of this income the Commission has two main duties. First, to see that the correct rates are applied within certain categories of revenue. Second, to ensure that the proper payments are made to the EU by the national authorities which act as the EU's collecting agents.

On the expenditure side, the administrative arrangements vary according to the type of expenditure concerned. The Commission must, however, always operate within the approved annual budget (the EU is not legally permitted to run a budget deficit) and on the basis of the guidelines for expenditure headings that are laid down in EU law. Of the various ways in which the EU spends its money two are especially important in that, together, they account for over 75 per cent of total budgetary expenditure.

First, there is the Guarantee section of the European Agricultural Guidance and Guarantee Fund (EAGGF). This takes up around 50 per cent of the annual budget and is used for agricultural price support purposes. General management decisions concerning the EAGGF – such as whether, and on what conditions, to dispose of product surpluses – are taken by the Commission, usually via an appropriate management committee (see below). The practical application of agricultural policy and management decisions occurs at national levels through appropriate agencies (see Chapter 13).

Second, there are the structural funds, which consist of the European Regional Development Fund (ERDF), the European Social Fund (ESF), and the Guidance Section of the EAGGF. Following the inclusion, via the SEA, of a new Title V in the EEC Treaty on 'Economic and Social Cohesion' and, in particular, of a new Article 130A under Title V which stated 'the Community shall aim at reducing disparities between the various regions and the backwardness of the least-favoured regions', it was decided in 1988 to double the size of the structural funds over a five year period so that they would account for 25 per cent of the budget by 1993. It was also decided in 1988 to reform the funds so that instead of each having its own rules and objectives they would be based on four shared principles: concentration (involving the collective use of the funds in areas of greatest need); programming (mostly based on medium-term programmes for regional development, rather than 'one-off' projects); partnership (preparation, decision-making, and implementation of programmes and projects to be a shared responsibility between the Commission, national governments, and sub-national bodies); and additionality (programmes and projects to be co-financed by the Community and appropriate national bodies). The funds were to concentrate their attention on five shared objectives: developing backward regions, converting or adjusting declining industrial regions, combatting long-term unemployment, integrating young people into the job market, and adjusting agricultural structures and developing rural areas.

When the structural funds came up for review in 1992–3 it was agreed that the arrangements which had been created in 1988 had worked reasonably well. Accordingly, the size of the funds was again significantly increased (see Chapter 12) and their principles, their objectives, and administrative arrangements were confirmed, subject to some fine tuning. This means that the structural funds are managed in the following way:

(1)   National governments, in consultation with both the Commission and with the competent regional and local authorities, submit to the Commission three to five year plans. The plans – which can be national, regional, or local in their scope – identify strategies and priorities for achieving the five objectives and indicate how EU financial assistance is to be used.

(2)   On the basis of the plans submitted by the member states, in dialogue with the appropriate national and sub-national representatives, and after consulting the appropriate advisory committee – either the Advisory Committee on the Development and Conversion of Regions, the Committee of the European Social Fund, or the Committee on Agricultural Structures and Rural Development – the Commission draws up what are known as Community Support Frameworks (CSFs). By setting out a statement of the priorities for action, outlining the forms of assistance that are to be made available, and indicating the financial allocations that are envisaged, CSFs provide a reference framework for the applications for assistance which are made to the funds.

(3)   Procedures for operationalising CSFs vary. The three main forms of implementation are through operational programmes (there may be several types of programme in a particular region), individual applications for large-scale projects, and global grants (whereby the Commission entrusts the administration of a budget to a national or regional intermediary).

(4)   Monitoring and assessment of CSFs and individual operations is undertaken by monitoring committees on which sit representatives both of the Commission and of national, regional, and local partners.

Moving beyond the different parts of the Commission's financial management functions to look at the overall financial picture, it is clear that the Commission's ability to manage EU finances effectively is greatly weakened by its reliance on the Council. The Council controls the upper limits of the revenue base, and framework spending decisions are taken by different groups of ministers. In the past this sometimes caused considerable difficulties because it meant that if it became obvious during the course of a financial year that expenditure was exceeding income the Commission could not step in at an early stage and take appropriate action by, for example, increasing the Value Added Tax (VAT) ceiling on revenue or reducing agricultural price guarantees. All the Commission could do, and regularly did, was to make out a case to the Council as to what should be done. This dependence on the Council still remains, but the general situation is not so fraught as it was, because since 1988 there have been planned and clearer controls on the growth of both income and expenditure, and there are provisions for the Commission to act quickly if expenditure expands beyond targets in the main 'problem' area of agriculture. The Commission is thus now more capable of effective financial management than formerly it was.

Before leaving the Commission's responsibilities for financial management it should also be noted that the Commission has some responsibilities for coordinating and managing finances which are not drawn exclusively from EU sources. These responsibilities mostly cover environmental programmes, scientific and technological research programmes, and educational programmes in which the member states are joined by non-member European states – mainly from the EFTA countries.

A particularly important programme area in which the Commission has assumed coordination and management responsibilities is not even exclusively European-based. The seven-nation Western Economic Summit of July 1989 called on the Commission to coordinate a programme of assistance from the twenty-four OECD countries to Poland and Hungary. This resulted in the PHARE programme (Poland and Hungary: Aid for the Restructuring of Economies), which has subsequently been extended to other countries of the former Soviet bloc. The PHARE programme is by no means the only channel via which Western aid is being made available to the fledgling democracies of Central and Eastern Europe, but it is an extremely important one, with billions of Ecus being made available for purposes such as increasing investment, expanding vocational training, and improving environmental standards.

(3) *Supervision of 'front line' policy implementation.* The Commission's role with regard to the implementation of EU policies is primarily that of supervisor and overseer. It does undertake a limited amount of direct policy implementation – in connection with competition policy, for example – but the bulk of the practical/routine/day-by-day/front line implementation of EU policies is delegated to appropriate agencies within the member states. Examples of such national agencies are: Customs and Excise Authorities (which deal with most matters in relation to movements across the EU's external and internal borders); veterinary inspection teams (which check quality standards on foodstuffs); and Ministries of Agriculture and Agricultural Intervention Boards (which are responsible for controlling the volume of agricultural produce on domestic markets and which deal directly with farmers and traders about payments and charges). To ensure that policies are applied in a reasonably uniform manner throughout the member states the Commission attempts to supervise, or at least hold a watching brief on, the national agencies and

the way they perform their EU duties, a task that carries with it many difficulties. Four of these are especially important.

First, the Commission is not, in general, sufficiently resourced for the job. There just are not enough officials in the DGs, and not enough money to contract the required help from outside agencies, to see that the agriculture, the fishing, the regional, and all the other policies are properly implemented. The Commission is, therefore, heavily dependent on the good faith and willing cooperation of the member states. However, even in those policy spheres where it is in almost constant communication with national officials, the Commission cannot know everything that is going on. And with respect to those areas where contacts and flows of communication between Brussels and national agencies are irregular and not well ordered, it is almost impossible for Commission officials to have an accurate idea as to what is happening 'at the front'. Even if the Commission comes to suspect that something is amiss with an aspect of policy implementation, lack of resources can mean that it is not possible for the matter to be fully investigated: at the end of 1993 there were only about 100 Commission officials specifically employed to combat fraud, with a mere 35 in the special fraud unit.

The second difficulty is that even where they are willing to cooperate fully, national agencies are not always capable of implementing policies as the Commission would ideally wish. One reason for this is that some EU policies are, by their very nature, extremely difficult to administer. For example, the Common Fisheries Policy is extremely difficult to police, with the provisions on fishing zones, total allowable catches, and conservation requiring surveillance measures such as obligatory and properly entered logbooks, port inspections, and aerial patrols. Another reason why national agencies are not always capable of effective policy implementation is that national officials are often poorly trained and/or are overburdened by the complexities of EU rules. The maze of rules which officials have to apply is illustrated by the import levy on biscuits which varies according to cereal, milk, fat and sugar content, while the export refund varies also according to egg content. Another example of rule complexity is seen in respect of the export of beef which, at the beginning of 1993, was subject to over forty separate regulations, which were themselves subject to an array of permanent and temporary amendments.

The third difficulty is that agencies in the member states do not always wish to see EU law applied. Competition policy, for example, is rich in such examples, but there is often little the Commission can do against a deliberately recalcitrant state given the range of policy instruments available to governments which wish to assist domestic industries, and given too the secretiveness with which these can often be arranged.

The fourth, and final, difficulty is that EU law can be genuinely open to different interpretations. Sometimes indeed it is deliberately flexible so as to allow for adjustments to national circumstances.

☐ *The role of management and regulatory committees.* As is clear from the above discussion, a number of different procedures apply with regard to how the Commission exercises its executive functions. An important dimension of these differences concerns the role of management and regulatory committees. These committees have some role to play with regard to each of the three aspects of the Commission's executive powers that have just been outlined, but particularly the first two. This is because the committees are very important with regard to how the Commission may act when it wishes to adopt appropriate implementing/adaptive measures in respect of Council and European Parliament and Council legislation.

Aware that the arrangements regarding the Commission's implementing powers were becoming ever more confusing and complex, and aware too that the projected completion of the internal market by 1992 would entail a host of implementing decisions, the Single European Act (SEA) provided for a clarification of the procedures. On the basis of the SEA, and of a Council decision of 13 July 1987, the Commission's management and implementing powers in respect of Council decisions were clarified and streamlined. While no new procedures were introduced, it was established what the possible procedures were, and some guidelines were laid down for which should apply in particular cases.

As can be seen from Table 4.2, there are significant differences between the powers of the different types of committee: advisory committees can only *advise*; management committees can *block* Commission decisions by a qualified majority; regulatory committees must give their *approval* for Commission decisions by a qualified majority. These differences have led to disputes on 'comitology', between the Council on the one hand and the Commission and the EP on the other, regarding which procedure should apply – as is perhaps inevitable given that when the 1987 reforms were being discussed, the EP only wanted Procedures I and II and the Commission did not want procedure IIIb or Safeguard Measure b. The main bone of contention is that the Council has made too much use of the regulatory committee procedure and insufficient use of the advisory committee procedure.

Concentrating attention now just on management committees and regulatory committees – advisory committees having been discussed earlier – both types of committee are chaired and serviced by the Commission. The committee members are governmental representatives with, in an average-sized committee, two or three middle-ranking officials from

Table 4.2　*Procedures to be used in respect of the Commission's implementing powers*[1]

Procedure I (Advisory Committee)	The Commission submits a draft of the measures to be taken to the committee. The committee delivers an opinion on the draft, by a simple majority if necessary. The Commission takes 'the utmost account' of the opinion delivered by the committee.
Procedure II (Management Committee)	The Commission submits a draft of the measures to be taken to the committee. If the Commission's measures are *opposed* by a qualified majority in the committee then either: Variant (a) The Commission *may* defer application of its decision for up to one month. Variant (b) The Commission *shall* defer application of its decision for up to three months. Within the one month and three month deadlines the Council may take a different decision by a qualified majority vote.
Procedure III (Regulatory Committees)	The Commission submits a draft of the measures to be taken by the committee. If the Commission's measures are not *supported* by a qualified majority in the committee, or if no opinion is delivered, the matter is referred to the Council. The Council may, within a period not exceeding three months, take a decision on the Commission's proposal by a qualified majority. If the Council does not act within the three month period then either: Variant (a) The proposal shall be adopted by the Commission. Variant (b) The proposal shall be adopted by the Commission except where a *simple* majority in the Council votes against adoption.

Safeguard Measures (Mainly trade)	No committee is appointed, but the Commission must notify, and in some cases must consult with, the member states in respect of a measure to be taken. If any member state asks for the Commission's measures to be referred to the Council, within a time limit to be determined, then either: Variant (a) The Council may take a different decision by a qualified majority within a time limit to be determined. Variant (b) The Council must confirm, amend, or revoke the Commission's decision. If the Council takes no decision within a time limit to be determined the Commission's decision is revoked.

[1] Which procedure applies is specified in the enabling legislation.

appropriate ministries attending on behalf of each state. There is no hard and fast distinction of either principle or policy responsibility between the two types of committee. Management committees in the past were mostly concerned with agriculture – there are currently over thirty of these, most of them having a specific sectoral responsibility for the CAP's product regimes – but there are now an increasing number of management committees in other areas too. The regulatory committees tend to be concerned with harmonisation and vary greatly in their sectoral interests. Some, such as the Standing Committee on Foodstuffs, the Steering Committee on Feedingstuffs and the Regulatory Committee on the Improvement of Information in the Field of Safety, Hygiene and Health at the Workplace, have fairly broad briefs. Others, such as the committees 'for the adaptation to technical progress of directives on the removal of technical barriers to trade', are highly specialised: they include committees on dangerous substances and preparations, on motor vehicles, and on fertilisers. All of these committees, management and regulatory, meet as appropriate, which means almost weekly in the case of agricultural products requiring frequent market adjustments such as cereals, sugar, and wines, and in other cases means hardly at all.

Both types of committees do similar things, with variations occurring not so much between management and regulatory committees as such, but rather between individual committees according to their terms of reference, the nature of the subject matter with which they are concerned, and how they are regarded by the Commission. In addition to considering proposed Commission decisions, agenda items for committee meetings could include analysing the significance of data of various kinds, looking at how existing legislation is working, considering how existing legislation may be modified to take account of technical developments (the particular responsibility of the technical progress committees), and assessing market situations (a prime task for the agricultural committees).

Those who criticise the EU on the grounds that it is undermining national sovereignties sometimes cite regulatory and management committees as part of their case. They point to the rarity of adverse opinions, the low number of no opinions, the frequency with which measures go through without unanimous support, and the ability of the Commission – especially under the management procedure – to ignore or circumvent unfavourable votes. There is, however, another side to this; a side which suggests that the power of the Commission to control the committees and impose its will on the states ought not to be exaggerated. Four points in particular ought to be noted. First, although some of the committees do exercise important powers, they tend, for the most part, to work within fairly narrowly defined limits. Anything very controversial is almost invariably referred to a Council meeting. Second, many negative votes by states are cast tactically rather than as part of a real attempt to stop a proposal. That is to say, a national delegation might well recognise that a measure is going to be approved but will vote against it or will abstain to satisfy a political interest at home. Third, as with all aspects of its activity, it is just not in the Commission's long-term interests to abuse its powers by forcing unwelcome or unpopular measures through a committee. It wants and needs cooperation, and if a proposal meets serious opposition in a committee a good chairman will, unless special circumstances prevail, suggest revisions rather than press a vote which may have divisive consequences. Finally, the Council tends to be jealous of its powers and would move quickly against the Commission if it thought committees of any sort were being used to undermine Council power.

☐ *The guardian of the legal framework*

In association with the Court of Justice, the Commission is charged with ensuring that the Treaties and EU legislation are respected. This role links closely with the Commission's supervisory and implementing responsibilities. Indeed, the lack of a full EU-wide policy implementing framework means that a legal watchdog role acts, to some extent, as a substitute for that detailed day-to-day application of policies that at national levels involves, as a matter of routine, such activities as inspecting premises, checking employee lists, and auditing returns. It is a role that is extremely difficult to exercise: transgressors of EU law do not normally wish to advertise their illegal actions, and they are often protected by, or themselves may even be, national governments.

The Commission may become aware of possible illegalities in one of a number of ways. In the case of non-incorporation or incorrect incorporation of a directive into national law that is obvious enough, since directives normally specify a time by which the Commission must be supplied with full details of national incorporation measures. A second way is through self-notification. States, for example, are obliged to notify the Commission about all national draft regulations and standards concerning technical specifications so that the Commission may satisfy itself that they will not cause barriers to trade. Similarly, under Article 93 of the EC Treaty, state aids must be referred to the Commission for its inspection. Self-notifications also come forward under Article 85 of the EC Treaty, because although parties are not obliged to notify the Commission of possible restrictive business practices, they frequently do, either because they wish for clarification as to whether or not a practice is in legal violation, or because they wish to seek an exemption. (If notifications are not made within specified time limits exemptions are not permissible.) A third way in which illegalities may come to the Commission's attention is from the many representations that are made by individuals, organisations, firms or member states who believe that their interests are being damaged by the alleged illegal actions of another party. For example, Germany has frequently complained about the amount of subsidisation given by many national governments to their steel industries. A fourth way is through the Commission's own efforts. Such efforts may take one of several forms: investigations by one of the small monitoring/investigatory/fraud teams that the Commission has in a few policy areas; careful analysis of the information that is supplied by outside agencies; or simply a Commission official reading a newspaper report that suggests a government or a firm is doing, or is not doing, something that looks suspicious under EU law.

Infringement proceedings are initiated against member states for not notifying the Commission of measures taken to incorporate directives into national law, for non-incorporation or incorrect incorporation of directives, and for non-application or incorrect application of EU law – most commonly in connection with internal market and industrial affairs, indirect taxation, agriculture, and environmental and consumer protection. Before any formal action is taken against a state it is informed by the Commission that it is in possible breach of its legal obligations. If, after the

Commission has carried out an investigation, the breach is confirmed and continued, a procedure comes into force, under Article 169 of the EC Treaty, whereby the Commission

> shall deliver a reasoned opinion on the matter after giving the State concerned the opportunity to submit its observations. If the State concerned does not comply with the opinion within the period laid down by the Commission, the latter may bring the matter before the Court of Justice.

Since most infringements have implications for the functioning of the market, the Commission usually seeks to ensure that these procedures operate according to a tight timetable: normally about two months for the state to present its observations and a similar period for it to comply with the reasoned opinion.

Most cases, it must be emphasised, are settled at an early stage. So, in an average year, the Commission issues around 800 letters of formal notice, delivers 200 reasoned opinions, and makes 80 references to the Court of Justice (see Table 11.2). Italy, France, and Greece consistently figure high in these lists. One reason for so many early settlements is that most infringements occur not as a result of wilful avoidance of EU law but rather from genuine differences over interpretation or from national administrative and legislative procedures which have occasioned delay. Although there are differences between member states in their enthusiasm for aspects of EU law they do not usually wish to engage in open confrontation with EU institutions.

If states do not wish to submit to an EU law it is, therefore, more customary for them to drag their feet rather than be openly obstructive. Delay can, however, be a form of obstruction, in that states know it could be years before the Commission, and even more the Court of Justice, brings them to heel. Environmental legislation illustrates this, with most states not having fully incorporated and/or implemented only parts of long-standing EU legislation – on matters such as air pollution, bathing water, and drinking water.

As regards what action the Commission can take if it discovers breaches, or prospective breaches, of EU law, that depends very much on the circumstances. Four different sorts of circumstances will be taken as illustrations of this point:

● *Non-compliance by a member state.* Until the entry into force of the TEU in 1993 the Commission was not empowered to impose sanctions against member states which were in breach of their legal obligations. Respect for Commission decisions was dependent on the goodwill and political judgement of the states themselves, backed up by the ability of the Commission to make a referral to the Court of Justice – though the Court too could not impose sanctions. However, under the TEU the Commission is now permitted, where a member state refuses to comply with a judgement of the Court, to bring the state back before the Court and in so doing to specify a financial penalty which should be imposed. The Court takes the final decision.

• *Firms breaching EU law on restrictive practices.* Treaty provisions (notably Article 85, EC), secondary legislation, and Court judgements have established a considerable volume of EU law in the sphere of restrictive practices. If at all possible, however, the Commission avoids using this law to take formal action against firms. This is partly because of the ill-feeling that can be generated by open confrontations, and partly because formal action necessitates the use of cumbersome and protracted bureaucratic procedures within the Commission itself. Offending parties are, therefore, encouraged to fall into line or to reach an agreement with the Commission during the extensive informal processes that always precede formal action. If this fails, however, fines can result. Thus, in 1989 fines totalling 60 million Ecu (£42 million) were imposed on 23 plastic groups for price-fixing in the early 1980s. (This subsequently led to appeals to the Court of Justice and to the reduction of some of the fines.) Less punitively, in December 1986, the Commission issued a token fine of 50,000 Ecu (£36,000) on three major acid manufacturers – Unilever, Henkel, and Oleofina – for exchanging confidential information between 1979 and 1982 about their sales of certain products. This was the first occasion the Commission had imposed fines for a pure exchange of information agreement. In explaining its action the Commission stated: 'This exchange of information, normally regarded as business secrets, provided each of them with a means to monitor the activities of its major competitors and to adjust its own behaviour accordingly.'

• *Firms breaching EU rules on state aids.* Articles 92–94 of the EC Treaty provide the Commission with powers to take action against what is deemed to be unacceptable state subsidisation of business and industry. These powers can take the form of requiring that the state aid in question be repaid, as was the case in July 1990 when the Commission instructed the UK Government to recover £44.4 million worth of concessions which had been given to British Aerospace at the time of its acquisition of the Rover car group in 1988. (Interestingly, this case then dragged on through appeals and legal technicalities, and when the money was eventually repaid, in May 1993, the total had risen to £57.6 million because of lost interest calculated from August 1990 – the first occasion aid repayment involved reimbursement of interest.)

• *Potential breaches of EU rules on company mergers.* Council Regulation 4064/89 – the so-called Merger Control Regulation – which came into effect in September 1990, specifies the Commission's powers in some detail: specified information regarding proposed mergers and takeovers above certain limits have to be notified to the Commission; on receipt of the information the Commission must decide within one month whether it proposes to either let the deal go ahead on the grounds that competition would not be harmed, or whether it wishes to 'open proceedings'; if it wishes to 'open proceedings' it has four months to carry out an investigation, during which it is entitled to enter the premises of firms and seize documents; any firm that supplies false information during the course of a Commission inquiry, or implements a merger or takeover without gaining clearance from the Commission, is liable to be fined up to 10 per cent of its annual sales.

In practice, up to the end of 1993 the Commission had given authorisation to all but one of the mergers referred to it – though sometimes conditions were laid down requiring, for example, some of the assets of the merging firms to be sold off. The first merger to be blocked was in 1991 when – to the background of a fierce disagreement within the Commission (between those who wished to apply the competition rules strictly and those who wished to be 'flexible' in the interests of building strong European-based global companies) the College of Commissioners voted by nine votes to eight to block the Aerospatiale (of France)/Alenia (of Italy) bid to buy De Haviland Canada from Boeing.

In exercising the role of guardian of the legal framework the Commission attempts to operate in a flexible and politically sensitive manner. It would not be in its, or the EU's, interests to use an overly heavy hand. A good example of the way in which political calculation, as well as legal interpretation, is employed by the Commission in the exercise of this role was seen in the much publicised Renault case: in March 1988 the Commission approved French Government aid to Renault subject to certain conditions; in November 1989 the approval was revoked, on the grounds that Renault had not kept its part of the bargain; in the deliberations which followed the Commission initially leant towards ordering Renault to pay back most of the aid, but following protracted negotiations at the highest levels – involving, at times, the Commissioner responsible (Sir Leon Brittan) and the French Prime Minister (Michel Rocard) a deal was struck under which Renault would pay back half of the FFr 12 billion (£1.26b) it had received.

As with most of its other activities, the Commission's ability to exercise its legal guardianship role is blunted by a number of constraints and restrictions. Three are especially important:

• The problem of limited resources means that choices have to be made about which cases are worth pursuing, and with what vigour. For example, only about fifty officials – in a specially created task force located in DGIV – have been appointed to undertake the detailed and highly complex work that is necessary to give effect to the 1989 Merger Control Regulation. As one Community official told the *Financial Times* in 1989 in connection with state aid: 'It is depressing to think that there are 30 of us here trying to control state aid, while in the Walloon region of Belgium alone there are 150 doling it out.'

• Relevant and sufficiently detailed information can be difficult to obtain – either because it is deliberately hidden from prying Commission officials, or because, as is the case with many aspects of market conditions, reliable figures are just not available. An example of an EU law which is difficult to apply because of lack of information is the *Council Directive of 2 April 1979 on the Conservation of Wild Birds* (79/409/EEC). Amongst other things, the Directive provides protection for most species of migrant birds and forbids killing for trade and by indiscriminate methods. Because the shooting of birds is popular in some countries, several governments were slow to transpose the Directive into national law, and were then reluctant to do much about applying the law once it had been transposed. On the first of these implementing problems – transposition – the Commission can acquire the information it needs since states are obliged to inform it of the measures they have taken. On the second of the implementation problems, however – application of the law by national authorities against transgressors – the Commission has been much less able to make judgements about whether states are exercising their responsibilities: it is very difficult to know what efforts are really being made by national authorities to catch shooters and hunters.

• Political considerations can inhibit the Commission from acting as vigorously as it could in certain problem areas and in particular cases. This is largely because it does not normally wish to upset or politically embarrass member states if it is at all avoidable: the Commission does, after all, have to work closely and continuously with the states both on an individual and – in the Council of Ministers – on a collective basis. An example of political pressures inhibiting the Commission is seen in the above cited Conservation of Wild Birds Directive: in addition to the practical problems it has in acquiring information about the killing of birds, the Commission's sensitive political antennae also serve to hold it in check in that it is well aware of the unpopularity and political difficulties that would be created for some governments if action was to be taken against the thousands who break this law. Another example of the inhibiting role of political pressures is seen in the cautious line that the Commission has traditionally adopted towards multinational corporations which appear to be in breach of EU competition law: to take action against multinationals is to risk generating political opposition from member states in which the companies are based, and also risks being self-defeating in that it may cause companies to transfer their activities outside the EU. (There are also, of course, practical problems of the sort noted in the previous point when seeking to act against multinationals: it is very difficult to follow investigations through when dealing with organisations which are located in several countries, some of which may be outside Europe.)

☐ *External representative and negotiator*

The different aspects of the Commission's role in respect of the EU's external relations are considered in some detail in Chapter 14, so attention here will be limited to simply identifying what those aspects are. There are, essentially, six.

First, the Commission is centrally involved in determining and conducting the EU's external trade relations. On the basis of Article 113 of the EC Treaty, and with its actions always subject to Council approval, the Commission represents and acts on behalf of the EU both in formal negotiations, such as those which are conducted under the auspices of GATT, and in the more informal and exploratory exchanges such as are common between, for example, the EU and the United States over world agricultural trade, and between the EU and Japan over access to each other's markets.

Second, the Commission has important negotiating and managing responsibilities in respect of the various special external agreements which the EU has with many countries and groups of countries. These agreements take various forms but the more 'advanced' – the economic cooperation agreements and the association agreements – go beyond the 'privileged' trading conditions which are invariably at their heart, to include provisions for such things as European Investment Bank loans, financial aid, and political dialogue.

Third, the Commission represents the EU at, and participates in the work of, a number of important international organisations. Four of these are specifically mentioned in the EC Treaty: the United Nations and its specialised agencies (Article 229); GATT (Article 229); the Council of Europe (Article 230); and the Organisation for Economic Cooperation and Development (Article 231).

Fourth, the Commission has responsibilities for acting as a key point of contact between the EU and non-member states. Over 140 countries have diplomatic missions accredited to the EU and the Commission is expected to keep them informed about EU affairs, either through the circulation of documents or by making its officials available for information briefings and lobbying. The EU, for its part, maintains an extensive network of diplomatic missions abroad, numbering 100 delegations and offices, and these are staffed by Commission employees.

Fifth, the Commission is entrusted with important responsibilities in regard to applications for EU membership. On receipt of an application the Council normally asks the Commission to carry out a detailed investigation of the implications and to submit an opinion (an opinion that the Council need not, of course, accept – as it did not in 1976 when it rejected the Commission's proposal that Greece be offered a pre-accession period of unlimited duration and instead authorised negotiations for full membership). If and when negotiations begin, the Commission, operating within Council approved guidelines, acts as the EU's main negotiator, except on show-piece ministerial occasions or when particularly sensitive or difficult matters call for an inter-ministerial resolution of differences. The whole process – from the lodging of an application to accession – can take years. Portugal, for example, applied in March 1977; the Commission forwarded a favourable opinion to the Council in May 1978; negotiations opened in October 1978 and were not concluded until March 1985; and Portugal eventually joined in January 1986 – eight years and ten months after applying.

Sixth, and finally, under the TEU the 'Commission shall be fully associated with the work carried out in the common foreign and security policy field' (Article J.9). Quite what this will mean in practice remains to be seen, though the creation in the 1993–5 Commission of a new portfolio of External Political Relations, and the subsequent splitting of DGI into two so as to create a separate DG for External Political Relations, signalled the Commission's desire to maximise its role. Clearly, however, political relations, coupled with the intergovernmental and non-EC nature of the CFSP pillar, suggest that the Commission's role will essentially be supportive and secondary to that of the Council, and not in any way comparable to the role it undertakes in regard to external trade. Indeed the TEU makes that virtually explicit by stating that the Council Presidency shall take the leading role in representing the EU on CFSP matters and should also assume responsibility for implementing measures.

☐ *Mediator and conciliator*

Much of EU decision-making, especially in the Council of Ministers, is based on searches for agreements between competing interests. The Commission is very much involved in trying to bring these agreements about and a great deal of its time is taken up looking for common ground which can create compromises that are somewhat more than the lowest common denominator. As a consequence, the Commission is often obliged to be guarded and cautious with its proposals. Radical initiatives, involving perhaps what it really believes needs to be done, are almost certain to meet with fierce opposition. More moderate proposals on the other hand, perhaps taking the form of adjustments and extensions to existing policy, and presented preferably in a technocratic rather than an ideological manner, are more likely to be acceptable. In other words, the Commission is often subject to an enforced incrementalism.

The Commission is not the only EU body that consciously seeks to oil the wheels of decision-making. As is shown in Chapter 5, the Council itself has taken steps to improve its own machinery. But the Commission is particularly well placed to act as mediator and conciliator. One reason for this is that it is normally seen as being non-partisan: its proposals may, therefore, be viewed less suspiciously than any which come from, say, the chairman of a Council working party. Another reason is that in many instances the Commission is simply in the best position to judge what proposals are likely to command support, both inside and outside the Council. This is because of the continuous and extensive discussions which the Commission has with interested parties from the earliest considerations of a policy proposal through to its enactment. Unlike the other institutions, the Commission is represented at virtually every stage and in virtually every forum of the EU's decision-making system.

Although there are naturally limitations on what can be achieved, the effectiveness with which the Commission exercises this mediating role can be considerably influenced by the competence of its officials. While, for example, one Commission official may play a crucial role in driving a proposal through a Council working party, another may be so incompetent as not only to prejudice the Commission's own position but to threaten the progress of the whole proposal. Many questions must be handled with care and political sensitivity: when should a proposal be brought forward, and in what form?; at what point will an adjustment in the Commission's position open the way to progress in the Council?; is there anything to be gained from informal discussions with 'awkward delegations'? These, and questions such as these, call for highly developed political skills.

☐ *The conscience of the Union*

In performing each of the above tasks the Commission is supposed to stand above and beyond sectional and national interests. While others might look to the particular, it should look to the general; while others might look to the benefits to be gained from the next deal, it should keep at least one eye on the horizon. As many have described it, the Commission should be the 'conscience' of the Union.

Christopher Tugendhat, a former Commissioner, has commented on this role. Among other things, he states, the Commission exists 'to represent the general interest in the welter of national ones and to point the way ahead, but also drawing the attention of member states to new and more daring possibilities' (Tugendhat, 1986). Ideally this may be so. But, in practice, it is very difficult to operationalise. One reason for this is that it is highly questionable whether such a thing as the 'general interest' exists: there are few initiatives which do not threaten the interests of at least some – were this not the case there would not be so many disagreements in the Council. Another reason is that many in the Commission doubt whether it is worth pursuing 'daring possibilities' if it is clear that they will be rejected and may even generate anti-Commission feelings.

In practice, therefore, the Commission tends not to be so detached, so far-seeing, or so enthusiastic in pressing the *esprit communautaire*, as some would like. This is not to say that it does not attempt to map out the future or attempt to press for developments that it believes will be generally beneficial. On the contrary, it is precisely because the Commission does seek to act in the general interest that the smaller EU states tend to see it as something of a protector and are consequently normally supportive of the Commission being given greater powers. Nor is it to deny that the Commission is sometimes ambitious in its approach and long-term in its perspective – as, for example, is demonstrated with the SEM programme, with the Social Charter, with the championing of the cause of EMU, and with the campaign which was launched in late 1992 and which produced a White Paper in late 1993 setting out a medium-term strategy for growth, competitiveness and employment. But the fact is that the Commission does operate in the real EU world, and often that necessitates looking to the short rather than to the long term, and to what is possible rather than what is desirable.

■ Concluding remarks

It is frequently stated that there has been a decline in the powers of the Commission since the mid-1960s. Commentators have particularly stressed a diminution in the Commission's initiating role and a corresponding weakening in its ability to offer real vision and leadership. It has become, it is claimed, too reactive in exercising its responsibilities: reactive to the pressures of the many interests to which it is subject; reactive to the immediacy of events; and above all, reactive to the increasing 'instructions' which are given to it by the Council of Ministers and the European Council.

Unquestionably, there is something in this view. The explanation for why it has happened is to be sought in a combination of factors. The rather rigid vertical lines within the Commission's own organisational structure sometimes make it difficult for a broad vision to emerge. The tensions which are seemingly present between the politically creative elements of the Commission's responsibilities and the bureaucratic roles of adminis-tering and implementing have perhaps never been properly resolved. Beyond such internal considerations, factors as varied as the accession of states which are anxious to protect their independence, the frequent appearance on the EU agenda of politically sensitive matters, and the desire of politicians not to cede too much power to others if it can be avoided, have resulted in the states being reluctant to grant too much autonomy to the Commission.

But the extent to which there has been a decline should not be exaggerated. Certainly the Commission has to trim more than it would like, and certainly it has suffered its share of political defeats – not least in regard to its wishes for stronger Treaty-based powers. But in some respects its powers have actually increased as it has adapted itself to the ever-changing nature of, and demands upon, the EU. As has been shown, the Commission exercises, either by itself or in association with other bodies, a number of crucially important functions. Moreover, it has been at the heart of pressing the case for, and putting forward specific proposals in relation to, all of the major issues which have been at the heart of the EU agenda in recent years: the SEM programme, EMU, the social dimension, institutional reform, enlargement, and a strategy for promoting growth. Perhaps the Commission is not quite the motor force that some of the founding fathers had hoped for, but in many ways it is both central and vital to the whole EU system.

■ *Chapter 5* ■

The Council of Ministers

The Council of Ministers is the principal meeting place of the national governments and is the EU's main decision-making institution.

When the Community was founded in the 1950s many expected that in time, as joint policies were seen to work and as the states came to trust one another more, the role of the Council would gradually decline, especially in relation to the Commission. This has not happened. On the contrary, by jealously guarding the responsibilities that are accorded to it in the Treaties, and by adapting its internal mechanisms to enable it to cope more easily with the increasing volume of business that has come its way, the Council has not only defended, but has in some respects extended, its power and influence. This has naturally produced some frustration in the Commission, and in the EP. It has also ensured that national governments are centrally placed to influence most aspects of EU business.

There was also a general expectation when the Community was founded that governments would gradually come to be less concerned about national sovereignty considerations and that this would be reflected in an increasing use of majority voting in the Council. Until the 1980s, however, there was little movement in this direction: even where the Treaties permitted majority votes, the Council normally preferred to proceed on the basis of consensual agreements. This preference for unanimity naturally bolstered the intergovernmental, as opposed to the supranational, side of the Community's nature and resulted in Council decision-making processes tending to be slow and protracted. As will be shown, this situation has changed considerably in recent years.

■ Responsibilities and functions

The principal responsibility of the Council is to take policy and legislative decisions. As is shown in Chapters 4, 7, and 11, the Commission and the EP also have such powers, but they are not comparable to those of the Council. Virtually all proposals for politically important and/or sensitive legislation have to receive Council approval in order to be adopted.

Normally, the Council has to act on the basis of proposals which are made to it by the Commission, and after receiving advice from the EP and the Economic and Social Committee (ESC) but, crucially, it alone decides, apart from under the co-decision legislative procedure where final decision-making powers are shared with the EP. The Council is, therefore, the legislature, or under the co-decision procedure the co-legislature, of the European Union. In 1993 it adopted 63 directives, 319 regulations and 164 decisions.

But, if the Council is the EU's legislature in the sense that it converts proposals into legal acts, its legislative capacity is significantly restricted by the requirement of the EC, ECSC and Euratom Treaties which state that the Council can usually act only on the basis of Commission proposals. This means that it does not have the constitutional power to initiate or draft proposals itself. In practice, ways have been found, if not to completely circumvent the Commission, at least to allow the Council a significant policy initiating role. Article 152 of the EC Treaty is especially useful: 'The Council may request the Commission to undertake any studies the Council considers desirable for the attainment of the common objectives, and to submit to it any appropriate proposals.' In the view of many observers, the use that has been made of Article 152, and the very specific instructions which have sometimes been issued to the Commission under its aegis, are against its intended spirit. Be that as it may, the political weight of the Council is such that the Commission is bound to pay close attention to what the ministers want.

In addition to Article 152, four other factors have also enhanced the Council's policy initiating role:

(1)   The increasing adoption by the Council of opinions, resolutions, agreements and recommendations. These are not legal texts but they carry political weight and it is difficult for the Commission to ignore them. Sometimes they are explicitly designed to pressurise the Commission to come up with proposals for legislation.

(2)   The movement of the EU into policy spheres which are not covered, or are not covered clearly, in the Treaties. This sometimes produces uncertainty regarding the exact responsibilities of decision-making bodies, and hence grey areas which the Council can exploit.

(3)   The increasingly developed Council machinery. There are now many places in the Council's network where ideas can be generated. The emergence of the Council Presidency as a key institutional actor has played a particularly important role in enabling the Council to influence policy directions and priorities.

(4)   The increasing willingness of the states to found aspects of their cooperation not on EU law but on non-binding agreements and

understandings. This is most obviously seen in the spheres of foreign policy and justice and home affairs, which constitute the second and third pillars of the EU Treaty, but it does sometimes also happen in other, more conventional, EU spheres where national differences make it very difficult for law to be agreed. Such non-legal arrangements do not have to be Commission initiated.

Not only has the Council encroached on the Commission's policy initiating function but it has also joined it in exercising important responsibilities in the key activities of mediation and consensus building. Of course, as the forum in which the national representatives meet, the Council has always served the function of developing mutual understanding between the member states. Moreover, a necessary prerequisite for successful policy development has always been that Council participants display an ability to compromise in negotiations. But, as the EC/EU has grown in size, as more difficult policy areas have come onto the agenda, and as political and economic change has broken down some of the pioneering spirit of the early days, so has positive and active mediation come to be ever more necessary: mediation primarily between the different national and ideological interests represented in the Council, but also between the Council and the Commission, the Council and the EP, and the Council and non-institutional interests. The Commission has taken on much of this task, but so too have agencies of the Council itself.

The Council has thus gained powers and responsibilities over the years, but it has lost some too. It has done so in two principal respects. First, the European Council – the body which brings together the Heads of Government two or three times a year – has assumed increasingly greater responsibilities for taking the final political decisions on such matters as new accessions, institutional reform, and the launching of broad policy initiatives (see Chapter 6). Second, under both the SEA and the TEU the legislative powers of the EP were increased, to such an extent that though it is not yet as powerful as the Council, it can, in respect of certain policy matters in certain circumstances, prevent the Council from overriding its wishes.

■ Composition

☐ *The ministers*

Ministerial meetings are at the apex of the Council machinery. Since the 1965 Merger Treaty entered into force in 1967 there has, legally, been only one Council of Ministers but, in practice, there are many in the sense that the work of the Council is divided into policy areas. The General Affairs Council, which is composed of Foreign Ministers, has the widest brief: it deals with general issues relating to policy initiation and coordination, with external political relations, and often too with matters which, for whatever reason, are particularly politically sensitive. More sectoral matters are dealt with in the twenty or so 'Technical Councils', which are made up of Ministers of Agriculture, of Energy, of Environment and so on (see Table 5.1, p. 129).

Often, the national representatives who attend ministerial meetings differ in terms of their status and/or their policy responsibilities. This can inhibit efficient decision-making. The problem arises because the states themselves decide by whom they wish to be represented, and their decisions may vary in one of two ways:

☐ *The level of seniority.* Normally, by prior arrangement, Council meetings are attended by ministers of a similar standing, but circumstances do arise when delegations are headed at different levels of seniority. This may be because a relevant minister has pressing domestic business or because it is judged that an agenda does not warrant his attendance. Occasionally, he may be 'unavoidably delayed' because he does not wish to attend an unwanted or a politically awkward meeting. Whatever the reason, a reduction in the status and political weight of a delegation may make it difficult for binding decisions to be agreed.

☐ *The sectoral responsibility.* Usually it is obvious which government departments should be represented at Council of Ministers meetings, but not always. Doubts may arise because agenda items may straddle policy divisions, or because member states organise their central government departments in different ways. As a result, it is possible for ministers from rather different national ministries, with different responsibilities and interests, to be present. The difficulties which this creates are sometimes compounded, especially in broad policy areas, by the minister attending not feeling able to speak on behalf of other ministers with a direct interest and therefore insisting on a reference back to national capitals.

States are not, therefore, always comparably represented at ministerial meetings. But whether a country's principal spokesman is a senior minister, a junior minister or, as occasionally is the case, the Permanent Representative or even a senior diplomat, care is always taken to ensure that national interests are defended. The main way in which this is done is by the attendance, at all meetings, not only of the national spokesmen, but of small national delegations. These delegations comprise national officials and experts plus, at important meetings or meetings where there is a wide-ranging agenda, junior ministers to assist the senior minister. (Trade Ministers, for example, usually accompany Foreign Ministers to meetings of the General Affairs Council when trade issues are to be considered.) Normally five or six officials and experts support the 'inner table team' (that is, the most senior national representatives who actually sit at the negotiating table), but this number can vary according to the policy area concerned (Foreign Ministers may be accompanied by teams of as many as eight or nine), the importance of the items on the agenda, and the size of the meeting room. The task of the supporting teams is to ensure that the head of the delegation is properly briefed, fully understands the implications of what is being discussed, and does not make negotiating mistakes. Sometimes, when very confidential matters are being discussed, or when a meeting is deadlocked, the size of delegations may, on a proposal from the President, be reduced to 'Ministers plus two', 'Ministers plus one', or, exceptionally, 'Ministers and Commission'.

Council of Ministers meetings are normally convened by the country holding the Presidency, but it is possible for the Commission or a member state to take the initiative. The Presidency rotates between the states on a six monthly basis: January until June, July until December (see Figure 5.1 and the Appendix for the order of rotation). The main tasks of the Presidency are as follows:

(1) Arranging (in close association with the Council Secretariat) and chairing, all Council meetings from ministerial level downwards (apart from a few committees and working parties which have a permanent chairman). These responsibilities give to the Presidency a considerable control over how often Councils and Council bodies meet, over agendas, and over what happens during the course of meetings.

(2) Launching and building a consensus for initiatives. A successful Presidency is normally regarded as one which gets things done. This can usually only be achieved by extensive negotiating, persuading, manoeuvring, cajoling, mediating and bargaining with and between the member states, and with the Commission and the EP.

(3) Ensuring some continuity and consistency of policy development. An important way in which this is achieved is via the so-called 'troika' arrangements which provide for cooperation between the preceding, the incumbent, and the succeeding Presidencies.

(4) Representing the Council in dealings with outside bodies. This task is exercised most frequently with regard to other EU institutions (such as

regular appearances before the EP), and with non-member countries in connection with certain external EU policies.

Holding the Presidency has advantages and disadvantages. One advantage is the prestige and status that is associated with the office: during the six month term of office the Presidential state is at the very heart of EU affairs; its ministers – especially its Head of Government and its Foreign Minister – meet with prominent international statesmen and dignitaries on behalf of the EU; and media focus and interest is considerable. Another advantage is that during its term of office a Presidency can do more than it can as an ordinary member state to help shape, and set the pace of, EU policy priorities. The extent of the potential of the Presidency in terms of policy development should not, however, be exaggerated: though Presidencies set out their priorities when they enter office, they do not start with a clean sheet but have to be much concerned with uncompleted business from previous Presidencies; related to this last point, an increasingly important part of the 'troika' arrangement is 'rolling work programmes' in which measures to be taken by the Council are coordinated between the three participating states, rather then being left solely to the preferences of the incumbent state; and, finally, six months just does not provide sufficient time for the full working through of policy initiatives – especially if legislation is required. As for the disadvantages of holding the Presidency, one is the blows to esteem and standing that are incurred when a state is judged to have had a poor Presidency, and another is the heavy administrative burdens that are attached to the job – burdens which some of the smaller states find difficult to carry.

Altogether there are around 90 Council meetings in an average year (95, for example, in 1993) with a certain bunching occurring in relation to key features of the EU timetable: the budgetary cycle, the annual agricultural price-fixing exercise, and the ending of a country's six month Presidency. Meetings are normally held in Brussels, except for April, June, and October when they are held in Luxembourg.

The regularity of meetings of individual Councils reflects their importance in the Council system and the extent to which there is an EU interest and activity in their policy area. So, as can be seen from Table 5.1, Foreign Ministers, Agriculture Ministers, and Economic and Finance Ministers (in what is customarily referred to as the Ecofin Council) meet most regularly: usually about once a month, but more frequently if events require it; Internal Market Ministers, Environment Ministers, Fisheries Ministers, and Transport Ministers follow next, with around four or five meetings per year; other Councils – such as Research, Social, Energy, and

Table 5.1   *Council Meetings in 1992*

Agriculture	14	Consumer Protection	2
General Council		Health	2
(Foreign Ministers)	12*	Education	2
Economic and Finance		Culture	2
(Ecofin)	10	Energy	2
Internal Market	7	Industry	2
Fisheries	5	Development	2
Environment	5**	Budget	2
Transport	4	Tourism	1
Research	3	Justice	1
Telecommunications	3		———
Labour and Social		Total Number of Council	
Affairs	3	Meetings	84

* Including 2 special meetings.
** Including 1 jointly with Development Ministers.

Source: R. Corbett (1993) 'Governance and Institutional Developments' in N. Nugent (ed.) *The European Community 1992: Annual Review of Activities* (Blackwell).

Industry – meet only two or three times a year, or even just once or twice a year in fringe areas such as Health and Cultural Affairs.

Unless there are particularly difficult matters to be resolved, meetings do not normally last more than a day. A typical meeting would begin about 10.00 a.m. and finish around 6.00 p.m. or 7.00 p.m. Foreign Ministers, Agriculture Ministers, and Budget Ministers are the most likely to meet over two days, and when they do it is common to start with lunch on Day 1 and finish around lunchtime on Day 2.

Outside the formal Council framework some groups of ministers, particularly Foreign Ministers and Ecofin Ministers, have periodic weekend gatherings, usually in the country of the Presidency, which are used for the purpose of discussing matters on an informal basis without the pressure of having to take decisions.

☐ *The Committee of Permanent Representatives*

Each of the states has a national delegation, or Permanent Representation as they are more usually known, in Brussels which acts as a kind of embassy to the EU. There was some debate as to whether, post-Maastricht, they were embassies to the European Union or the European Communities. Most states decided upon Union, but the UK preferred

Communities, doubtless mainly because the word 'Union' is not much liked, though the formal explanation was a legalistic one: in the words of a spokesman 'The EU does not have the legal status to send or receive ambassadors. [The UK Ambassador] cannot be accredited to the Union because it does not have the legal personality to receive his accreditation.'

The Permanent Representations are headed by a Permanent Representative, who is normally a diplomat of very senior rank, and are staffed, in the case of the larger states, by thirty to forty officials, plus back-up support. About half of the officials are drawn from the diplomatic services of the member states with the others being seconded from appropriate national ministries such as Agriculture, Trade, and Finance.

Of the many forums in which governments meet 'in Council' below ministerial level, the most important is the Committee of Permanent Representatives (COREPER). Although no provision was made for such a body under the Treaty of Paris, ministers established a coordinating committee of senior officials as early as 1953, and under the Treaties of Rome the Council was permitted to create a similar committee under its Rules of Procedure. Under Article 4 of the Merger Treaty these committees were merged and were formally incorporated into the Community system: 'A committee consisting of the Permanent Representatives of the Member States shall be responsible for preparing the work of the Council and for carrying out the tasks assigned to it by the Council.'

There are, in fact, two COREPERs. Each normally meets once a week. COREPER 2 is the more important and is made up of the Permanent Representatives plus supporting staff. Because of its seniority it is the more 'political' of the two COREPERs and works mainly for the Foreign Ministers (and through them for the European Council) and Ecofin. It also usually deals with issues for other Council meetings that are particularly sensitive or controversial. COREPER 2 is assisted in its tasks by the Antici Group, which is made up of senior officials from the Permanent Representations and which, in addition to assisting COREPER 2, acts as a key information gathering and mediating forum between the member states. COREPER 1 consists of the Deputy Permanent Representatives and supporting staff. Amongst the policy areas it normally deals with are environment, social affairs, transport and the internal market. Agriculture, because of the complexity and volume of its business, is not normally dealt with by COREPER except in regard to certain aspects, of which the most important are finance, harmonisation of legislation, and commercial questions in relation to non-EU countries. Most agricultural matters are dealt with by the Special Committee on Agriculture (SCA) which is staffed by senior officials, either from the Permanent Representations or from national Ministries of Agriculture. Like the two COREPERs the SCA normally meets at least once a week.

☐ *Committees and working parties*

A complicated network of committees and working parties assists and prepares the work of the Council of Ministers, COREPER and the SCA. The *committees* are of different types. They include:

• Council committees in the strict sense of the term are those standing committees which are serviced by Council administrators. There are only a handful of these, of which the Energy Committee and the Committee on Education are examples. Council committees are composed of national officials and their role is essentially to advise the Council and the Commission as appropriate and, in some instances, as directed. A particularly important and rather special Council committee is the Article 113 Committee which deals with commercial policy. Any significant action undertaken by the EU in international trade negotiations is preceded by internal coordination via this Committee. It normally meets once a week: the full members – who are very senior officials in national Ministries of Trade or the equivalent – meet monthly, and the deputies – who are middle-ranking officials from the Ministries, or sometimes from the Permanent Representations – meet three times a month. The Committee performs two main functions: it drafts the briefs on which the Commission negotiates on behalf of the EU with third countries (the Committee's draft is referred, via COREPER, to the Ministers for their approval); and it acts as a consultative committee to the Council and the Commission – by, for example, indicating to the Commission what it should do when problems arise during the course of a set of trade negotiations.

• The Standing Committee on Employment is also a Council serviced committee, but its membership is unusual in two respects: first, it is composed not only of governmental representatives but also of sectional interest representatives – the latter being drawn from both sides of industry; and, second, the governmental representations are headed by the Ministers themselves – or, if they are unable to attend, by their personal representatives. The Committee meets twice a year to discuss matters of interest and, where possible, to make recommendations to the Labour and Social Affairs Council. The nature of the membership of the Committee, with ministerial representation, means that where general agreement can be found, the matter is likely to be taken up by the Council.

• Various committees which are, technically, Commission committees, report to, or feed into, the Council, as well as the Commission, in an advisory capacity. In practice, they are as much Council committees as Commission committees. Their access to the Council usually stems either from their founding mandates, the importance of their policy competences, the eminence of their memberships, or from some combination of all three.

The most important of these committees is the Monetary Committee which was established under Article 105 of the EEC Treaty and which saw its position consolidated by Article 109c of the TEU: 'In order to promote coordination of the policies of the Member States to the full extent needed for the functioning of the internal market, a Monetary Committee with advisory status is hereby set up.' The Committee's prestige and power is explained by four main factors. First, it is given a broad brief in very important policy areas. The main focus of its work covers the European Monetary System (EMS), (it can be crucial when realignments of currencies in the Exchange Rate Mechanism (ERM) are being considered), capital movements, international monetary relations, and the many issues that arise in connection with Economic and Monetary Union (EMU). (On most of these matters the Committee works closely with another very important committee, the Committee of Governors of Central Banks.) Second, the Committee enjoys unusually privileged access to both the Commission and the Council. Indeed, in relation to the latter, the Committee's chairman normally reports several times a year directly to the Ecofin Council on the Committee's work. Third, the Committee meets regularly – including, normally, before Ecofin Council meetings – and is supported in most aspects of its work by an Alternates Committee and a small number of working parties. Finally, the members of the Committee – of which there are two from each member state, plus two from the Commission – are mostly senior and influential figures from Finance Ministries and Central Banks: people, in other words, who can normally communicate directly with whomsoever they wish, and people who are customarily listened to. If, and when, the third stage of EMU begins, the Monetary Committee will, under provisions laid down by the TEU, be replaced by an Economic and Financial Committee.

• In addition to the 'formally constituted' committees that have just been described – formally constituted in the sense that they have been established by the Treaties or by EU legislation – many other committees also assist the work of the Council. Not always referred to as committees, but sometimes as groups or simply meetings, these are most often found in policy areas which are now part of the EU but not of the EC. Such committees perform a variety of tasks: in the foreign policy field there is a well established committee structure – made up of the Political Committee, the Correspondents Group, and about twenty specialised working groups – which seeks to facilitate the exchange of information, coordinate positions, and prepare the work of the Foreign Ministers; in the internal security field, officials meet to perform similar functions in connection with their areas of responsibility – reporting in their case to Interior Ministers; and there has been an increasing tendency in recent years for *ad hoc* committees of senior national officials – usually referred to as *High*

Level Groups – to be established for the purpose of developing initiatives and policies (though not, of course, for the purpose of drafting legislation) in new, and sometimes sensitive areas – the control of drugs, for example.

The role of the *working parties* (or working groups) is more specific than that of most of the committees in that they are responsible for carrying out a detailed analysis of formally tabled Commission proposals for Council, and EP and Council, legislation. The number of working parties in existence at any one time varies according to the overall nature of the EU's workload and the preferences of the Presidency in office, but in recent years there have usually been somewhere in the region of 150. (It is impossible to give a precise figure because over half of the working parties are *ad hoc* in nature.) Members of the working parties, of whom there may be up to three or four per member state, are almost invariably national officials and experts based either in the Permanent Representations or in appropriate national ministries. Occasionally governments appoint non-civil servants to a working party delegation when highly technical or complex issues are under consideration.

Working parties meet as and when they are required, usually with an interval of at least three weeks between meetings so as to allow the Council's Secretariat time to circulate minutes and agendas – in all the languages of the member states. For permanent working parties with a heavy workload meetings may be regular, for others, where nothing much comes up within their terms of reference, there may be very few meetings at all. Up to ten or eleven different working parties can be in session in Brussels on some days. On completion of their analyses of the Commission proposals, groups report to COREPER or to the SCA.

☐ The Council Secretariat

The main administrative support for the work of the Council is provided by the General Secretariat. This has a staff of just over 2000, of whom around 200 are at 'A' grade, that is diplomatic level. The Secretariat's base, which also houses Council meetings, is near to the main Commission and EP buildings in Brussels.

The Secretariat's main responsibility is to service the Council machinery – from ministerial to working party levels. This it does by activities such as preparing draft agendas, keeping records, providing legal advice, processing and circulating decisions and documentation, translating, and generally monitoring policy developments so as to provide an element of continuity and coordination in Council proceedings. This last task includes seeking to ensure a smooth transition between Presidencies by performing a liaising role with officials from the preceding, the incumbent, and the incoming Presidential states.

In exercising many of its responsibilities, the Secretariat works closely with representatives from the member state of the President-in-office. This is essential because key decisions about such matters as priorities, meetings, and agendas are primarily in the hands of the Presidency. Before all Council meetings at all levels Secretariat officials give the Presidency a full briefing about subject content, about the current state of play on the agenda items, and about possible tactics – 'the Danes can be isolated', 'there is strong resistance to this in Spain and Portugal so caution is advised', 'a possible vote has been signalled in the agenda papers and, if taken, will find the necessary majority', and so on.

The extent to which Presidencies rely on the Council Secretariat varies considerably, with smaller countries, because of their more limited administrative resources, tending to be most reliant. Even the larger countries, however, have much to gain by making maximum use of the Council's resources, as the United Kingdom discovered – somewhat late in the day – during its Presidency in the second half of 1992: for the first few months of its Presidency the UK Government made little headway in dealing with the problems which arose from the first Danish referendum on the TEU, but progress was made after it started using the Council Secretariat, which had long had a solution lined up but which was not consulted until mid-November. (This episode led, in December 1992 at Edinburgh, to a Council official – the head of the Legal Department – addressing a European Council meeting for the first time.)

The main reason why Presidencies are sometimes a little reluctant to make too much use of the Council's Secretariat is that there is a natural tendency for them to rely heavily on their own national officials as they seek to achieve a successful six month period of office by getting measures through. It is largely for this reason that the staff of a state's Permanent Representation increases in size during a Presidential tenureship. Something approaching a dual servicing of the Presidency is apparent in the way at Council meetings, at all levels, the President sits with officials from the Council's General Secretariat on his one side and national advisers on the other.

■ The operation of the Council

□ *The hierarchical structure*

As indicated above, a hierarchy exists in the Council consisting of the General Affairs Council, the Technical Councils, COREPER and SCA, and the committees and working parties. The European Council is also sometimes thought of as being part of this hierarchy but, in fact, it is not properly part of the Council system, even though it does have the political capability of issuing what amount to instructions to the ministers.

The Council's hierarchical structure is neither tight nor rigidly applied. The General Affairs Council's seniority over the Technical Councils is, for example, very ill-defined and only very partially developed, whilst important committees and working parties can sometimes communicate directly with Technical Councils. Nonetheless, the hierarchy does work in many important respects. This is best illustrated by looking at the Council's procedures for dealing with a Commission proposal for Council, or EP and Council, legislation.

The first stage is initial examination of the Commission's text. This is normally undertaken by a working party, or if it is of very broad application, several working parties. If no appropriate permanent working party exists, an *ad hoc* one is established.

As can be seen from Table 5.2, several factors can affect the progress of the proposal. A factor that has greatly increased in importance in recent years is whether the proposal will be subject to qualified majority voting rules (see below) when it appears before the ministers (votes are not taken below ministerial level). If it is not, and unanimity is required, then working party deliberations may take as long as is necessary to reach an agreement – which can mean months, or even years. If, however, it is, then delegations which find themselves isolated in the working party are obliged to anticipate the possibility of their country being outvoted when the ministers consider the proposal, and so they must seek to engage in damage limitation. This usually involves adopting some combination of three strategies: (1) if the proposal is judged to be important to national interests, then this is stressed during the working party's deliberations, in the hope that other delegations will take a sympathetic view and will either make concessions or will not seek to press ahead too fast; (2) if the proposal is judged to be not too damaging or unacceptable, then attempts will be made to amend it, but it is unlikely that too much of a fuss will be made; and (3) an attempt may be made to 'do a deal' or 'come to an understanding' with other delegations so that a blocking minority of states is created.

The General Secretariat of the Council is always pressing for progress and tries to ensure that a working party does not need to meet more than three times to discuss any one proposal. The first working party meeting normally consists of a general discussion of key points. Subsequent meetings are then taken up with a line by line examination of the Commission's text. If all goes well, a document is eventually produced indicating points of agreement and disagreement, and quite possibly

Table 5.2   *Principal factors determining the progress of a proposal through the Council machinery*

- The urgency of the proposal
- The controversiality of the proposal and support/opposition amongst the states
- The extent to which the Commission has tailored its text to accommodate national objections/reservations voiced at the pre-proposal stage
- The complexity of the proposal's provisions
- The ability of the Commission to allay doubts by the way it gives clarifications and answers questions
- The judgements made by the Commission on whether, or when, it should accept modifications to its proposals
- The competence of the Presidency
- The agility and flexibility of the participants to devise (usually through the Presidency and the Commission) and accept compromise formulae
- The ability and willingness of the states to use majority voting

---

having attached to it reservations that states have entered to indicate that they are not yet in a position formally to commit themselves to the text or a part of it. (States may enter reservations at any stage of the Council process. These can vary from an indication that a particular clause of a draft text is not yet in an acceptable form, to general withholdings of approval until the text has been cleared by appropriate national authorities.)

The second stage is the reference of the working party's document to COREPER or, in the case of agriculture, to the SCA. In being placed between the working parties and the Council of Ministers COREPER acts as a sort of filtering agency for ministerial meetings. It attempts to clear as much of the ground as possible so as to ensure that only the most difficult and sensitive of matters will detain the ministers in discussion. So, where the conditions for the adoption of a measure have been met in a working party, COREPER is likely to confirm the working party's opinion and advance it to the ministers for formal enactment. Where, however, agreement has not been possible in a working party, COREPER can do one of three things: try to resolve the issue itself (which its greater political status might permit); refer it back to the working party, perhaps with accompanying indications of where an agreement might be found; or pass it upwards to the ministers.

Whatever progress proposals have made at working party and COREPER levels, formal adoption is only possible at ministerial level. Ministerial meetings thus constitute *the third and final stage* of the Council's legislative procedure.

Items on ministerial meeting agendas are grouped under two headings: 'A' points and 'B' points. Matters which have been agreed at COREPER level, and on which it is thought Council approval will be given without discussion, are listed as 'A points'. These can cover a range of matters – from routine 'administrative' decisions to controversial new legislation which was agreed in principle at a previous ministerial meeting but on which a formal decision was delayed pending final clarification or tidying up. 'A points' do not necessarily fall within the policy competence of the Council that is meeting but may have been placed on the agenda because the appropriate Technical Council is not due to meet for some while. Ministers retain the right to raise objections on 'A points', and if any do the proposal may have to be withdrawn and referred back to COREPER. Normally, however, 'A points' are quickly approved without debate. Such is the thoroughness of the Council system that ministers can assume they have been thoroughly checked in both Brussels and national capitals to ensure they are politically acceptable, legally sound, and not subject to outstanding scrutiny reservations. Ministers then proceed to consider 'B points', which may include items left over from previous meetings, matters which it has not been possible to resolve at COREPER or working party levels, or proposals which COREPER judges to be politically sensitive and hence requiring political decisions. All 'B points' will have been extensively discussed by national officials at lower Council levels, and on most of them a formula for an agreement will have been prepared for the ministers to consider.

As can be seen from Exhibit 5.1, ministerial meetings – in this case a meeting of Agriculture Ministers – can have very wide and mixed agendas. Four observations are particularly worth making about the sorts of agenda items which arise.

- There are variations regarding what ministers are expected to do. The range of possibilities includes the taking of final decisions, the adoption of common positions (see below and Chapter 11), the approval of negotiating mandates for the Commission, the resolution of problems that have caused difficulties at lower levels of the Council hierarchy, and – simply – the noting of progress reports.
- Some items concern very general policy matters, whilst others are highly specialised and technical in nature.
- Most items fall within the sectoral competence of the ministers who have been convened, but a few – such as that on a technology initiative for disabled and elderly people in Exhibit 5.1 – do not.

Exhibit 5.1   A Council of Ministers meeting: items considered and decisions taken

1683rd meeting of the Council – Agriculture – Brussels, 21 September 1993

Agri monetary sector

The Council adopted the following conclusions:

The Council discussed in depth the agri-monetary situation following the decision taken on 2 August 1993 by the Ministers for Finance and the governors of the central banks to widen the fluctuation ranges in the EMS.

It took note of all the observations made by the Member States.

In the light of that discussion it invited the Commission to submit, before the next Council meeting on agriculture, a proposal for the agri-monetary system to be applied following the decision of 2 August.

In that context it stressed the need to take account of all relevant factors, including budgetary ones.

Meanwhile the Council noted the Commission's intention of taking appropriate steps to suspend any change in agricultural conversion rates, while ensuring that any deflection of trade was avoided.

The Council saw no need at this stage to examine the Commission proposal laying down the arrangements for implementing the agri-monetary compensatory aid decided on by the Council in December 1992.

Supply of milk to schoolchildren

The Council discussed the Commission proposal concerned which, following discontinuation of the 'normal' co-responsibility levy on milk, is designed to reduce the amount of Community aid given for the school milk scheme. The proposal seeks to cut this aid, which up to now has been largely financed from that levy, from 125% to 62.5% of the guide price for milk.

At the close of its debate the Council, acting by a qualified majority (the German and Portuguese delegations wanted to keep the aid at its current level and voted against), agreed to a compromise text alleviating the adverse impact on the original proposal by setting the level of aid at 95% of the guide price for milk. The Community aid is not to be reduced before the end of 1993.

The Commission will make the necessary technical adjustments under the powers vested in it.

The Regulation will be formally adopted shortly, once the relevant texts have been finalized.

Development and future of wine-sector policy

The Council held a wide-ranging exchange of views on the Commission communication concerning the development and future of wine-sector policy. The Commission discussion paper in question sets out guidelines for future wine-sector reform further to the undertaking given by the Commission during discussion of the 1993/1994 prices package to make a thorough analysis of the present situation and likely trends in this sector.

Delegations endorsed the Commission's analysis of the situation and the view that the wine-sector CMO needed a comprehensive overhaul in order to balance this market in the medium term; they gave their opinions on the broad range of measures which the Commission advocated for achieving this goal.

In conclusion, the Presidency asked the Commission to submit its formal proposals in this area at an early date.

Support for producers of certain arable crops (set-aside)

Pending the European Parliament's Opinion, the Council held a preliminary exchange of views on the Commission proposal which seeks to introduce more flexibility into the rules adopted as part of the arable crops reform. The proposal follows up the review of the reform of the arable crops arrangements carried out in the course of fixing the 1993/1994 prices and the Commission's discussion paper on possible changes in its set-aside policy . . .

At the close of its debate on this complex technical dossier, the Council instructed the Special Committee on Agriculture to expedite its work on this matter so that the Council would be able to take a decision once it received the European Parliament's Opinion.

Implementation of the memorandum of understanding on oilseeds

Pending the European Parliament's Opinion, the Council held a preliminary exchange of views on the Commission proposal concerned, which follows on from the formal approval by the Council last June on the Memorandum of Understanding on Oilseeds between the Community and the United States concluded on 3 December 1992 . . .

Closing its debate – which revealed a need for more thorough discussion – the Council instructed the Special Committee on Agriculture to continue examining the matter.

Further decisions relating to agriculture

Imports of wine from Hungary

The Council adopted the Regulation amending Regulation No 3677/89 in regard to the total alcoholic strength by volume of certain quality wines imported from Hungary. . .

Special report No 4/93 of the Court of Auditors

The Council took note of Special report No 4/93 of the Court of Auditors on the implementation of the quota system intended to control milk production, accompanied by the Commission's replies.

Fees for health inspectors and controls of fresh meat

The Council adopted by a qualified majority (the French delegation having voted against) the Decision deferring until 31 December 1993 the deadline laid down in Decision 88/408/EEC, *inter alia* for applying the standard fee for poultrymeat to be charged when carrying out health inspections and controls of fresh meat. The extension is intended to enable an in-depth study to be made of all the arrangements relating to fees with a view to a decision on the future regime.

Fruit juices and similar products

Following the European Parliament's approval of its common position, the Council finally adopted the Directive relating to juices and certain similar products. That Directive is a consolidated version of Directive 75/726/EEC and subsequent amendments thereto.

This consolidation is designed to simplify the whole body of Community legislation already in force in this area and to make it more understandable to both consumers and business.

More specifically, the Directive provides that Member States must take all measures necessary to ensure that the products can be marketed only if they conform to the Directive's rules. These rules cover, *inter alia*, substances, treatments, processes, additives and descriptions authorized in the manufacture of each type of fruit juice.

Marketing standards for eggs

Acting by a qualified majority (the United Kingdom delegation having voted against), the Council adopted the Regulation amending Regulation (EEC) No 1907/90 on certain marketing standards for eggs. The aim is to replace the indication of the packaging date by the recommended limit date for consumption and also to provide for the possibility of advertizing on egg packs.

Miscellaneous decisions

Importation of Mediterranean products

The Council adopted the Regulations suspending, within the limits of the quota volumes and for the periods indicated, customs duties applicable to imports into the Community of:

– melons originating in Israel: 10 789 tonnes – from 1 November 1993 to 31 May 1994;
– cut flowers and flower buds, fresh, originating in:

• Morocco: 325.5 tonnes; Jordan: 54.2 tonnes; Israel: 18 445 tonnes – from 1 November 1993 to 31 May 1994;
• Cyprus: 70 tonnes – from 1 June 1994 to 31 October 1994.

Technology initiative for disabled and elderly people (TIDE) (1993–1994)

The Council adopted the Decision on a Community technology initiative for disabled and elderly people (TIDE) (1993–1994). The initiative is aimed at promoting and applying technology with a view to encouraging the creation of an internal market in rehabilitation technology and assisting the economic and social integration of disabled and elderly people . . .

Source: General Secretariat of the European Communities, *Press Release* 8696/93 (147) (extracts).

• As well as policy issues, agenda items can also include administrative matters – such as appointments to advisory committees.

The position of the General Council rather suggests that there would, in certain circumstances – such as when a policy matter cuts across sectoral divisions, or when Technical Councils cannot resolve key issues – be a fourth legislative stage involving the Foreign Ministers. In practice, though recourse to such a stage would frequently be desirable, it is by no means common. A principal reason for this is that the theoretical seniority enjoyed by the General Affairs Council over other Councils has no legal basis. Rather it stems only from an ill-formulated understanding that the General Affairs Council has special responsibility for dealing with disputes which cannot be resolved in the Technical Councils, for tackling politically sensitive matters, and for acting as a general coordinating body at ministerial level. Another factor limiting the role of the General Affairs Council is that often the Foreign Ministers are not able, or willing, to act any more decisively in breaking a deadlock than is a divided Technical

Council. Members of the General Council may, indeed, have no greater seniority in rank, and may even be junior, to their national colleagues in, say, the Budget or the Agriculture Councils. In any case, Technical Councils are often not willing to refer their disputes 'upwards': Ministers of Agriculture, Trade, Environment, etc. have as much authority to make EU law as do Foreign Ministers and they normally prefer to take their own decisions – unless something which is likely to be very unpopular can be passed on elsewhere. The General Council is thus of only limited effectiveness in resolving issues that have created blockages in the Technical Councils and in counteracting the fragmentation and sectoralism to which the Council of Ministers is unquestionably prone. The same is true of joined or 'jumbo' Councils, which bring together, but only on an occasional basis, different groups of ministers.

This absence of clear Council leadership and of an authoritative coordinating mechanism has had the consequence of encouraging the European Council to assume responsibilities in relation to the Council of Ministers, even though it is not formally part of the Council hierarchy. Increasingly at their meetings the Heads of Government have gone beyond issuing general guidelines to the Council of Ministers, which was intended to be the normal limit of European Council/Council of Ministers relationships when the former was established in 1974. Summits have sometimes been obliged to try and resolve thorny issues that have been referred to them by the Council of Ministers, and have also had to seek to ensure – principally via policy package agreements of the sort that were agreed at Fontainebleau in 1984, Luxembourg in 1985, Brussels in 1988, and Edinburgh in 1992 – that there is some overall policy direction and coherence in the work of the Council of Ministers. The European Council can only go so far, however, in performing such problem solving, leadership, and coordinating roles: partly because it is timetabled to meet only twice a year; partly because many national leaders prefer to avoid getting too involved in detailed policy discussions; but, above all, because the Heads of Government are subject to the same national and political divisions as the ministers.

☐ *Decision-making procedures*

The Treaties provide for three basic ways in which the Council can take a decision: unanimously; by a qualified majority vote; or by a simple majority vote.

● *Unanimity* used to be the normal requirement where a new policy was being initiated or an existing policy framework was being modified or further developed. However, the SEA and the TEU have greatly reduced the circumstances in which a unanimity requirement applies and it is now largely confined to the CFSP and JHA pillars of the TEU (though even here some implementing decisions may be taken by qualified majority vote), and to various 'constitutional' and financial matters which fall under the EC Treaty (see Table 11.1 for details). Unanimity is also required when the Council wishes to amend a Commission proposal against the Commission's wishes. Abstentions do not constitute an impediment to the adoption of Council decisions that require unanimity.

• *Qualified majority voting* now applies to most types of decisions in most policy areas. As regards variations in the usage of qualified majority voting between the EU's various legislative procedures, it applies invariably under the cooperation procedure (except for certain specified circumstances at second reading stage), almost invariably under the co-decision procedure (except for decisions in the spheres of culture and research frameworks), commonly under the consultation procedure, and sometimes under the assent procedure (see Chapter 11 and Table 11.1 for details).

Under the qualified majority voting rules, France, Germany, Italy and the United Kingdom have 10 votes each; Spain has 8; Belgium, Greece, the Netherlands and Portugal have 5; Denmark and Ireland have 3; and Luxembourg has 2. Of this total of 76 votes, 54 votes (that is 71 per cent of the total) constitutes a qualified majority vote. This means that the five larger states cannot outvote the smaller seven, and also that two large states cannot by themselves constitute a blocking minority. An abstention has the same effect as a negative vote, since the total vote required to achieve a majority is not reduced as a result of an abstention. (See Appendix for voting arrangements following accessions to the EU by EFTA states.)

• *Simple majority voting*, in which all states have one vote each, is used mainly for procedural purposes and, since February 1994, for anti-dumping and anti-subsidy tariffs within the context of the Common Commercial Policy (CCP).

Until relatively recently, proposals were not usually pushed to a vote in the Council when disagreements between the states existed, even when majority voting was perfectly constitutional under the Treaties. To appreciate the reasons for this it is necessary to go back to the institutional crisis of 1965.

In brief, events unfolded in the following way. The Commission, in an attempt to move progress in areas which had almost ground to a halt, put forward a package deal which had important policy and institutional implications. The most important aspects of its proposals were the completion of the CAP, changing the basis of Community income from national contributions to own resources, and the granting of greater powers of control to the EP over the use of those resources. The French Government objected to the supranational implications of these proposals. It also used the occasion to register its opposition to what it saw as the increasing political role of the Commission and to the imminent prospect of the Community moving into a stage of its development in which there was to be more majority voting in the Council. When no agreement could be reached on these matters in the Council, France withdrew its representatives from the Community's decision-making institutions in July 1965, though it continued to apply Community law. This so-called 'policy of the empty chair' continued for six months and was ended only after the French Government, under strong domestic pressure, accepted a fudged deal at a special Council meeting in Luxembourg in January 1966. The outcome of that meeting is usually referred to as the *Accords de Luxembourg* or the Luxembourg Compromise. In fact, there was little agreement or genuine compromise but rather a registering of differences. This is apparent from the official communiqué:

I   Where, in the case of decisions which may be taken by majority vote on a proposal of the Commission, very important interests of one or more partners are at stake, the Members of the Council will endeavour, within a reasonable time, to reach solutions which can be adopted by all the Members of the Council while respecting their mutual interests and those of the Community, in accordance with Article 2 of the Treaty.

II   With regard to the preceding paragraph, the French delegation considers that where very important interests are at stake the discussion must be continued until unanimous agreement is reached.

III   The six delegations note that there is a divergence of views on what should be done in the event of a failure to reach complete agreement.

IV   The six delegations nevertheless consider that this divergence does not prevent the Community's work being resumed in accordance with the normal procedure.

Although it had no constitutional status, the Luxembourg Compromise came to profoundly affect decision-making in the Council at all levels. It did so because point II of the communiqué came to be interpreted as meaning that any state had the right to exercise a veto on questions which affected its vital national interests – and the states themselves determined when such interests were at stake.

The Luxembourg Compromise did not, it should be emphasised, replace a system of majority voting by one of unanimous voting. On the contrary, before 1966 majority voting was rare and, indeed, it was its proposed phasing-in that the French were most concerned about. After 1966, the norm became one not of unanimous voting but one of no voting at all – except in a few areas where decisions could not be indefinitely delayed and postponed, such as during the annual budgetary cycle and on internal staffing matters. Most decisions, even on routine issues, came to be made by letting deliberations and negotiations run until an agreement finally emerged. As a result there was rarely a need for the veto to be formally invoked, and it was so only very occasionally – no more than a dozen times between 1966 and 1985.

Because it had produced a norm of consensual, and therefore very slow, decision-making, in which decisions were all too often of a lowest common denominator type, the Luxembourg Compromise had naturally never been liked by those who wished for an efficient and dynamic Community. By the mid-1980s the damaging effects of the Compromise were coming to be generally acknowledged and the practice of majority voting began to develop where it was so permitted by the Treaties. The 1986 SEA, which greatly increased the circumstances in which majority votes were permitted by the Treaties, seemed to signal the final demise of the Compromise. In the event it has not quite done so in that Greece attempted – with only marginal success – to invoke the Compromise in 1988 in connection with a realignment of the 'green drachma', and in 1992–3 France threatened to invoke it in connection with the GATT Uruguay Round trade settlement which was proposed by the Commission. These are, however, isolated incidents and on many occasions where it might have been expected that the Compromise would have been invoked had it still had bite – such as by the United Kingdom in connection with unwanted social legislation – it has not been so. Everything thus indicates that whilst the Compromise may not be quite completely dead, it is in the deepest of sleeps and is subject only to very occasional and partial awakenings.

Clearly, the most visible aspect of the Luxembourg Compromise was the national veto – a veto to which some still make reference when they wish to claim that Community membership has not fundamentally undermined national sovereignty. A less visible, but in practice much more significant effect, was in the stimulus it gave to the Council of Ministers to take virtually all of its decisions unanimously. But the preference for unanimity, which still exists today despite the greatly increased use of majority voting, was not, and is not, just a consequence of an unofficial agreement made in the mid-1960s. There are strong positive reasons for acting only on the basis of unanimity. In many ways the functioning and development of the EU is likely to be enhanced if policy-making processes are consensual rather than conflictual. Thus, national authorities (which may be governments or parliaments) are unlikely to undertake with much enthusiasm the necessary task of transposing EU directives into national law if the directives are perceived as domestically damaging, or if they are being unwillingly imposed following a majority vote in the Council. Nor is it likely that national bureaucracies will adopt helpful attitudes towards the implementation of unwanted legislation. More generally, the over-use of majority votes on important and sensitive matters could well create grievances that could have disruptive implications right across the EU's policy spectrum.

For good reasons, as well as perhaps some bad, decision-making in the Council thus usually proceeds on the understanding that difficult and controversial decisions are not imposed on dissenting states without full consideration being given to the reasons for their opposition. Where it is clear that a state or states have serious difficulties with a proposal, they are normally allowed time. They may well be put on the defensive, asked to fully explain their position, pressed even to give way or at least to compromise, but the possibility of resolving an impasse by a vote is not the port of first call. Usually, the item is held over for a further meeting, with the hope that in the meantime informal meetings or perhaps COREPER will find the basis of a solution. All states, and not just the foremost advocates of the retention of the veto (initially France, more latterly Denmark, the United Kingdom, and, to a more limited extent, Greece and Ireland) accept that this is the only way Council business can be done without risking major divisions.

But though there are good reasons for preferring unanimity, it is now generally accepted that the principle cannot be applied too universally or too rigidly. Were it to be so decision-making would, as in the 1970s, be determined by the slowest, and many much needed decisions would never be made at all. Qualified majority voting has thus become common where the Treaties so allow.

Several – in practice closely interrelated – factors explain this increased use of majority voting:

- The 'legitimacy' and 'mystique' of the Luxembourg Compromise were dealt a severe blow in May 1982 when, for the first time, an attempt to invoke the Compromise was overridden. The occasion was an attempt by the British Government to veto the annual agricultural prices settlement by proclaiming a vital national interest. The other states did not believe that such an interest was at stake (and with some reason given that the United Kingdom had already approved the constituent parts of the package). The view was taken (correctly) that the British were trying to use agricultural prices to force a more favourable outcome in concurrent negotiations over UK budgetary contributions. Agricultural ministers regarded this attempted linkage as quite invalid. They also thought it was over-demanding, since the dispute was played out to the background of the Falklands crisis in which the UK Government was being supported by her

Community partners even though some were unenthusiastic. Prompted by the Commission, the Belgian Presidency proceeded to a vote on the regulations for increasing agricultural prices and they were approved by seven (of the then ten) states. Denmark and Greece abstained, not because of any sympathy for Britain but because of reservations about the possible supranational implications of the majority vote.

● Attitudes have changed. There has been an increasing recognition, even amongst the most rigid defenders of national rights and interests, that decision-making by unanimity is a recipe not only for procrastination and delay, but often for unsatisfactory, or even no decision-making. The situation whereby consensus is the rule, even on issues where countries would not object too strongly to being voted down, has increasingly been seen as unsatisfactory in the face of the manifest need for the EU to become efficient and dynamic in order, for example, to assist its industries to be able to compete successfully on European and world markets.

● The 1981 and 1986 enlargements of the Community, which brought the membership to twelve, clearly made unanimity on policy issues all the more difficult to achieve and hence increased the necessity for majority voting.

● The SEA, and later the TEU, extended the number of policy areas in which majority voting was constitutionally permissible. Crucially, under the SEA the extension included most of those matters that were covered by the priority programme of completing the internal market by 1992: harmonisation of technical norms, opening up public procurement, removing restrictions in banking, insurance, capital controls and so forth. Moreover, the discussions which accompanied the SEA and the TEU were based on the assumption that the new voting procedures would be used.

● In July 1987, the General Council, in accordance with an agreement it had reached in December 1986, formally amended the Council's Rules of Procedure. Among the changes was a relaxation of the circumstances by which votes could be initiated: whereas previously only the President could call for a vote, under the new Rules any national representative and the Commission also have the right, and a vote must be taken if a simple majority agrees.

In 1986, the last full year before the SEA came into force, over 100 decisions were taken by majority vote, most of them in the three main areas provided for in the EEC Treaty: budget, agriculture, and external trade. Since 1986 the number has increased enormously, though to exactly what figure is impossible to say. It is impossible to say because though Council minutes, unlike previously, now record when formal votes have taken place (see Exhibit 5.1, p. 138), what really amounts to majority voting often occurs without a formal vote being taken. This may take the form of a state which is opposed to a proposal that otherwise commands general support preferring to try and extract concessions in negotiations – perhaps at working party or COREPER stage – rather than run the risk of pressing for a vote and then finding itself outvoted. Or it may take the form of the Presidency simply announcing 'we appear to have the necessary majority here', and that being left unchallenged by a dissenting state, and not therefore formally voted on. Unless an important point of principle or a damaging political consequence is at stake, a country in a minority thus often chooses not to create too much of a fuss.

Important, however, though this development of majority voting is, consensual decision-making remains, and can be expected to remain, a key feature of Council processes. Quite apart from the fact that unanimity is still required by the Treaties in some important areas, there is still a strong preference for trying to reach general agreements where 'important', 'sensitive', and 'political' matters, as opposed to 'technical' matters, are being considered. This may involve delay, but the duty of the national representatives at all Council levels is not only to reach decisions but also to defend national interests.

The formal processes by which Council meetings are conducted and business is transacted are broadly similar at ministerial, COREPER, and working party levels. As can be seen from Figure 5.1, at one end or one side of the table sits the Presidency – whose delegation is led by the most senior figure present from the country currently holding the Presidency; at the other end or side sit the Commission representatives; and ranged between the Presidency and the Commission are the representatives of the twelve member states – with the delegation from the country holding the Presidency sitting to the right of, but separate from, the President.

As indicated earlier, the Presidency plays a key role in fixing the agenda of Council meetings, both in terms of content and the order in which items are considered. The room for manoeuvre available to the Presidency should not, however, be exaggerated for, quite apart from time constraints, there are several factors which serve to limit options and actions: it is difficult to exclude from the agenda of Council meetings items which are clearly of central interest or which need resolution; the development of rolling programmes means that much of the agenda of many meetings is largely fixed; and anyone in a COREPER or a ministerial meeting can insist a matter is discussed provided the required notice is given. A Presidency cannot, therefore, afford to be too ambitious or the six month tenureship will probably be seen to have been a failure. With this in mind the normal pattern for an incoming President of a reasonably

Figure 5.1 *Rotation of Council Presidency between the states and seating arrangements in Council meetings*

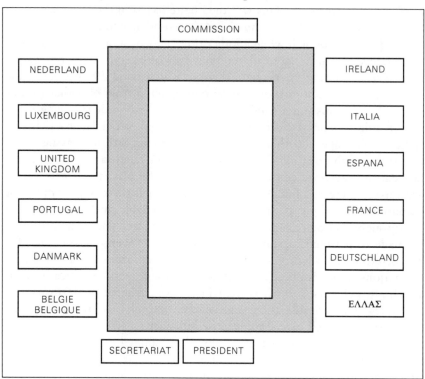

Notes:
1. Figure 5.1 shows the seating arrangements when Greece holds the Presidency (which it last did January–June 1994). National delegations sit according to the order in which they will next assume the Presidency – which rotates in an anti-clockwise direction. With each change of Presidency all states move round one place in a clockwise direction.
2. In the round of Presidencies which began with Belgium in the first half of 1987 and ended with the United Kingdom in the second half of 1992, the Presidency rotated in alphabetical order, according to how countries names were spelt in their own language. Because of variations in the responsibilities of Presidencies between the first half and the second half of the year – most of the work on agricultural prices, for example, is done in the first half and most of the work on the budget is done in the second half – the round of Presidencies which began in the first half of 1993 saw pairs of countries' reversing their alphabetical order: so, Denmark assumed the Presidency for the first half of 1993 and Belgium did so for the second half.
3. The arrangements apply to all Council meetings at all levels.
4. See Appendix for the rotation of the Presidency in the event of accessions from EFTA states.

important Technical Council is to take the view that of, say, twenty proposed directives in his policy area, he is going to try and get eight particular ones through. This will then be reflected in the organisation of Council business, so that by the end of the Presidency four may have been adopted by the Council, while another three may be at an advanced stage.

At ministerial level Council meetings can often appear to be chaotic affairs: not counting interpreters there can be around 100 people in the room – with each national delegation putting out a team of perhaps six or seven, the Commission a similar number, and the Presidency being made up of both General Secretariat and national officials; participants frequently change – with ministers often arriving late or leaving early, and some of the officials coming and going in relation to items on the agenda; ministers are constantly being briefed by officials as new points are raised; there are huddles of delegations during breaks; requests for adjournments and postponements are made to enable further information to be sought and more consideration to be given; and telephone calls may be made to national capitals for clarifications or even, occasionally, for authorisation to adopt revised negotiating positions. Not surprisingly, delegations which are headed by ministers with domestic political weight, which are well versed in EU ways, which have mastered the intricacies of the issues under consideration, and which can think quickly on their feet, are particularly well placed to exercise influence.

A device which is sometimes employed at Council meetings, especially when negotiations are making little progress, is the *tour de table* procedure. By this, the President invites each delegation to give a summary of its thinking on the matter under consideration. This ensures that discussion is not totally dominated by a few and, more importantly, establishes the position of each member state. It can thus help to clarify the possible grounds of an agreement and provide useful guidance to the President as to whether a compromise is possible or whether indeed he can attempt to move to a decision. As well as advantages there are, however, also drawbacks with the procedure: in particular, states can find it more difficult to alter their position once they have 'gone public', and it is very time-consuming – even if each state restricts itself to just five minutes a *tour* takes an hour. Presidencies do then tend, and are normally advised by the General Secretariat, to be cautious about using the procedure unless there seems to be no other way forward. It is usually better to use another approach, such as inviting the Commission to amend its proposal, or seeking to isolate the most 'hard line' state in the hope that it will back down.

This last point highlights how important the Presidency can be, not only at the agenda setting stage but also during meetings themselves. An astute and sensitive chairman is often able to judge when a delegation that is making difficulties is not terribly serious: when, perhaps, it is being awkward for domestic political reasons and will not ultimately stand in the way of a decision being made. A poor chairman, on the other hand, may allow a proposal to drag on, or may rush it to the point that a state which, given time, would have agreed to a compromise may feel obliged to dig in its heels.

An extremely important feature of the whole Council network is the role of informal processes and relationships. Three examples demonstrate this. First, many understandings and agreements are reached at the lunches that are very much a part of ministerial meetings. These lunches are attended only by ministers and the minimum number of translators. (Most ministers can converse directly with one another – usually in French or English – although the entry of Greece, Spain, and Portugal did reduce this capacity.)

Second, where difficulties arise in ministerial negotiations a good chairman can make advantageous use of scheduled and requested breaks in proceedings to explore possibilities for a settlement. This may involve holding off-the-record discussions with a delegation that is holding up an agreement, or it may take the form of a *tour* of all delegations – perhaps in the company of the relevant Commissioner and a couple of officials – to ascertain 'real' views and fall-back positions.

Third, many of the national officials based in Brussels come to know their counterparts in other Permanent Representations extremely well: better, sometimes, than their colleagues in their own national capitals or Permanent Representations. This enables them to make judgements about when a country is posturing and when it is serious, and when and how a deal may be possible. A sort of code language may even be used between officials to signal positions on proposals. So if, for example, a national representative states 'this is very important for my minister', or 'my minister is very strongly pressurised on this', other participants recognise that signals are being given to them that further deliberations are necessary at their level if more serious difficulties are to be avoided when the ministers gather.

■ Concluding comments

The structure and functioning of the Council is generally recognised as being unsatisfactory in a number of important respects. In particular: power is too dispersed; there is insufficient cohesion between, or sometimes even within, the sectoral Councils; and decision-making processes are still often too cumbersome and too slow.

Many have argued that what the Council structure most needs to deal with these weaknesses is some sort of 'super' Council, with authority to impose an overall policy pattern on subsidiary 'Technical Councils'. Such a Council may indeed be useful for identifying priorities and knocking a few heads together, but it would be unwise to hold out too many hopes for it, even if the practical obstacles in the way of establishing it could be overcome. As the experience of the European Council demonstrates (see Chapter 6), the dream of authoritative national leaders rationally formulating policy frameworks in the 'EU interest' just does not accord with political realities.

But if fundamental structural reforms are unlikely, it should be recognised that the Council has undergone, and is undergoing, quite radical changes in an attempt to deal with the increasing demands on it. The most important of these changes are the greatly increased use of majority voting, the enhancement of the role of the Presidency, and the increased cooperation which occurs between Presidencies – of which the development of rolling policy programmes is especially important. Further changes can be expected in the future – not least because of questions which arise in connection with the projected enlargement of the EU.

■ *Chapter 6* ■

The European Council

■ Origins and development

Although no provision was made in the Founding Treaties for summit meetings of Heads of Government, a few such gatherings did occur in the 1960s and early 1970s. In 1974, at the Paris summit, it was decided to institutionalise these meetings with the establishment of what soon became known as the European Council.

The main reason for the creation of the European Council was a growing feeling that the Community was failing to respond adequately or quickly enough to new and increasingly difficult challenges. Neither the Commission, whose position had been weakened by the intergovernmental emphasis on decision-making that was signalled by the Luxembourg Compromise, nor the Council of Ministers, which was handicapped both by sectoralism and by its practice of proceeding only on the basis of unanimous agreements, were providing the necessary leadership. A new focus of authority was seen as being required to try and make the Community more effective, both domestically and internationally. What was needed, argued France's President Giscard d'Estaing who, with West Germany's Chancellor Schmidt, was instrumental in establishing the European Council, was a body which would bring the Heads of Government together on a relatively informal basis to exchange ideas, to further mutual understanding at the highest political level, to give direction to policy development, and perhaps sometimes to break deadlocks and clear logjams. It was not anticipated that the leaders would concern themselves with the details of policy.

The formal creation of the European Council was very simple: a few paragraphs were issued as part of the Paris communiqué. The key paragraphs were these:

Recognising the need for an overall approach to the internal problems involved in achieving Europe, the Heads of Government consider it essential

153

to ensure progress and overall consistency in the activities of the Communities and in the work on political cooperation.

The Heads of Government have therefore decided to meet, accompanied by the Ministers of Foreign Affairs, three times a year and, whenever necessary, in the Council of the Communities and in the context of political cooperation. The administrative secretariat will be provided for in an appropriate manner with due regard for existing practices and procedures.

Two points about this communiqué are particularly worth emphasising. First, it was vague and left a number of questions largely unanswered, especially as regards the precise role and functioning of the European Council.

Second, the communiqué had no constitutional or legal standing. It announced a political agreement between the national leaders but it did not formally or legally integrate the European Council into the Community framework.

In a somewhat similar fashion to the Luxembourg Compromise and European Political Cooperation (EPC), the European Council was thus to be part of the 'unofficial' approach to integration rather than the 'official' Treaty-based approach. Over the years, however, there has been something of a formalisation of the position and role of the European Council, albeit on a tentative and cautious basis. This has occurred in three steps. First, declarations by the European Council itself in the late 1970s and early 1980s – notably London (1977) and Stuttgart (1983) – did something, though not a great deal, to clarify its role. Second, in 1986 the European Council was given legal recognition for the first time via the SEA, though it was so only in two short paragraphs that were confined to clarifying membership and reducing the minimum number of meetings per year from three to two. Moreover, the paragraphs were not incorporated into the Community Treaties. Third, the TEU, expanding on the SEA, contained three 'sets of references' to the European Council:

● The Common Provisions of the Treaty specified the following under Article D:

> The European Council shall provide the Union with the necessary impetus for its development and shall define the general political guidelines thereof. The European Council shall bring together the Heads of State or of Government of the Member States and the President of the Commission. They shall be assisted by the Ministers for Foreign Affairs of the Member States and by a Member of the Commission. The European Council shall meet at least twice a year, under the chairmanship of the Head of State or of Government of the Member State which holds the Presidency of the Council.

The European Council shall submit to the European Parliament a report after each of its meetings and a yearly written report on the progress achieved by the Union.

For the first time, the role of the European Council was thus laid down in a legal document. It was so, however, in only very general terms and – because the Common Provisions are not incorporated into the Community Treaties – on a legal basis which meant that whatever interpretation the European Council gave to its role, or indeed to any of the other provisions of Article D, it could not be challenged in the Court of Justice.

• In Title VI of the EC Treaty, which deals with Economic and Monetary Policy, the Heads of Government are brought into the framework of the Communities for the first time. There are two references to the European Council under Title VI: under Article 103 it is given an important role in determining the recommendations which are to be made, as part of the movement to EMU, on 'the broad guidelines of the economic policies of the Member States and of the Community'; and under Article 109b it is required to be presented with the annual report of the European Central Bank (which is to be established under stage three of EMU). Under Title VI the Heads of Government are also mentioned in a capacity separate from their membership of the European Council. In one formulation, under Articles 109a and 109f, leading members of the European Central Bank and of the Bank's forerunner the European Monetary Institute are to be appointed 'by common accord of the Governments of the Member States at the levels of Heads of State or of Government'. In the other formulation which is used, in Articles 109j and 109k, the final decisions on the third stage of EMU, on the adoption of the single currency, and on the suitability of countries to join the third stage, are to be taken by qualified majority vote in the Council of Ministers 'meeting in the composition of Heads of State or of Government'.

• Under Article J.3 of the CFSP pillar of the Treaty, the European Council is given a quite specific role: 'The Council shall decide, on the basis of general guidelines from the European Council, that a matter should be the subject of joint action.'

It might have been thought that the lack of clarity as to the precise role of the European Council, coupled with its non-legal (pre-SEA) and then quasi-legal (post-SEA) base, would have been hindrances in terms of the European Council exercising influence and establishing itself as an important decision-making institution. In practice, they have not been hindrances at all because the status of those who attend meetings – particularly the national leaders – is such that they can more or less decide amongst themselves what the European Council will and will not do. As a result, the evolution, the operation, and the influence of the European Council has owed much more to the preferences of participants and to political and practical necessities than they have to agreed rules and requirements. Indeed, so as to give itself maximum flexibility and manoeuvrability, the European Council has been careful to avoid being based on, or being subject to, rules and requirements – especially those which might arise, not least from Court of Justice jurisdiction, if the European Council was to be placed firmly within the context of the Community Treaties.

The opportunity to decide for itself what it does, has resulted in the European Council coming to exercise a number of roles and perform a number of functions. The precise nature of these roles and functions are explained in some detail below, so suffice it to note here that they add up to an extremely important and impressive portfolio. Indeed, they put the European Council at the very heart of EU decision-making: not on a day-to-day basis in the manner of the other four main EU institutions, but rather from a more distanced position where it is centrally involved in setting the overall parameters of the EU system. Final and legally binding EU decisions may be made by other EU institutions, but major political decisions concerning the institutional and policy development of the EU are now generally taken by, or at least are given clearance by, the European Council.

■ Membership

As Article D of the Common Provisions of the TEU makes clear (see above) there are twenty-six negotiating participants at European Council meetings: two from each member state (the Head of Government and Foreign Minister – apart from France whose delegation is always led by the President, who is Head of State, accompanied by either the Prime Minister or the Foreign Minister), plus two from the Commission. Apart from these twenty-six, only a very restricted number of other people are permitted to be present at the formal sessions of the European Council: interpreters; six officials – two from the country holding the Presidency, one from the Council Secretariat (a major job of these three officials is to make an accurate record of proceedings), and three from the Commission – including the Secretary General of the Commission; and national civil servants, but only on the basis of one adviser per country being allowed entrance at any one time.

In recent years the practice has developed of Ecofin Council ministers also travelling to European summits and holding parallel meetings when economic and financial issues constitute an important part of the summit agenda. This happened, for example, at the December 1992 Edinburgh summit and the December 1993 Brussels summit.

Each state has a suite in the vicinity of the summit meeting room which is available to its official delegation and from which officials may be summoned as required. Official delegations are normally restricted in number, but states always supplement their official delegations with numerous other officials who make up what are customarily described as the non-official or technical delegations.

The membership of the European Council is thus based on the Council of Ministers model in the sense that it is made up of national delegations, plus the Commission. Unlike in the Council of Ministers, however, the participants in European Council sessions are not physically accompanied by teams of national officials.

■ Organisation

□ *Preparing European Council meetings*

Much of the responsibility for preparing European Council meetings rests with the Presidency – a post that is held concurrently with the Presidency of the Council of Ministers. How closely the Head of Government of the incumbent Presidency becomes involved in these preparations depends very much on circumstances, style and personal preference. Some act in a low-key manner and do little more than circulate the other summit participants with a letter indicating topics to be discussed and ways in which it is proposed to try and deal with them. Others, especially those who are faced with a difficult meeting or who are looking for media attention, may well play a very active and public role – including making a tour of some or all of the national capitals.

Whatever the preparatory work that Heads of Government themselves choose to do, national officials and Foreign Ministers are invariably extensively engaged in pre-European Council preparations. The 'standard' procedure is for senior officials from the Presidency, working in liaison with the Secretariat of the Council of Ministers (the European Council does not have its own Secretariat), the Antici Group (see Chapter 5), and the Commission, to identify topics that can be, ought to be, or need to be discussed. These are then channelled through COREPER or, in the case of

CFSP matters, through the Political Committee (which is made up of Political Directors from Foreign Offices). Finally, about ten days before the European Council meeting, Foreign Ministers meet to finalise the general shape of the agenda and, usually, to engage in exploratory pre-summit negotiations. To this 'standard' procedure may well be added – especially when it looks as though a European Council meeting will be difficult – numerous preparatory meetings of officials and the convening of extra meetings of the Foreign Ministers and of appropriate Technical Councils.

☐ *Setting the agenda*

The subject matter of European Council meetings depends on many factors:

- Some issues are almost always on the agenda because of their intrinsic importance. So, time is usually allowed for a discussion of the general economic situation in the EU, and in recent years time has usually also been set aside for some consideration of developments relating to the SEM and EMU.
- The Commission may be pressing an initiative which the Presidency and at least some of the states are sympathetic to. This was the background to the discussion on the Social Charter at the 1989 Strasbourg summit, and to the establishment of a plan of action at the December 1992 Edinburgh summit to promote growth and to combat unemployment.
- The Presidency, perhaps supported by, or even pressed by, the Commission and all or some of the other member states, may wish to use a European Council meeting to make or to formalise an important policy or institutional breakthrough. The events leading to the TEU illustrate this: the decision to call an IGC on EMU was taken at the 1989 Strasbourg summit; the decision to call a parallel IGC on Political Union was taken at the special April 1990 Dublin summit; the setting of dates for the opening of the two IGCs was taken at the June 1990 Dublin summit; the IGCs were formally opened at the December 1990 Rome summit; and the IGCs reported to, and the final decisions on the contents of the TEU, were taken at, the December 1991 Maastricht summit.
- Decisions may be urgently needed on matters which the Council of Ministers has been unable to resolve. This is the reason why there were so many summit discussions in the 1980s on budgetary and agricultural reform.
- Business may be left over from, or have been referred from, a previous summit. Such was the case at the December 1993 Brussels summit which was much taken up with a Commission White Paper on a medium-term

strategy for growth, competitiveness and unemployment which had been requested by the June 1993 Copenhagen summit.

• International circumstances may require discussions, declarations, and decisions. So, the December 1990 Rome summit decided to send emergency food aid to the Soviet Union, lifted the voluntary ban on EC investments in South Africa, urged the negotiating parties in the suspended GATT world trade talks to reach a balanced agreement as soon as possible, and re-affirmed Community support for the UN–US stance on the Gulf crisis. Summits in 1992–3 all addressed the situation in the former Yugoslavia.

The regular, twice yearly, European Council meetings contain on their agendas a mixture of most of the factors that have just been itemised. When special summits are held, however – and there is normally at least one a year – the situation is rather different for they are usually convened for a specific purpose, last no more than one day, and therefore inevitably have a much narrower agenda. So, for example, the February 1988 Brussels summit was called to try and resolve pressing budgetary, and budgetary-related, problems. The special Dublin summit of April 1990 was called to discuss German unification – though in the event the much broader question of political unification in the Community also featured prominently on the agenda. The special Rome summit of October 1990 – which many thought was not really required and suspected had been called because the Italians wanted the prestige and status of an extra summit during their Presidency – focused mainly on EMU. And the special Birmingham summit of October 1992 was nominally convened to discuss the recent crisis in the ERM – though by the time the summit was held the immediacy of the crisis had passed, the other states had intimated their unwillingness to examine what the UK government was referring to as 'the fault lines in the ERM', and so the agenda was broadened to include a discussion on subsidiarity and transparency.

☐ *Location and timing of meetings*

The six-monthly meetings of the European Council that are specifically provided for in the TEU are held in the country of the Presidency. When the provision for only twice yearly meetings was first established, in the SEA, it had been anticipated that extra meetings would be held in Brussels, but when both Ireland and Italy arranged for an extra meeting during their Presidencies in 1990 they held them not in Brussels but in their national capitals. (The four 1990 summits have come to be referred to as Dublin 1 and Dublin 2, and Rome 1 and Rome 2.) Subsequent extra meetings have also been held in the country of the Presidency.

The regular meetings of the European Council take place towards the end of a Presidency – in June and December. They are held over a two day period and normally – though by no means always – begin in the morning of day 1 and end in the late afternoon of day 2. The timing and length of special summits depends largely on the reasons for which they have been called – Dublin 1, for example, was held on a Saturday in April.

☐ *The conduct of business*

The customary, though by no means rigid, format for the regular European Council meetings is as follows:

● Participants gather after breakfast. On the basis of the (normally loose) agenda that has been agreed in advance, a full plenary session is held. Since 1987 this opening session has included an address from the President of the European Parliament.
● Lunch is a drawn-out affair, which allows time for informal discussions and bilateral meetings.
● In the afternoon another full plenary is usually held, although sometimes the Heads of Government and the Foreign Ministers separate into two meetings.
● In the evening, dinner provides another opportunity for further informal discussions. Sometimes the Heads of Government and the President of the Commission, and the Foreign Ministers and the other representative of the Commission, take dinner separately.
● What happens after dinner rather depends on what progress has been made during the day. The customary format used to be that the Heads would hold informal 'fireside chats', whilst Foreign Ministers would discuss EPC (now CFSP) business. At several recent summits, however, informal sessions have been replaced with reconvened plenaries in an attempt to make progress with uncompleted business.
● During the night Presidency and Council Secretariat officials prepare a draft of conclusions on the first day's business and/or work on a form of words that can serve as a basis for further negotiations the next day.
● Another plenary session is held in the morning, and perhaps afternoon, of day 2. This usually picks up from the previous day's discussions, but with the draft that has been worked on during the night now tabled. With the leaders now trying to move towards conclusions, breaks in proceedings may be called for, most usually by the Presidency, so as to permit delegations to carefully study the implications of proposals or so as to allow for informal discussions.

• The summit normally ends some time in the afternoon with the publication of a statement which is issued in the form of a 'Conclusions of the Presidency'. The statement is customarily agreed to by all, but there are two sets of circumstances in which unanimity may be lacking. First, since 1985 there has been some limited use of voting in European Council meetings. This has largely been because of irritation with UK opposition to integrationist developments. It is no coincidence that on each occasion a vote has been taken the United Kingdom has been in the minority: at Milan in 1985 when Denmark, Greece and the United Kingdom were outvoted on the establishment of the IGC which led to the SEA; at Strasbourg in 1989 when the United Kingdom was in a minority of one on both the adoption of the Social Charter and on the calling of the IGC on EMU; and at the special Rome summit in 1990 when the United Kingdom was again in a minority of one on the setting of a date for Stage 2 of EMU. Second, some states may attach reservations to the statement: thus, the preamble to the conclusions of the 1985 Luxembourg summit which, in effect, agreed the SEA, included the following – 'Denmark has stated that it was unable to take a position on these texts. A blanket reservation on the part of Denmark therefore remains. Italy has made its final acceptance conditional upon examination by the Italian Parliament. There are also a few reservations on specific points.'
• Press conferences are held for the hundreds of journalists who attend European Councils, and who do so much to turn the summits into major media events. The President of the European Council and the President of the Commission normally hold a joint press conference, and each delegation holds one of its own. Different versions of what has happened are often given on these occasions.

The negotiating, the bargaining, and the compromising which can be such a part of European Council meetings, and the variable forms that meetings can take, is worth illustrating with an example. The 1992 Edinburgh summit – one of the most important summits of recent years because of the many decisions it produced – will be used for the purpose:

• Several key issues were on the agenda and needed resolution. Likened by the summit's chairman, UK Prime Minister John Major, to taking the form of a Rubik Cube, these issues included: a strategy to assist the Danish Government to 'overturn' the referendum of June in which the Maastricht Treaty had not been approved (the Danish government hoped to be able to hold a second referendum in which it could say, amongst other things, that it had firm guarantees that Denmark would not be obliged to participate in EMU or in a common defence policy); clarification of how the concepts of subsidiarity and transparency – which were emerging, post-Maastricht, almost as guiding principles for the future – were to be operationalised; agreement on the size and composition of the budget for the period 1993–7 (it was ten months since the Commission had put forward proposals – in the so-called 'Delors II' budgetary package); what action was to be taken on the Commission's plans for the adoption of measures designed to promote growth and employment; whether to authorise the opening of enlargement negotiations with EFTA applicants (the June 1992 Lisbon summit had said negotiations could begin once the budgetary issue was settled and the TEU was ratified); and the siting of several new EU institutions.

• Much of the plenary session on the morning of day 1 was taken up discussing the problem of the Danish ratification. The focus of the debate was a paper by the Presidency which had been circulated two days before the meeting. This paper was based on an earlier Presidential draft which had been amended at a Foreign Ministers meeting five days before the summit. By the lunchtime of day 1 the Danes were largely satisfied with the form of words that was emerging. The Director-General of the Council's Legal Service was called into the plenary to give assurance that the decision – not declaration – which it was proposed be issued on Denmark, would be legally binding but would not require re-ratification of the Treaty by those ten member states which had already ratified.

The morning plenary also made progress with subsidiarity and transparency.

• Over lunch, taken at Edinburgh Castle, the Commission's plans for an economic growth initiative provided the main focus for discussion.

• The afternoon plenary was mainly taken up with the budgetary issue. Sharp differences existed over both the overall size of the budget (with the United Kingdom taking the most restrictive line) and the shape of the budget (with the four poorer countries – Greece, Ireland, Portugal, and Spain – pressing for large increases in the redistributive structural funds).

• Running parallel with the summit meeting there was an all-day meeting of Finance Ministers. In the morning this meeting reviewed the general economic situation in the Community and in the afternoon considered the Commission proposals for an investment package to promote growth.

• The evening dinner was ceremonial rather than working, with the summit participants joining the Royal Family on the Royal Yacht Britannia. Seating arrangements went through a reported twenty-four drafts!

• Before breakfast on day 2 all delegations were presented with Presidential drafts covering day 1 business.

• The morning plenary was delayed for nearly three hours whilst the Presidency consulted individual delegations on issues which were proving to be difficult. During this period, Foreign Ministers (who focused mainly on the former Yugoslavia) and Finance Ministers (who wrestled with the budgetary issue) met separately. President Mitterrand went shopping!

• By early afternoon it was clear that most issues had been settled – either in the previous day's plenary sessions, in the meetings of Finance and of Foreign Ministers, or in bilateral meetings. However, Spain led the poorer countries in pressing for a more favourable settlement on the budgetary issue and made it clear that final agreement on all issues was conditional on this particular issue being settled. This led to protracted negotiations in which the hand of the main player – the Spanish Prime Minister Felipe González – was extremely strong for he knew that all other participants, especially the UK Presidency, wanted a deal and the summit to be a success.

• As negotiations dragged on into the evening, and 'technical' points were referred to officials, the question of the siting of EU institutions, which it had been thought might be postponed until the next summit, was raised. It produced two hours of discussions, but only limited progress was made with the many competing claims which were being pressed: the site of existing institutions was confirmed (to the satisfaction of France, Belgium and Luxembourg), but no decision was taken on the location of new institutions.

• Eventually at 10.30 p.m. – instead of at lunchtime as had been planned – the summit ended and the press conferences began. Extracts from key points of the 113 page final communiqué are included in Exhibit 6.1.

• Three aspects of the final agreement merit particular comment in regard to the light they throw on the functioning of the European Council. First, compromise is a central feature of the agreement. This is seen most obviously in the budgetary deal in which the finally agreed size and distribution of planned future expenditure was higher and more generous than the United Kingdom would have liked but not quite so high or so generous as the Commission and the poorer countries were advocating (see Chapter 12 for details). Secondly, whilst all participants played a part in influencing the shape of the final agreement, the hand of Chancellor Kohl and of Germany was especially apparent: in, for example, giving clear support to the poorer countries on the budgetary issue on day 2 of the summit and thereby obliging the United Kingdom to give more ground than it had anticipated, and in not pressing the case for a final agreement on the siting of the new institutions – in the (as it turned out correct) belief that a future summit would agree to the European Monetary Institute (and therefore, in time, the European Central Bank) being located in Germany. Thirdly, further evidence was provided of how much the European Council is completely its own master when it decided not to apply the two conditions which it had laid down itself only six months earlier at the Lisbon summit in respect of the opening of accession negotiations with the

Exhibit 6.1   European Council in Edinburgh 11–12 December 1992:
Conclusions of the Presidency

Introduction
1.   The European Council met in Edinburgh on 11–12 December 1992 to discuss the central problems on the Community's agenda. The meeting was preceded by an exchange of views between the members of the European Council and the President of the European Parliament on the various issues of the agenda.
2.   The European Council agreed on solutions to a very wide range of issues which are essential to progress in Europe. This paves the way for a return to confidence by its citizens in European construction which will contribute to the recovery of the European economy.
In particular the European Council reached agreement on the following major issues:

–   The problems raised by Denmark in the light of the outcome of the Danish referendum on 2nd June 1992 on the Maastricht Treaty
–   Guidelines to implement the subsidiarity principle and measures to increase transparency and openness in the decision making process of the Community
–   The financing of Community action and policies during the rest of this decade
–   The launching of enlargement negotiation with a number of EFTA countries
–   The establishment of a plan of action by the Member States and the Community to promote growth and to combat unemployment.

Treaty on European Union – state of the ratification process
3.   The members of the European Council reaffirmed their commitment to the Treaty on European Union. Ratification is necessary to make progress towards European Union and for the Community to remain an anchor of stability in a rapidly changing continent, building on its success over the last four decades.
4.   Having reviewed the state of the ratification process the European Council agreed to the texts set out in Part B of these Conclusions concerning the issues raised by Denmark in its memorandum 'Denmark in Europe' of 30 October 1992. This will create the basis for the Community to develop together, on the basis of the Maastricht Treaty, while respecting, as the Treaty does, the identity and diversity of Member States.

Subsidiarity
5.   On the basis of a report from Foreign Ministers the European Council agreed the overall approach, set out in Annex 1, to the application of the subsidiarity principle and the new Article 3b. The European Council invited the Council to seek an inter-institutional agreement between the European Parliament, the Council and the Commission on the effective

application of Article 3b by all institutions. The European Council discussed this aspect with the President of the European Parliament. It welcomed the ideas in the draft of an Inter-Institutional Agreement presented by the European Parliament. . . .

Openness and transparency
7. The European Council reaffirmed its commitment at Birmingham to a more open Community and adopted the specific measures set out in Annex 3. . . .

Accession of new Member States to the Union
8. The European Council in Lisbon agreed that official negotiations with EFTA countries seeking membership of the Union will be opened immediately after the Treaty on European Union is ratified and the agreement has been achieved on the Delors II package.

Given the agreement reached on future financing and the prospects for early ratification of the Treaty on European Union by all Member States, the European Council agreed that enlargement negotiations will start with Austria, Sweden and Finland at the beginning of 1993. . . .

Promoting Economic Recovery in Europe
10. The European Council heard a report from the President of the Commission about the economic situation. It discussed the prospects for growth and the rise in unemployment. It agreed to carry forward the action and initiatives set out in the declaration in Annex 4. . . .

Size of the European Parliament
26. The European Council agreed – based on the proposal of the European Parliament – on the . . . number of members of the European Parliament, from 1994, to reflect German unification and in the perspective of enlargement. . . .

Seats of the Institutions
27. On the occasion of the European Council Member States reached agreement on the seats of the European Parliament, the Council, the Commission, the Court of Justice and the Court of First Instance, the Economic and Social Committee, the Court of Auditors, and the European Investment Bank. The formal decision is set out in Annex 6. . . .

Source: European Council, *Conclusions of the Presidency*, 11–12 December 1992.

EFTA applicants: although the TEU was still some months away from being ratified and one of the conditions had not yet been met, it was agreed that the negotiations could open early in 1993.

■ Role and activities

As was noted above, the European Council has a relatively free hand with regard to what it may, and may not, do. Such constitutional and other legal provisions as there are which refer to its responsibilities are, for the most part, vague, whilst the political status of its members is such as to put it generally beyond much challenge.

As a result, the activities undertaken by the European Council have tended to vary, according both to the preferences of the personalities involved and changing circumstances and requirements. So, in the second half of the 1970s, when President Giscard d'Estaing and Chancellor Schmidt determined much of the direction and pace, considerable time was given over to general discussions of major economic and monetary problems. For much of the 1980s, by contrast, when some participants – notably Mrs Thatcher and the representatives of the Commission – began to press particular distributional questions, and when policy issues were increasingly referred 'upwards' from the Council of Ministers for resolution, the summits came to be much concerned with quite detailed decision-making. Towards the end of the 1980s another shift began to occur as summits devoted increasing time and attention to the general direction and development of the Community. This shift has continued into the 1990s and has resulted in the European Council increasingly assuming the role of a sort of board of directors: setting the overall framework and taking decisions about the major initiatives to be pursued, but leaving the operationalisation of its pronouncements and decisions to management (which in this case is essentially the Commission and the Council of Ministers).

The main topics and areas with which the European Council concerns itself can be grouped under five headings:

☐ *The evolution of the European Union*

Although this item appears only occasionally on European Council agendas as a topic in its own right, reviewing and guiding the evolution of the European Union is what several specific items are, in effect, concerned with. The most important of these items – constitutional and institutional reform, EMU, and enlargement – are dealt with separately below, but others which are worth noting include: the monitoring of progress in the creation of the Single European Market; 'troubleshooting' when progress towards European Union is threatened – as with the measures agreed at the Edinburgh summit to deal with 'the Danish problem'; and setting out framework principles when that seems to be necessary – as with statements on subsidiarity in 1992 at the Lisbon, Birmingham and Edinburgh summits.

☐ *Constitutional and institutional matters*

These come up in the European Council in three main forms. First, summits take all key decisions relating to new accessions. So, for example, in the latest enlargement round – dealing with applications from EFTA countries – the December 1991 Maastricht summit requested the Commission to produce a report on the applicant countries, the June 1992 Lisbon summit accepted that report and laid down conditions for negotiations to open, and the December 1992 Edinburgh summit authorised the opening of negotiations. Second, the summits consider, and sometimes take action on, a range of specific institutional matters. For example: the Edinburgh summit took the final decision (which confirmed a proposal made to it by the EP) on the size of the EP following German unification and the prospect of enlargement, whilst the location of EU institutions was settled partially at Edinburgh (for established institutions) and partially at the special October 1993 Brussels summit (for new institutions). Third, the European Council takes important decisions in the context of the movement towards the 'constitutionalisation' of European integration. To date, this has occurred in connection with the two major revisions of the Founding Treaties: (a) the June 1985 Milan summit established the IGC that paved the way for the SEA which was agreed at the December 1985 Luxembourg summit; (b) the IGCs which worked on what became the TEU were established over a series of four summits in 1989 and 1990 (two regular and two special), and the final negotiations on the TEU were conducted at the December 1991 Maastricht summit.

☐ *The economy and economies of the European Union*

Summits usually review both the overall economic and social situation within the EU, and also look at particular questions relating to economic growth, trade patterns, inflation, exchange rates, and unemployment. Until relatively recently differences between the member states on what should be done, coupled with a widely shared determination to ensure that national hands remained firmly placed on key economic controls, meant that these discussions were not usually able to produce very much beyond general exhortations on topics such as controlling inflation, tackling unemployment, and encouraging investment. However, as EMU has gathered momentum three developments have come to give these economic deliberations rather more bite. First, the European Council is the place where the major features and timetable of the EMU programme are finalised. Secondly, since EMU requires convergence between key national economic policies, proposals for concerted economic action are now more regularly made in the European Council and are taken more seriously than hitherto. Thirdly, and this has been stimulated by economic recession as well as the impulsion of EMU, it is now widely accepted that the EU should itself be directly tackling economic problems with programmes of its own.

The June 1993 Copenhagen summit illustrates just how important this issue area now is at European Council meetings. Building on principles which had been set out six months earlier at the Edinburgh summit, the Copenhagen summit sought to promote growth and combat unemployment through a series of recommendations to the member states and a range of EU sponsored measures. The recommendations to the member states included giving priority to investment in national budget planning for 1994, and making fiscal adjustments to lower the cost of labour and to reduce consumption of scarce energy resources. The measures at EU level included authorising the European Investment Bank and the Commission to increase by 3 billion Ecu the temporary facility of 5 billion Ecu that had been agreed at Edinburgh to promote European infrastructure and competitiveness, and inviting the Commission to present a White Paper on a medium-term strategy for growth, competitiveness and employment for consideration at the December 1993 Brussels summit.

☐ *External relations*

The European Council is involved in the EU's external relations in three principal ways.

First, many economic issues are not purely internal EU matters. They have vitally important global dimensions and summits often look at these: usually either with a view to considering whether and how pressures should be put on other economic powers (especially the USA and Japan), or with a view to coordinating the EU's position in international negotiations (such as Western Economic Summits or – a matter which was regularly considered at summits in 1992–3 in the context of the troubled Uruguay Round negotiations – GATT).

Second, the European Council has long issued declarations on important aspects of international political affairs: for example, South Africa, the Middle East, East–West relations, the break up of the Soviet Union, and the civil war in the former Yugoslavia. Sometimes the declarations have had policy instruments attached to them, but because these have been 'soft' instruments – usually taking the form of mild economic sanctions or modest economic aid – there is little evidence of summits having had much effect on world political events. They may, however, do so in the future under the CFSP pillar of the TEU if the stated intention of the EU developing a more coherent foreign policy, and linking that in time to a common defence policy and possible common defence, is realised. The guidance role specifically allocated to the European Council under Article J.3 of the CFSP pillar (see p. 155 above) should ensure that all major policies, initiatives and actions are at its behest, or at least are with its general approval.

Third, the European Council has played an extremely important role since the break up of the former Soviet bloc in setting the guidelines for the EU's relations with the countries of Central and Eastern Europe (CCEE). Initially this took the form of authorising aid programmes, encouraging economic liberalisation and political democratisation, and promoting cooperation and association agreements. However, at the June 1993 Copenhagen summit it was decided to give the EU–CCEE relationships a significant advance by: (1) agreeing for the first time 'that the associated countries in Central and Eastern Europe that so desire shall become members of the European Union (though no dates were specified); and (2) proposing that the associated countries enter into a structured relationship with the institutions of the EU.

☐ *Specific internal policy issues*

Despite the original intention that the European Council should operate at a fairly general level it does, in practice, often concern itself with quite specific internal policy issues. There are three main reasons for this: (1) some issues are so sensitive and/or are so intractable that it requires the authority of national leaders to deal with them; (2) the European Council is, because of its non-sectoral nature, often the best placed institution to put together the package deals that are sometimes required to reach agreements on issues that cut across policy sectors, or which can be resolved only by linking up issues in one sector with issues in another; and (3) the status of the European Council in the EU system is now such that the general expectation and assumption is that most policy matters of great significance ought at least to be given clearance, if they are not to be determined, at European Council level.

These differing reasons for the European Council involving itself in specific policy issues results in three broad types of involvement. First, the European Council sometimes plays a significant role in policy initiation. This was the case, for example, with the creation of the New Community Instrument at the Brussels 1977 summit, the establishment of the Integrated Mediterranean Programmes at Dublin in 1984, and the adoption of the Social Charter at Strasbourg in 1989. Since the late 1980s several initiatives have been taken in such areas as immigration, drugs, and terrorism, and it is likely that these will continue to figure prominently on summit agendas as the JHA pillar of the TEU becomes established. Second, policy involvement can take the form of tackling issues that the Council of Ministers have been unable to resolve. For example, at summits in the early 1980s, CAP reform, UK budgetary rebates, and budgetary resources were constantly on European Council agendas until a package deal was eventually agreed at the Fontainebleau summit in 1984. Within a couple of years of Fontainebleau all these issues had reappeared as problems and, along with demands for expanding the size of the social and regional funds, dominated two unsuccessful summits in 1987 and the ultimately successful special summit at Brussels in 1988. When the five year budgetary plan which had been agreed at Brussels came up for renewal, the final agreement on the most intractable issues was concluded at the 1992 Edinburgh summit. Third, and this has been of increasing importance in recent years as the number of policy issues which are 'referred up' from the Council of Ministers for final resolution has declined (a consequence of qualified majority voting resulting in fewer blockages at Council of Ministers level), the European Council has become less concerned with arbitrating and acting as a final court of appeal on internal policy issues and more concerned with encouraging and guiding. This is illustrated by the frequent messages it sends to other EU institutions in its communiqués with the use of such phrases as 'invites a report on', 'calls for action to be taken in regard to', 'confirms its full support for', 'welcomes the progress made by', and 'endorses the steps taken in connection with. . .'.

The European Council thus concerns itself with various matters, the relative importance of which can vary from summit to summit. Six functions, which can be analytically separated but which in practice greatly overlap, are associated with these matters. First, the European Council is a forum, at the highest political level, for building mutual understanding and confidence between the governments of the EU member states. Second, it identifies medium- and long-term EU goals. Third, it is a policy initiator and dispenser of policy guidelines. Fourth, it makes an important contribution to the coordination of EU policy goals and activities. Fifth, it is a decision-maker – both on matters which have come to be accepted are its ultimate responsibility (most notably constitutional and major institutional issues), and on matters which, because of their importance or their political complexity and sensitivity, are not resolved by the Council of Ministers. Sixth, it exercises responsibilities in the sphere of external relations: responsibilities which will increase as EU foreign policy, and in time security and defence policy, develops under the CFSP pillar of the TEU.

One function, it must be emphasised, that the European Council does not exercise is that of legislator. It does have the potential to make EU law – by transforming itself into a special Council of Ministers – but it has never done so. Its decisions are thus political decisions. Where it is intended that its decisions should be given legal effect, the customary EU legislative procedures have to be applied. (There is, it should be said, no guarantee that an agreement in the European Council will automatically produce ease of passage through these procedures. One reason for this is that the guidelines laid down by the European Council are sometimes insufficiently precise to clear all political obstacles. Another reason is that governments occasionally decide after a summit that their delegations gave too much away and that ground must be recovered by taking a tough line in the Council of Ministers.)

■ The European Council and the European Union system

Institutionalised summitry in the form of the European Council has inevitably strengthened the position of national governments in the EU system. It has also added an extra intergovernmental element to the nature of the EU by virtue of the fact that the leaders usually act on the basis of unanimous agreements – either because they prefer to or, where subsequent Council legislation is required to give their decisions effect, because they may in effect be required to.

However, although the European Council has unquestionably become an important EU institution, its role, or more accurately roles, are still shifting. Certainly it has, since the mid-to-late 1980s, come to approximate more to the original idea that it would provide overall strategic direction and not become too involved in policy detail, but this position is by no means fixed or, indeed, applied with complete consistency. What happens at individual summits is not part of any regularised or consistent pattern. So, some summits are relatively low key affairs and do little more than pronounce on some aspects of current international developments, indicate one or two policy initiatives in fringe policy areas, and cobble together a concluding statement exuding general goodwill. Other summits, by contrast, are surrounded by atmospheres of crisis and by prophecies of catastrophe should they fail to produce firm decisions on key and pressing issues: occasionally they do fail, but the catastrophes never quite happen, and the next summit, or next but one, is usually able to find an agreement via the customary EU method of compromise.

The creation and development of the European Council has inevitably had implications for the roles and functioning of the other principal EU institutions.

- The Commission has seen some further undermining of its special position regarding policy initiation. ('Further' because, as was shown in Chapters 4 and 5, the Council of Ministers has also increasingly exercised policy initiating and mediating responsibilities.) However, the Commission has, to some extent, been compensated for this slippage by being permitted to enter into political discussions with national leaders at the summits, and also by being able – and sometimes being required – to submit reports and documents to the summits. (See Chapter 4 for examples of influential Commission submissions to summits.)
- The Council of Ministers has lost power to the European Council by virtue of the increasing tendency of most major issues to go through the summits in some form. However, the extent of the loss should not be exaggerated. One reason why it should not be so is that there is no rigid hierarchical relationship between the two bodies in the sense that the Council of Ministers always feels obliged to refer all significant matters 'upwards' for final decisions. It is true that most broad-based or very significant initiatives are referred to the European Council, but as often as not that is for little more than political approval or for noting. Certainly it would be quite erroneous to suppose that the European Council takes all 'first-order' decisions and the Council of Ministers is confined to 'second-order' decisions. A second reason why the extent of the loss should not be overstated is that there is no consistent line of division between the two regarding who does what, other than the Council of Ministers being responsible for making legislation. And a third reason is that since the European Council only meets for four, or perhaps six, days a year, it cannot normally hope to do anything more than sketch outlines in a restricted number of areas.
- The EP has been largely by-passed by the European Council and so could be regarded as having experienced some net loss of power. It is true

that the President of the European Council gives a verbal report on each summit meeting to the next EP plenary session, and it is also the case that the EP President addresses the opening sessions of summits so as to inform the national leaders of the Parliament's thinking on key issues. However, there is no evidence of either of these procedures producing much in the way of influence. Far more important is the almost complete lack of input by the EP onto European Council agendas or deliberations, and the tendency of the Council of Ministers to take the view that legislation which stems from European Council decisions is non-negotiable.

• Since the European Council operates largely on an extra-constitutional basis, and since its decisions are political rather than legal in character, its existence has had few implications for the Court of Justice. Or, rather, it has had few direct implications. It can, however, be argued that any increase in a non-constitutional approach to integration necessarily constitutes a corresponding decrease in the influence of the Court of Justice, given its attachment to, indeed its restriction to, questions that have a legal base.

■ Concluding comments

The record of the European Council is mixed. On the one hand there have been failures, or at least the non-fulfilment of hopes. This was particularly so in the period from about 1980 to 1988: summits became rather routinised and immersed in detail; too often time was devoted to policy detail rather than to mapping out the future; and disputes about distributional issues were seemingly always on agendas. On the other hand there have been positive achievements: understandings between national leaders have been furthered; important goals have been identified/given an impetus/brought to a conclusion (such as on enlargements, the internal market, the social dimension, institutional reform, and EMU); and agreements have been worked out on matters that were either unsuitable for, or could not be resolved by, the Council of Ministers.

That there should be pluses or minuses in the record is not altogether surprising. The summits are, after all, conducted on a very loose and ill-defined basis and it is thus perhaps inevitable, given the status of the participants, that they should be drawn into attempting to do a host of different things. It is also perhaps inevitable, given the composition and mode of functioning of the summits, that they should experience some of the problems of intergovernmental conflict that are so characteristic of the Council of Ministers.

■ *Chapter 7* ■

The European Parliament

■ Powers and influence

Since it was first constituted, as the Assembly of the European Coal and Steel Community, the European Parliament – the title it adopted for itself in 1962 – has generally been regarded as a somewhat ineffective institution. It is a reputation which, today at least, is not entirely justified. For whilst it is true that the EP's constitutional powers are not comparable with those of national legislatures, developments over the years have come to give it, in practice, a not inconsiderable influence in the EU system. As with national parliaments this influence is exercised in three main ways: through the legislative process, through the budgetary process, and through control and supervision of the executive.

□ *Parliament and EU legislation*

The EP has a number of opportunities to influence EU legislation.

First, it sometimes participates in policy discussions with the Commission at the pre-proposal legislative stage. The Commission may, for example, float a policy idea before an EP committee, or committee members themselves may suggest policy initiatives to the Commission.

Second, the EP can formally adopt its own ideas for suggested legislation. There are two main ways in which it can do this. First, it can adopt own initiative reports – which are reports that the Parliament itself initiates. There is, however, a major weakness with these reports, which is that whilst the Commission may feel pressurised by them it is not obliged to act upon them. Second, the TEU created a new Article 138b of the EC Treaty, which states 'The European Parliament may, acting by a majority of its members, request the Commission to submit any appropriate proposal on matters which it considers that a Community

174

act is required for the purpose of implementing this Treaty'. Clearly Article 138b considerably strengthens the EP's initiating powers, for political realities would make it difficult for the Commission not to act if there was the necessary majority in Parliament (though it should be said that poor attendance often makes such majorities difficult to obtain).

Third, the annual budgetary cycle provides some opportunities for exercising legislative influence. In large measure this dates back to the *Joint Declaration of 30 June 1982 by the European Parliament, the Council and the Commission on various measures to improve the budgetary procedure.* Amongst the 'various measures', it was agreed that if the EP put appropriations into the budget for items for which there was no legal base – in other words, the EP opened new budget lines – the Commission and the Council would seek to provide the necessary base by drafting new legislation. It was further agreed that expenditure limits in respect of legislation should not be set in the legislative process, but in the budgetary process – where the EP has more power.

Fourth, the annual legislative programme, which is essentially a planning tool of an indicative nature, is a matter for agreement between, and if necessary negotiation between, the Commission and the EP. The procedure is as follows: (1) The Commission adopts its legislative programme for the following year by November. Several factors determine the contents of the programme, most notably: commitments which are pending, priorities which have been identified in the Commission's work programme for the year (this is normally issued in October), and views expressed in inter-institutional meetings between the Commission, the EP and the Council. (The priorities of the Council Presidency for the first half of the year are likely to be known, but not the priorities for the second half Presidency.) (2) The programme is formally presented to the EP. It is then discussed in the EP's committees and a resolution is voted on in plenary session. (3) As soon as possible a declaration on the legislative programme is agreed by the EP and the Commission, in the presence of the Council.

Fifth, and most important of all, the EP's views must be sought – though its approval is only required in certain circumstances – in connection with most of the EU's important/significant/sensitive legislation. If the Council of Ministers – in whose name most legislation is made – acts prematurely and does not wait for Parliament to make its views known, the 'law' will be ruled invalid by the Court of Justice. Any uncertainty on this point was removed by the isoglucose case ruling in 1980 when the Court annulled a Council regulation on the grounds that it had been issued before Parliament's opinion was known. The isoglucose case ruling does not give the EP an indefinite veto over Council legislation, for it is obliged by Treaty to issue opinions and the Court in some of its judgements has referred to the duty of loyal cooperation among Community institutions, but it does give it a very useful delaying power.

Until July 1987, and the entry into force of the Single European Act (SEA), all legislation referred to the EP was subject to what is known as the consultation procedure. However, the SEA created two new procedures – the cooperation procedure and the assent procedure – and the TEU introduced a further one – the co-decision procedure. There are thus now four possible procedures to which legislation may be subject (plus some variations within these procedures). Which procedure applies to a particular legislative proposal depends on the Treaty Article(s) on which the proposal is based. The nature of these procedures, and the policy areas to which they apply, are described in some detail in Chapter 11, so attention here will be restricted to describing how they affect the EP.

- *The consultation procedure*. Under this procedure Parliament is asked for an opinion on Commission proposals for Council legislation on only one occasion. Once that opinion is given the Council may take a decision. What use the EP is able to make of this single referral depends, in part at least, on its own subject competence and its tactical skills. The standard way of proceeding is to take advantage of Article 189a(2) of the EC Treaty which states: 'As long as the Council has not acted, the Commission may alter its proposals during the procedures leading to the adoption of a Community act.' If the Commission can be persuaded to alter a proposal so as to incorporate the EP's views, the prospects of those views becoming part of the text that is finally approved by the Council are greatly enhanced. With this in mind, the EP attempts to convince and to pressurise the Commission. Normally, pressurising takes the form of voting on amendments to proposals, but not voting on the resolution which formally constitutes the opinion until after the Commission has stated – as it is obliged to do – whether or not it accepts the amendments. If the Commission does accept the amendments the EP votes for the legislative resolution and the amendments are incorporated into the Commission's proposal. If the Commission does not accept the amendments, or at least not all of them, the EP may judge the Commission position to be unsatisfactory and, as a result, may seek to delay the progress of the proposal by referring it back to the appropriate Parliamentary committee for further consideration.
- *The cooperation procedure*. Whereas under the consultation, or single reading, procedure the Council can take final decisions after the EP has issued its opinions, under the cooperation procedure there is a second reading process. On first reading the Council is confined to adopting 'common positions' which must then be referred back to the EP. In making the reference back, the Council is obliged to provide the EP with

explanations for common positions – including giving reasons for any EP amendments that have been rejected – and if the EP is dissatisfied it can exert further pressure at its second reading by amending or rejecting common positions by votes that include an absolute majority of its members. Such votes do not amount to vetoes, but because they carry considerable political weight, and because too they can only be overcome in the Council by unanimous votes, they put considerable pressure on the Commission and the Council to take the EP's views seriously and to engage in inter-institutional bargaining.

● *The co-decision procedure*. This procedure is similar to the cooperation procedure up to the point when the EP issues its second reading position. The procedure then changes, for if the Council cannot accept the EP's position as indicated by a vote of a majority of its component members, and if the differences between the two institutions cannot be resolved in a Conciliation Committee composed of an equal number of representatives from both the Council and the Parliament, the EP can prevent that text from being adopted (again by a vote of an absolute majority of its members) if the Council seeks to press ahead. In other words, the EP has a potential veto on legislative proposals which are subject to this procedure. The significance of the EP's powers under the co-decision procedure is symbolised by the fact that legislation which is subject to the procedure is made in the name of the EP and the Council.

● *The assent procedure*. Under this procedure the EP must give its approval, at a single reading and with no provision for amendments, to proposals. In some circumstances the assent requires an absolute majority of Parliament's members. Again, the EP thus has veto powers under this procedure.

It will be some time before the pattern of the EP's legislative activity under the TEU settles down and becomes clear. However, some indication of how active the EP is on the legislative front can be gained by considering its 'output' in 1992, the last full year before the TEU came into effect: it participated in 390 legislative procedures – 243 consultations, 70 first readings and 66 second readings under the cooperation procedure, and 11 assents. Under the TEU, consultations will fall (the scope of the procedure having been considerably narrowed), assents will grow (this procedure having been widened), and co-decision first and second readings and conciliation meetings will begin.

It is very difficult to estimate the precise effect of EP deliberations on the final form of legislative acts. One reason for this is that a great deal of EP persuading and lobbying is impossible to monitor because it is carried out via informal contacts with Commission and Council representatives.

Another reason is that the Commission and the Council often go halfway in agreeing to the sense of EP amendments, but object to the way in which they are phrased or to specific parts of them. But though it is impossible to be precise, two things are quite clear. First, the EP is centrally involved in a process of legislative bargaining with the Commission and the Council – both on an informal basis and in formal inter-institutional meetings. Second, figures show that a very significant percentage of EP amendments are accepted by the Commission and the Council, with the former being generally more sympathetic than the latter. This may be illustrated by looking at the 332 legal instruments which were adopted under the cooperation procedure from the entry into force of the SEA in mid-1987 to the end of 1993: of the amendments requested by the EP at first reading, 55 per cent were accepted by the Commission and 43 per cent by the Council; on second reading – when many amendments are, in effect, rejected first reading amendments – 44 per cent were accepted by the Commission and 24 per cent by the Council. These figures need to be interpreted with caution – they do not, for example, indicate the extent to which EP 'political', as opposed to 'technical' amendments are accepted – but they do indicate real legislative influence: an influence, indeed, which few national parliaments can match.

Having established that the EP does have a genuine legislative role, the weaknesses to which it is subject will now be outlined.

The first, and most obvious, weakness, is that the EP does not carry full constitutional legislative authority. Unlike national parliaments, it does not have the final say over what is, and what is not, to become law. On the one hand it does not have the capacity to exercise a fully 'positive' legislative role by initiating, developing, and passing into law its own proposals. On the other hand, its 'negative' legislative role is also considerably circumscribed, for whilst the co-decision and assent procedures do give it a veto over certain legislative proposals, under both the consultation and cooperation procedures the Council has the power to overturn EP amendments which have and have not been accepted by the Commission, and to ignore EP rejections of legislative proposals. The Council can also choose not to act at all on legislative proposals it does not like – at any one time there are usually around 400–500 proposals on which the Parliament has given an opinion that still await a Council decision. (Proposals subject to the cooperation and co-decision procedures are not exempt from such Council inaction, since the restricted timetable that is attached to the procedures only comes into play once the Council has adopted its common position.)

The second weakness is that although the EP usually attempts to deliver opinions as soon as possible, so as to ensure they are available to the Council at an early stage of its deliberations, it is by no means unusual for the Council, before the opinion of the EP has been delivered, to take decisions or to adopt common positions 'in principle' or 'pending the opinion of the European Parliament'. This is especially common where the initial referral to the EP is delayed, where there is some urgency about the matter, or where a Council Presidency is anxious to push the proposal through. Whatever the reason, in such circumstances the EP's opinion, especially under the consultation procedure, is likely to have only a very limited effect.

The third weakness is that the EP is not consulted on all Council legislation. The greatest gaps in this regard are its lack of any right to be consulted on most of the external agreements which the Council concludes with third countries on behalf of the EU. Most importantly, trade agreements which are concluded under Article 113 (EC Treaty) do not require EP approval. In practice the Council, and more particularly the Commission (which conducts the actual trade negotiations) do usually discuss upcoming and ongoing trade matters with the EP on an informal basis, but they are not obliged to do so and there is not much evidence of Parliament bringing much influence to bear on the EU's negotiating stance. In only two sets of circumstances where EU law is being made with regard to external agreements is EP approval necessary, in both cases by the assent of an absolute majority of Parliament's members: under Title VII Article O of the TEU, for new accessions to the EU; and under Article 228 of the EC Treaty, for certain specific types of agreements, including association agreements, cooperation agreements, and agreements which have important budgetary implications. The first of these circumstances is obviously only for very occasional use. The second, however, has a more recurring application and has been used to some effect, notably in putting pressure on countries to improve their human rights records if they wish to receive the financial assistance which is usually an important component of association and cooperation agreements. (It should, perhaps, be added here that the EP also has the right to be informed and consulted about various other forms of EU external relations – notably under the CFSP pillar of the TEU – but these do not involve legislation, and the EP's powers are purely advisory.)

The fourth and final weakness is that the EP does not have to be consulted on – although, in practice, it is notified of – Commission legislation. This is despite the fact that, numerically, Commission legislation makes up most of EU legislation. There are different views on the significance of this. Pointing to the political and expenditure implications of some Commission legislation, critics argue that this is another example of executive power and of legislative and democratic weakness. Others, however, emphasise that Commission legislation is usually highly technical and of a kind that needs quick decisions; as such, it is similar to the decrees, ordinances and other minor legislative acts that national administrations issue and which are commonly accepted as an inevitable aspect of decision-making in the modern world.

☐ *Parliament and the EU budget*

Thanks mainly to the 1970 *Treaty Amending Certain Budgetary Provisions of the Treaties* and the 1975 *Treaty Amending Certain Financial Provisions of the Treaties* the EP enjoys considerable Treaty powers in relation to the EU's budget. These include:

(1)   The right to propose 'modifications' to compulsory expenditure. (This principally means agriculture – which comprises around half of the total budget.) Modifications that entail increases in total expenditure require qualified majority support in the Council to be accepted. Where increases are not involved, owing perhaps to a proposed increase being offset by a proposed decrease, a qualified majority vote is required for rejection – a negative majority as it is called.

(2)   The right to propose 'amendments' to non-compulsory expenditure (which means most things apart from agriculture) subject to the ceilings set by the financial perspective (see below). Acting by a qualified majority the Council may modify these amendments, but Parliament can reinsert and insist on them at its second reading of the budget.

(3)   Under Article 203(8) of the EC Treaty, Parliament, 'acting by a majority of its members and two thirds of the votes cast may, if there are important reasons, reject the draft budget and ask for a new draft to be submitted to it'. In other words the EP may reject the whole budget if it does not like the Council's final draft.

Following the introduction of direct elections for MEPs in 1979, extensive use was made of the powers just listed in the 1980s. Virtually every aspect of the rules, including the power of rejection, were tested to see how far they could be taken. Major confrontations with the Council, far from being avoided, seemed at times almost to be sought as the EP attempted to assert itself. For most of the 1980s, however, this assertion was limited in its effect. It was so because although the EP formally enjoyed joint decision-making powers with the Council on the budget, the powers of the two bodies were not equally balanced. Parliament was still very much restricted in what it could do: restricted by the Treaty which gave it very little room for manoeuvre in the major budgetary sector, compulsory expenditure; restricted by the Council's attitude, which tended to be one of wishing to limit Parliament's influence as much as possible; and restricted by its own inability – because of conflicting loyalties and pressures – to be wholly consistent and resolved in its approach.

For the most part, these restrictions still apply. However, developments occurred in 1988 which increased the EP's influence. Following decisions taken by the European Council in February 1988 on budgetary matters, the EP, together with the Commission and the Council of Ministers, put its name, in June 1988, to *The Interinstitutional Agreement on Budgetary Discipline and Improvement of the Budgetary Procedure*. This committed all three institutions to a financial perspective for the years 1988 to 1992. Key features of the perspective were provisions for a significant increase in non-compulsory expenditure and a significant decrease in compulsory expenditure (thus realising aims for which the EP had been pressing for years), and the setting of clear ceilings for both types of expenditure. The main benefits of the *Interinstitutional Agreement*, in power terms, for the EP were twofold. First, its influence over compulsory expenditure, which in the past had been very limited, was potentially increased. It was so because Parliament's approval was now required for any upward movement of the ceiling. Second, the very act of the Council agreeing to sign a financial perspective with the EP gave to the latter an extra element of leverage in budgetary discussions.

When the 1988–92 financial perspective came to be revised in 1992–3, the EP's influence was not, it must be said, as great as MEPs had hoped or anticipated. Whilst it was accepted by the Commission and the Council that a precedent had been set in 1988 and that the next financial perspective would require the EP's endorsement, the key institutions in determining the size and shape of what became a seven year financial perspective covering the years 1992–9 were the Commission, the Council of Ministers, and the European Council. As it turned out there was much in the new financial perspective of which the EP approved – most notably further cuts in agricultural expenditure and further increases in non-agricultural expenditure – but these were largely the outcome of battles fought in the Council of Ministers and at the decision-making European Council meeting at Edinburgh rather than EP influence. Dissatisfied with the negotiating role it had been allowed, the EP delayed ratifying the agreement until November 1993 – though this did enable it to wring concessions from the Council in regard to its future influence over compulsory expenditure.

☐ *Control and supervision of the executive*

Virtually all parliaments have difficulties in attempting to exercise controlling and supervisory powers over executives. On the one hand, they are usually hampered by the executives themselves, which do not welcome the prospect of being investigated and which therefore seek to protect themselves behind whatever constitutional, institutional and party political defences are available. On the other hand, parliamentarians themselves tend not to have the requisite information, the specialist knowledge, or the necessary resources that are required effectively to monitor, and if necessary to challenge, executive activity.

The EP shares these problems but additionally has two particular ones of its own. First, a key aspect of control and supervision of executives is with regard to policy implementation: is policy being implemented efficiently and for the purposes intended by relevant law? The Commission is the most obvious body to be called to account on these questions. But in many policy spheres the Commission's executive role is very limited and consists essentially of attempting to coordinate the work of outside agencies operating at different administrative levels. Such agencies, of which national governments are the most important, are often reluctant to open the books or to adopt cooperative attitudes towards EP investigators. Certainly there is little question of government ministers allowing themselves to be grilled by the EP on the competency and honesty of their national bureaucracies.

The second problem specific to the EP is that on broad controlling and supervisory issues – such as whether the EU executive is acting responsibly in the execution of its duties, and whether it is fulfilling its Treaty obligations – problems arise from the blurring of roles between the Commission, the Council of Ministers, and the European Council. Insofar as the Council of Ministers and the European Council have assumed an increasing importance in what are theoretically Commission functions, the EP's supervisory powers have been weakened. This is because Parliament is not so constitutionally strong in relation to the Council of Ministers as it is to the Commission, nor does it have the access to the former that it does to the latter. As for the European Council, the EP has virtually no constitutional powers in relation to it, and only very limited access.

The EP's ability to control and supervise the Commission, the Council of Ministers, and the European Council will now be considered separately.

In relation to the Commission, the EP has seven main powers and channels at its disposal.

First, the TEU established, under Article 158(EC), the right of the EP to be consulted on the person whom the governments of the member states intend to appoint as President of the Commission. This does not explicitly give the EP the right to vote on the nominee for President, and therefore does not formally amount to the EP having the right of confirmation, but in practice it adds up to much the same thing: partly because under Jacques Delors such votes were already being held; partly because revised EP Rules of Procedure provide for such a vote; and partly because it is virtually inconceivable that a nominee who failed to receive Parliament's approval would proceed with his/her candidature.

Second, the TEU also established under Article 158(EC) that the 'President and the other members of the Commission thus nominated shall be subject as a body to a vote of approval by the European Parliament' before they are formally appointed by the governments of the member states. Again, this power formalises a confirmation process which developed in the 1980s, but Parliament now intends to make much more use of it by calling Commissioners-designate before its committees in a manner somewhat like the confirmation hearings that occur in the US Senate. Unlike the US Senate, however, the EP cannot vote on individual Commissioners but only on the Commission collectively.

Third, the EP can dismiss the College of Commissioners – but not individual Commissioners – by carrying a motion of censure by a two-thirds majority of the votes cast, including a majority of all MEPs. In practice it has never done so, although several votes of no confidence have been held. The main reason why it has not done so is that the power of dismissal is really too blunt a controlling instrument for most purposes. In all normal circumstances the EP has no wish to dismiss the Commission. Rather it just wishes to encourage the Commission to bring forward specified policy initiatives and to find out what are its plans, what it is up to, and how effectively it is managing EU policies. In any event, up to the TEU entering into force, even if the Commission were to be dismissed the EP had no formal say in the appointment of a new Commission: now that the EP does have a say, the threat of possible dismissal may be a more potent weapon and a strong inducement to the Commission to be accommodating.

Fourth, under Article 143 of the EC Treaty, the Parliament 'shall discuss in open session the annual general report submitted to it by the Commission'. This debate used to be one of the highlights of the Parliamentary year, but there is not much evidence of it ever having produced any concrete results. It has come to be superseded in importance by debates on the Commission's annual work programme and annual legislative programme.

Fifth, under Article 205a of the EC Treaty 'The Commission shall submit annually to the Council and to the European Parliament the accounts of the preceding financial year relating to the implementation of the budget. The Commission shall also forward to them a financial statement of the assets and liabilities of the Community'. On the basis of an examination of the accounts and the financial statement, and having examined also the annual report of the Court of Auditors, Parliament 'acting on a recommendation from the Council which shall act by a qualified majority, shall give a discharge to the Commission in respect of the implementation of the budget' (Article 206, EC). Under its discharge powers the EP can require the Commission and other institutions to take appropriate steps so as to ensure action on the comments appearing in the decision giving discharge.

Sixth, Parliament's standing committees have remits that are broad enough to allow them to attempt to exercise supervisory functions if they choose to do so. However, the Commission is not anxious to encourage investigations of itself, and the committees are not sufficiently well resourced to be able to probe very far. The Committee on Budgetary Control, which is specifically charged with monitoring policy implementation, is in a typically weak position: with only a handful of A-grade officers employed to assist it, it cannot hope to do anything other than cover a small fraction of the Commission's work.

Finally, questions can be asked of the Commission. These take different forms: written questions – of which 3588 were tabled in 1993; oral questions in question time – 850 in 1993; and oral questions with or without debate – 170 in 1993.

The EP is less able to control and supervise the Council of Ministers than it is the Commission. There are three main reasons for this.

The first reason arises from the role of the Council as the meeting place of the member states. To make it, or any of its members, directly responsible to the EP would be to introduce a measure of supranationalism into the EU that has been, and is, unacceptable to most governments. The view has been taken that insofar as Council members are to be responsible it should be principally to their national parliaments. In other words, the Council as a collective body is not to be responsible to anyone, whilst individual members are not to be responsible to another EU institution. (It might be added that this does not always stop ministers, if they find themselves being pressed too hard in their national legislatures, from hiding behind Council meetings and 'immovable' EU partners.)

Second, in respect of certain key policy sectors – most notably the CFSP and JHA pillars of the TEU and aspects of EMU – the EP's powers are relatively weak. This is partly because decisions in these spheres sometimes need to be made quickly and in secret. It is partly also, however, because some member states wish intergovernmentalism to be the prevailing decision-making mode in these sensitive areas. The EP is thus left to make the best it can of its powers to be consulted, to be kept informed, to ask questions, and to make recommendations.

Third, the very nature of the Council – with its ever-changing composition, its specialist Councils, and its rotating Presidency – makes continuity of relations between it and the EP difficult to establish.

The amount of access the EP gets to the Council depends in large part on the attitude of the country holding the Presidency. There are, however, certain set points of contact which, if they do not enable the EP to exercise an overall control on the Council, at least provide it with opportunities to challenge the Council on its general conduct of affairs. First, the Presidency of the Council, in the form usually of the Foreign Minister, appears before EP plenaries at the beginning and at the end of each six month term of office. On the first occasion the Presidency's priorities are explained and on the second occasion an assessment of the Presidency is given. On both occasions, MEPs are given the opportunity to ask questions. Second, ministers from the Presidency usually attend the EP committees that deal with their spheres of responsibility at least twice during their country's Presidency. MEPs can seek to use these occasions for informal discussions with the Council, or to have wide-ranging question and answer sessions on the Council's priorities and performance. Third, ministers from the Presidency also regularly attend EP plenary sessions and participate in important debates. Fourth, the EP can, through the Presidency, ask questions of the Council and of the Council of Foreign Ministers on CFSP matters (the two are distinct because of their different constitutional positions). The procedures used for asking questions are similar to those used for questions to the Commission. In 1993, 354 written questions, 316 oral questions in question time, and 87 oral questions with or without debate were asked of the Council, and 169 written questions, 159 oral questions in question time, and 22 oral questions with or without debate were asked of the Council of Foreign Ministers.

If the EP is not able to call the Commission fully to account and is greatly restricted in its ability to exercise control over the Council of Ministers, it is almost wholly bereft of any supervisory power over the European Council. This is largely because of the nature of the European Council: it is an intergovernmental institution which is largely outside of the framework of the Treaties; it meets for only between four and six days a year; and most of its more important members, the Heads of Government, not only have no great wish to be accountable to MEPs but can ensure that they are not so since it is at European Council meetings that final decisions on the contents of the Treaties – which set out the main operating principles of the EU – are taken.

The TEU makes provision in a few instances – in regard to EMU under the EC Treaty – for the European Council, or the Heads of Government meeting in the composition of the Council of Ministers, to inform or consult with the EP, but these are anticipated as being for only very occasional use. In only two sets of circumstances does the European Council come into regular contact with the EP, and these are a consequence of political practice rather than legal requirement. The first is at the opening session of European Council meetings when the EP's President is permitted to address the summit so as to inform it of the views of MEPs on current issues. The second is after European Council meetings when the President of the European Council delivers a report, and answers questions, on the outcome of the summit before an EP plenary session.

What this all adds up to is very little influence indeed by the EP on the European Council, let alone control over what it does. The fact is that there are only very limited linkages between the two institutions, and there are no reasons at all for supposing that the participants at summits make a habit of looking over their shoulders in anticipation of how the EP will view the outcome of their deliberations and negotiations.

■ Elections

Until 1979 MEPs were nominated by national parliaments from amongst their members. Various consequences followed from this: parties not represented in their national legislature could not be represented in the EP; virtually all MEPs were pro-integrationists, since sceptics and opponents in national parliaments were generally unwilling to allow their name to be considered for nomination; and MEPs were limited in the time they could give to their European responsibilities.

However, Article 138 of the EEC Treaty included the following provision: 'The Assembly shall draw up proposals for elections by direct universal suffrage in accordance with a uniform procedure in all Member States.' The Assembly approved such proposals as early as 1960, but found itself frustrated by another Article 138 requirement which stated: 'The Council shall, acting unanimously, lay down the appropriate provisions, which it shall recommend to Member States for adoption in accordance with their respective constitutional requirements.' That the first set of direct elections were not held until 1979 is witness to the feeling of some member governments – initially mainly the French, later the Danes and the British – that direct elections were rather unwelcome: unwelcome because they had supranational overtones, and unwelcome too because they might be followed by pressures for institutional reform in the EP's favour. Even after the principle of direct elections was eventually won and it was agreed they would be held on a fixed five year basis, no uniform electoral system could be agreed, nor has been agreed since. Consequently, the four sets of direct elections to have been held to date – in 1979, 1984, 1989, and 1994 – have all been contested on the basis of different national electoral arrangements (see Table 7.1). Eleven of the twelve states have used one of several different forms of proportional representation; the United Kingdom has used its traditional single member constituency 'first past

Table 7.1   *National arrangements for the 1994 elections to the European Parliament*

	Number of MEPs	*Entitle- ment to vote*	*Eligibi- lity for election*	*Electoral system*	*Number of constituencies*
Belgium	25	18	21	PR with PV[1]	4
Denmark	16	18	18	PR with PV	1
Germany	99	18	18	PR without PV[2]	16
Greece	25	18	21	PR without PV	1
Spain	64	18	18	PR without PV	1
France	87	18	23	PR without PV	1
Ireland	15	18	21	PR with STV[3]	4
Italy	87	18	21	PR with PV	5
Luxembourg	6	18	21	PR with vote splitting	1
Netherlands	31	18	25	PR with PV	1
Portugal	25	18	18	PR without PV	1
United Kingdom	87	18	21	Majority vote system (except Northern Ireland – PR with STV)	84 + 1 (Northern Ireland: 3 seats)
Total	567				

Notes:
[1] Proportional representation with preferential vote.
[2] Proportional representation without preferential vote.
[3] Proportional representation with single transferable vote.

See Appendix for numbers of MEPs to be allocated to EFTA countries on their accession to the EU.

the post' system, apart from in Northern Ireland where proportional representation has been used to ensure that the Catholic minority wins a seat. It seems likely that if the United Kingdom were to concede on the principle of proportional representation, a common form of proportional representation could be agreed between the states.

In addition to the differences between their electoral systems, there are also other differences between the states regarding their EP electoral arrangements which merit noting. One is that candidate eligibility ranges from 18 years to 25 years. A second is that voting takes place not on one day but on two – with, in 1994, Denmark, Ireland, the Netherlands and the United Kingdom voting on Thursday 9 June and the other countries voting on Sunday 12 June. And a third difference, and one which is important in terms of the democratic base of the EP, is that there is a considerable variation in size of population per MEP: in 1994 the range was from 1:819,156 voters in Germany to 1:64,967 voters in Luxembourg. The reason for this imbalance is that EP seats are distributed not just on grounds of national equitability but also with an eye to ensuring that the representations of small states are not totally swamped in EP decision-making processes. In most states the 1994 ratio was between 1:350,000 and 1:650,000

A subject that has been much discussed in the context of EP elections is voter turnout. Many have argued that a high turnout would serve to enhance the EP's legitimacy and democratic base and, partly in consequence of this, would also place the EP in a strong position to press for increased powers.

In the event, turnout has been relatively low. In 1979 only 62 per cent of those eligible to vote did so, in 1984 the figure was 61 per cent, in 1989 the figure was 58 per cent, and in 1994 it was 56.5 per cent. Belgium and Luxembourg have displayed the highest national turnouts, with around 90 per cent on each occasion, whilst the United Kingdom has displayed the lowest turnouts, with figures of 33 per cent in 1979, 33 per cent in 1984, and 36 per cent in 1989 and 1994

Three main factors combine to explain the low turnouts. First, because EP elections do not offer any prospect of a change of government, of switches in policy, or of the making or unmaking of political reputations, they do not provide much of a base for the generation of popular interest or political excitement. Second, the election campaigns have had little overall coherence or coordination. They have essentially been national contests, but of a secondary sort. 'European' issues have never made much of an impact. 'In 1989, for example, there was little sense of the 1984–9 Centre-Right EP majority defending its record, or of the Left seeking to gain control. Third, many of the actors who do much to focus attention and generate interest in national electoral campaigns have approached the EP elections in, at best, a half-hearted manner: national political parties have been generally reluctant to commit resources to their Euro-campaigns; party activists have tended to be uninterested; a conscious attempt has been made by some governments to play down the importance of the elections because they are frequently interpreted as being, in part at least, 'mid-term' national elections, or unofficial referenda on the government's performance in office; and media interest has been limited.

■ Political parties and the European Parliament

Party political activity is seen at three main levels in relation to the EP: the transnational, the political groups in the EP, and the national.

☐ *The transnational federations*

Very loosely organised transnational federations, grouped around general principles, exist for coordinating, propagandist, and electioneering purposes. The three main federations were created in similar circum-stances in the mid-1970s: out of existing, but extremely weakly-based, liaising and information exchanging bodies, and as a specific response to the continuing development of the EC and the anticipated future use of direct elections for the EP. These three federations are: the European People's Party (EPP), which is composed primarily of Christian Democratic parties and their offshoots; the European Liberal, Democrat and Reform Party (ELDR); and the Party of European Socialists (PES).

Some supporters of European integration have hoped that the federations might develop into organisations providing leadership, vision and coordination at European level, and perhaps might even serve as agents of unification to their heterogeneous memberships. They have failed to do so. Their principal weakness is that, unlike national parties or the EP political groups, they are not involved in day-to-day political activity in an institutional setting. They have, therefore, no very clear focus and cannot develop attachments and loyalties. From this, other weaknesses flow: low status; limited resources – they are heavily dependent on the EP political groups for administrative and financial support; and loose organisational structures based on periodic congresses and bureaux meetings.

The federations have not, therefore, been able to do very much, even though there certainly are tasks that EU-wide transnational parties could usefully perform, such as long-term policy planning, the harmonisation of national party differences, and educating the electorate about Europe. Such influence as they have exercised has been largely confined to very loose policy coordination (effected partly through periodic meetings – often before European Council meetings – of national leaders), and to EP elections when manifestos have been produced and a few joint activities have been arranged. Even the manifestos, however, have reinforced the general picture of weakness for they have usually been somewhat vague in content (necessarily so given the need to reconcile differences), and have been utilised by only a few of the constituent member parties (because EP elections are contested, for the most part, along national lines).

Beyond the three main federations, other groupings of an even looser nature have surfaced from time to time, usually to try and coordinate election activities. They have included Green, Regional, Communist, and Extreme Right alliances. All have been internally divided and have been hard pressed to put together even minimalist common statements.

☐ *The political groups in the European Parliament*

Partisan political activity in the EP is mainly channelled via the political groups. Under the current Rules of Procedure (9th edition, 1993) the minimum number of MEPs required to form a political group is 26 if they come from one member state, 21 if they come from two member states, 16 if they come from three member states, and 13 if they come from four or more member states.

Groups have been formed and developed for a number of reasons. The principal basis and unifying element of most of the groups is ideological identification. Despite the many differences which exist between them, MEPs from similar political families and traditions are naturally drawn to one another. All the more so when cooperation serves to maximise their influence, as it does in the EP in all sorts of ways – from electing the President to voting on amendments.

Organisational benefits provide another inducement to political group formation. For example, funds for administrative and research purposes are distributed to groups on the basis of a fixed amount per group (the non-attached being regarded as a group for these purposes), plus an additional sum per member. No-one is, therefore, unsupported, but clearly the larger the group the more easily it can afford good back-up services.

There are also advantages in the conduct of Parliamentary business that stem from group status, since the EP arranges much of what it does around the groups. Although non-attached members are not formally excluded from anything by this – indeed they are guaranteed many rights under the Rules of Procedure – they can, in practice, be disadvantaged: in the distribution of committee chairmanships for example, or in the preparation of the agendas of plenary sessions.

In recent years there have usually been between eight and ten political groups in the EP. The main reason there have been so many is that, with proportional representation electoral systems used for EP elections in all EU states apart from the United Kingdom, MEPs reflect the wide range of political opinion that exists across the EU, both as regards ideological and national orientation. Since direct elections were introduced in 1979, the number of national political parties represented in the EP has never been less than sixty.

The political groups – as of before, and just after, the 1994 elections (see Figure 7.1) – are as follows:

- *Group of the Party of European Socialists (PES)*. The Socialists are the largest single group in the EP. They include amongst their membership at least one MEP from each member state. Reflecting the breadth of European Socialism, the members of the group have sometimes found cooperation difficult. In part this has been because of ideological diversity within the group, with opinions ranging from 'far left' state interventionists to 'moderate' social democrats. In part it has been caused by national party groups being reluctant to concede national interests to wider European interests. And in part it has stemmed from differences within the group on the very bases and direction of European integration.
- *Group of the European People's Party (EPP)*. The EPP draws its main ideological roots from European Christian Democracy. It used to be dominated by the German CDU/CSU and the Italian DC, but since 1989 it has had a broader base and, like the PES, has included in its ranks at least one MEP from every EU country. The group is broadly Centre-Right in its political orientation but internal differences do exist, notably on social issues. These issues were sharpened in 1992 when British Conservative MEPs, who previously had been excluded from the group because of the perceived Euro-scepticism and over zealous economic liberalism of the UK Conservative Government, were permitted to associate themselves with (though not to become full members of) the group.
- *Liberal Democratic and Reformist Group (LDR)*. In some respects this is the most divided group of all, and the most difficult to pinpoint in terms of its ideas. It contains certain Leftist elements, but it is basically a combination of parties of the Centre and the Right.
- *Group of the Greens in the European Parliament*. In the 1984–9 Parliament, Environmentalists and Ecologists sat with 'non-Green' MEPs of various sorts as part of an extremely heterogeneous Rainbow Group (RBW, see below). In the 1989 elections the Green representation was considerably increased and they were able to constitute their own group.

Figure 7.1 *Political groups in the European Parliament: before and after the 1994 elections*

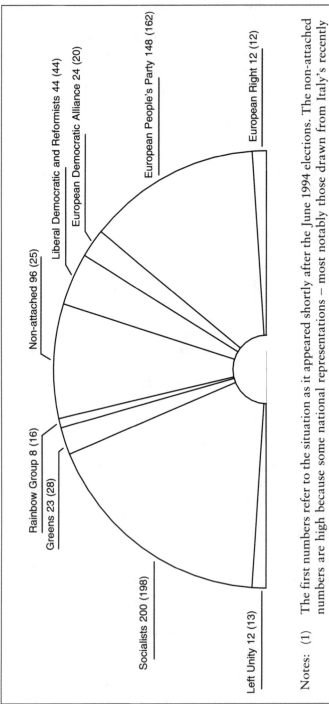

Socialists 200 (198)

Rainbow Group 8 (16)

Greens 23 (28)

Non-attached 96 (25)

Liberal Democratic and Reformists 44 (44)

European Democratic Alliance 24 (20)

European People's Party 148 (162)

European Right 12 (12)

Left Unity 12 (13)

Notes: (1) The first numbers refer to the situation as it appeared shortly after the June 1994 elections. The non-attached numbers are high because some national representations – most notably those drawn from Italy's recently elected right-wing government – had not decided how they were going to constitute themselves in the EP.

(2) The numbers inside the brackets refer to the situation in February 1994.

(3) There were 518 MEPs in the 1989–94 EP, and 567 in the EP which was elected in June 1994.

Beyond their common concern with 'green issues', the Greens are not very homogeneous, with some of their MEPs coming from a clear Left background and others thinking of themselves as neither Left nor Right.

● *Group of the European Democratic Alliance (EDA)*. The two main component parties of the EDA – the French Gaullists and the Irish Fianna Fail – share a general Centre-Right political outlook and a firm commitment to the CAP. Neither has been large enough to constitute a group on its own, but both, for different reasons, have been reluctant to link up with one of the more established Centre-Right groups. The EDA has, therefore, served as a useful marriage of convenience for both of them.

● *Rainbow Group (RBW)*. In the 1984–9 Parliament the RBW group brought together, on a very loose basis, Greens, Anti-EC Danes, and Regionalists. Following the departure of the Greens after the 1989 elections to constitute their own group, the RBW group was greatly reduced in size. Insofar as the group has any coherence it is in its attempts to protect regional and minority interests.

● *Technical Group of the European Right (ER)*. An Extreme Right group was formed in the 1984–9 Parliament based on the French National Front (FN) and the Italian Social Movement (MSI). In 1989, when newly elected German MEPs from the Republican Party joined the group, the MSI MEPs decided to sit as Independents. The main disagreement with the Republicans was over the South Tyrol issue, where the MSI have been fierce defenders of the Italian-speaking minority. The ER group is highly nationalistic in its attitudes, and has focused particularly on what it sees as unacceptably liberal attitudes to ethnic and immigration issues. The group is virtually completely ostracised by the other groups in the EP.

● *Left Unity (LU)*. The LU group consists of MEPs from the more hard-line communist parties of France, Greece, and Portugal. The group's rigid stance on many issues, coupled with its generally hostile attitude to further European integration, results in it being somewhat distanced from the other groups on the Left.

The political groups thus all contain significant internal divisions, usually of both an ideological and a national character. Inevitably this has a weakening effect. So, for example, it is difficult, whatever their ideological principles might suggest to them, for French MEPs to vote for a cut in agricultural prices or for Portuguese MEPs not to support increases in the Regional Fund.

Three other factors also make for looseness and a limited ability on the part of the groups to control and direct their members. The first of these factors arises from the political powers of the EP and the institutional setting in which it is placed. With no government to sustain or attack, no government-sponsored legislation to pass or reject, MEPs do not have the same semi-automatic 'for' or 'against' reaction that is so typical of much national parliamentary behaviour. The second factor is structural. Unlike parties in national legislatures, the political groups are not part of a wider organisational framework from which emanate expectations of cooperative and united behaviour, and generally recognised notions of responsibility and accountability. Rather most of them are weak, quasi-federal bodies functioning in a multicultural environment. This is seen in a number of ways: the constituent member parties of the larger groups hold their own separate meetings and have their own leaderships; in seeking to encourage group unity, group leaders can invoke no effective sanctions against, and can withhold few rewards from, MEPs who do not fall into line; and, in looking to their political futures, it is not only their political group or its leadership that MEPs must cultivate but also their national parties at home. The third factor is that MEPs can have claims on their loyalties and their votes which compete with the claims of the political groups. One source of such claims are the numerous interest groups with which many MEPs are closely associated. Another source is the EP's intergroups which bring together, usually on a relatively informal basis, MEPs from different political groups who have similar views on particular issues. (About 80 intergroups exist, of which 30 or so meet on a regular basis. The intergroups come in many different forms and vary considerably in the nature and range of their policy focus. Amongst their number are the Federalist Intergroup for European Union, the Friends of Israel Intergroup, the Central American Intergroup, the Media Intergroup, the Rural Areas Intergroup, the Animal Welfare Intergroup, and the Elderly People Intergroup).

However, despite the many weaknesses of the groups, it is important to emphasise that they are still of considerable importance in determining how the EP works.

Some of the functions and tasks they fulfil and the privileges they enjoy are specifically allocated to them under the Rules of Procedure or by decisions of Parliament. These include guaranteed representation on key EP bodies and committees, and speaking rights in plenary sessions.

Other functions have not been formally laid down, but have developed more out of political necessity, advantage, and convenience. This is most obviously seen in the way the groups are the prime determiners of tactics and voting patterns in the EP – decisions on which are normally taken in the week prior to plenary sessions, which is set aside for political group meetings. At these meetings efforts are made to agree a common group position on matters of current importance: should a deal be attempted with another political group on the election of the President?; what is the group's attitude to a Commission proposal for a Council directive?; what tactics can the group employ to prevent an unwelcome own initiative report being approved by a committee? In dealing with such questions internal group differences may have to be tackled, and sometimes they may not be resolved. But, of the many influences bearing down on MEPs, political group membership is normally the single most important factor correlating with how they vote.

Before leaving the political groups a few comments about the overall political balance of the EP are required.

From 1979 to 1989 a nominal Centre-Right majority existed, but in the 1989 elections this was replaced by a nominal Left–Green, or Red–Green, majority. The nature of the nominal majority existing at any one time unquestionably affects the interests and priorities of the EP, as is demonstrated by the greater attention given to social and environmental issues after 1989. But the word 'nominal' has to be attached to 'majority' because majorities have not existed at all in any formal sense, and majorities have not, in practice, displayed much political coherence or consistency. There are three main reasons for this. The first is the many and varied divisions between, and sometimes within, the political groups. Various liaising channels and mechanisms exist via which groups attempt to reach agreements and strike deals, but these are of limited effectiveness where fundamental policy differences exist. On some issues it is by no means unusual for the views of political groups on the Centre-Left and Centre-Right, or at least of some MEPs within these groups, to be closer to each other than to the views of other Left and Right groups. The second reason is that a number of issues which have taken up much of the EP's time have cut across the ideological spectrum and have attracted support from virtually all of the political groups. Examples of such issues are action on combatting racism in Europe, the provision of assistance to the countries of the developing world, and the need for the further development of European integration. And the third reason is that the EP frequently and consciously attempts to avoid being divided along Left–Right lines when it votes, especially on important issues. If it can present itself as united, it is in a stronger position to pressurise the Commission and the Council to accept its views.

☐ *National parties*

National political parties are involved in EP-related activities in three main ways. First, most candidates in the EP elections, and virtually all of those who are elected, are chosen by national parties. This means that MEPs inevitably reflect national party concerns and are normally obliged, if they wish to be reselected, to continue to display an awareness of these concerns.

Second, EP election campaigns are essentially national election campaigns conducted by national parties. Use may be made of the transnational manifestos, but voters are directed by the parties primarily to national issues and the results are assessed primarily in terms of their domestic implications. That the European dimension is limited is no more clearly seen than in the lack of any consistent Left–Right movement in voting patterns across the member states in European elections.

Finally, in the EP itself, national party groups exist within the political groups. This is an obvious potential source of political group disharmony and sometimes does create strains. Problems do not arise so much from the national groups having to act on specific domestic instructions. This does sometimes occur but, generally, organisational links between the national groups and national party leaderships are weak and the former have a reasonably free hand within general party guidelines. The problem is simply that each national party group inevitably tends to have its own priorities and loyalties.

■ Composition

In addition to party political attachments there are other aspects of the composition of the EP which are also of interest and importance. Three are particularly worthy of comment.

□ *The dual mandate*

After the 1979 elections some 30 per cent of MEPs were also members of their national legislature. This figure was inflated, however, because many MEPs had contested the election primarily for domestic political reasons and had no firm commitment to completing their terms of office. By the end of the Parliament the number of dual mandates had been more than halved. What, therefore, seemed to be a big drop after the 1984 elections, to around 12 per cent of MEPs holding a dual mandate, in fact reflected a trend that was already well under way; a trend that has been assisted since 1984 by some parties actively trying to discourage dual mandates and by Belgium and Spain forbidding them altogether under national law.

Among the consequences of this decline in the dual mandate has been a weakening of links between the EP and national parliaments. Most parties have procedures of some kind for maintaining contact between the two levels but they tend to be weak, and frequently the EP group is seen as something of a poor relation. A more positive outcome of the decline of dual mandates has been that MEPs with one mandate rather than two have more time and energy for their EP duties. This has been reflected in more days spent in plenaries and committees, more Parliamentary questions, and more reports.

Continuity

The degree of change and turnover in personnel affects the way most organisations work. The EP is no exception to this: the more effective MEPs tend to be those who have developed policy interests and expertise in European affairs over time, and who have come to know their way around the EU system.

Lack of continuity in membership was a problem during the 1979–84 Parliament, with nearly one-quarter of MEPs being replaced before the 1984 elections. However, as was noted above, that was always likely to be an inflated figure, with many prominent politicians standing in 1979 who had no intention of making a political career in the EP. Events since have, indeed, shown the anticipated settling down, with only a relatively small proportion of MEPs now resigning before they end their term of office.

As for turnover of MEPs between elections, it is certainly higher than is common in national parliaments, but not alarmingly so: around half of the MEPs who were elected in 1984 had sat in the 1979–84 Parliament, and over half of those who were elected in 1989 were returning. Of the 1989 intake, 110 first took their seats between 1979 and 1984, 96 first sat in 1984, 2 in 1985, 38 in 1986, 28 in 1987, 4 in 1988, and 240 in 1989. (1986 was exceptional because of the Spanish and Portuguese accessions, and 1987 was so because Spain and Portugal held their first direct elections to the EP.)

Competence and experience

It is sometimes suggested that MEPs are not of the same calibre and do not carry the same political weight as their counterparts in national legislatures. Because the EP is weak, the argument runs, it attracts mostly weak members, or members who regard it merely as a stepping stone to a national career or advancement.

There is something in this view. Major national figures have tended either not to contest EP elections or not to have completed their terms of office. (The provision in the 1976 'Direct Elections Act' making national governmental office incompatible with EP membership has not helped in this regard.) Additionally, a few MEPs have transferred from the EP to national legislatures.

But the situation should not be exaggerated. Competition to be an MEP is normally fierce, requiring all the customary political skills. Most MEPs do have considerable public experience, either in national or regional politics, or in an executive capacity with a major sectional interest. Amongst the MEPs who were elected in 1989 there were thirty-five former ministers from national governments.

Perhaps the key point to be emphasised is that it should not be assumed that those who choose to stand for, and work in, the EP are necessarily settling for second best. Many are firmly committed to their responsibilities and have developed a competence and an experience which is different from, but which is not necessarily inferior to, that of national parliamentarians.

■ Organisation and operation

□ *The multi-site problem*

The work of the EP is carried out on three sites in three different countries. Full plenary sessions are held in Strasbourg whilst mini-plenary sessions are held in Brussels. Committees usually meet in Brussels. Most of the 3000 staff who work in the Secretariat of the Parliament are based in Luxembourg (this figure does not include the 450 who work in the Secretariats of the political groups).

This situation is clearly unsatisfactory, and it is a source of grievance and annoyance amongst most MEPs. A reasonably conscientious MEP may well have to change his working location half a dozen times in an average month. His work diary is likely to look something like this: one week attending the monthly plenary at Strasbourg; from two to five days in committee(s), probably in Brussels but sometimes elsewhere; two to four days in political group meetings and group working parties, probably in Brussels; whatever time remains, in his constituency (if he has one), visiting somewhere as part of an EP delegation, in Luxembourg consulting with officials on a report, or at home.

If the EP had one base, and especially if that was Brussels, it is likely that Parliament's efficiency, influence and visibility would all be increased. However, the Council has the power of decision on the matter, and hard lobbying from the Luxembourg and French governments has ensured that arguments for 'sense to prevail' and a single site to be agreed have not been acted upon.

☐ *Arranging parliamentary business*

Compared with most national parliaments the EP enjoys a considerable independence in the arrangement of its affairs. That is not to say it can do whatever it likes. The Treaties oblige it to do some things – such as deliver opinions on Commission proposals for Council legislation – and prevent it from doing others – such as censuring the Council. But, on many agenda, timetable and other organisational matters it remains, to a considerable degree, its own master.

A major reason for this independence is, once again, the special institutional setting in which the EP operates. The EU executive does not have to be as concerned to control what the EP does as do national governments with their legislatures. This is because although EP pronouncements and activities can be unwelcome to the Council and the Commission, they do not normally have politically damaging or unmanageable consequences.

A second, and closely related, reason is the lack of any clear and consistent identification, of either a positive or negative kind, between the EP and the EU executive. In national parliaments business is shaped to a considerable degree by political attachments. But the Commission is made up of officials who are nominally non-partisan, whilst the Council is multi-party, multi-ideological, and multi-national in its membership. As for the 'persuasive devices' that national executives have at their disposal to further encourage loyalty, neither the Commission nor the Council has patronage to dispense.

A third reason is that the EP is entitled to adopt its own Rules of Procedure. This it has done, amending and streamlining the Rules in such ways as to make itself both more efficient and more influential.

Most decisions by the EP about its operation and functioning are not taken in plenary session but are delegated to either the President, the Bureau, or the Conference of Presidents.

The President of the EP is elected to office for a two and a half year term. According to Rule 19 of the Rules of Procedure the President 'shall direct all the activities of Parliament and of its bodies under the conditions laid down in these Rules'. In practice, this means that the President has many functions, such as presiding over debates in the chamber, referring matters to committees as appropriate, and representing the EP in dealings with other EU institutions and outside bodies. An effective President must be an administrator and a politician, skilled in organising and also in liaising and bargaining.

The Bureau consists of the President and Parliament's fourteen Vice-Presidents. Like the President, the Vice-Presidents are elected for a two and a half year period of office, though by tradition the posts are distributed amongst the member states. Various financial and administrative organisational matters are dealt with by the Bureau, such as drawing up the EP's draft estimates and deciding on the composition and structure of the Parliament's Secretariat. To assist it in the performance of its duties, and in particular to take responsibility for financial and administrative matters concerning members, five Quaestors, who are also elected, sit in the Bureau in an advisory capacity.

Organisational matters, other than matters of routine which are dealt with by the Bureau have, since the 1993 Rules of Procedure were introduced, been the responsibility of the Conference of Presidents. This is composed of the EP President and the chairmen of the political groups. MEPs who are not attached to any political group can delegate two of their number to attend meetings. Matters which fall within the remit of the Conference of Presidents include the following: deciding on the seating arrangements in the Chamber – a potentially sensitive and highly symbolic issue when groups do not wish to be seated too far to the left or too far to the right of the hemicycle; drawing up the draft agendas for plenary sessions; and authorising the drawing up of own initiative reports. Decisions are made by a consensus whenever possible, but if none exists matters are put to the vote, with group chairmen (though not the non-attached delegates who do not have voting rights) having as many votes as there are members of the group.

Two other Conferences were also created under the 1993 Rules of Procedure: the Conference of Committee Chairmen and the Conference of Delegation Chairmen (the latter brings together the chairmen of the EP's delegations to the interparliamentary delegations and joint parliamentary committees which have been established with the parliaments of thirty or so non-EU states). These Conferences are essentially advisory in character, though they can also have certain tasks assigned to them by the Conference of Presidents.

☐ *The committees of Parliament*

Much of the EP's work is carried out by committees. These are of two types. The first, and by far the most important, are standing or permanent committees. There are 19 of these (see Table 7.2). The second are *ad hoc* committees which are established to investigate special topics.

Assignment of MEPs to the permanent committees occurs at the beginning and half way through each five year term. Assignment to the *ad hoc* committees is as required. According to the Rules of Procedure, all committee members are elected to their positions on the basis of proposals made by the Conference of Presidents to Parliament which are 'designed to ensure fair representation of Member States and of political views'. What this means, in practice, is that the political groups negotiate the share-out of committee memberships on a basis proportionate to their size. Most MEPs become a member of one standing committee – though a few are on as many as three – and a substitute member of another.

The permanent committees perform various duties, such as explore ideas with the Commission, foster own initiative reports, and discuss developments with the President-in-Office of the Council. Their most important task, however, is to examine legislative proposals on which an EP opinion is required. The standard way of proceeding (other than where a proposal is completely straightforward and uncontroversial, which may

Table 7.2   *Standing committees of the European Parliament*

	Title
1	Foreign Affairs and Security
2	Agriculture, Fisheries and Rural Development
3	Budgets
4	Economic and Monetary Affairs and Industrial Policy
5	Energy, Research and Technology
6	External Economic Relations
7	Legal Affairs and Citizen's Rights
8	Social Affairs, Employment and the Working Environment
9	Regional Policy, Regional Planning and Relations with Regional and Local Authorities
10	Transport and Tourism
11	Environment, Public Health and Consumer Protection
12	Culture, Youth, Education and the Media
13	Development and Cooperation
14	Civil Liberties and Internal Affairs
15	Budgetary Control
16	Institutional Affairs
17	Rules of Procedure, the Verification of Credentials and Immunities
18	Women's Rights
19	Petitions

result in it being dealt with by special procedures allowing for rapid approval) is as follows:

(1)   Each proposal is referred to an appropriate committee. Should a proposal overlap the competency and interest of several committees, up to three may be asked for their views, but one is named as the committee responsible and only it reports to the plenary session.

(2)   The responsibility for drawing up the committee's report is entrusted to a *rapporteur*. Though formally chosen by their fellow committee members, *rapporteurs* are, in practice, like committee chairman and many others in the EP who hold nominally elected positions, appointed as a result of negotiations between the political groups: negotiations that, in this case, are carried out by group 'coordinators' from the different committees. In drawing up the report the *rapporteur* can call on assistance from various places: from Parliament's Secretariat, from his own research services (the EP provides funds to enable each MEP to have at least one research assistant), from the Secretariat of his political group, from research institutes, and even from the Commission. Some *rapporteurs* hardly use these facilities and do most of the work themselves; others do little more than present what has been done on their behalf.

(3)   A first draft is produced for consideration by the committee according to an agreed timetable. Drafts are normally presented in four main parts: Amendments to the Commission Proposal (if there are any); a Draft Legislative Resolution; an Explanatory Statement; and Annexes (if there are any), including opinions of other committees. How much discussion the draft provokes, and how many committee meetings are required before a text is adopted that can be recommended to the plenary, depends on the complexity and controversiality of the subject matter. Factors likely to shape the reactions of committee members include national and ideological perspectives, lobbying by outside interests, and views expressed by the Commission.

(4)   The *rapporteur* acts as the committee's principal spokesman when the report is considered in the plenary. In this capacity he may have to explain the committee's view on amendments put forward by non-committee members, or he may be called upon to use his judgement in making recommendations to Parliament on what it should do when the Commission goes some, but not all, of the way in accepting committee-approved amendments. Occasionally – when, for example, the Commission offers a mixed package – committee meetings may be hurriedly convened during plenary sessions.

(5)   Where the cooperation and co-decision procedures apply, the role and activity of committees at the second reading stage is similar to that at the first reading. That is to say, they examine a proposal – which is now in

the form of the Council's common position – and make recommendations to the plenary. The responsibility for drawing up reports is conferred automatically on the committees involved in the first reading and the *rapporteur* remains the same. The reports normally have two main sections: Recommendations for the Second Reading (which may provide for approval of, rejection of, or amendments to, the common position – amendments often having the intention of re-establishing the EP's position as defined at the first reading, or to produce a compromise with the Council); and Justifications or Explanatory Statements.

(6) The committees which have dealt with proposals at first and second readings are not directly concerned with proceedings if a Conciliation Committee is convened under the co-decision procedure. However, the presumption is that the political groups, who make the nominations to the EP's delegation to the Conciliation Committee, will select at least some members of the committees concerned.

A number of factors help to determine how the EP committees work, and how much influence they exercise. The most important of these factors are:

- *The significance of the policy area within the EU system.* The Committee on Agriculture, for example, deals with matters which loom much larger in the EU scale of things than the Committee on Women's Rights.
- *The power of Parliament within the policy area.* The influence of the Committee on Budgets is enormously enhanced by the real budgetary decision-making powers that the Treaties give to Parliament. Similarly, the Committee on Budgetary Control would be much weaker if the EP did not have the statutory responsibility to grant, postpone, or refuse a discharge to the Commission in respect of the implementation of the EU's budget.
- *Committee expertise.* Many committee members just do not have the requisite specialised skills to be able to explore relevant issues in depth or to question the Commission on the basis of a fully informed understanding of policy. For example, few members of the Committee on Energy, Research and Technology have an appropriate technical background (though they may, of course, have, or may develop as a result of their committee membership, a great knowledge of relevant subject material). The Committee on Legal Affairs and Citizen's Rights, on the other hand, is composed mainly of lawyers or legal experts.
- *Secretariat support.* In terms of numbers, all committees are thinly resourced in their administrative back-up. Each has, on average, only about five or six senior officials and these, because of the EP's recruitment

policy, usually have a generalist rather than a specialist background. However, amongst these small teams there do appear to be, in variable quantities perhaps, high degrees of competence and enthusiasm.

● *Committee chairmanship*. The role of committee chairmen can be vital in guiding the work of committees. They can help to push business through; they can assist *rapporteurs* in rallying support for reports that are to be debated in plenaries; they can help to create committee harmony and a constructive working atmosphere; and they can do much to ensure that a committee broadens its horizons beyond simply reacting to initiatives that others present to it.

● *Committee cohesiveness*. One of the reasons why, for example, the Committee on Development and Cooperation is rather more influential than a number of other committees is that it tends to display a high degree of cohesiveness. With members of the committee being united on the desirability of improving conditions in the developing countries, discussions tend to revolve around questions of feasibility rather than ideological desirability. The Agriculture Committee, on the other hand, attracts MEPs who are both supportive and critical of the CAP and hence it tends often to be sharply internally divided.

☐ *Plenary meetings*

There are usually eleven full plenary meetings, or part-sessions as they are properly known, per year: one each month apart from August. Part-sessions are held in Strasbourg and last from Monday afternoon to Friday midday. Since September 1993, when a new EP building was opened in Brussels, mini-plenaries, normally lasting two days, have also been held. It seems likely that in the future four or five, Brussels-based, mini-sessions will be held each year.

The agenda for plenaries is drafted by the President and the Conference of Presidents in consultation with the Conference of Committee Chairmen and the EP's Secretariat. Their recommendations have to be approved by the plenary itself. With time so tight, items which many MEPs consider to be important inevitably do not get onto the agenda, whilst those that do make it normally have to be taken at pace. Strict rules govern who can speak, when, and for how long: the effect of the rules is often to restrict speakers to committee and political group spokesmen.

Full plenaries have three standard elements. First, the bread and butter business is the consideration of reports from committees. As indicated earlier, these reports usually lead to either resolutions embodying opinions or to resolutions embodying own initiatives. Second, time is set aside for debates on topical and urgent matters. These debates also frequently result in the adoption of resolutions. Finally, there is a 1½ hour Commission Question Time and a 1½ hour Council Question Time. Who answers on behalf of the Commission and the Council depends on the policy content of the questions (which are known in advance), preferences expressed by the Parliament, and who is available.

A few figures may be cited to illustrate what these elements of EP activity produce. In 1993 Parliament adopted 727 resolutions and decisions, amongst which were included: 249 embodying its opinion; 345 own initiative resolutions, of which 120 were on the basis of reports, 146 were by urgent procedure, and 79 followed an early vote to conclude debates on Commission or Council Statements or on oral questions; and 25 were on budgetary matters. As for questions to the Commission and the Council, in 1993 there was a total of 4111 written questions and 1325 oral questions (see above for details).

In addition to the three standard activities, there are a number of other possible agenda items. For example: statements by the Commission and the Council; addresses by distinguished foreign guests; and – at least twice a year – a report on European Council meetings by the Head of Government of the incumbent Presidency.

The EP in plenary does not, it should be said, give the impression of being the most dynamic of places. Attendance in the chamber is poor, the translation problem limits spontaneity, and much immediacy is lost by the practice of taking most votes in clusters at allocated voting times rather than at the end of debates. (These times are often not even on the same day as the debate.) Nonetheless, working procedures have been gradually improved over the years, most notably by the removal of much minor business from the floor of the chamber.

▌ Concluding remarks: is the EP becoming a 'proper' parliament?

The EP has clearly assumed an increased role in the EU in recent years. Several factors account for this, not least the Parliament's own efforts to increase its powers.

In attempting to enhance its role and influence, the Parliament has pursued a dual strategy. On the one hand there has been a *maximalist* approach, which has been directed towards achieving fundamental reform of inter-institutional relations, and especially increasing the powers of the Parliament vis-a-vis the Council of Ministers. In 1984 this approach led to the EP approving the *Draft Treaty establishing the European Union*, which played a part – though not perhaps as important a part as its supporters have claimed – in helping to bring about the SEA. In the 1990s, in the context of the increasingly heard debate about the 'democratic deficit', and as part of its submissions to the IGC on Political Union, the approach led to the EP approving reports – the so-called Martin Reports – which called, amongst other things, for co-decision-making legislative powers with the Council, for the ability to initiate legislation, and for the right to elect the President of the Commission on a proposal from the European Council. On the other hand there has been a *minimalist* approach, in which the EP has used its existing powers to the full and has done whatever it can to see how far these powers can be pressed. As part of this approach the EP has made use of the enhanced status and increased vigour that has stemmed from direct elections, has taken advantage of favourable Court judgements, and has contracted a number of formal and informal understandings with other EU institutions which have brought it certain benefits.

But notwithstanding all its efforts and the increased influence it has achieved, the EP is still commonly regarded as being a rather special sort of advisory body rather than a proper parliament. The main reason for this is that its constitutional powers remain considerably weaker than those of national parliaments. It does not have full legislative powers, its budgetary powers are circumscribed, and it cannot overthrow a government.

However, in assessing the importance of the EP, attention should not be restricted to its constitutional capabilities. For when the comparison with national parliaments is extended to encompass what actually happens in practice, the powers exercised by the EP are, in several key respects, comparable with the powers exercised by many national parliaments. Indeed, it is not difficult to make out a case that in exercising some of its functions – scrutinising legislative proposals, for example, and contributing to the debate about future developments – the EP exerts a greater influence over affairs than do the more executive-dominated parliaments of some member states.

■ *Chapter 8* ■

European Union Law and the Court of Justice

■ The need for European Union law

An enforceable legal framework is the essential basis of decision-making and decision application in all democratic states. Although not itself a state, this also applies to the EU. It does so because the EU is more than merely another international organisation in which countries cooperate with one another on a voluntary basis for reasons of mutual benefit. Rather it is an organisation in which states have voluntarily surrendered their right, across a broad range of important sectors, to be independent in the determination and application of public policy.

If there was no body of law setting out the powers and responsibilities of the institutions and the member states of the EU, and if there was no authority to give independent rulings on what that law is and how it should be interpreted, effective EU decision-making would not be possible. Of course, law is not the only factor shaping the EU's decision-making processes. As in any organisation, practice evolves in the light of experience of what is possible and what works best. The tendency to often not press for a vote in the Council even when it is legally permissible is an obvious example of this. But the law does provide the basic setting in which decisions are made. It lays down that some things must be done, that some cannot, and that some may be. So, for example, it is by virtue of EU law that agricultural prices can no longer be fixed in national capitals but must be agreed at EU level, that the Commission is entitled to take certain types of decisions without reference to other institutions, and that the EP is permitted to increase the annual budget within specified limits.

The existence of EU law is also crucial with regard to policy implementation. For if decisions took the form only of vague intergovernmental agreements, and if those agreements could be interpreted by member states in whatever way was most beneficial and convenient for them, common policies would not, in practice, exist and the whole rationale of the EU would be undermined. The likes of the *common* agricultural policy, the *common* competition policy, the *common* commercial policy, and the harmonisation of matters as diverse as maximum axle weights of lorries and minimum safety standards at work, can be fully effective only if they are based on *common laws* that are capable of *uniform* interpretation in *all* member states.

■ The sources of European Union law

An EU legal order is thus an essential condition of the EU's existence. The sources of that order are to be found in a number of places: the Treaties, EU legislation, international law, the general principles of law, and judicial interpretation.

□ The Treaties

The Treaty on European Union is, as was shown in Chapter 3, made up of several component parts. Some of these parts have the status of law and are subject to the jurisdiction of the Court of Justice, whilst other parts do not have the status of law and are not subject to the jurisdiction of the Court. The parts of the TEU which are subject to the jurisdiction of the Court are: the three Founding Community Treaties as amended over the years, notably by the SEA and by the TEU itself; protocols of the TEU which are attached to the Community Treaties; Article K.3(2)(c) of the Justice and Home Affairs (JHA) pillar, which deals with conventions; and Articles L to S of the Final Provisions which include matters relating to Treaty amendments and accessions to the EU. The parts of the TEU which are not subject to the jurisdiction of the Court are: the Common Provisions – which include general objectives of the Union, the membership and role of the European Council, and respect for fundamental human rights as guaranteed by the 1950 European Convention for the Protection of Human Rights and Fundamental Freedoms; the Common Foreign and Security Policy (CFSP) pillar; the JHA pillar apart from Article K.3(2)(c); and Declarations attached to the Treaty.

Clearly this all makes for a rather messy and untidy legal framework. It also makes for a rather confusing and potentially contentious one since in some circumstances there is considerable legal ambiguity and uncertainty. So, for example, to take the principle of subsidiarity, which has been widely hailed as one of the key innovative features of the TEU, it is established as a principle in the Common Provisions, but the only definition of it is in Article 3b of the EC Treaty – and that definition is so vague as to provide no real guide as to how the principle should be applied in practice.

One of the consequences of the complicated legal nature of the TEU is that commentators on the EU have adopted different positions as to whether to use the term 'EU law' or 'Community law'. Since there is not much that falls outside the three Community Treaties that is subject to the jurisdiction of the Court, many commentators – especially lawyers – prefer to stay with the established term of 'Community law'. Others, however, prefer to use the term 'EU law': partly because the Communities are part of the EU; partly because some, albeit very limited, spheres of law under the TEU are not based on the Communities; and partly because to keep moving between 'EU' and 'Community' is a recipe for confusion. In this chapter, as elsewhere in the book, the term 'EU law' is used, except in circumstances where it is clearly inaccurate to do so.

Those parts of the TEU which are subject to the jurisdiction of the Court constitute the so-called primary law of the EU. They may also be regarded as making up the EU's written and legal constitution. (It could be argued that the TEU as a whole makes up the EU's political constitution.)

National constitutions in liberal democracies normally do two main things: they establish an institutional structure for decision-making, and they set out – often in a bill of rights – freedoms of the individual and restrictions on the power of decision-makers over the citizenry. The relevant component parts of the TEU exercise the first of these tasks, but only in a very restricted way the second. The establishment of the institutional structure is seen, most obviously, in the identification of the Commission, the Council, the Court and the Parliament as the key decision-making institutions, and by the laying down of rules governing relations between them and also between them and the member states. As for the establishment of individual rights, the scope is largely restricted to certain economic freedoms – a reflection of the concerns of the EU and of the fact that it does not carry the comprehensive responsibilities of nation states. (As noted above, the references in the TEU to fundamental rights are not subject to the jurisdiction of the Court of Justice.)

But if the TEU does not fulfil all of the tasks of national constitutions, it is much concerned with something that is normally not considered to be appropriate subject matter for constitutions: policy. This takes the form of enunciation of general principles on the one hand and the identification of policy sectors that are to be developed on the other. The main general principles are those of the EC Treaty that are designed to promote competition and the free movement of goods, persons, services, and capital, all behind a common external tariff (CET) and a common commercial policy (CCP). The policy issues and sectors that are identified, with varying degrees of precision regarding how they are to be developed, include: coal and steel (ECSC Treaty); atomic energy (Euratom Treaty); agriculture, social, transport, regional, the environment, research and technological development, and economic and monetary union (EC Treaty).

□ *European Union legislation*

Laws adopted by the EU institutions constitute secondary legislation. They are concerned with translating the general principles of the Treaties into specific rules and are adopted by the Council, by the European Parliament and the Council, or by the Commission according to the procedures that are described in other chapters of this book. While there is no hard and fast distinction between Council, EP and Council, and Commission legislation, the first two tend to be broader in scope, to be concerned with more important matters, and to be aimed often at laying down a legal framework in a policy sphere. Commission legislation, of which there is, in terms of volume, much more than Council and European Parliament and Council legislation, is largely administrative/technical in nature, and is usually subject to tight guidelines laid down in enabling Council, or EP and Council, legislation.

The Treaties distinguish between different types of legislation (Article 14, ECSC; Article 189, EC; Article 161, Euratom): regulations, directives, decisions, and recommendations and opinions.

□ *Regulations* (called general decisions under the ECSC). A regulation is:

(1)   Of 'general application'; that is, it contains general and abstract provisions which may be applied to particular persons and circumstances.

(2)   'Binding in its entirety'; that is, it bestows rights and obligations upon those to whom it is addressed, and member states must observe it in full and as written.

(3)   'Directly applicable in all Member States'; that is, without the need for national implementing measures, it takes immediate legal effect right across the EU on the date specified in the regulation. (Normally this is the same day as, or very shortly after, the regulation is published in the

Official Journal of the European Communities. This, in turn, is usually only a day or two after the regulation has been adopted.)

Most regulations are adopted by the Commission and concern highly specific and technical adjustments to existing EU law. The majority relate to the CAP. Exhibit 8.1 is a typical regulation.

☐ *Directives* (recommendations under the ECSC). 'A directive shall be binding, as to the result to be achieved, upon each Member State to which it is addressed, but shall leave to the national authorities the choice of form and method' (Article 189 EC).

In theory, a directive is thus very different from a regulation: it is not binding in its entirety but only in 'the result to be achieved'; it is addressed to member states and does not claim general applicability; it is not necessarily addressed to all member states; and appropriate national measures need to be taken to give the directive effect. As a consequence directives tend to be rather more general in nature than regulations. They are not quite so much concerned with the detailed and uniform application of policy, as with the laying down of policy principles which member states must seek to achieve but which they can pursue by the appropriate means under their respective national constitutional and legal systems. (Such appropriate means can vary from administrative circulars to new laws approved by national legislatures.)

The distinction between regulations and directives should not, however, be exaggerated because, in practice, a number of factors often result in a blurring. First, directives are almost invariably addressed to all states and are so because they are usually concerned with the harmonisation or approximation of laws and practices in fields of EU activity. Exhibit 8.2 is a typical harmonising directive. Second, some directives are drafted so tightly that there is very little room for national authorities to incorporate adjustments. Third, directives contain a date by which the national procedures to give the directive effect must have been complied with. The Commission has to be notified of national implementing measures, and states which do not comply by the due date are liable to have proceedings initiated against them which can, ultimately, result in a case before the Court of Justice. Fourth, the Court has ruled that in some instances directives are directly applicable; for example, where national implementing legislation has been unduly delayed or where it has departed from the intent of the original directive.

☐ *Decisions* (called individual decisions under the ECSC). 'A decision shall be binding in its entirety upon those to whom it is addressed' (Article 189, EC). It may be addressed to any or to all member states, to undertakings, or

Exhibit 8.1   Commission Regulation (EC) No 270/94 of 4 February 1994 fixing the import levies on white sugar and raw sugar

THE COMMISSION OF THE EUROPEAN COMMUNITIES,

Having regard to the Treaty establishing the European Community,

Having regard to Council Regulation (EEC) No 1785/81 of 30 June 1981 on the common organization of the markets in the sugar sector([1]), as last amended by Regulation (EC) No 133/94([2]), and in particular Article 16 (8) thereof,

Having regard to Council Regulation (EEC) No 3813/92 of 28 December 1992 on the unit of account and the conversion rates to be applied for the purposes of the common agricultural policy([3]), as amended by Regulation (EC) No 3528/93([4]), and in particular Article 5 thereof,

Whereas the import levies on white sugar and raw sugar were fixed by Commission Regulation (EEC) No 1695/93([5]), as last amended by Regulation (EC) No 246/94([6]);

Whereas it follows from applying the detailed rules contained in Commission Regulation (EEC) No 1695/93 to the information known to the Commission that the levies at present in force should be altered to the amounts set out in the Annex hereto;

Whereas, in order to make it possible for the levy arrangements to function normally, the representative market rate established during the reference period from 3 February 1994, as regards floating currencies, should be used to calculate the levies,

HAS ADOPTED THIS REGULATION:

Article 1

The import levies referred to in Article 16 (1) of Regulation (EEC) No 1785/81 shall be, in respect of white sugar and standard quality raw sugar, as set out in the Annex hereto.

Article 2

This Regulation shall enter into force on 5 February 1994.

This Regulation shall be binding in its entirety and directly applicable in all Member States.

Done at Brussels, 4 February 1994.

For the Commission
René STEICHEN
Member of the Commission

([1]) OJ No L 177, 1. 7. 1981, p. 4.
([2]) OJ No L 22, 27. 1. 1994, p. 7.
([3]) OJ No L 387, 31. 12. 1992, p. 1.
([4]) OJ No L 320, 22. 12. 1993, p. 32.
([5]) OJ No L 159, 1. 7. 1993, p. 40.
([6]) OJ No L 30, 3. 2. 1994, p. 45.

ANNEX

to the Commission Regulation of 4 February 1994 fixing the import levies on white sugar and raw sugar

(ECU/100 kg)

CN code	Levy([3])
1701 11 10	33,95([1])
1701 11 90	33,95([1])
1701 12 10	33,95([1])
1701 12 90	33,95([1])
1701 91 00	40,12
1701 99 10	40,12
1701 99 90	40,12([2])

(^{1}) The levy applicable is calculated in accordance with the provisions of Article 2 or 3 of Commission Regulation (EEC) No 837/68 (OJ No L 151, 30. 6. 1968, p. 42) as last amended by Regulation (EEC) No 1428/78 (OJ No L 171, 28. 6. 1978, p. 34).

(^{2}) In accordance with Article 16 (2) of Regulation (EEC) No 1785/81 this amount is also applicable to sugar obtained from white and raw sugar containing added substances other than flavouring or colouring matter.

(^{3}) No import levy applies to OCT originating products according to Article 101 (1) of Decision 91/482/EEC.

Source: Official Journal of the European Communities, L32, Vol.37 (5 February 1994).

to individuals. Many decisions are highly specific and are, in effect, administrative rather than legislative acts. Others are of a more general character and can be akin to regulations or even, occasionally, directives.

Decisions are adopted in a whole range of circumstances. For example: to enforce competition policy; to institute a pilot action programme; to authorise grants from one of the EU's funds; to allow an exemption from an existing measure; or to counter dumping from a third country.

☐ *Recommendations and opinions* (opinions only under the ECSC). Recommendations and opinions have no binding force and so, strictly speaking, do not formally constitute part of EU law. However, the Court of Justice has on occasions referred to them, so their legal status is not always completely clear. The same applies to some of the other non-binding devices which the EU institutions use for such purposes as floating ideas, starting a legislative process, promoting coordination, and encouraging harmonisation. These include memoranda, communications, conventions, programmes, guidelines, agreements, declarations, resolutions, and decisions not made under Article 189 (EC).

In order to accommodate the mosaic of different national circumstances and interests which exist on many policy issues the EU's legislative framework needs to be creative, flexible, and capable of permitting differentiation. There are four main ways in which it is so:

● As has just been shown, the EU makes use of a variety of formal and quasi-formal legislative instruments.

● There are considerable variations between directives regarding the time periods permitted for incorporation into national law. So, for example, amending directives may have to be incorporated almost immediately, whereas innovative or controversial directives, or directives which involve substantial capital expenditure in order to be properly applied – as is

Exhibit 8.2   Council 93/93/EEC Directive of 29 October 1993 on the masses and dimensions of two or three-wheel motor vehicles

THE COUNCIL OF THE EUROPEAN COMMUNITIES,

Having regard to the Treaty establishing the European Economic Community, and in particular Article 100a thereof,

Having regard to Council Directive 92/61/EEC of 30 June 1992 relating to the type-approval of two or three-wheel motor vehicles([1]),

Having regard to the proposal from the Commission([2]),

In cooperating with the European Parliament([3]),

Having regard to the opinion of the Economic and Social Committee([4]),

Whereas the internal market comprises an area without internal frontiers in which the free movement of goods, persons, services and capital is ensured; whereas the measures necessary for its operation should be adopted;

Whereas with regard to their masses and dimensions, in each Member State two or three-wheel vehicles must display certain technical characteristics laid down by mandatory provisions which differ from one Member State to another; whereas, as a result of their differences, such provisions constitute barriers to trade within the Community;

Whereas those barriers to the operation of the internal market may be removed if the same requirements are adopted by all the Member States in place of their national rules;

Whereas it is necessary to draw up harmonized requirements concerning the masses and dimensions of two or three-wheel motor vehicles in order to enable the type-approval and component type-approval procedures laid down in Directive 92/61/EEC to be applied for each type of such vehicle;

Whereas given the scale and impact of the action proposed in the sector in question, the Community measures covered by this Directive are necessary, indeed essential, to achieve the aim in view, which is to establish Community vehicle type-approval; whereas that aim cannot be adequately achieved by the Member States individually;

Whereas the provisions of this Directive should not oblige those Member States which do not allow two-wheel motor vehicles on their territory to tow a trailer to amend their rules,

HAS ADOPTED THIS DIRECTIVE:

Article 1

This Directive together with its Annex shall apply to the masses and dimensions of all types of vehicle as defined in Article 1 of Directive 92/61/EEC.

Article 2

The procedure for the granting of component type-approval in respect of the masses and dimensions of a type of two or three-wheel motor vehicle and the conditions governing the free movement of such vehicles shall be as laid down in Chapters II and III of Directive 92/61/EEC.

Article 3

Any amendments necessary to adapt the requirements of the Annexes to technical progress shall be adopted in accordance with the procedure laid down in Article 13 of Directive 70/156/EEC([5]).

Article 4

1.   Member States shall adopt and publish the provisions necessary to comply with this Directive before 1 May 1993. They shall forthwith inform the Commission thereof.

When the Member States adopt these provisions, they shall contain a reference to this Directive or shall be accompanied by such a reference on the occasion of their official publication. The methods of making such a reference shall be laid down by the Member States.

2.   From the date mentioned in paragraph 1 Member States may not, for reasons connected with masses and dimensions, prohibit the initial entry into service of vehicles which conform to this Directive.

They shall apply the provisions referred to in paragraph 1 as from 1 November 1995.

3.   Member States shall communicate to the Commission the texts of the provisions of national law which they adopt in the field covered by this Directive.

Article 5

This Directive is addressed to the Member States.

Done at Brussels, 19 October 1993.

For the Council

The President

R. URBAIN

(¹) OJ No L 225, 10. 8. 1992, p. 72.
(²) OJ No C 293, 9. 11. 1992, p. 1.
(³) OJ No C 337, 21. 12. 1992, p. 104 and Decision of 27 October 1993 (not yet published in the Official Journal).
(⁴) OJ No C 73, 15. 3. 1993, P. 22.

(⁵) Council Directive 70/156/EEC of 6 February 1970 on the approximation of the laws of the Member States relating to the type-approval of motor vehicles and their trailers (OJ No L 42, 23. 2. 1970, p. 1) Directive as last amended by Directive 92/53/EEC (OJ No L 225, 10. 8. 1992, p. 1).

Source: Official Journal of the European Communities, L311, Vol.36 (14 December 1993).

common with environmental directives – may not be required to be incorporated for some years.

• Devices which allow for adaptation to local conditions and needs are often either attached to legal texts or are authorised by the Commission after an act has come into force. Examples of such devices include exemptions, derogations, and safety clauses.

• Provided the Commission is satisfied that the relevant provisions 'are not a means of arbitrary discrimination or a disguised restriction on trade between Member States' (Article 100A EC), states are permitted to apply national legislation which is 'tougher' than EU legislation in respect of certain matters – notably protection of the environment and of the working environment.

The complexity of EU legislation is closely linked with its considerable volume. In an average year as many as 7000–8000 instruments of all types are adopted, of which around 4000 are regulations, 2500 are decisions, and 120 are directives. The vast majority of these instruments consist of administrative measures of a routine, non-political, recurring kind.

□ *International law*

International law is notoriously vague and weak, but the Court of Justice has had occasional recourse to it when developing principles embodied in EU law. Judgements have also established that insofar as the EU is increasingly developing an international personality of its own and taking over powers from the states, the same rules of international law apply to it as apply to them: regarding treaty law, for example, and the privileges and immunities of international organisations.

The many international agreements to which the EU is a party are sometimes viewed as another dimension of international law. However, since they are implemented by legislative acts they are probably better viewed as constituting part of EU legislation.

☐ *The general principles of law*

All three Community Treaties charge the Court of Justice with the task of ensuring 'that in the interpretation and application of this Treaty the law is observed' (Article 164, EC; Article 136 Euratom; Article 31 ECSC). The implication of this, and of certain other Treaty articles (notably 173 and 215 EC), is that the Court need not regard written EU law as the only source of law to which it may refer.

In practice, this has meant that the Court, in making its judgements, has had regard to the general principles of law when they have been deemed to be relevant and to apply. Now, exactly what the general principles of law are, gives rise to controversy. Suffice to note here that principles which have been cited by the Court include proportionality (the means used to achieve a given end should be no more than is appropriate and necessary to achieve the end), non-discrimination (whether between nations, product sectors, firms, or individuals), adherence to legality, and respect for procedural rights. As for fundamental human rights, the Court has referred to them on several occasions: so, for example, in *Hauer* v. *Land Rheinland-Pfalz* (Case 44/79) the Court ruled that fundamental rights are an integral part of the general principles of law and the Court must ensure their observance.

☐ *Judicial interpretation*

Although case law has traditionally not played a major role as a source of law in most of the member states of the EU (the United Kingdom and Ireland are the main exceptions), the rulings of the Court of Justice have played an important part in shaping and making EU law. This stems partly from the Court's duty of ensuring that law is interpreted and applied correctly. It stems also from the fact that much of EU statute law is far from clear or complete.

The lack of precision in much of the EU's statute law arises from a number of factors: the relative newness of the EU and its constituent

Communities; the problems of the decision-making processes that so often lead to weak compromises and to avoidance of necessary secondary legislation; and the speed of change in some spheres of EU activity which makes it very difficult for the written law to keep abreast of developments. In many fields of apparent EU competence the Court thus has to issue judgements from a less than detailed statutory base. In the different types of cases that come before it – cases of first and only instance, cases of appeal, cases involving rulings on points of EU law that have been referred by national courts – the Court, therefore, inevitably and frequently goes well beyond merely giving a technical and grammatical interpretation of the written rules. It fills in the gaps in the law and, in so doing, it not only clarifies the law, but it creates new law. This is seen both in the way national courts are expected to – and generally do – respect its judgements, and in the way the Court has increasingly come to cite its own case law.

In short, the Court is, in effect, extending EU law through its interpretations and judgements.

■ The content of European Union law

The content of EU law is described at some length in Chapter 10, in the context of the examination that is presented there of EU policies. Attention here will, therefore, be confined to briefly noting some points of general significance.

The first point is that EU law does not range as widely as national law. It is not, for instance, directly concerned with criminal law or family law. Nor does it have much to do with policy areas such as education or health. What EU law is primarily concerned with – and, in this, it reflects the aims and the provisions of the Treaties – is economic activity. More particularly, EU law is strongly focused in the direction of the activities of the EC which, as set out in Article 3 of the EC Treaty, include

a common commercial policy . . . an internal market characterised by the abolition, as between Member States, of obstacles to the free movement of goods, persons, services and capital . . . a common policy in the spheres of agriculture and fisheries . . . a system ensuring that competition in the internal market is not distorted . . . the approximation of the laws of Member States to the extent required for the functioning of the common market . . . a policy in the sphere of the environment.

The second point is that no policy area, with the exception of the common commercial policy, contains a comprehensive code of EU law. Even in areas where there is a high degree of EU regulation, such as with the functioning of agricultural markets, national laws covering various matters still exist. As Figures 10.2 and 10.3 show, EU law thus sits side-by-side with national law, constituting an important part of the overall legal framework of member states in some policy spheres, being of only marginal significance in others.

The third point is that the range of EU law has broadened considerably over the years. Certainly, as already noted, EU law is primarily economic in character but less dominantly so than it was. A good illustration of this is seen in the considerable volume of EU environmental law that now exists, which deals with matters as diverse as air and water pollution, disposal of toxic wastes, and protection of endangered bird species. This expansion of EU law into an increasing number of policy areas has occurred, and is still occurring, for several reasons. Prominent amongst these reasons are: sectional interest pressures; increasing recognition of the benefits which can accrue in many fields of activity from joint action; and an increasing acceptance that the SEM can function smoothly, efficiently, and equitably only if there are common rules covering not just directly related market activities but also matters such as health and safety at work, entitlements to social welfare benefits, and mutual recognition of educational and professional qualifications.

■ The status of European Union law

In Case 6/64 *Costa* v. *ENEL* the Court of Justice stated:

> By creating a Community of unlimited duration, having its own institutions, its own personality, its own legal capacity of representation on the international plane and, more particularly, real powers stemming from limitation of sovereignty or a transfer of powers from the states to the Community, the Member States have limited their sovereign rights, albeit within limited fields, and have thus created a body of law which binds both their individuals and themselves.

EU law thus constitutes an autonomous legal system, imposing obligations and rights on both individuals and member states, and limiting the sovereignty of member states. There are three main pillars to this legal system: direct applicability, direct effect, and primacy.

□ *Direct applicability*

EU law is directly applicable where there is no need for any national measures to be taken in order for the law to have binding force within member states. Of the different statutory sources of EU law only regulations are always directly applicable. However, it has been established, principally via Court of Justice judgements, that other legal acts may also be directly applicable when their structure and content so allow and certain conditions are satisfied.

☐ *Direct effect*

This term refers to the principle whereby certain provisions of EU law may confer rights or impose obligations on individuals which national courts are bound to recognise and enforce. Having initially established the principle in 1963 in the case of *Van Gend en Loos* (Case 26/62), the Court, in a series of judgements, has gradually strengthened and extended the scope of direct effect so that it now applies to most secondary legislation except where discretion is explicitly granted to the addressee. Many of the provisions of the Treaties have also been established as having direct effect, although the Court has ruled that it does not apply in some important spheres, such as free movement of capital.

(Although the details of what is an extremely complicated legal debate cannot be rehearsed here, it should be noted that the distinction that has just been drawn between direct applicability and direct effect is not one that all lawyers accept. A consequence of this is that the terms have given rise to considerable confusion and much debate. Even official EU sources, including the Court itself, have not always used the terms consistently or with precision.)

☐ *Primacy*

Somewhat surprisingly, there is no explicit reference in the Treaties to the primacy or supremacy of EU law over national law. Clearly the principle is vital if the EU is to function properly, since if member states had the power to annul EU law by adopting, or giving precedence to, national law, then there could be no uniform or consistent EU legal order: states could apply national law when EU law was distasteful or inconvenient to them. The Court, therefore, from an early stage, took an active part in establishing the primacy of EU law. National courts, it has consistently asserted, must apply EU law in the event of any conflict, even if the domestic law is part of the national constitution. An example of Court statements on primacy may be taken from *Simmenthal* v. *Commission* (Case 92/78) where the Court concluded:

> Every national court must, in a case within its jurisdiction, apply Community law in its entirety and protect rights which the latter confers

on individuals and must accordingly set aside any provision of national law which may conflict with it, whether prior or subsequent to the Community rule.

In general, national courts have accepted this view of the Court and have given precedence to EU law. A few problems do still remain – notably in relation to fundamental rights guaranteed by national constitutions – but for the most part the authority and binding nature of EU law is fully established.

▌ Powers and responsibilities of the Court of Justice

The Court of Justice – which is based in Luxembourg and which must not be, though it often is, confused with the Strasbourg-based European Court of Human Rights – has two main functions. First, it is responsible for directly applying the law in certain types of cases. Second, it has a general responsibility for interpreting the provisions of EU law and, in so doing, it must attempt to ensure that the application of the law, which on a day-to-day basis is primarily the responsibility of national courts and agencies, is consistent and uniform.

Inevitably, for the reasons that were explained earlier, these duties result in the Court making what is, in effect, judicial law. This is most clearly seen in four respects.

First, as was noted above, the Court has clarified and strengthened the status of EU law. The landmark decisions of the 1960s and 1970s – such as *Van Gend en Loos* – were crucial in paving the way to the establishment of a strong legal system, but later decisions have also been important. For example, in its 1992 judgement in *Francovich and Bonifaci* v. *Italy* (Joined Cases 6/90 and 9/90) the Court ruled that individuals are entitled to financial compensation if they are adversely affected by the failure of a member state to transpose a directive within the prescribed period.

Second, EU policy competence has been strengthened and extended by Court judgements. Social security entitlements illustrate this. Most governments have not wished to do much more about entitlements than coordinate certain aspects of their social security systems. The Court, however, through a number of judgements, has played an important part in pushing the states in the direction of harmonising some of their practices – with regard to the rights of migrant workers for example. It has also extended the provisions of certain laws in ways the states did not envisage when they gave them their approval in the Council. Interestingly, in issuing judgements in social security cases, the Court has often used the EEC (now

EC) Treaty and not legislation as its legal base – because the Council can change legislation much more easily than it can the Treaty.

Another example of the Court strengthening and extending policy competence is seen in a judgement it gave in May 1990 in a preliminary ruling case. The case – *Barber* v. *Guardian Royal Exchange Assurance Group* (Case 262/88) – had been referred by the UK Court of Appeal. The Court of Justice ruled that occupational pensions are part of an employee's pay and must therefore comply with Article 119 of the EEC Treaty (unamended in the EC Treaty) which deals with equal pay for men and women. Regarding the particular issue that gave rise to the case, the Court stated that it was contrary to Article 119 to impose different age requirements for men and women as conditions for obtaining pensions on compulsory redundancy under a private pension scheme.

The area where the Court has exercised the greatest influence in strengthening and extending EU policy competence is in regard to the SEM. In some instances this has been a result of practices being ruled to be illegal by the Court, and in others it has been a consequence of Court judgements pressurising, enabling or forcing the Commission and the Council to act – as, for example, in de-regulating transport services.

Third, and of crucial importance in respect of the SEM, Court judgements have saved the EU the need to make law in existing areas of competence. A particularly influential judgement was issued in February 1979 in the *Cassis de Dijon* case (Case 120/78) which concerned the free circulation of the French blackcurrant liqueur. The Court ruled that national food standards legislation cannot be invoked to prevent trade between member states unless it is related to 'public health, fiscal supervision and the defence of the consumer'. The principle of 'mutual recognition' – whereby a product lawfully produced and marketed in one member state must be accepted in another member state – was thus established, with the result that the need for legislation to harmonise standards so as to facilitate trade was much reduced. Of course, the *Cassis de Dijon* judgement does not rule out challenges to the principle of 'mutual recognition' or to its application. For example, in the much publicised case *Commission* v. *Germany* (Case 178/84), the German Government attempted to protect its brewers by arguing that whereas their product was pure, most so-called foreign beers contained additives and needed to be excluded from the German market on health grounds. In March 1987 the Court upheld the 'mutual recognition' principle and ruled that a blanket ban on additives to beer was quite disproportionate to the health risk involved; the German insistence on its own definition of beer amounted to a barrier to trade. In a similar ruling in July 1988 (Case 407/85) the Court ruled against an Italian prohibition on the sale of pasta products which are not made (as all Italian pasta is) from durum (hard) wheat; the Court stated that the importation of German pasta – which is made from a mixture of hard and soft wheat – was not prejudicial to consumers' health, nor was its use misleading to consumers.

Fourth, the powers and functioning of the institutions have been clarified, and in important respects have been significantly affected, by the Court. Four judgements will be cited to illustrate this. (1) In October 1980, in the isoglucose case (Case 138/79), the Court ruled that the Council could not adopt legislation until it had received Parliament's opinion (see Chapter 7 for further consideration of this case). (2) In July 1986, in a case brought by the Council and supported by Germany, France and the United Kingdom against the Parliament (Case 34/86), the Court specified limitations on the EP's budgetary powers. (3) In October 1988, in the 'Wood Pulp' cases (Joined Cases 89, 104, 114–117, 125–129/85), the Court upheld and strengthened the power of Community institutions to take legal action against non-EC companies. (In this case the Commission had imposed fines on a number of American, Canadian and Finnish producers of wood pulp in respect of concerted practices which had affected selling prices in the Community. The Court ruled that the key factor in determining the Community's jurisdiction was not where companies were based, nor where any illegal agreements or practices were devised, but where illegalities were implemented.) (4) In 1992, in *Spain, Belgium and Italy* v. *Commission* (Joined Cases 271, 281, and 289/90) – which involved the liberalisation of the monopolistic telecommunications services market – the Court ruled that the Commission's powers in relation to competition policy under the EEC Treaty were not limited to surveilling rules already in existence, but extended to taking a pro-active role to break monopolies. The fact that the Council could have taken appropriate measures did not affect the Commission's competence to act.

In fulfilling its responsibilities the Court cannot itself initiate actions. It must wait for cases to be referred to it. This can happen in one of a number of ways, the most important of which are:

☐ *Failure to fulfil an obligation*

Under Articles 169 and 170 EC, the Court rules on whether member states have failed to fulfil obligations under the Treaty. Actions may be brought either by the Commission or by other member states. In either eventuality, the Commission must give the state(s) concerned an opportunity to submit observations and must then itself deliver a reasoned opinion. Only if this fails to produce proper compliance with EU law can the matter be referred to the Court of Justice.

In practice, failures to fulfil obligations are usually settled well before they are brought before the Court. When an action is brought the Commission is almost always the initiator. It is so partly because if a member state is behind the action it is obliged to refer the matter to the Commission in the first instance, and partly because member states are extremely reluctant to engage in direct public confrontations with one another (though they do sometimes try to encourage the Commission to, in effect, act on their behalf). Such cases in recent years have led to rulings against Italy that its duties on imported gin and sparkling wine were discriminatory, against the United Kingdom that it had taken insufficient national measures to give full effect to the 1976 directive on sexual discrimination, and against Belgium for failing to implement three directives which harmonise certain stock exchange rules. (See Table 8.1 for an indication of the volume of Court business under this and other headings.)

☐ Application for annulment

Under Article 173 EC, the Court of Justice 'shall review the legality of acts adopted jointly by the European Parliament and the Council, of acts of the Council, of the Commission and of the ECB, other than recommendations and opinions, and of acts of the European Parliament intended to produce legal effects *vis-à-vis* third parties'. The Court cannot conduct reviews on its own initiative but only when actions are brought by a member state, by the Council, by the Commission, or – where their prerogatives are concerned – by the EP and by the European Central Bank (when it is established). Reviews may be based on grounds of 'lack of competence, infringement of an essential procedural requirement, infringement of this Treaty or of any rule relating to its application, or misuse of powers'. If an action is well founded, the Court is empowered – under Article 174 – to declare the act concerned to be void.

An increasingly important aspect of Court activity under this heading arises in connection with the Treaty base(s) on which EU legislation is proposed and adopted. Following the SEA and the TEU there are now several procedures by which EU law can be made (see Chapter 11 for details), each of which is different in terms of such key matters as whether qualified majority voting rules apply in the Council and what are the powers of the EP. Which procedure applies in a particular case depends on the article(s) of the Treaty on which the law is based. So, for example, if a legislative proposal concerned with the competitiveness of industry in the internal market is based on Article 100a (EC) (approximation of laws – internal market), the co-decision procedure applies, which means that

Table 8.1 Cases brought before the European Court of Justice in 1993: analysed by type (EC Treaty)

			Proceedings brought under								Art.220		
	Art. 93(2)	Art. 169	Art. 173				Art. 175	Art. 177	Arts. 178 and 215	Art. 181	Conventions	Appeals	Total
			By governments	By Community institutions	By individuals	Total							
Actions brought	3	36	13	7	42	62	2	194	161	2	9	17	486
Cases not resulting in a judgement	–	22	6	1	1	8	–	29	–	–	–	2	61
Cases decided:	1	36	11	3	42	56	3	160	2	2	3	7	269
In favour of applicant	1	33	2	–	15	17	–	–	–	1	–	1	53
Dismissed on the merits	–	2	7	1	8	16	1	–	2	1	–	6	28
Rejected as inadmissible	–	–	2	2	19	23	2	–	–	–	–	–	25

Note: Types of proceedings covered by the Treaty articles are explained in the text of this book.

Source: XXVIIth General Report on the Activities of the European Communities: 1993.

qualified majority voting can be used in the Council and the EP has a potential veto over the proposal. If, however, it is brought forward on the basis of Article 130 (EC) (industry), unanimity applies in the Council and the EP's powers are weak. It thus naturally follows that if a legislative proposal is brought forward by the Commission on a legal base which the Council or the EP believe to be both damaging to their interests and legally questionable, and if political processes cannot bring about a satisfactory resolution to the matter, they may be tempted to appeal to the Court. Similarly, governments which find themselves outvoted on legislative proposals to which they are opposed may, if they think they have a case, appeal to the Court for the annulment of the legislative act on the grounds that the Commission should have used a legal base where unanimity was required. The Greek Government, for example, made such an application to the Court in respect of a regulation which was adopted in December 1987 which set the standards for maximum levels of radioactive contamination for agricultural goods imported into the Community. The Greek case rested on the claim that the regulation should not have been treated as falling under trade policy (where qualified majority voting rules apply), but as falling under environmental policy (where, prior to the TEU, unanimity was required for adoption). The Court did not agree with the Greek Government. In giving its judgement in May 1990 the Court ruled that the regulation concerned trade in goods and was therefore a trade policy regulation even if it did contain elements of environmental protection.

Article 173 also allows any 'natural or legal person' (that is to say, private individuals or companies) to institute proceedings for annulment, although only on a restricted basis. Rulings under this provision have tended to serve as useful underpinnings to some EU policies, notably competition policy, commercial policy, and the highly controlled and directed policies for steel that were pursued in the early 1980s and then again in the mid-1990s.

☐ The imposition of a penalty

In certain limited spheres of activity, notably competition policy, the Commission is empowered to impose financial penalties to ensure compliance with EU regulations. Under Article 172, the regulations may grant unlimited jurisdiction to the Court regarding the penalties. This means that aggrieved parties may appeal to the Court against Commission decisions and the penalties it has imposed. As such, this is another form of action for annulment. The Court may annul or confirm the decision and increase or decrease the penalties. In the great majority of judgements, the Commission's decisions are upheld.

The TEU gave to the Court, for the first time, powers to impose penalties on member states. Under Article 171 (EC), the Commission can initiate action against a state which it believes has not complied with a judgement of the Court in a case involving failure to fulfil an obligation under the Treaty. The first stages of the action involve giving the state concerned the opportunity to submit its observations, and issuing a reasoned opinion which specifies the points on which the state has not complied with the judgement of the Court and which also specifies a time limit for compliance. If the state does not comply with the reasoned opinion, the Commission may bring a case against the state before the Court. In so doing, the Commission must specify the amount of the lump sum or penalty payment to be paid by the member state concerned 'which it considers to be appropriate in the circumstances'. If the Court finds that the member state has indeed not complied with its judgement, it may impose a lump sum or penalty payment – with unlimited jurisdiction applying with regard to penalties.

☐ *Failure to act*

Under the three Community Treaties there are provisions, which vary in nature between the Treaties, for institutions to be taken before the Court for failure to act. So, under the EC Treaty, should the European Parliament, the Council or the Commission fail to act on a matter provided for by the Treaty, the member states, the institutions of the Community and, in restricted conditions, 'natural or legal persons', may initiate an action before the Court under Article 175 to have the infringement established. Such actions are not common, but one that attracted much attention was initiated by the Parliament, with the support of the Commission, against the Council in 1983. The case concerned the alleged failure of the Council to take action to establish a Common Transport Policy, despite the provision for such a policy in the EEC Treaty. The judgement, which was delivered in May 1985, was not what the Parliament or the Commission had hoped for. The Court ruled that whilst there was a duty for legislation to be produced, it had no power of enforcement because the Treaty did not set out a detailed timetable or an inventory for completion; it was incumbent upon the national governments to decide how best to proceed.

☐ *Action to establish liability*

'In the case of non-contractual liability, the Community shall, in accordance with the general principles common to the laws of the

Member States, make good any damage caused by its institutions or by its servants in the performance of their duties' (Article 215, EC). Under Article 178, the Court has exclusive jurisdiction to decide whether the Community is liable, and if so, whether it is bound to provide compensation.

This means that the Community may have actions brought against it on the grounds of it having committed an illegal act. The complex mechanisms of the CAP have produced by far the greatest number of such cases, threatening indeed to overwhelm the Court in the early 1970s. As a consequence the Court became increasingly unwilling to accept non-contractual liability cases, at least on the basis of first instance, and made it clear that they should be brought before national courts.

In the 1970s the Court also ruled that the circumstances in which the Community could incur non-contractual liability and be liable for damages were strictly limited. Of particular importance in this context were judgements in 1978 on two joined cases concerning skimmed milk (Cases 83 and 94/76 and 4, 15 and 40/77). Community legislation obliged the food industry to add skimmed milk to animal feed as part of an effort to reduce the surplus on powdered milk. A number of users challenged the legality of this, on the grounds that the Community's solution to dealing with the problem was discriminatory. In its first judgement, the Court ruled that the powdered milk regulations were, indeed, invalid because they did not spread the burden fairly across the agricultural sector. In its second judgement, however, it ruled that it was only exceptionally and in special circumstances, notably when a relevant body had manifestly and seriously exceeded its powers, that the Community should be liable to pay damages by virtue of a legislative measure of a political and economic character being found to be invalid.

□ Reference for a preliminary ruling

The types of cases referred to in the sections above are known as direct actions. That is to say, the Court is called upon to give a judgement in a dispute between two or more parties who bring their case directly before the Court. References for preliminary rulings are quite different, in that they do not involve the Court itself giving judgements in cases, but rather require it to give interpretations on points of EU law to enable national courts to give judgement in cases which they are hearing.

References are made under Article 177 (EC) which states that national courts may, and in some circumstances must, ask the Court to give a preliminary ruling where questions arise concerning the interpretation of the Treaty or the validity and interpretation of acts of the institutions of the Community. The Court cannot make a pronouncement on a case which happens to have come to its attention unless a reference has been made to it by the appropriate national court, and parties to a dispute have no power to insist on a reference or to object to one being made. It is the exclusive prerogative of the national court to apply for a preliminary ruling. Once a reference has been made, the Court is obliged to respond, but it can only do so on questions which have been put to it and it may not pronounce on, or even directly attempt to influence the outcome of, the principal action. Interpretations made by the Court during the course of preliminary rulings must be accepted and applied by the national court that has made the referral.

Preliminary rulings now constitute the largest category of cases that come before the Court. With only occasional dips, references have progressively increased: from 1 in 1961, to 32 in 1970, to 106 in 1979, to 194 in 1993. Preliminary rulings serve three principal functions. First, they help to ensure that national courts make legally 'correct' judgements. Second, because they are generally accepted by all national courts as setting a precedent, they promote the uniform interpretation and application of EU law in the member states. Third, they provide a valuable source of access to the Court for private individuals and undertakings who cannot directly appeal to it, either because there is no legal provision or because of inadequacy of funds.

☐ *The seeking of an opinion*

Under Article 228 EC, the Council, the Commission, or a member state may obtain the opinion of the Court on whether an international agreement that is envisaged is compatible with the provisions of the Treaty. Where the opinion of the Court is adverse, the agreement cannot enter into force without being suitably amended or without the Treaty being amended.

An opinion which created considerable publicity and difficulties was issued in December 1991 when the Court, after considering – at the Commission's request – the Agreement between the Community and the EFTA countries to establish the European Economic Area, issued opinion 1/91 declaring that the judicial review arrangements envisaged by the Agreement were incompatible with the EEC Treaty. This necessitated further Community–EFTA negotiations and a further reference to the Court when revisions had been agreed. The revisions were subsequently approved by the Court and the Agreement was finally signed, several months later than had been anticipated, in May 1992.

■ Membership and organisation of the Court

The Court consists of one judge from each member state, plus an extra judge when there is an even number of EU member states. Each judge is appointed for a six year term of office which may be, and frequently is, renewed. To ensure continuity turnover is staggered in three-yearly cycles.

According to the Community Treaties, judges are to be appointed 'by common accord of the Governments of the Member States' from amongst persons 'whose independence is beyond doubt and who possess the qualifications required for appointment to the highest judicial offices in their respective countries or who are juriconsults of recognised competence'. In practice, there is something of a gap, in spirit at least, between these Treaty provisions and reality. First, because each state is permitted one nomination that is automatically accepted, leaving only the extra judge, if there is one, to be appointed by a common accord. (Though see the Appendix, p. 446, for changed arrangements in appointing the extra judge when EFTA states accede to the EU.) Second, because in making their choices governments have tended not to worry too much about the judicial qualifications or experience of their nominations, but have looked rather for a good background in professional activities and public service. There is no evidence of 'political' appointments being made, in the way in which they are to the United States Supreme Court, but the fact is that soundness and safeness seem to be as important as judicial ability. At the time of his initial appointment the typical judge is a legally qualified 'man of affairs' who has been involved with government in his native country in some way, but who has, at best, served in a judicial capacity for only a limited period.

The judges elect one of their number to be President of the Court for a term of three years. His principal function is to see to the overall direction of the work of the Court by, for example, assigning cases to the Court's chambers, appointing judge-*rapporteurs* to cases, and setting schedules for cases. He is also empowered, on application from a party, to order the suspension of Community measures and to order such interim measures as he deems to be appropriate.

Assisting the judges in the exercise of their tasks are six advocates-general (to be increased to eight after EFTA state accessions). The duty of advocates-general is 'acting with complete impartiality and independence, to make, in open court, reasoned submissions on cases brought before the Court of Justice' (Article 166, EC). This means that an advocate-general, on being assigned to a case, must make a thorough examination of all the issues involved in the case, take account of all relevant law, and then present his conclusions to the Court. The conclusions are likely to include observations on the key points in the case, an assessment of EU law touching on the case, and a proposed legal solution.

In principle, advocates-general are appointed on the same Treaty terms and according to the same Treaty criteria as the judges. In practice, since not all states can claim an advocate-general, appointments are more genuinely collective than is the case with judges – but only up to a point, since the larger states have usually been able to ensure that they have one post each. (See the Appendix for new arrangements for the appointment of advocates-general following the accession of EFTA states.) At the same time, the judicial experience of advocates-general tends to be even more questionable than is that of the judges; certainly few have ever served in a judicial capacity in their own states.

In addition to the judges and the advocates-general, each of whom is assisted by two legal secretaries, the Court employs a staff of around 750. Most of these are engaged either in administrative duties – such as registering and transmitting case documents – or in providing language services.

The increasing number of cases coming before the Court – in the 1960s there were around 50 in an average year, today there are between 400 and 500 – has made it impossible for everything to be dealt with in plenary session. There has, therefore, been an increasing tendency for cases to be assigned to one of the Court's six chambers. In general, a matter is referred to a chamber of three judges if it is based upon relatively straightforward facts, raises no substantial points of principle, or where the circumstances are covered by existing case law. Cases involving complex findings of fact, or novel or important points of law, which do not require to be heard by the full Court, are assigned to a chamber of five judges.

Following amendments made by the TEU, the only circumstances in which the Court is required to sit in plenary session is 'when a Member State or a Community institution that is a party to the proceedings so requests' (Article 165, EC). In practice, the Court sometimes also chooses to sit in plenary session when cases are deemed to be especially important. A quorum for the plenary Court is seven judges.

■ The procedure of the Court

The procedure of the Court of Justice involves both written and oral stages. The former are more important, with cases being conducted largely away from the public eye via the communication of documents between interested parties and Court officials. Not much happens in open court.

Without going into all the details and possible variations, direct action cases proceed broadly along the following lines:

• Relevant documentation and evidence is assembled. The Court, under the direction of a duly appointed judge-*rapporteur*, may have to take a very proactive role in gathering the information that it needs and in soliciting the views of interested parties. This may involve holding a preparatory inquiry at which oral and documentary evidence is presented. (In preliminary ruling cases the procedure is very different: the national court making the reference should have provided with its submission a summary of the case and of all relevant facts, a statement of the legal problem, and the (abstract) question it wishes the Court to answer.)

• A public hearing is held at which the essentials of the case are outlined, at which the various parties are permitted to present their views orally, and at which the judges and advocates-general may question the parties' lawyers.

• Following the public hearing, the advocate-general appointed to the case examines it in detail. He and his staff look at all relevant EU law and then come to a decision that appears to them to be correct in legal terms. A few weeks after the public hearing the advocate-general presents his submission to an open session of the Court.

• Acting on the advocate-general's submission, and on the basis of a draft drawn up by the judge-*rapporteur*, the Court prepares its decision. Deliberations are in secret and decisions are made, where there is a disagreement, by majority vote (hence the need for an odd number of judges). Judgements must be signed by all the judges who have taken part in the proceedings and no dissenting opinions may be published. (In their oath of office members swear to preserve the secrecy of the deliberation of the Court.)

Three problems associated with the Court's proceedings ought to be mentioned. First, there is a lengthy gap between cases being lodged at the Court and final decisions: on average, about eighteen months for preliminary rulings and just over two years for direct actions. In special cases, however, interim judgements are issued and accelerated procedures are used. Second, lawyers' fees usually mean that going before the Court can be an expensive business, even though there is no charge for the actual proceedings in the Court itself. This does not, of course, place much of a restriction on the ability of member states or EU institutions to use the Court, but it can be a problem for individuals and small firms. There is a small legal aid fund, but it cannot remotely finance all potential applicants. Third, the use of majority voting, coupled with the lack of opportunity for dissenting opinions, has encouraged a tendency, which perhaps is inevitable given the different legal backgrounds of the judges, for judgements sometimes to be less than concise; occasionally even to be fudged.

■ The Court of First Instance

Under the SEA the Court was given an additional means of enabling it to deal more expeditiously and more effectively with its constantly expanding workload: the Council was empowered to establish, at the request of the Court, a Court of First Instance. Such a request was quickly made and in 1988 the Court of First Instance was established by Council Decision 88/ 591. The Court began to function in November 1989.

The Court is made up of one judge from each member state. The conditions of appointment and the terms of office of the judges are similar to those of the judges of the Court of Justice. Most of the work of the Court of First Instance is undertaken in one of five chambers, which have a membership of between three and five judges. Unlike in the Court of Justice, no advocates-general are appointed to the Court of First Instance. Where the exercise of the function of advocate-general is seen as being necessary – which it is not in all cases – the task is undertaken by one of the judges; the judge so designated cannot take part in the judgement of the case.

The jurisdiction of the Court of First Instance was initially limited to three areas: under Article 179 of the EC Treaty, disputes between the Community and its staff (79 of the 115 actions brought before the Court in 1992); actions brought against the Commission under the ECSC Treaty (no actions in 1992); and certain aspects of the competition rules (36 actions in 1992). However, in 1993 the Council of Ministers (General Affairs) agreed to give the Court jurisdiction to hear and determine at first instance all actions brought by natural or legal persons other than anti-dumping cases, on which a decision was deferred; jurisdiction in anti-dumping cases was agreed in February 1994. The June 1993 extension of the Court's jurisdiction did not extend to preliminary rulings under Article 177 EC. (See Table 8.2 for a list of cases brought before the Court in 1993.)

All decisions of the Court of First Instance are subject to appeal to the Court of Justice on points of law.

Table 8.2 Cases brought before the Court of First Instance in 1993: *analysed by type (EC Treaty)*

	Proceedings brought under					Costs	Total
	Art. 173 (individuals)	Art. 175 (individuals)	Art. 178 and 215	Art. 179	Art. 181		
Actions brought	89	3	412	83	–	–	587
Cases not resulting in a judgment	8	1	–	16	–	–	25
Cases decided:	10	1	–	64	–	1	76
In favour of applicant	1	–	–	17	–	1	19
Dismissed on the merits	2	–	–	28	–	–	30
Rejected as inadmissible	7	1	–	19	–	–	27

Note: Types of proceedings covered by the Treaty articles are explained in the text of this book.

Source: XXVIIth *General Report on the Activities of the European Communities: 1993.*

■ Concluding comments

The legal framework described in the previous pages constitutes the single most important feature distinguishing the EU from other international organisations. The member states do not just cooperate with one another on an intergovernmental basis but have developed common laws designed to promote uniformity. The claim to legal supremacy in the interpretation, application and adjudication of these laws constitutes a central element of the supranational character of the EU.

This has necessarily involved the member states in surrendering some of their sovereignty since they are obliged to submit to a legal system over which they have only partial control and, as a corollary, their governments are sometimes prevented from introducing national laws they themselves desire.

The Court of Justice has played, and continues to play, an extremely important part in establishing the EU's legal order. Ensuring that EU law is interpreted in a uniform manner is the most obvious way in which it does this. But whether it is acting as an international court, a court of review, a court of appeal, or a court of referral (roles which, in practice, greatly overlap) the Court is also frequently a maker of law as well as an interpreter of law. Of course, judges everywhere help to shape the law, but this is especially so in the EU where the Court has had much more manoeuvrability available to it than is customary within states. It has used this potential to considerable effect: to help clarify relations between the institutions and between the institutions and the member states; to help determine, clarify and extend policy content in many different spheres; and to help develop and foster the *esprit communautaire*.

■ *Chapter 9* ■

Other Institutions and Actors

■ The Economic and Social Committee

☐ *Origins*

In the negotiations which led to the Rome Treaties it was decided to establish a consultative body comprised of representatives of socio-economic interests.

There were four principal reasons for this decision. First, five of the six founding states – West Germany was the exception – had such bodies in their own national systems. The main role of these bodies was to provide a forum in which sectional interests could express their views, and in so doing could supplement the popular will as expressed via parliaments. Second, the essentially economic nature of the Community meant that sectional interests would be directly affected by policy developments and would be key participants in, and determiners of, the development of integration. Third, it was not thought that the Assembly (as the EP was then called) would be an effective forum for the expression of sectional views. Fourth, the institutional framework of the Rome Treaties was based on the Treaty of Paris model, and that had provided for a socio-economic advisory body in the ECSC Consultative Committee.

Accordingly, the EEC and Euratom Treaties provided for a common Economic and Social Committee (ESC). It was to have an advisory role and it was to be made up of representatives of various types of economic and social activity.

☐ *Membership*

Since the 1986 Community enlargement the ESC has had 189 members. These are drawn from the member states as follows:

Belgium	12	Italy	24
Denmark	9	Luxembourg	6
France	24	Netherlands	12
Germany	24	Portugal	12
Greece	12	Spain	21
Ireland	9	United Kingdom	24

Arrangements for the composition of the ESC in the event of accessions by EFTA states are set out in the Appendix (p. 446).

Members of the Committee are proposed by national governments and are formally appointed by the Council of Ministers. The term of office lasts for four years, which may be renewed.

To ensure that a broad spectrum of interests and views are represented, the membership is divided into three, more or less equally sized, groups. Each national complement of members is supposed to reflect this tripartite division. The three groups are:

☐ *Group I – Employers.* Just less than half of this group are drawn from industry. The rest are mostly from public enterprises, commercial organisations, banks, insurance and so forth.

☐ *Group II – Workers.* The great majority in this group are members of national trade unions.

☐ *Group III – Various interests.* About half of this group are associated either with agriculture, small and medium-sized businesses, or the professions. The rest are mostly involved with public agencies and local authorities, consumer groups, environmental protection organisations etc.

All members are appointed in a personal capacity and not as delegates of organisations. However, since most members are closely associated with, or are employees of, national interest organisations (organisations that are, in many cases, affiliated to Euro-organisations) it is inevitable that they do tend to act as representatives of, and spokesmen for, a cause.

The administrative support for the Committee is provided by a Secretariat which employs a staff of around 520, more than a third of whom are engaged in language work.

☐ *Organisation*

The Committee elects a Chairman and a Bureau from amongst its members, each for a term of two years. The main responsibility of the

Chairman is to act as the ESC's principal representative in relations with other EU institutions, member states, and non-EU organisations and states. The Bureau, which has 30 members – the President, two Vice-Presidents, and nine members from each group – assists with outside relations and is also responsible for the general organisation of the Committee's work.

The groups operate in a somewhat similar fashion to the political groups in the EP. That is to say, they meet on a regular basis – there is a total of around 90 group meetings per year – to review matters of common concern, to discuss their work, and (particularly in the more cohesive groups I and II) to attempt to agree voting positions on proposals and issues that are due to be considered in plenary sessions. Group representatives in sections and study groups (see below) also sometimes meet together to coordinate their activities.

Most of the work of the ESC consists of giving opinions on EU-related matters. In a manner similar to the way in which the detailed work on opinions in the EP is undertaken by committees, so in the ESC it is undertaken by sections, each of which draws its membership from the groups. There are nine sections:

Agriculture and Fisheries

Industry, Commerce, Crafts and Services

Economic, Financial and Monetary Questions

Social, Family, Educational and Cultural Affairs

Transport and Communications

External Relations, Trade and Development Policy

Energy, Nuclear Questions, and Research

Regional Development and Town and Country Planning

Protection of the Environment, Public Health and Consumer Affairs

The sections appoint *rapporteurs* to prepare draft opinions on their behalf. How *rapporteurs* go about this depends on circumstances and preferences. Usually use is made of a sub-committee or a study group; assistance may be called for from the ESC Secretariat – though resources for this purpose are thin; and – a common occurrence – help may be sought, or be offered from, Euro or national sectional interests. In the sections an attempt is usually made to develop a common position on opinions, though on controversial issues this is not always possible to achieve. In an average year there are usually around 70–80 section meetings and some 300 meetings of sub-committees and study groups. (In addition, there are 300–400 miscellaneous meetings and meetings sponsored by the three groups. Many of these are concerned in some way with the preparation of opinions.)

Plenary meetings are held in Brussels, over a two-day period, usually nine or ten times a year. Agendas are dominated by consideration of reports from the sections. The standard procedure for dealing with reports is for each to be introduced by its *rapporteur*, for a debate to be held, and for a vote to be taken. On uncontroversial items the vote may be taken without discussion or debate.

□ *Functions*

The ESC engages in a number of activities:

(1)   It issues information reports on matters of contemporary interest and concern.

(2)   It liaises, via delegations, with a host of other international bodies and groupings.

(3)   It seeks to promote understanding between sectional interests by, for example, organising conferences, convening meetings, and being represented at congresses and symposia.

(4)   It seeks to take advantage of various contacts it has with other EU institutions to press its views. The most regularised of these contacts is with the Commission: Commission officials, and sometimes Commissioners themselves, attend plenaries and meetings of sections. Occasionally ministers address plenaries.

(5)   Above all, as noted above, it issues opinions on a range of EU matters. Opinions are issued in one of three sets of circumstances:

● *Mandatory referral.* Under Article 198 (EC) and Article 170 (Euratom) 'The Committee must be consulted by the Council or by the Commission where this Treaty so provides'. Compared with the EP there are not so many policy areas where the Treaties do so provide, but extensions made by the SEA and the TEU have resulted in most important policy areas now being subject to ESC mandatory referral. So, under the EC Treaty, amongst the policy spheres on which the ESC must be consulted are agriculture, freedom of movement of workers, internal market issues, economic and social cohesion, social policy and the European Social Fund (ESF), regional policy and the European Regional Development Fund (ERDF), the environment, and research and technological development. Under the Euratom Treaty the Committee has to be consulted on such matters as research and training programmes, health and safety, and investment.

● *Optional consultation.* The Committee may be consulted by the Council or the Commission 'in all cases in which they consider it appropriate' (Article 198, EC; Article 170, Euratom). Until the entry into force of the SEA some 80 per cent of ESC opinions were based on optional consultation. With the widening of the scope of mandatory referral this figure has fallen to around 60 per cent.

• *Own initiatives*. Following pressure over a long period, the 1972 summit of Community leaders granted the ESC the right to issue opinions on its own initiative. It can, in theory, thus pronounce on almost any matter it wishes, other than those which fall under the ECSC.

The reason for the exclusion of the ESC from ECSC matters is, as noted above, that the ECSC has a separate Consultative Committee. With 96 members – who are divided into three equal groups of producers, workers, consumers and dealers – the Consultative Committee performs similar functions for the ECSC as does the ESC for the EEC and Euratom. The Consultative Committee meets about six times a year.

The ESC normally issues 150–180 consultative documents per year, of which the vast majority are opinions on Commission proposals and communications, 10–15 are own initiative opinions, and 3–4 are information reports. Amongst the 1992 opinions on Commission proposals were ones on the reform of the CAP, farm prices, collective redundancies, fair pay, and participation in company profits. (Exhibit 9.1 is a typical example of an ESC opinion on a Commission proposal for a Council directive.) Own initiative reports in 1992 included ones on economic and social cohesion, adoption, the citizen's Europe, and economic cooperation with the Maghreb countries.

A point of contrast worth noting between ESC and EP opinions is that the ESC is not as concerned as the EP to reach a single position which excludes all minority views. It is quite possible for minority positions to be attached as annexes to ESC opinions which have received majority support in the plenary.

□ *Influence*

The influence exercised by the ESC on EU policy and decision-making is limited. Evidence of this is seen, for example, in the follow-up reports to ESC opinions which the Commission produces: these tend to include relatively few unambiguous acceptances of ESC recommendations, but include many evasive comments along the lines 'The Commission has taken note of the ESC opinion' or 'The opinion will be useful to the

> ## Exhibit 9.1
> ### An opinion of the Economic and Social Committee
>
> Opinion on the proposal for a Council Directive amending for the fourteenth time Directive 76/769/EEC on the approximation of the laws, regulations and administrative provisions of the Member States relating to restrictions on the marketing and use of certain dangerous substances and preparations([1]) (93/C 304/02)
>
> On 17 May 1993 the Council decided to consult the Economic and Social Committee, under Article 100 A of the Treaty establishing the European Economic Community, on the above mentioned proposal.
>
> The Section for Protection of the Environment, Public Health and Consumer Affairs, which was responsible for preparing the Committee's work on the subject, adopted its Opinion on 9 July 1993. The Rapporteur was Mr Beltrami.
>
> At its 308th Plenary Sessuion (meeting of 22 September 1993), the Economic and Social Committee adopted the following Opinion unanimously.
>
> 1. The Committee approves the proposal to amend for the fourteenth time Annex I to Directive 76/769/EEC.
>
> 2. The Committee endorses the purpose of the amendment, which is to harmonize restrictions on the marketing and use of certain personal items containing nickel, thus avoiding the creation of barriers to trade and ensuring a high level of consumer protection.
>
> 3. The aim is to ensure that people who come into 'direct and prolonged contact' with articles of jewellery and other personal items containing nickel do not become sensitized to nickel and suffer allergic reactions.
>
> 4. The Committee notes with approval that the test methods for checking conformity with the essential requirements [being drawn up by the European Committee for Standardisation (CEN)] will be the subject of a European standard which is to be incorporated in an annex to the proposed Directive. This should ensure that checks and evaluations are uniform.
>
> 5. Since test methods already exist for points 1 and 2 of Annex I but not for point 3, the Committee recommends that Member States should not be required to apply the provisions of point 3 until the CEN has devised an appropriate test method. This should take the form of a European standard based on the experience acquired in certain Member States and on dermatologists' findings.
>
> 6. Lastly, the Committee calls on the Member States to take steps to ensure that the Directive's provisions are respected by all links in the distribution chain, including the importer and retailer, and that consumers are properly informed about the risks of sensitization.
>
> Done at Brussels, 22 September 1993.
>
> ---
> ([1]) OJ No C 116, 27. 4. 1993, p. 18.
>
> *The Chairman*
> *of the Economic and Social Committee*
> *Susanne TIEMANN*

Source: *Official Journal of the European Communities*, C304, Vol.36 (10 November 1993).

Commission staff in their exchanges of views with the Council'. Such ESC recommendations as are taken up usually cover relatively minor points and, in any event, are often as much a consequence of pressure that is exerted by other institutions and interests as by ESC pronouncements (this point is discussed further in Chapter 11).

There are a number of reasons why the ESC is in a relatively weak position to exercise power. First, the Council and the Commission are not obliged to act upon its views. This also, of course, applies to the EP outside of the co-decision procedure, but at least in its case it *has* to be consulted on *most* important proposals, its opinion *must* be delivered before proposals can be given legislative effect, and delaying powers are available to strengthen its bargaining position. The ESC is not so well placed: the range of issues on which consultation is mandatory is more restricted; the deliverance of its opinion is often therefore not necessary for further progress; and even when its opinion is required it can be made subject to a timetable that is so tight as not to allow sufficient time for a considered response – the Council and the Commission can, if they consider it necessary, set a time limit as short as one month for the submission of an ESC opinion.

The second weakness follows on from this last point: it is by no means uncommon for proposals to be referred to the ESC at a stage of policy advancement when agreements between the key decision-makers have already been made in principle and are difficult to unscramble.

Third, the ESC is not the only, and in many circumstances is not even the most important, channel available to sectional interests wishing to exert pressure on EU decision-makers. Direct access to Council representatives and to Commission officials, and representation in advisory committees, is seen by many as being more useful than activity in the ESC – not least because these other channels often offer greater opportunities than does the ESC for influencing policy proposals at the pre-proposal stage.

Finally, members of the ESC serve only on a part-time basis and are, therefore, very limited in what they can do. In addition, the fact that they serve – in theory at least – in a personal rather than a representational capacity means that there are rarely any very strong reasons why the Commission or the Council should listen to them if they do not wish to do so.

The ESC is perhaps best thought of as a functional complement to the EP. It should not, however, be thought of as being in any significant way comparable to the EP, for it simply does not have anything like the same degree of capacity, influence or power.

What the ESC basically does is two things. First, it provides a useful forum in which representatives of sectional interests can come together on a largely cooperative basis to exchange views and ideas. Second, it is a consultative organ that gives some limited – but in most cases only very limited – opportunities for interests to influence EU policy and decision-making.

■ The Committee of the Regions

□ *Origins*

Regionalism, regional issues, and regional politics have come to assume a not insignificant role and importance in the EU. The main factors accounting for this are as follows:

- There are considerable variations in wealth and income in the EU between member states and between regions of member states. In the mid-1990s the ten most prosperous regions, headed by Groningen in the Netherlands and Hamburg in Germany, were three times as rich and were investing three times as much in their basic economic fabric as the ten poorest regions in Greece and Portugal. Such disparities have long produced pressures for compensatory and rectifying measures to be taken at EU level, and these pressures have increased since the SEM programme was launched in the mid-1980s.
- Since the ERDF was established in 1975, regional and local groupings have had a clear focus for their attention at EU level: attraction of funds. The Commission has encouraged sub-national levels of government to play a full part in ERDF management, especially since the launching of its partnership programme under the 1988 reform of the Structural Funds.
- Partly in consequence of the financial opportunities offered by the ERDF and other funds, but partly too because they do not wish to be wholly controlled by their national governments, many sub-national levels of government have established direct lines of communication with decision-makers in Brussels. In those states where sub-national levels of government have strong constitutional positions – most obviously Germany with its quasi-federal system – it is customary for the regional governments to have their own offices in Brussels.
- Over the years several transnational organisations bringing together sub-national levels of government in different member states have been established to promote common interests and, where appropriate, to make representations and to seek to exert pressure at EU level. These organisations include the Association of European Border Regions, the

Assembly of European Regions, the Association of Regions of Traditional Industry, and the Association of Frontier Regions.

In response to this developing regional dimension of Community affairs, the Commission established in 1988 the Consultative Council of Regional and Local Authorities. For some governments, notably the German and Belgian, the Consultative Council did not go far enough and they took advantage of the 1990–1 IGC on Political Union to press the case for a stronger body to be established. Differing views were expressed in the IGC – with France, Spain and the UK putting up some resistance to the creation of a new body – but it was eventually agreed to establish, as part of the EC Treaty, a Committee of the Regions (COR).

☐ *Membership, organisation, functions and powers*

The size and national composition of the *membership* of the COR is the same as that of the ESC: a total of 189 members, with the 'big four' states each having 24 members, Spain having 21, Belgium, Greece, the Netherlands and Portugal each having 12, Denmark and Ireland each having 9, and Luxembourg having 6. (See the Appendix, p. 446, for the composition of the COR after EU enlargement to EFTA states.) The members are appointed for a four year term of office, which is renewable, by the Council of Ministers on proposals from the member states.

As to the qualities and characteristics of the COR's members, the EC Treaty simply states the Committee shall consist of 'representatives of regional and local bodies' (Article 198a). The implications of the lack of insistence in the Treaty that members should be *elected* representatives on regional and local bodies led to considerable debate in some member states but, in the event, virtually all of those who were nominated to the first four year term of the Committee – covering the years 1994–7 – were elected representatives of sub-national levels of government of some kind. Those countries with clear regional structures – Belgium, France, Germany, Italy, the Netherlands and Spain – allocated at least half of their places to regional representatives. The more centralised countries mostly sent representatives from local councils and authorities. In all, when the COR met for the first time in March 1994, 93 of its members were regional representatives and 96 were local representatives.

The *organisation* of the Committee will take some time to settle down, but it will generally resemble that of the ESC. That is to say, plenary sessions will take final decisions, but the work of plenaries will be prepared by specialised committees and groups.

The Committee shares the administrative services of the ESC.

The *functions and powers* of the Committee are, like those of the ESC, of an advisory nature. The key Treaty references to what the COR can do are set out in Article 198c (EC):

> The Committee of the Regions shall be consulted by the Council or by the Commission where this Treaty so provides and in all other cases in which one of these two institutions considers it appropriate . . .
>
> Where the Economic and Social Committee is consulted . . . the Committee of the Regions shall be informed by the Council or the Commission of the request for an opinion. Where it considers that specific regional interests are involved, the Committee of the Regions may issue an opinion on the matter.
>
> It may issue an opinion on its own initiative in cases in which it considers such action appropriate.

Further to the first paragraph of Article 198c, the Treaty does 'so provide' for consultation of the Committee in respect of: education, training and youth; economic and social cohesion – specific actions; aims and rules of the Structural Funds; implementing decisions of the ERDF; trans-European networks – guidelines and implementation; public health; and culture.

As they can with the ESC, the Council or the Commission can set a time limit on the COR, which can be as short as one month, for the delivery of its opinion. Upon expiry of the time limit, the absence of an opinion cannot prevent the Council or the Commission proceeding.

It will be some time before a proper assessment of the influence of the COR will be possible. The likelihood is, however, that within the spheres of its competence, and especially where mandatory consultation applies, its position will be at least comparable with that of the ESC. Many of the COR's members are experienced politicians at regional and local level and will doubtless press hard to ensure that the Committee is not confined to the role, which some governments would like to see, of a marginal sounding board.

■ The European Investment Bank

The European Investment Bank (EIB) was created in 1958 under the EEC Treaty. Its members are the member states of the EU. The Bank is located in Luxembourg.

☐ *Responsibilities and functions*

Under the TEU, the responsibilities and functions of the EIB are referred to in several articles of the EC Treaty. Article 198e is especially important: it sets out the task of the Bank as being to contribute, on a non-profit making basis, via the granting of loans and the giving of guarantees, to the 'balanced and steady development of the common market in the interests of the Community'. What this means, in practice, is that the Bank's main job is to act as a source of investment finance for projects which further certain EU goals. In so doing, it is by far the largest provider of EU loan finance. In 1993 Bank lending totalled 19.6 billion Ecu. Around 90 per cent of EIB loans are for projects within the member states and the remainder for projects outside. The latter mainly involves the Bank in operations in Eastern and Central Europe, the Mediterranean countries, and the ACP states which are linked with the EU via the Lomé Convention.

In respect of the loans which are made within the EU, two main conditions have to be satisfied for the Bank to consider providing finance. First, projects must comply with the policy objectives laid down in Article 198e and with credit directives from the Bank's Board of Governors. These objectives are interpreted fairly broadly but at least one of the following criteria normally has to be met:

(1) Projects must further economic and social cohesion by contributing to the economic development of the EU's less prosperous regions. Around two-thirds of loans are now used for regional development purposes and for aiding the EU's poorest areas. This finance is used primarily to assist with communications and other infrastructure, the productive sector, and capital spending on energy installations.

(2) Projects must involve modernisation and must contribute to the competitiveness of EU industry. Under this heading, particular support is given to the introduction and development of advanced technology, and to the integration of industry at a European level.

(3) Projects must be of common interest to several member states or to the EU as a whole. In this connection, major transport and telecommunications developments and the EU's energy objectives are given a high priority. The EU's environmental policies also receive considerable support – with around half of the 'environmental loans' being made available to the water sector (catchment, treatment and supply), and the rest going to projects dealing with such problems as atmospheric pollution, waste management, land conservation, and urban improvement.

Second, projects must be financially and technically viable, and loans must be guaranteed by adequate security. This is because although the EIB is not a profit-making body it is not a loss-making one either: apart from in certain specified and strictly limited circumstances, the Bank's loans are not subsidised from the EU budget but must be financed from the Bank's own capital. This capital comes from two sources: paid in or due to be paid in capital by the member states, and borrowing – in the EIB's own name and on its own credit – on capital markets inside and outside the EU. Of these two sources, borrowing is by far the largest element, and since the sums raised must be repaid from the Bank's own financial operations the Bank must take appropriate steps to protect itself.

A major attraction for potential EIB borrowers is that loans are offered at very competitive rates. They are so because the Bank enjoys a first class international credit-rating and is thus itself able to borrow at favourable rates, and also because the bank is not profit-making and is thus able to pass on its favourable rates. Other advantages of EIB loans are that they are generally made available at fixed interest rates, repayments can often be deferred for the first two or three years, and the repayment periods are usually medium- to long-term (between five and twelve years for industrial projects and up to twenty years or more for infrastructure projects).

Two other features of EIB loans are also worth noting. First, the Bank does not usually lend more than 50 per cent of the investment cost of a project (though see below for special arrangements under 'the Edinburgh facility'). Borrowers need to find additional sources of loan finance, with the consequence that the Bank very frequently operates on a co-financing basis with other banks. Second, the Bank generally only deals directly with large loans – of more than about 10m Ecu. This does not, however, mean that only large-scale investment is supported because, mainly via its global loan facility, the Bank opens lines of credit to intermediary institutions – such as regional development agencies and, more commonly, national financial institutions – which then lend the money on in smaller amounts. Global loans account for around 25 per cent of total EIB lending and are directed principally towards small and medium-sized enterprises (SMEs). An administrative problem with global loans is that the intermediary agencies which act on the EIB's behalf, and which are delegated responsibility for appraising applications and negotiating with potential borrowers on the basis of the EIB's lending criteria, tend sometimes to make their decisions according to traditional banking criteria and not with much of an eye to EU objectives.

In addition to the activities which have just been described – which may be thought of as the Bank's 'standard' activities – certain other activities should also be mentioned:

• The Commission also borrows funds on capital markets in connection with certain ECSC and Euratom activities. The Commission decides on the granting of loans, and the Bank is responsible for financial appraisal and management.

• Some projects are eligible for both EIB loan finance and for EU grant aid. Where this is the case – and it applies mainly in connection with the European Regional Development Fund (ERDF) and the Cohesion Fund – the Bank works closely with other interested parties, especially the Commission, to work out appropriate financial arrangements.

• As part of a series of measures designed to promote economic recovery in Europe, the European Council at its meeting in Edinburgh in December 1992 authorised a new lending facility of 5 billion Ecu within the EIB. The purpose of this 'Edinburgh facility' is primarily to accelerate the financing of capital infrastructure projects, notably those connected with trans-European networks of transport, telecommunications, and energy. For projects financed by this facility the normal ceiling on loans is raised from 50 per cent to 75 per cent and the combined ceiling on loans and grants from 70 per cent to 90 per cent. The June 1993 Copenhagen summit raised the lending facility by 3 billion Ecu: a further 2 billion for trans-European networks and 1 billion Ecu for SMEs.

• The Edinburgh European Council also laid the foundations for a European Investment Fund (EIF) which was given as its purpose the provision of guarantees for loans intended to finance projects of common European interest and also projects promoted by SMEs. The Fund, which was scheduled to be operational from mid-1994, has a subscribed capital of 2 billion Ecu – 40 per cent provided by the EIB, 30 per cent by other EU sources (channelled through the Commission), and 30 per cent by public and private banks. The EIF has its own administrative and decision-making structure within the Bank.

☐ *Organisation*

The Bank's main decision-making bodies are as follows:

The *Board of Governors* decides on the Bank's subscribed capital and lays down general directives on the Bank's activities. It is also responsible for formally appointing members of the Board of Directors and the Management Committee. The Board of Governors is composed of one minister per member state – usually the Minister of Finance – and normally meets once a year. Certain major decisions of the Board have to be made unanimously, others can be made by a majority of members representing at least 45 per cent of subscribed capital.

The *Board of Directors* has a general responsibility for ensuring that the Bank is managed according to the provisions of the EC Treaty, the Bank's Statute, and directives issued by the Governors. More specifically, the Board has sole responsibility for deciding on loans and guarantees, raising funds, and fixing interest rates. There are 22 Directors: 21 are nominated by the member states and are senior figures in national financial institutions or national Ministries of Finance/Economics/Industry; one is nominated by the Commission. The Board of Directors normally meets every four to six weeks.

The *Management Committee* controls current operations, makes recommendations to the Board of Directors and is responsible for implementing decisions made by the Directors. The Committee is a full-time body consisting of the Bank's President and six Vice-Presidents. It meets at least weekly.

Supporting, and operating under, these decision-making bodies is the EIB's administration. This is divided into seven Directorates: General Administration; Operations in the Community 1; Operations in the Community 2; Operations Outside the Community; Finance and Treasury; Research; and Legal. There is also a Technical Advisory Service. In all, the EIB employs around 800 staff.

☐ Concluding comments

The EIB is a bank, not a grant-dispensing body. This means that it must observe certain basic banking principles. At the same time, however, it is an EU institution charged with furthering a number of policy objectives. These two roles – of banker and EU institution – do not always sit easily together.

The scale of EIB borrowing and lending is small when compared with the total operations of commercial banks across the member states. The role of the Bank should not, however, be underestimated. Indeed, it is the largest international financial institution on capital markets, and within the EU it is an important source of finance for capital investment. Between 1989 and 1993 it lent a total of 73 billion Ecu for projects in member states. In 1993 alone, EIB financing within the EU helped to support, on the basis of an average 30 per cent coverage of total costs, overall investment estimated at 52 billion Ecu, which corresponds to about 5 per cent of aggregate gross fixed capital formation. This percentage was naturally much higher in those lower income countries and regions where EIB loans are concentrated – Portugal, Greece, Spain, Ireland, and southern Italy.

The EIB thus acts as a useful source of medium and long-term finance for EU-oriented projects. It complements other public and private funding resources for the promotion of capital investment projects that, in general terms, promote economic development and further integration within the Union.

■ The Court of Auditors

The 1975 *Treaty amending Certain Financial Provisions of the Treaties . . . ,* which entered into force in 1977, replaced the then two existing Community audit bodies – the Audit Board of the EEC and Euratom and the ECSC Auditor – with a single Court of Auditors. The TEU enhanced the Court's standing by raising it, in Article 4 of the EC Treaty, to the rank of a fully fledged Community institution. The Court is based in Luxembourg.

□ *Membership and organisation*

There are as many members of the Court as there are EU states. Each member is appointed by a unanimous vote of the Council of Ministers on the basis of one nomination per member state and after there have been consultations with the EP. At its November 1989 part-session the EP, for the first time, voted to reject nominations – one made by France and one by Greece. The EP vote was not binding on the Council, but France nonetheless submitted a new name. Greece claimed it had difficulties in finding a suitable alternative candidate so the EP decided, at the following December part-session, to accept both appointments in order to enable both posts to be filled by the new year.

At the time of their appointment, members of the Court must belong to, or have belonged to, an external audit body in their own country, or be persons who are appropriately qualified in some other capacity. Appointment is for a six year period, which may be renewed. As with other 'non-political' EU bodies, a condition of appointment is that the members will act in the general interest and will be completely independent in the performance of their duties.

The members elect one of their number to be the President of the Court. His term of office is for three years and is renewable. The President sees to the general efficient running of the Court and also represents it in its external relations.

Members are assigned a specific sector of activity for which they hold a particular responsibility regarding the preparation and implementation of the decisions of the Court. Each sector falls under one of three audit groups which act primarily as coordinating agencies and filters for plenary sessions of the whole Court. All important decisions are taken in plenaries, by majority vote if need be.

As with several other EU institutions, the administration supporting the Court is rather small in size given the potential importance of the work to be done. In 1993 there were just over 400 people employed by the Court, of whom around 250 were directly engaged in audit duties, 70 were in the language service, and 80 were in administrative departments. Inevitably such modest staffing resources greatly restricts the number of things the Court can attempt to do.

☐   *Activities of the Court*

The task of the Court is to examine the accounts of all revenue and expenditure of the Communities and of bodies set up by the Communities insofar as the relevant legal instruments do not preclude such examination. In exercising this responsibility the Court engages in two main types of activity.

The first is to carry out annual audits to see whether revenue has been received and expenditure has been incurred in a lawful and regular manner, and also to examine whether the financial management of EU authorities has been sound. The auditing powers of the Court cover the general budget of the EU, plus certain financial operations that are not included in the budget such as borrowing and lending facilities of the ECSC and aid to developing countries that is financed by national contributions.

The auditing of the general budget, which is the Court's most important single task, and the related process of granting a discharge to the Commission on its implementation of the budget, proceed as follows:

● The Commission is required to draw up, for each financial year, accounts relating to the implementation of the budget, a financial statement of the assets and liabilities of the EU, and an analysis of the financial year. The main responsibility for collecting and presenting this information (the internal audit) lies with DGXX (Financial Control). The documentation must be forwarded to the Council, the EP, and the Court of Auditors by no later than 1 June of the following financial year.
● The Court undertakes its audit (the external audit) partly on the basis of an examination of the Commission documentation and partly on the

basis of its own independent investigations. The latter, which begin before the Commission documentation arrives, involve examining records supplied by, and requested from, EU institutions and member states (which in the latter case means liaising closely with national audit bodies and appropriate national agencies) and also, where necessary, carrying out on-the-spot investigations. The purpose of this Court audit is not to replicate what has already been covered by the internal audit, but rather to add an extra dimension to the EU's overall auditory control by examining the adequacy of internal procedures – particularly with regard to their ability to identify significant irregular and unlawful transactions and to properly evaluate the extent to which correct financial management (in terms of economy, efficiency and effectiveness) is being practised. By 15 July, the Court transmits to all relevant institutions any comments which it proposes to include in its annual report to which it believes there should be, or there may wish to be, a reply. After the receipt of replies, which must be submitted by 31 October, the Court adopts the final version of its annual report. This has to be communicated to the EU's other institutions by 30 November.

• The EP, acting on a recommendation of the Council, is supposed to give discharge to the Commission in respect of the implementation of the budget by 30 April of the following year. To this end, the EP's Budgetary Control Committee examines all relevant documentation, particularly that produced by the Court of Auditors. Normally, discharge is given by the due date, but not always. In 1987, for example, dissatisfaction with several matters resulted in the discharge for the 1985 financial year being deferred and it was only after the Commission had taken remedying measures that discharge was eventually given in January 1988.

The second main activity of the Court is to submit observations and deliver opinions on a range of subjects. This it does in three sets of circumstances: special reports on specific aspects of the audit are prepared, either on the Court's own initiative or at the request of another institution; an EU institution may ask the Court to submit an opinion on a matter, usually concerning financial aspects of draft legislation; and when the Council enacts a financial regulation it is obliged to seek an opinion from the Court on the draft text. From its establishment in 1977 to the end of 1992 the Court adopted 68 special reports and delivered 71 opinions.

☐ *The effectiveness of financial controls*

Unquestionably, controls over EU revenue and expenditure could be improved if the political will to do so existed. For example, procedures could be tightened so as to prevent member states from imposing the limitations they occasionally apply to the audit enquiries considered necessary by the Court of Auditors. The Court's own attempts to extend its influence beyond questions of financial rectitude into considerations of policy efficiency could be encouraged, and even formalised. And the particular problem of fraud – which is generally thought to account for at least 10 per cent of the EU budget, most of it in connection with agriculture payments – could be tackled more effectively if resources at both EU and member state levels were expanded and if proposals that have long been advocated by the Court for streamlining administrative practices were adopted.

A few sentences from the Introduction to the Court's *Annual Report Concerning the Financial Year 1992*, which was published in the C series of the *Official Journal* on 16 November 1993, may be cited to illustrate the sort of financial weaknesses the Court identifies and seeks to remedy:

> Examples of insufficient checking by the Commission of legality and regulatory aspects of transactions are to be found throughout this report . . . In the Structural Funds, several programmes were in general poorly controlled by the Commission, both in records and on the spot . . . The Commission needs to take urgent action to raise the level of financial competence and awareness of those officials to whom it has delegated authorizing officer powers, as well as improving their knowledge of the correct procedures and practices . . . The Court once again reports many instances of inadequate control of Community expenditure by national agencies. In the case of the Guarantee Section of the European Agricultural Guarantee and Guidance Fund [EAGGF – Guarantee] there are in addition the risks for Community funds that result from the complexity of the national systems, insufficient coordination between regional organizations and the central paying agencies and the need to strengthen the control of export refunds and related guarantees.

Observations of this kind make it clear that the EU's financial control mechanisms need to be improved. However, the extent of the short-comings should not be overstated. One reason why they should not be is that the internal and external audits have resulted over the years in a tightening of many procedures and an improvement in many adminis-trative practices. Another reason is that total EU expenditure is still relatively modest in size (see Chapter 12 for details), which means that EU decision-makers, far from being able to be financially profligate with surplus funds are, for the most part, obliged to work to tight budgets and within limited resources.

■ Interests

□ *Different types*

A vast range of non-governmental interests cluster around EU processes. These interests are of four main types.

□ *Sub-national levels of government.* As was noted above in the examination of the Committee of the Regions, many sub-national levels of government in the member states seek to influence, or even to exercise a direct role in, EU decision-making processes. The degree of their involvement and activity depends particularly on the amount of autonomy and manoeuvrability they enjoy at national level. Where regional government with real powers exists, then several direct lines of communication have usually been opened up with EU institutions, notably the Commission, and promotion offices have often been established in Brussels. More usually, however, regional and local authorities work with the EU through their national governments and also, where appropriate, through *ad hoc* delegations and the locally-based EU liaison officers which many have appointed.

□ *Private and public companies.* Many large business firms, especially multinational corporations, are very active in lobbying EU institutions. Adopting, usually, multiple strategies, their lobbying is both mediated by national and Euro interest groups (see below), and is also conducted on a direct basis. Direct lobbying has the advantage of not requiring the need to search for a collective view with other firms, and also enables sensitive issues to be pursued where there is no desire to 'go public' – as, for example, where competition and trading matters are involved. The car industry is an example of a sector where direct lobbying by firms – and not just European firms – is common. (As is indicated by the fact that 10 of the 15 largest car firms in Europe have lobbying/information offices in Brussels.)

□ *National interest groups.* Many circumstances result in nationally-based interest groups attempting to involve themselves in EU processes. For example, an environmental interest group may want to see more effective implementation of existing EU legislation on disposal of sewage into the sea. In seeking to play a part in EU processes, most national interest groups are confined to working from their national offices or via a European interest group, but a few of the larger industrial and agricultural groups have, in addition to a domestic and a European group base, their own representatives and agents permanently based in Brussels.

☐ *Euro-groups.* There are somewhere in the region of 550 Euro-groups. These are groups which draw their membership from several countries and which operate at, and in so doing seek to represent the interests of their sector or cause at, the EU level. Given their particular EU orientation it is worth looking at the Euro-groups in a little detail.

Their *policy interests* naturally reflect the policy priorities and policy concerns of the EU. Of the 550 or so Euro-groups, around 50 per cent represent industry and commerce, about 25 per cent agriculture and food, about 20 per cent services, and about 5 per cent trade unions, environmental causes, and other interests. Within these broad categories a multiplicity of specific interests and groups are to be found. So, taking agriculture for example, Euro-groups range in nature from the broadly-based Committee of Professional Agricultural Organisations of the European Community (COPA), which seeks to represent most types of farmers on most issues, to highly specialised groups representing the likes of yeast producers and pasta manufacturers.

The reason that such an array of Euro-groups have been constituted and are active at EU level is, quite simply, that pressure groups go where power goes. As policy responsibilities – in agriculture, in the regulation of the market, in the protection of the environment etc. – have been transferred from national capitals to the EU, then so has a Euro-lobby developed to supplement – not to replace – the domestic lobbies.

The *membership* of Euro-groups also varies considerably. It does so in four main respects. First, there are variations in the breadth of the membership base. Some groups – the so-called umbrella groups – have a broad membership base and seek to represent a whole sector or area of activity. Examples of umbrella groups are COPA, the Union of Industrial and Employers Confederation of Europe (UNICE), the European Trade Union Confederation (ETUC), the European Environmental Bureau (EEB), and the European Bureau of Consumers' Associations (BEUC). Because of the breadth of their membership some of these umbrella groups have considerable difficulty in maintaining internal cohesion and presenting a common front: ETUC, for example, has traditionally had to try and reconcile differences between socialist, communist, and christian trade unions, whilst COPA has had problems in recent years in managing the varying agricultural sectoral implications of reforms in the CAP. Most groups, however, are more narrowly focused than the umbrella groups and seek to speak on behalf of a specific industry, process, service, or product. Examples of such groups are the European Union of Fruit and Vegetable

Wholesalers, Shippers, Importers and Exporters (EUCOFIL), the European Association of Manufacturers of Business Machines and Data Processing Equipment (EUROBIT), and the Federation of European Explosive Manufacturers (FEEM).

Second, there are variations in terms of whether membership is via affiliation or is direct. In most cases membership is based on affiliation by national sectoral or, in the case of a few of the larger Euro-groups, national peak (cross-sectoral) organisations. Since the mid-1980s, however, there has been a growth in direct membership groupings and organisations. The most important development in this regard has seen major industrial, often multinational, companies coming together, frequently as a supplement to, rather than as an alternative to, their involvement in affiliation-based sectoral groups. Examples of Euro-groups which are dominated by large companies are the Association of European Automobile Constructors (ACEA), which represents all of the EU's major non-Japanese car manufacturers other than Peugeot, and the Association of Petrochemical Producers in Europe (APPE). A few lobbying-related linkages between major companies are relatively informally based and in some respects are perhaps thought of as think tanks and forums for the generation of ideas rather than as Euro-groups. The best known example of such a 'think tank' is the European Round Table of Industrialists which brings together fifty or so heads of major European industrialists. The Round Table produces reports that are designed to identify how the right conditions can be created for business to flourish.

Third, there are variations in the representativeness of groups. Since most Euro-groups are based on national affiliates, the number of people they can claim to represent naturally reflects the factors determining group membership at national levels. So, sectional interests are usually better placed than promotional interests. Similarly, amongst sectional interests, Euro-groups representing interests which are well mobilised at national levels, such as dairy farmers and textile manufacturers, naturally tend to be much more genuinely representative than groups acting on behalf of poorly mobilised sections of populations such as agricultural labourers or consumers.

Fourth, there are variations in the width of the EU base of groups. At one end of the spectrum, many Euro-groups draw their members from only a few states – which, in the case of activities which are carried on throughout the EU, can weaken a group's representational claims. At the other end of the spectrum, some groups are not EU specific and draw members from many European states: ETUC, for example, has thirty affiliates from twenty countries, whilst UNICE represents thirty-two business federations from twenty-two European countries. Membership of this latter sort, which goes beyond the geographical borders of the EU, has advantages and disadvantages: on the one hand, it can help to promote international cooperation and increase group resources; on the other hand, and this is a charge that has frequently been laid against ETUC, it can serve to dilute group concentration on, and therefore influence within, the EU.

In terms of *resources*, only a few large umbrella groups have well appointed offices with a full-time staff that is numbered in double figures. Amongst these are COPA (by far the best resourced, with a full-time staff of around 50), UNICE, ETUC, CEA (European Insurance Committee), and GCECEE (Savings Banks Group of the EEC). More commonly, groups rely heavily on the resources of national affiliates and themselves employ only one or two full-time officials – who often do not have their own separate offices but work either from home or from accommodation that is made available to them by an affiliate (usually the Belgian) or an appropriate umbrella group. Many groups do not even stretch to one permanent employee and work purely through affiliates, consultants, or through part-time and temporary representatives and agents whose services are called upon as and when the need arises.

The *organisational structure* of most Euro-groups is extremely loose. The central group organs usually enjoy only a very limited independence from the national affiliates, whilst the affiliates themselves are autonomous in most respects and are not subject to central discipline. In addition, key decisions made at central level are frequently taken only on the basis of unanimous votes, though some groups – including COPA and ACEA – do have provisions for weighted majorities on some issues. These loose structures can weaken the effectiveness of Euro-groups, by making them slow to react and making it difficult for them to put forward collective views which are anything more than rather vague lowest common denominators. At the same time, however, moves to create stronger structures risks groups not affiliating, or national affiliates concentrating almost exclusively on their national level activities.

The extent and complexity of groups' organisational structures varies. The more specialised and poorly resourced groups usually operate on a fairly rudimentary basis, often merely via an annual meeting and an executive committee which meets as required. The large umbrella groups, by contrast, usually have an extensive structure, typically made up of a general meeting which meets at least once a year, an executive committee which meets once every four to six weeks, specialist policy committees whose frequency of meetings depends on the business in hand, a President, and a full-time Secretariat which is headed by a Secretary General. COPA has the most developed structure (see Figure 9.1).

Finally, with regard to their *functions*, Euro-groups normally attempt to do two main things. First, they seek to gather and exchange information –

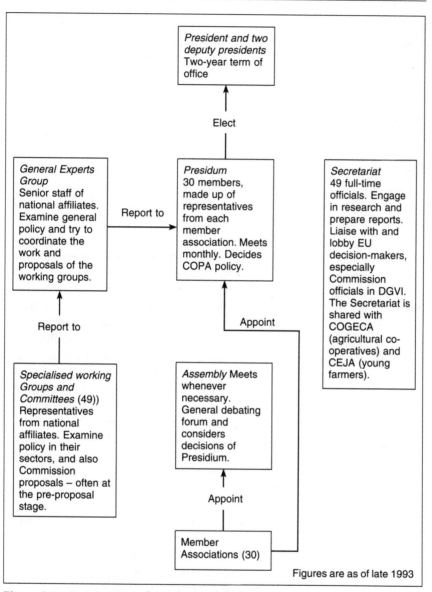

Figure 9.1 *Organisational structure of COPA*

both in a two-way process with EU organs and with and between national affiliates. Second, they seek to have their interests and views incorporated into EU policy, by persuading and pressurising those who make and implement policy. Not all Euro-groups, of course, attempt or are able to exercise these functions in equal measure: for example, in those sectors where EU policy is little developed, Euro-groups often choose to give a higher priority to the first than to the second function.

☐ Access to decision-makers

The long, complex and multi-layered nature of EU processes provides many points of access for interests, and so many opportunities for them to keep themselves informed about developments and to press their cases with those who influence, make, and implement decisions. The points of access can be grouped under three broad headings: national governments, the Commission, and the European Parliament and the Economic and Social Committee.

☐ *National governments.* A major problem for interests is that they cannot normally directly approach either the European Council or the Council of Ministers. This is partly because there are practical problems involved in lobbying what are, in effect, international negotiations, it is partly because the meetings are held behind closed doors, but it is mainly because neither body has wished to make itself available, as a collective entity, for regularised or intensive interest targeting. Only a few direct linkages therefore exist, and these are largely restricted to the most powerful of interests. So, the President-in-Office of a Technical Council may occasionally meet the president of a powerful Euro-group, or a written submission from an influential interest may be officially received and circulated prior to a European Council or Council of Ministers' meeting. More usually, however, the only way an interest can hope to establish contact with, and perhaps exert pressure on, the European Council or the Council of Ministers is indirectly: through a government or governments looking favourably on its cause or feeling obliged to act on its behalf.

Much time and effort is, therefore, spent by interests, especially national interests, attempting to influence the positions adopted by governments in EU negotiations. In the case of the European Council, this task usually has to be undertaken at least at one stage removed because national leaders do not normally allow themselves to be directly lobbied. With the Council of Ministers, however, one of a number of factors may result in doors being opened. Amongst such factors are: some interests, such as most of the major national agricultural groups, enjoy – for a mixture of political, economic, technical, and other reasons – an insider status with relevant government departments, which means that they are consulted as a matter of course on proposals and developments within their sphere of interest; when a technically complicated matter is under consideration, governments usually seek the advice of relevant interests at an early stage of the

Council process – with perhaps Council working party or management committee members communicating directly with interest representatives; and when the cooperation of an interest is important for the effective implementation of an EU proposal, its views may well be actively sought, or received and listened to if an approach is made.

This last point touches on another reason, in addition to trying to influence Council decision-making, why interests may approach national governments: they may wish to influence the way EU decisions are implemented. One way in which they can attempt to do this is by making their views known to governments when measures are being devised to incorporate EU directives into national law. And if relevant ministries can be persuaded to delay, or not to monitor too closely, the implementation of directives on, say, disposal of pollutants, or safety standards in the workplace, some interests may well have much to gain financially.

☐ *The Commission.* The Commission is the main target for most interests. It is so, primarily, because of its central importance in so many different respects: in policy initiation and formulation; in taking many final decisions; in following proposals through their legislative cycle; in managing the EU's spending programmes; and in policy implementation. An important contributory reason why the Commission attracts so much interest attention is simply that it is known to be approachable.

The Commission makes itself available to interests because several advantages can accrue to it from so doing. First, interests often have access to specialised information and to knowledge of how things are 'at the front' which the Commission needs if it is to be able to exercise its own responsibilities efficiently. Second, the Commission's negotiating hand with the Council of Ministers is strengthened if it can demonstrate that its proposals are supported by influential interests – as, for example, many of its attempts to approximate European standards are supported by multinational corporations, and indeed in some cases may have originated from having been pressed by multinational corporations. Third, and this is in some ways the other side of the coin of the previous point, if the Commission does not consult with and try to satisfy interests, and comes forward with proposals to which influential interests are strongly opposed, the proposals are likely to meet with strong resistance at Council of Ministers level. Fourth, with regard specifically to Euro-groups, where groups come forward with broadly united and coherent positions, they can greatly assist the Commission by allowing it to deal with already aggregated views and by enabling it to avoid becoming entangled in national and ideological differences between sectional interests. For this reason Commission DGs generally keep Euro-groups which are 'recognised' informed about matters which are of interest to them and usually are prepared to consult with them too. (There are no explicit Commission rules on recognition, in the sense that there is no proper system of accreditation or registration, but informal consultation lists do exist. The main reasons for non-recognition are either that the Commission does not regard the group as a proper Euro-group – perhaps because it consists just of two or three large companies – or that it is not seen as very effective in 'delivering' aggregated and coordinated views to the Commission.)

Until about the mid-1970s the Commission displayed a strong preference for talking to Euro-groups rather than national groups, and to national governments rather than sub-national levels of government. This attitude, however, has since been relaxed and most interests of significance, and most interests which can provide useful information that is presented in a clear manner, have been able to have their views at least considered by the Commission. The procedures by which the contacts and communications occur are many and are of both a formal and an informal nature. They include:

- The extensive advisory committee system that is clustered around the Commission. This primarily exists for the precise purpose of allowing interests to make their views known to EU authorities, and in particular to the Commission (see Chapter 4).
- The Social Dialogue – or, as it is also known, the Val Duchesse Dialogue – provides for an exchange of views between the Commission and the two sides of industry. It has, since 1985, regularly brought together, at the most senior and at working group levels, representatives from the Commission, trade union representatives from ETUC, and representatives from the two main employers' and industrial organisations – UNICE and the European Centre of Enterprises with State Holdings (CEEP). As part of the TEU Agreement on Social Policy concluded between eleven member states, the scope of the Commission's consultations with management and labour are being greatly extended (see Chapter 11).
- Commissioners and DG officials receive numerous delegations from interests of all sorts.
- Representatives of the Commission travel to member states to meet interests and to attend conferences and seminars where interests are represented.
- A few of the larger Euro-groups invite Commission representatives to attend some of their working parties and committee meetings.
- Informal meetings and telephone conversations between Commission and interest representatives occur constantly.

- Interests present the Commission with a mass of written documentation in the form of information, briefing, and policy documents.

Naturally, the extent and nature of the communications between any one interest and the Commission vary considerably according to a number of factors. A small national interest in a specialised area may only require occasional contact at middle-ranking official level with one particular DG. By contrast, an active umbrella group may wish to be permanently plugged into the Commission at many different points. As an indication of how extensive the links can be, some of the access channels available to COPA are worth noting: about every four to six weeks the Presidium of COPA meets the Commissioner for Agriculture; the Secretary General of COPA and the Director General of DGVI (Agriculture) meet regularly and often speak to each other several times a week on the telephone; at all levels, the staff of COPA are in almost constant touch with staff in DGVI and, less frequently, are also in close contact with staff in other DGs – notably DGXIX (Budgets); and COPA is strongly represented, both in its own right and via affiliates, on all the agricultural advisory committees and also on certain other leading advisory committees such as the Standing Committee on Employment and the Harmonisation of Legislation Committee.

☐ *The European Parliament and the Economic and Social Committee.* The special advisory positions held by the EP and the ESC in the EU make them natural, albeit generally second-ranking, targets for interests.

In the case of the ESC there are, of course, factors which put it in a special position *vis-à-vis* interests: its membership is largely made up of interest representatives and its very *raison d'être* is to act as the EU's principal forum for interest representation and expression. The ways and the extent to which the ESC exercises these representative and expressive roles were examined earlier in the chapter.

With regard to the EP, it has been very noticeable, not least in the swelling ranks of lobbyists who attend the Strasbourg plenaries, that as the role and influence of the Parliament in the EU system has grown, so has it increasingly attracted the attention of interests. Among the lobbying possibilities available to interests in respect of the EP are the following:

- The powers conferred on the EP by the TEU in Article 138b of the EC Treaty, which enable it to request the Commission to submit legislative acts, create the possibility of interests using MEPs to get legislative initiatives off the ground.
- Attempts can be made to encourage MEPs to draw up own initiative reports. If progress is made – and prospects may be better than under the Article 138b procedure which requires majority support of the EP's

members – then this could, given a fair wind, incline the Commission and/ or the Council into action of a desired sort.

• A general circulation of literature amongst MEPs may have the effect of improving the image of an interest or changing the climate of opinion in the interest's area of concern.

• MEPs can be directly approached with a view to persuading them to vote in a particular way on a particular issue (which may well be possible given the lack of voting discipline in the EP), or with a view to persuading them to support the interest's view in a committee or a political group.

• Interests have some opportunities for direct contacts with EP committees and political groups. Committees, for example, sometimes hold 'hearings' and occasionally travel to member states for the precise purpose of meeting interest representatives, whilst political groups sometimes allow themselves to be addressed when they judge it to be appropriate.

• Officials and MEPs engaged in preparing reports for EP committees often approach appropriate interests for their views, or allow themselves to be approached.

• Attempts can be made to persuade individual MEPs to take matters up with governments and with the Commission.

Many possible avenues are thus available to interests to enable them to promote their causes. Which are the most suitable, the most available, and the most effective, naturally varies according to circumstances. A local authority, for example, wishing to attract ERDF funds, would be well advised to establish contacts with DGXVI (Regional Policy), but it should also court good relations with regional and national civil servants since the ERDF functions on an EU/national/regional partnership basis. By contrast, an environmental group in a country where the government is not noted for its sympathy to 'green issues' might be most effective working as part of a Euro-group: from the broad base of a Euro-group it might be possible to launch public information and relations campaigns that help persuade the EP to pass a resolution; it may be possible to pressurise the Commission to produce legislative proposals and to increase its efforts to ensure that existing legislation is properly implemented; and it may be possible to find a route to the Council of Ministers via at least some of the national affiliates being able to lean on their governments.

☐ *Influence*

The factors which determine the influence exercised by interests in the EU are similar to those which apply at national levels. The more powerful and more effective interests tend to be those which have at least some of the following characteristics:

☐ *Control of key information and expertise.* Effective policy-making and implementation requires a knowledge and understanding of matters which can often be provided to EU authorities only via interests. This obviously puts some interests in potentially advantageous positions – as is seen, to some extent, in the way in which the influence interests exercise via official forums is often much greater in specialised advisory committees than it is in more general settings such as the ESC or the Standing Committee on Employment.

☐ *Adequate resources.* The better resourced an interest is, the more likely it is to be able to make use of a variety of tactics and devices at a number of different potential access points. So, regarding proposed legislation, a well resourced interest is likely to be in a position to feed its views through to the Commission, the EP, and perhaps the Council from the initiating stage to the taking of the final decision. Similarly, a regional or local authority hoping for EU funds is more likely to be successful if it employs people who know what is available, how to apply, and with whom it is worth having an informal word.

☐ *Economic weight.* Important economic interests – whether they be major companies or representational organisations – usually have to be listened to by EU decision-makers, not least because their cooperation is often necessary in connection with policies designed, for instance, to encourage EU-wide investment, to expand employment in the less prosperous regions, to stimulate cross-border rationalisations, or to improve industrial efficiency. Examples of economic weight being an important factor in contributing to political influence include the way in which the chemical industry – via its Euro-group CEFIC – has managed to persuade the Commission to investigate numerous cases of alleged dumping, and the way in which EUROFER – the steel manufacturers' association – has worked closely with the Commission and governments to limit the damage to its members caused by steel rationalisation programmes.

☐ *Political weight.* Many interests have political assets which can be used to advantage, usually via governments. So, for example, a national pressure group which is closely linked with a party in government may be able to get that government to virtually act on its behalf in the Council of Ministers. At a broader level, electoral factors can be important, with ministers in the

Council not usually anxious to support anything which might upset key voters – especially if an important national or local election is looming. Farmers' organisations in France, Italy, Germany and elsewhere are the best examples of interests which have benefited from having electoral significance.

☐ *Genuine representational claims.* National pressure groups and Euro-groups which genuinely represent a sizeable proportion of the interests in a given sector are naturally in a stronger position than those which do not. The representativeness of CEFIC, for example, is one important reason why the chemical industry has been permitted to exercise a certain degree of self-regulation.

☐ *Cohesion.* Some interests find it difficult to put forward clear and consistent views and are thereby weakened. As was noted earlier, this often applies to Euro-groups, especially umbrella Euro-groups, because of their varied membership and their loose confederal structures.

☐ *Access to decision-makers.* Most of the characteristics just described play some part in determining which interests enjoy good access to decision-makers and which do not. Clearly, those interests which do have good access – especially if it is at both national and EU levels – are more likely than those which do not to be fully aware of thinking and developments in decision-making circles, and to be able to present their case to those who matter. At the EU level, COPA is the most obvious example of such an 'insider' interest, whilst at national levels COPA affiliates usually also enjoy advantageous positions (see Chapter 13 for an examination of the access enjoyed by – and, indeed, for an examination of the general influence of – agricultural interests).

☐ *Concluding comments*

There are both positive and negative aspects to the involvement of interests in EU processes. Of the positive aspects, two are especially worth emphasising. First, interest activity broadens the participatory base of the EU and ensures that policy and decision-making is not completely controlled by politicians and officials. Second, interests can provide EU authorities with information and viewpoints which improve the quality and effectiveness of their policies and decisions. Of the negative aspects, the most important is that some interests are much more powerful and influential than others. This lack of balance raises questions about whether interests unduly, perhaps even undemocratically, tilt EU policy and decision-making in certain directions – towards, for example, producing a legislative framework which tends to favour producers more than such 'natural' opponents as consumers and environmentalists.

But whether interest activity is judged to be, on the whole, beneficial or not, its importance is clear. Interests are central to many key information flows to and from EU authorities, and they bring considerable influence to bear on policy and decision-making processes from initiation right through to implementation. There are few, if any, EU policy sectors where interests of at least some significance are not to be found.

■ PART 3 ■

POLICIES AND POLICY PROCESSES OF THE EUROPEAN UNION

■ Introduction

Part 3 examines what the EU does and how it does it. Chapter 10 looks at EU policies. The origins, the range, and the context of the policies are all considered. Particular themes of Chapter 10 are the breadth and diversity of EU policy interests, and the less than complete nature of many of the policies.

Chapter 11 focuses on patterns, practices and features of the EU's policy-making and decision-making machinery. Having examined the EU's institutions and political actors in Part 2, Chapter 11 considers how the various pieces fit together. What sort of policy-making and decision-making system are they part of and have they helped to create? A central concern of Chapter 11 is to emphasise that even the most general statements about how the EU operates normally have to be qualified. For one of the few things that can be said with certainty about EU processes is that they are many, complex, and varied. A truly accurate account of how the EU functions therefore requires something which just cannot be attempted here: an analysis of the procedures and practices which apply in every policy area with which the EU is involved.

In Chapter 12 the EU budget is examined. Where does the EU get its money from, and what does it spend it on? The budgetary decision-making process, which in several important respects is distinctly different from the processes which apply in policy areas, is also examined.

Chapter 13 considers one particular policy area in depth. As such, the chapter offers something of a contrast to the necessarily rather general approach of Chapters 10 and 11. Agriculture has been selected for this special examination, not because of any suggestion that it is typical – the variability of the EU's policy processes precludes any policy area being described as such – but simply because of its significance in the EU context.

The external relations of the EU are increasingly important and these constitute the subject matter of Chapter 14. The examination is undertaken on the basis of the three main component parts of the EU's external policies: trade policy, foreign and security policy, and development cooperation policy.

Finally, Chapter 15 focuses on one of the most important and certainly one of the most distinctive, features of EU processes: the mechanisms and arrangements used by the member states to control their relations with the EU and, insofar as it is possible, to control the EU itself.

■ *Chapter 10* ■

Policies

■ The origins of EU policies

The origins of EU policies are to be found in a number of places. At a general level, the changed post-war mood in Western Europe has played a part. So also has the increasingly interdependent nature of the international system which has resulted in national borders becoming ever more ill-matched with political and economic forces and realities. This interdependence has helped to persuade West European states to transfer policy responsibilities to a 'higher' level in an attempt to shape, to manage, to control, to take advantage of, and to keep apace with, the modern world.

At a more specific level, the Treaties are generally seen as key determinants of EU policy. However, their influence is not as great as is commonly supposed. Certainly they are important stimuli to policy development and they also provide the legal base on which much policy activity occurs. So, for example, such 'core' EU policies as the Common Commercial Policy (CCP), the Common Agricultural Policy (CAP), and the Competition Policy find their roots – though by no means all their principles – in the EEC (now EC) Treaty. Similarly, EU involvement with coal and steel cannot possibly be fully understood without reference to the Treaty of Paris. But Treaty provision for policy development does not guarantee that it will occur. The very limited progress made towards the establishment of a Common Transport Policy, despite it being provided for in Part 2 Title 4 of the EEC/EC Treaty, illustrates this. So too does the non-fulfilment of most of the hopes which were held out for Euratom. And a third, and in its implications for the nature of the EU crucially important, example of limited development of Treaty provisions is the only very partial implementation, until the late 1980s, of Part 3 Title 2 of the EEC Treaty, under which member states were supposed to regard their macroeconomic policies 'as a matter of common concern' and were to coordinate, cooperate and consult with one another on key economic and financial questions. In practice, it is quite clear that although there was cooperation and consultation in these areas – carried out mainly under the Ecofin Council of Ministers by committees of very senior national officials – the states did not work and act as closely together as the Treaty envisaged. Furthermore, one of the key steps towards financial cooperation – the creation in 1979 of the European Monetary System (EMS) which, amongst other things, was designed to fix maximum and minimum rates of exchange for currencies in the system – was created outside the Treaty system because of concern in some quarters about the rigidities that a Treaty-based approach might entail, and also because not all member states (notably the United Kingdom) wished to be full participants. It was only in 1987–8, thirty years after the EEC Treaty was signed, that clear, significant, formal, and Community-based moves towards economic and monetary integration between the member states began to be initiated and implemented.

If Treaty provision is no guarantee of policy development nor is lack of provision a guarantee of lack of development. Environmental policy illustrates this. Until it was given constitutional status by the Single European Act (SEA), environment was given no specific mention in the Treaties. Yet, from the early 1970s Community environmental policy programmes were formulated and legislation was approved. Legal authority for this was held to lie in the (almost) catch-all Articles 100 and 235 of the EEC/EC Treaty. The former allows the Community to issue directives for the approximation of laws 'as directly affect the establishment or functioning of the common market' and the latter enables it to take 'appropriate measures' to 'attain in the course of the operation of the common market, one of the objectives of the Community'. Environmental policy was, therefore, able to find a tentative constitutional base. However, even the most liberal readings of Articles 100 and 235 cannot stretch to some policy areas, but this has not prevented policy development from occurring. Foreign policy cooperation prior to the SEA illustrates this. Aware that there were no Treaty provisions for such cooperation, and unenthusiastic about subjecting such a sensitive area to the formalities and restrictions of Treaty processes, the EC member states in the early 1970s simply created a new machinery – which they entitled European Political Cooperation (EPC) alongside, but outside the formal framework of, the Treaties.

EPC was first given legal (but not EEC Treaty) status by the SEA, and it subsequently provided much of the basis for the Common Foreign and Security Policy (CFSP) pillar of the TEU. This 'constitutional evolution' of foreign policy highlights a key feature of the nature of EU policy development: the Treaties are facilitators and enablers of policy development, but they are not always the main causes. Indeed many of the amendments made to the Founding Treaties by the SEA and the TEU have taken the form of acknowledging and giving level recognition to changes which have been occurring outside their frameworks. If the Treaties thus provide only a partial explanation for policy development, what other factors have been influential? Three have been especially important: the leadership offered by the Commission; the perceptions of the member states of what is desirable; and the individual and collective capacities of the member states to translate their perceptions into practice.

To begin with Commission leadership, it is generally recognised that the Commissions which were led by Walter Hallstein (1958–66), Roy Jenkins (1977–80), and Jacques Delors (1985–94) were more dynamic and forceful than other Commissions. This is not to suggest that these Commissions saw all their ideas and proposals translated into practice – given the reliance of the Commission on other institutions that would be an unfair criterion on which to judge Commission success – but it is to say that they were particularly innovative in helping to bring issues onto the policy agenda and in pointing to what could, and perhaps should, be done. The ability of the Commission, in favourable circumstances, to have a real effect on policy development is no more clearly illustrated than in the way the Delors-led Commissions helped to force the pace on such key issues as the Single European Market (SEM) programme, EMU, and the social dimension.

Regarding the perceptions of the states – or, to be more precise, of national governments – a fundamental precondition of successful policy development is a judgement that the advantages of acting together outweigh the disadvantages. The advantages are mainly, though as the CFSP and JHA pillars of the TEU show, not entirely, economic in kind: those that stem from having, in an increasingly interdependent and competitive world, a single and protected market, a common external trading position, and some collective action and some pooling of resources in particular functional and sectoral areas. The principal disadvantage is the loss of national decision-making powers and sovereignty that transfers of power and responsibilities to the EU inevitably entail. Some states are more concerned about this than others, but even the strongest supporters of integration are hesitant about ceding powers that may, at a later stage, result in their own national room for manoeuvre being limited in areas that are important to them.

As for the capacities of the states to operationalise their perceptions of what is desirable, there are many problems. At the individual state level, a government may be favourably disposed towards an EU initiative but be inhibited from supporting it in the Council of Ministers because of opposition from a powerful domestic interest or because it could be electorally damaging. Following this through to the EU level, opposition from just one state, whether it is principled or pragmatic, can make policy development difficult to achieve, given the continuing Treaty requirement of unanimity in the Council of Ministers on several issues, and the preference in the Council for progress through consensus – especially on major issues – even where majority decisions are legally permissible.

■ The EU's policy interests and responsibilities

The EU's main policy interests and responsibilities can be grouped under five headings: establishing the Single European Market, economic and financial policies, functional policies, sectoral policies, and external policies.

☐ *Establishing the Single European Market*

The single most important reason why the dynamism and profile of the EC was so raised in the 1980s was that the Community embarked on a programme to 'complete the internal market by 1992'.

This programme was really a development of the Community's long-established goal of creating a common market. After years in which only modest progress had been made in this direction, a number of factors combined in the 1980s to convince the governments of the member states that a greater thrust was needed: the sluggish economic growth of the second half of the 1970s was continuing; the Community was clearly falling behind its competitors, notably Japan and the United States, in the new technologies; there was an increasing appreciation that the continuation of still essentially fragmented national markets was having a damaging effect on the economic performances of the member states; and the accession of three new countries (Greece in 1981, and Spain and Portugal in 1986) made it clear to all that to continue on the same path and in the same way would mean that the common market would never be properly established.

To this background the Commission in April 1985 produced the White Paper *Completing the Internal Market* (see also Chapters 4, 6, and 11). What the White Paper did was to identify some 300 measures which would have to be taken to enable the internal market to be completed, and to suggest also that 31 December 1992 should be set as the deadline for the adoption of the measures. The European Council, at its June 1985 Milan meeting, accepted the White Paper, and at its December 1985 Luxembourg meeting agreed that both the internal market objective and the 1992 deadline be included in the Single European Act. Crucially, the inclusions in the SEA involved additions and amendments to the EEC Treaty. Article

13 of the SEA, incorporating a new Article 8A of the EEC Treaty, was especially important:

> The Community shall adopt measures with the aim of progressively establishing the internal market over a period expiring on 31 December 1992 . . . The internal market shall comprise an area without internal frontiers in which the free movement of goods, persons, services and capital is ensured in accordance with the provisions of this [the EEC] Treaty.

The Commission's White Paper sought, in essence, to establish the conditions in which market activities – buying and selling, lending and borrowing, producing and consuming – could be done as easily on a Community basis as they can on a national basis. The hope was that by removing the obstacles and barriers which sectionalised and fragmented the Community market, efficiency, growth, trade, employment, and prosperity could all be promoted. In the context of a general de-regulatory approach, three sorts of obstacles and barriers were identified as needing to be removed: physical, technical, and fiscal.

The Commission was not, of course, starting from scratch with its internal market programme. A free and open market had been provided for in the EEC Treaty and much progress had been made. What the White Paper was intended to do was to inject a new focus, impetus, and dynamism into a fundamental Treaty objective which was proceeding far too slowly and, indeed, in some respects, had gone rather off the rails. Much of what was proposed in the White Paper, therefore, was not new, but had been around for some time – awaiting decisions by the Council of Ministers.

The White Paper thus needs to be placed in the context of the Community's long-standing aim to create a common market – or, as it has come to be more generally known in recent years, an internal market or a Single European Market (SEM). That aim was being pursued, but with only limited success, before the White Paper appeared, and has continued to be pursued since, not only via the implementation of the White Paper but also via new measures which did not appear in the White Paper. There are four main pillars on which this continuing process to establish a Single European Market rests.

The first pillar is the guarantee of *free movement of goods, persons, services and capital* between the member states. Of these, the free movement of goods has received the greatest attention. It is a freedom which, it might be thought, could be fairly easily realised: all barriers to trade must be dismantled according to the guiding principles of the EC Treaty which states that customs duties, quantitative restrictions, and measures having equivalent effect are not permitted. Great steps were quickly made in the 1960s with the first two of these and by 1968 customs duties and quantitative restrictions were removed. Measures having equivalent effect, however, have been more difficult to deal with and have frequently acted, and been used, as obstacles to trade. Attempts to eliminate such measures have generated a considerable amount of secondary legislation, much activity in the Court of Justice, and constituted a central part of the White Paper programme.

In seeking to establish the conditions for the free movement of persons, the Treaty provides for both the employed and the self-employed. The free movement of the former is to be attained by 'the abolition of any discrimination based on nationality between workers of the Member States as regards employment, remuneration and other conditions of work and employment' (Article 48, EC). The free movement of the latter is concerned principally with rights of establishment, that is with the right of individuals and undertakings to establish businesses in the territory of other member states. As with the free movement of goods, secondary legislation and Court rulings have done much to clarify and extend the free movement of persons. They have done so in two main ways. First, by providing for mutual recognition of many educational, professional, and trade qualifications. Second, by providing key facilitators, notably in the form of the establishment of various legal entitlements, irrespective of nationality and place of domicile, to education and job training, health care, and social welfare payments.

Some of the legislation and Court judgements which have promoted the free movement of persons, and more particularly rights of establishment have, of course, also helped to give effect to the Treaty declaration that restrictions on the provisions of services should be abolished. Until recently financial services were a particular problem, but legislation has now been passed – on, for example, banking, on insurance, and on insider trading – which is having the effect of opening up this hitherto highly protected and fragmented sector.

Until the late 1980s only limited progress was made in establishing the free movement of capital. Treaty provisions partly explain this, since the elimination of restrictions on the movement of capital, under Article 67 of the EEC Treaty was (and indeed still is under the EC Treaty) required only 'to the extent necessary to ensure the proper functioning of the common market'. More importantly, however, and notwithstanding the creation of the European Monetary System (EMS) in the late 1970s, the necessary political will did not exist in the first three decades of the Community's life. For many states control of capital movements was an important economic and monetary instrument and they preferred it to remain largely in their own hands. However, as part of the SEM programme, much of this former resistance was withdrawn or overcome, and all the major capital markets have – subject to a few derogations and some national protective measures – been more or less open since 1990.

The second pillar of the SEM involves *the approximation of such laws, regulations or administrative provisions of the Member States as directly affect the establishment or functioning of the common market* (Article 100, EC). Prior to the TEU, Article 100 referred to 'the approximation, *or harmonisation* of such legal provisions in the Member States' (my italics), but the word harmonisation was dropped from the amended EC Treaty to reflect the more flexible and less rigid approach which has been taken in recent years towards differences in national standards and requirements.

The need for approximation arises because, as noted above, the dismantling of barriers is not in itself sufficient to guarantee free movement. This is most clearly seen with regard to movement of goods where, prior to the 1992 programme, many non-tariff and non-quantitative barriers existed which inhibited, even prevented, free movement across the Community's internal borders. These barriers had, in the words of the Treaty, the 'equivalent effect' of tariffs and quantitative restrictions, and as such were obstacles to the creation of a market based on free and open competition. They tended, moreover, to be barriers of a kind that could not be removed simply by issuing general prohibitions. Many took the form of different national standards, national requirements, and national provisions and practices that had been adopted over the years. Sometimes they had been adopted for perfectly good reasons, but sometimes they had been adopted as a deliberate attempt to protect a domestic market from unwanted competition without actually infringing Community law. Whatever the intent, the effect was often the same: because of the need to adapt products to meet the different national standards of different states, and because also of the need for products to be subject to retesting and recertification procedures, efficiency was not maximised and producers in one member state often could not compete on an equal basis with producers in another. Examples of non-tariff barriers (NTBs) included different national technical specifications for products, different health and safety standards, charges for inspections on categories of imported goods, and taxes which though nominally general in their scope were discriminatory against imported goods in their effect.

Approximation, and before it harmonisation, is concerned with the removal of barriers of this type and as such is vital if free movement across national boundaries is to be achieved. Council directives and EP and Council directives are the main instruments for achieving approximation, although Court of Justice rulings have also been supportive and helpful.

Most approximation law is naturally to be found in relation to the free movement of goods, and consists largely of matters such as the setting of common standards on technical requirements, design specifications, product content, and necessary documentation. Critics of the EU often present such measures as harmonisation for harmonisation's sake, and from time to time proposals do indeed appear to smack of insensitivity to national customs and preferences. Sight should not be lost, however, of what approximation – or harmonisation as some still insist on calling it – is all about: creating conditions which allow, encourage and increase the uniform treatment of persons, goods, services and capital throughout the EU.

As was briefly explained in Chapter 8, and as is further explained in Chapter 11, the Community's approach to harmonisation changed in the 1980s. Following the 'breakthrough' *Cassis de Dijon* case in 1979 – when the Court of Justice ruled that products which conform with the standards of one member state cannot be excluded from the markets of other member states unless they can be shown to be damaging to health, safety, the environment, or other aspects of the public interest – the Community began to concern itself less than formerly with harmonising technical details. Under the 'new approach' a simpler and speedier process applies. There are three main aspects to this process: (1) whenever possible, legislation does not seek to harmonise but rather seeks to approximate in that it is restricted to laying down the essential requirements which national standards and specifications must meet – on health and safety requirements, for example; (2) as long as the essential conditions are met, member states must mutually recognise each other's specifications and standards; and (3) national specifications and standards are gradually being replaced by European specifications and standards – which are drawn up by the appropriate European standards organisations.

Competition policy is the third pillar of the SEM. The basic rules on competition are outlined in Articles 85–94 of the EC Treaty. They have three principal aspects to them. First, under Article 85, 'all agreements between undertakings, decisions by associations of undertakings and concerted practices which may affect trade between Member States and which have as their object or effect the prevention, restriction or distortion of competition within the common market are prohibited'. Second, under Article 86, 'Any abuse by one or more undertakings of a dominant position within the common market or in a substantial part of it shall be prohibited or incompatible with the common market insofar as it may affect trade between Member States'. Third, under Article 92, state aid 'which distorts or threatens to distort competition by favouring certain undertakings or the production of certain goods shall, insofar as it affects trade between Member States, be incompatible with the common market'.

All of these Treaty prohibitions – on restrictive practices, dominant trading positions, and state aids – have been clarified by subsequent EC/EU law, mainly in the form of Council legislation and Court judgements. It has been established, for example, that a 'dominant position' cannot be held to apply on the basis of an overall percentage market share, but only in relation to factors such as the particular product, the structure of its market, and substitutability. Similarly, exemptions to state aid prohibitions, which are only generally referred to in the Treaty, have been confirmed as legally permissible if they are for purposes such as regional development, retraining, and job creation in potential growth industries. Much of the work and time of DGIV (Competition) is taken up examining allegations of breaches in competition law and considering applications for exemptions.

An effective competition policy is, of course, necessary for an open and integrated market. To try and improve the policy and ensure that it is sufficiently effective the EU has adopted a twin-track approach in recent years. First, the Commission has become much more active in examining cases of apparent malpractice. For example, using its powers as investigator, prosecutor, judge, and jury (though with its decisions subject to appeal to the Court of Justice) it has been more willing to take action against member states in connection with state aids. Second, legislation designed to broaden the competition policy base has been approved. An important instance of such legislation is the 1989 Company Merger Regulation which gives considerable powers to the Commission to disallow mergers which it judges will have an adverse effect on competition. Other examples, in a very different area of competition policy, are the directives that are designed to open up public procurement – an area of activity that accounts for around 15 per cent of EU GDP.

The fourth pillar of the SEM is the *Common External Tariff* (CET), or, as it is also known, the *Common Customs Tariff* (CCT). The purpose of the CET is to further the course of fair and equal trading by surrounding all the member states with common trade barriers so that goods entering the EU via, say, Liverpool or Rotterdam, do so on exactly the same conditions as they do via Athens or Marseilles. No member state can therefore gain a competitive advantage by having access to cheaper raw materials and none can make a profit from exporting imported goods to an EU partner. The CET takes the EU beyond being just a free trade area – where, at best, external tariffs are only approximated – and makes it a customs union.

Establishing the CET was relatively easily achieved and maintaining it has not been too difficult. The external tariffs were in place by 1968, to coincide with the removal of the internal tariffs, and since then governments have had no independent legal authority over the tariffs to be charged on goods entering their country. The terms of trade of the member states are established and negotiated on a EU-wide basis via a Common Commercial Policy (CCP). If a member state wishes to seek exemptions from, or changes to, these terms of trade it must go through the appropriate EU decision-making processes. Naturally, there have been frequent disagreements between the states over different aspects of external trade and the CCP – tariff rates, trade protection measures, and alleged dumping are amongst the issues that have created difficulties – but the existence of a clear and binding legal framework has ensured that, for the most part, the common external protection and front system has worked.

Clearly much has been, and is being, achieved in establishing the SEM. Even some of the most intractable problems – such as removing internal border controls and setting limitations on the rates of indirect taxation – have largely been resolved. However, it is clear that it will be some years yet before the SEM is as open or as integrated as national markets. This is because not all of the barriers to free movement are being removed, and not all of the national policies which serve to fragment the market are being made common. The obstacles to a completely open and integrated market which will continue in at least some form for the foreseeable future fall into three categories.

First, there are the somewhat intangible, but nonetheless very important, obstacles arising from different historical experiences, cultures, traditions, and languages. These obstacles are unquestionably being gradually broken down, but only slowly. EU laws may, for example, oblige public authorities to receive tenders for contracts from throughout the EU, but laws cannot control the many informal processes that often incline decision-makers to award contracts whenever possible to fellow national, or even locally-based, companies.

Second, member states are still resisting – almost invariably for reasons of national interest – some aspects of market integration. As a result, much needed legislation is either held up, or is loosened so as to overcome resistance. (This is most likely to occur where decision-making rules in the Council of Ministers require unanimity.) So, for example, although 95 per cent of the White Paper proposals had been adopted by the Council by the end of 1993 and 84 per cent had been transposed into national law, there were still problems in such areas as veterinary and phytosanitary controls, public procurement, pharmaceuticals, and the recognition of diplomas and professional qualifications.

Third, there are many economic factors which were not included in the White Paper and which are not formally part of the SEM programme which nonetheless exist as obstacles to a completely open and integrated market. Economists and politicians dispute exactly what economic factors do constitute such obstacles, and what their relative importance is, but prominent amongst the factors that are generally recognised are the following: the lack of closely coordinated – some would say the lack of common – economic and monetary policies; the lack of fixed exchange rates, and in the view of many the lack of a common currency; the only partial development of common regional, social, environmental, and consumer policies; and the diversity of personal and corporate direct taxation systems.

As is shown below, many of these obstacles are increasingly being addressed, notably in the context of the movement towards Economic and Monetary Union, but their complete removal cannot be anticipated in the short-term.

☐ *Macroeconomic and financial policies*

Notwithstanding certain EEC Treaty provisions, and despite declarations by the Heads of Government in 1969 and 1972 that their intention was to establish an economic and monetary union by 1980, only limited practical progress was made prior to the late 1980s in moving towards Economic and Monetary Union (EMU).

Ministers and senior national officials did regularly convene to consult and to exchange ideas on macroeconomic policy, and at their meetings they periodically considered Commission submissions for the adoption of common guidelines and for short-term and medium-term strategies. But, ultimately, it was up to the states themselves as to what they did. When, for example, the Commission, in its quarterly economic report published in February 1987, stated that Germany had the greatest margin for manoeuvre to stimulate domestic demand, and France and the United Kingdom could do more to boost productive capacity, there was no guarantee that national policies would thereby be adjusted. A state may have been unwise to fall too much out of step with its partners – as the French Government was in 1981–2 when it attempted to stimulate its economy against the general trend – but it was perfectly entitled, and able, to embark on such a course of action.

Financial policy (which, of course, in practice, is inextricably linked with economic policy) was also the subject of frequent contacts between the states – at ministerial, official and central bank levels – but, like economic policy, most of what came out of such exchanges was of an exhortive rather than a directionist nature. That said, however, the creation in 1979 of the European Monetary System (EMS) did give to Community financial policy some central structure and some powers, since amongst its features were: a common reserve fund to provide for market intervention; the European Currency Unit (Ecu) to act as a reserve asset and a means of settlement; and, in the Exchange Rate Mechanism (ERM) of the EMS, fixed – though adjustable when necessary – bands of exchange for participating currencies.

Until the late 1980s the Community's macroeconomic and financial policies thus had only relatively weak policy instruments attached to them. Attempts to strengthen these instruments, so as to build up a more effective policy framework, traditionally met with at least four obstacles. First, there were differences as to which – the economic or the financial – naturally came first and should be accorded priority. Second, the Community's rather sectionalised policy-making mechanisms inhibited an overall and coordinated approach. Third, different aspects of economic and monetary integration had different implications for the states, which resulted in them being viewed with different degrees of enthusiasm. Fourth, for some states the possibility of ceding key macroeconomic and financial powers to the Community raised fundamental sovereignty questions.

But notwithstanding the many obstacles in the way of policy development, real progress towards EMU began to be made in the late 1980s. As a result of a number of factors – notably, an increasing appreciation by governments of the benefits for the SEM of economic and financial integration, the enthusiasm of the Commission for progress, and the amendment of the EEC Treaty by the SEA to include a new chapter on 'Co-operation in Economic and Monetary Policy' – the Community formally embarked on the road to EMU. Differences remained between the states both as regards what precisely EMU should consist of, and what should be the timetable for its full implementation, but all (apart from the United Kingdom) subscribed to the broad outlines of the scheme that was put forward in April 1989 by the Delors Committee in its *Report on Economic and Monetary Union* (see Chapter 6 for the circumstances in which the Committee was established). The Committee proved to be the forerunner of the 1990–1 IGC on EMU, in that not only did it clear much of the ground for the establishment of the IGC, but many of its proposals – including the principle of a three stage transition to EMU – were accepted by the IGC and incorporated in the TEU.

The TEU provisions on EMU were set out in Chapter 3 and so will not be repeated here. Suffice it to say that they established a scheme and a timetable for progression to EMU. The main features of the scheme are increasing coordination and convergence of the economic and monetary policies of the member states, leading to a single currency and the establishment of a European Central Bank (ECB) operating within the framework of a European System of Central Banks (ESCB). The main features of the timetable are a three stage transitional process leading to the adoption of the single currency by 1997 at the earliest (for those countries which are willing and which meet the specified conditions) and by 1999 at the latest (for those countries which meet the specified conditions – except for the United Kingdom and Denmark which are not committed to entering the single currency).

Some progress in realising the EMU objectives of the TEU is undoubtedly being made: stage one began on 1 July 1990 and stage two did so on 1 January 1994; member states are working more closely together – not least by trying to coordinate their macroeconomic policies and by agreeing national convergence programmes in the Council of Ministers; and EU intervention to tackle economic problems is developing – as witnessed by decisions taken at European Council meetings in 1992 and 1993 to make substantial funds available to support Commission initiatives to promote growth, competitiveness and employment.

However, there have also been developments which have brought the TEU scheme and timetable for EMU seriously into question. Two of these developments are especially important. First, few, if any, EU member states look as though they will meet, by the mid- to late-1990s, all of the conditions for progression to the third stage of EMU. (The conditions are low inflation, public finances without excessive deficits or debt, a stable currency, and stable interest rates.) Second, the ERM of the EMS, which was envisaged as being a key mechanism in the projected movement to EMU because of its role in promoting currency stability, has lost much of its usefulness following chronic instability in the Mechanism in 1992–3. The first in what became a series of ERM crises occurred in September 1992 when the lira was devalued (the first realignment in the ERM since 1987) and shortly afterwards both sterling and the lira suspended their ERM membership. Eleven months later, in August 1993, the ERM virtually ceased to exist in a recognisable form when it was decided that the bands for most of the currencies still in the system (which then stood at either 2.5 per cent or 6 per cent), would be widened to, what in effect became an almost free-floating, 15 per cent. (Only the Deutschmark and the Dutch Guilder did not move to this broad band.)

EMU is thus proceeding in some respects, but has been damaged in others. Several future scenarios can be envisaged, with some sort of intensification of the variable speed EMU that was envisaged in the TEU being perhaps the most likely.

☐ *Functional policies*

The EU has interests and responsibilities in many functional policies: policies, that is, which have a clear functional purpose, and which are more specific in nature than the policies considered under the previous heading.

Probably the best known of the EU's functional policies, and in budgetary terms by far the most important, are the regional policy – aspects of which are financed by the European Regional Development Fund (ERDF) – and the social policy – aspects of which are financed by the European Social Fund (ESF). (There is some discussion of these funds in Chapters 4 and 12.) Less prominent functional policies include educational policy, cultural policy, and consumer protection policy. Since it is not possible to examine all of the EU's functional policies here, attention will be directed to five of the more important. The examinations which follow will, in addition to explaining the features of the five policy spheres which are considered, also illustrate the range, and varying depth, of EU involvement in different functional areas.

☐ *Justice and home affairs policy.* In the mid-1970s the EC member states began to exchange information and to cooperate with one another on matters relating to the monitoring and control of terrorism, drugs, and organised crime. A series of mechanisms, which were quite outside the framework of the Community Treaties and which came to be known as the Trevi process, developed, which brought together, often on a semi-secret basis, officials from Interior and Justice ministries, senior police and intelligence officers, and ministers. Over the years the issues covered by Trevi developed – due in no small part to the need to dismantle internal border controls as part of the SEM programme – so that by the late 1980s the original 'threats' of terrorism, drugs and organised crime had been joined on the agenda by a variety of matters relating to immigration, visas, public order, computer systems, and customs controls.

This array of policy interests, and the plethora of *ad hoc* arrangements which had developed to deal with them, were brought together and strengthened by the TEU. They were so mainly under the third pillar of the Treaty – dealing with Provisions on Cooperation in the Fields of Justice and Home Affairs – which laid down objectives and rules in respect of three aspects of Justice and Home Affairs (JHA). Since these aspects were described at some length in Chapter 3, they will be only summarised here. First, the member states were to regard nine JHA areas as 'matters of common interest': asylum policy, rules governing the crossing of the EU's external borders by persons, immigration policy, combatting drug addiction, combating international fraud, judicial cooperation on civil matters, judicial cooperation on criminal matters, customs cooperation, and police cooperation for the purpose of preventing and combating terrorism, drug trafficking and other serious forms of international crime. It will be noted that these nine areas do not explicitly include visa policy – the reason being that the TEU dealt with this by making it the subject of a new Article 100c of the EC Treaty. Amongst the requirements of Article 100c (EC) is that a common visa policy shall be adopted, by qualified majority voting rules in the Council, by 1 January 1996. Second, the Council was empowered to adopt joint positions and joint actions, and to draw up conventions. Third, new institutional arrangements to promote cooperation and coordination, and to enable the EU to fulfil its obligations under the Treaty, were to be established. Central to these arrangements was to be a new Coordination Committee of senior officials – the K.4 Committee. This new Committee is now functioning and is divided into three sub-committees: immigration and asylum; security and law enforcement and police and customs cooperation; and judicial coopera- tion. Each of these sub-committees has its own working groups.

The TEU thus not only consolidated, but also significantly extended, the EU's responsibilities in the JHA sphere. This is most obviously seen in the way in which the foundations were laid for a common visa policy, a common asylum policy, a common immigration policy, increased police cooperation, and the establishment of a European information system. These are all highly sensitive issues which, it can be anticipated, will be the subject of much debate in the years ahead. If pressures increase on the EU to allow permanent entry to significantly increased numbers of people from third countries, they are issues which are likely to become highly charged and the focus of intense controversy.

☐ *Social policy.* The EEC Treaty provided for the development of a Community social policy. It did so in two ways: Articles 117–122 stated that there should be closer cooperation between the member states in the social field, and specified particularly (in Article 119) that member states should apply the principle that men and women should receive equal pay for equal work; Articles 123–128 laid the foundation for a European Social Fund (ESF) which was to be used primarily for the purpose of assisting the unemployed by means of vocational retraining, resettlement allowances, and temporary financial aid.

The ESF was quickly established and has, over the years, made an important contribution to employment training and retraining in the member states, especially in respect of young people and the long-term unemployed to whom it has been mainly directed. But until relatively recently not a great deal was done to give effect to Articles 117–122, apart from some developments – via both legislation and Court of Justice judgements – in areas such as working conditions, entitlements to benefits, and equal opportunities. However, in 1989 a major boost was given to Community social policy when the Commission – believing that the SEM programme should have a 'social dimension' – produced *The Community Charter of Fundamental Social Rights for Workers*. The Charter was inevitably somewhat general in its character and terminology but it contained the fundamental principles which should apply to twelve main themes. Amongst these themes were: free movement of workers on the basis of equal treatment in access to employment and social protection; employment on the basis of fair remuneration; improvement of living and working conditions; freedom of association and collective bargaining; and protection of children and adolescents. The Charter was adopted by eleven member states (the United Kingdom was the exception) at the December 1989 Strasbourg European Council meeting. The Strasbourg summit also took 'note of the fact that the Commission has drawn up an action programme on the application of the Charter and calls upon the Council to deliberate upon the Commission's proposals in the light of the social dimension of the internal market and having regard to the national and Community responsibilities' (Conclusions of the Presidency).

Amongst the 47 measures which were listed in the action programme were proposals for directives on employment and working conditions, on employment contracts, on health and safety at work, on the protection of pregnant women and young people at work, and on travel conditions for the disabled. By the end of 1993 the Commission had presented detailed proposals on all of the 47 measures, including 29 which required legislative action. Included amongst those which required legislation were several very controversial proposals, such as the Directive on the Organisation of Working Time to which the UK government was strongly opposed. The Working Time Directive, which had been first presented in 1990, was eventually approved by the Council in December 1993, with the United Kingdom, after winning several concessions and derogations, abstaining. The Directive lays down provisions on such matters as: maximum weekly working time, daily rest, breaks, weekly rest, annual paid leave, and night-time working hours.

The opposition of the UK Government to much of the Social Charter and the action programmes was carried into the negotiations which led to the TEU. As was noted in Chapter 3, the UK was unwilling to sanction Treaty extensions of the remit and the decision-making powers of the EU in the social field, with the consequence that the other eleven member states contracted a separate Protocol and Agreement on Social Policy. Important features of the Agreement between the eleven include: a recalling and a strengthening of 'traditional' social policy interests; a broadening of the scope of social policy to embrace new matters relating to human resources, social protection, social exclusion, and employment (with 'employment' being extended to include the protection of workers where their employment contract is terminated, and the representation and collective defence of the interests of workers and employers); and management and labour are offered greater consultation, and also the opportunity to negotiate agreements at EU level which are to be implemented either on the basis of established national procedures or – at the joint request of the signatory parties – by a Council decision on a proposal from the Commission.

It will be some time before the impact of the Protocol and Agreement is clear. In all probability, however, the relevant EC Treaty articles will be used as the legal bases for social policy wherever possible, both because there is no great wish to fracture the EU more than is necessary and because different social standards in the EU will have distorting effects on the functioning of the market.

☐ *Energy policy.* Given the existence of the ECSC and Euratom Treaties, given the centrality of energy to any modern economy, given the disruption and damage that was caused by oil price increases in the 1970s, and given the immense savings that the Commission has for years identified as accruing from have an integrated energy market, it is perhaps surprising that until the late 1980s very little progress was made in developing a common energy policy – as opposed to having some policies for particular energy sectors. The main obstacle to progress was that the member states – with their differing domestic energy resources, their differing energy requirements, and their large/state owned/monopolistic energy industries – preferred essentially national solutions.

Since the late 1980s, however, there has been a greater receptivity to the idea of a common energy policy. This has been stimulated in no small part by a realisation that energy cannot be isolated from the increasingly integrated SEM, and also by an increased appreciation (which the Gulf War encouraged) of the over-reliance of the EU on external suppliers – the EU depends on non-member countries for almost half of its energy requirements, with the dependence being as high as 70 per cent in the case of oil. Attitudes have thus been changing, and this is bringing about a rapid evolution in energy policy. The evolution is focused around three basic objectives:

• *Developing an internal market in energy.* Progress has been made in the fields of public procurement in the energy equipment sector, tax structures, standardisation of energy equipment and products, and liberalisation of the electricity and gas markets.

- *Developing external energy relations and ensuring security of supply.* Initiatives in this sphere include efforts to establish a pan-Europe energy agreement (via the European Energy Charter which was signed by 47 countries in 1991), attempting to slow the growth in total energy consumption, and promoting domestic energy production.
- *Minimising the negative impact on the environment of energy use and production.* Measures here include a variety of programmes with such purposes as developing alternative sources of non-polluting energy, reinforcing domestic and industrial efficiency, and several fiscal proposals including a carbon/energy tax and incentives for investments in energy-saving and carbon dioxide reducing measures.

☐ *Research and technological development policy.* The EU's research and technological development (R & TD) policy and activities take four main forms:

(1)   Research is undertaken directly by the EU itself at its Joint Research Centre (JRC). The JRC consists of four establishments and employs around 2250 people. Most of the work of the JRC is concentrated on nuclear energy (especially safety issues), materials, remote sensing and, increasingly, industrial research related to the SEM.

(2)   The largest part of EU R&TD consists of shared-cost or contract research. This research is not undertaken by Commission employees but by tens of thousands of researchers in universities, research institutes, and public and private companies. The EU's role is to develop and agree the principles, aims, and conditions of the programmes under which the research is conducted, to coordinate activities, and to provide some of the finance (usually around 50 per cent of the total cost of the research). The better known programmes in this approach to research activity include ESPRIT (information technology), BRITE (industrial technology), and RACE (advanced telecommunications).

(3)   There are concerted action-research projects where the EU does not finance the actual research, but facilitates and finances coordination of work being done at national level. The EU's medical research programme takes this form.

(4)   Some of the research activity takes none of the above three 'conventional' forms, but consists of arrangements in which, for example, only some member states participate, or in which the EU cooperates with non-member states and international organisations. A particularly important research activity of this type is the Joint European Torus (JET) project, in which non-EU states participate with the EU in joint-venture research into controlled nuclear fusion.

❊   ❊   ❊   ❊

R & TD was not mentioned in the original EEC Treaty but the SEA rectified this by amending the Treaty to add a new Title on 'Research and Technological Development'. The TEU developed the SEA provisions a little, whilst preserving the same broad objective of 'strengthening the scientific and technological bases of Community industry and encouraging it to become more competitive at international level', (Article 130f, EC).

A particularly important aspect of the SEA amendments was to legitimise, and give a boost to, a development that the Community initiated in 1984: using multi-annual framework programmes to coordinate and give a strategic view to its many specific R & TD policies and activities. The First Framework Programme covered 1984–7, the Second 1987–91, the Third (which overlapped with the second) 1990–4, and the Fourth 1994–8. The Fourth Framework Programme has been allocated a budget of not less than 12 billion Ecu, of which 28 per cent is directed to information and communication technologies, 18 per cent to non-nuclear energy, 16 per cent to industrial technologies, 13 per cent to life sciences and technologies, and 9 per cent to environmental sciences and technologies. The main themes of the Fourth Framework Programme include improving the coordination of research activities amongst the EU member states, concentrating funding on key technologies which could benefit many industrial sectors, and better dissemination of R & TD findings via a European Technology Assessment Network.

☐ *Environmental policy*. As with R & TD policy, there was no mention of environmental policy in the original EEC Treaty, but it was incorporated by the SEA through a new Title – 'Environment'. The TEU built on the SEA provisions, though not so much in terms of objectives – which remain so vague as to be virtually meaningless – but in terms of operating principles. The key EC Treaty article is now Article 130r(2), which states:

> Community policy on the environment shall aim at a high level of protection taking into account the diversity of situations in the various regions of the Community. It shall be based on the precautionary principle and on the principles that preventive action should be taken, that environmental damage should as a priority be rectified at source and that the polluter should pay. Environmental protection requirements must be integrated into the definition and implementation of other Community policies.

Since Community legislation began to appear in the early 1970s, over 200 legal instruments have been adopted – most of them in the form of directives. They cover matters as important and as diverse as water and air pollution, disposal of chemicals, waste treatment, and protection of species and natural resources. Alongside, and supporting, the legislation are several other policy instruments, ranging from information campaigns to arrangements for the collection of environmental data – the latter being the particular responsibility of the European Environment Agency which, after long delays caused by disagreements in the Council over its siting, was eventually established in Copenhagen in 1994.

Many of the environmental policy instruments, both legislative and non-legislative, have been designed to give effect to the series of Environmental Action Programmes which have been adopted since 1973. The current Programme – which is the Fifth, which is to run from 1993–2000, and which is entitled *Towards Sustainability* – is by far the most ambitious. Drawing on the principles set out in the EC Treaty as amended by the TEU, it seeks to bring about major innovations in EU environmental policy. These innovations include:

- A greater focus on the sources rather than the receptors of pollution.
- An identification of five 'main target sectors' where an EU-level approach is seen as being particularly necessary – industry, energy, transport, agriculture, and tourism.
- A more holistic approach based on addressing the behavioural patterns of producers, consumers, governments and citizens, and also on ensuring that all EU policies are assessed in terms of their environmental impact.
- An increased emphasis on the shared responsibilities of different levels of government – European, national, regional and local – towards the environment.

This last innovation, emphasising shared responsibilities, touches on a very important and unsatisfactory aspect of environmental policy: implementation. Because of the way in which the EU is structured, and because of the Commission's limited resources, implementation of policies and laws is a problem in several EU policy spheres and sectors. It is so, however, particularly in respect of the environment. There are a number of reasons for this, of which expense is frequently the most crucial. It is, for example, very costly to take the measures which are required to meet the standards set out in the 1975 bathing water directive – a directive which not one member state has fully or properly implemented.

☐ *Sectoral policies*

Some EU policies are directed towards specific economic sectors. A few such policies – for coal and steel, for atomic energy, for agriculture, and for transport – were explicitly provided for in the Founding Treaties. Others have their origins in a combination of factors: difficulties in adjusting to changed trading conditions; rapid sectoral decline; and effective political lobbying by interested parties.

The most obvious example of a sectoral policy is the Common Agricultural Policy (CAP) which consumes by far the largest proportion of EU expenditure and where most policy-making responsibilities have been transferred from the member states to the EU. (The CAP is examined in some detail in Chapter 13.) Other, though more modest and less comprehensive, examples of sectoral policies include atomic energy, where important work is undertaken in areas such as research and safety standards, and shipbuilding, where a code of practice includes specified limitations on governmental subsidies and aids.

Two important sectoral policies will be taken to illustrate EU sectoral activity:

☐ *Fishing*. Following years of discussion and the periodic issuing of laws regulating aspects of the industry, a legally enforceable Common Fisheries Policy (CFP) was agreed in 1983. In December 1992, the 1983 agreement was revised by a new framework regulation on fisheries and aquaculture. The main purpose of the 1993 revision was to extend and improve the existing CFP – by, most notably, making provision for 'the Council to set, on a multiannual basis . . . the objectives and detailed rules for restructuring the Community fisheries sector with a view to achieving a balance on a sustainable basis between resources and their exploitation, taking account of possible economic and social consequences and of the special characteristics of the various fishing regions' (Council Press Release, 11171/97).

The essential rationale of the CFP is to ensure that, with resources diminishing, existing fish stocks are exploited responsibly, with due care for the marine ecosystem, and with the interests of fishermen and consumers protected as far as possible. There are four main aspects to the CFP.

● *Access and conservation*. All waters within the EU's 200 mile zone are open to all EU fishermen, but within a 12 mile limit of their own shores member states may reserve fishing to their own fishermen and to those with traditional rights. All conservation measures and conservation implementation measures are agreed at EU level. The key feature of the conservation measures is that Atlantic and North Sea fish stocks are controlled by the setting, on an annual basis, of total allowable catches (TACs) that are divided into national quotas. These TACs and quotas are notorious for evasion and for difficulties in enforcement, so policy implementation procedures were strengthened in a series of Council decisions in 1992–3. The most important decision, which was taken as part of the December 1992 revision of the CFP, was to require that as from 1 January 1995 all EU fishing vessels should have a fishing licence on board. Other implementing decisions taken in 1992–3 included allowing Commission inspectors (of which there are only a few) the right of unannounced arrival and free movement in the member states, and greater use of satellite technology to monitor fishing activities.

• *Market management.* There is a market organisation for fish which covers a price system, marketing arrangements, and an external trade policy.

• *Structural measures.* Funding is made available from the EU budget for matters such as processing and market development projects, conversion and modernisation schemes, and redeployment.

• *External negotiations.* Negotiations with non-EU countries on fishing – which mostly concern access to waters and conservation of fish stocks – are conducted by EU representatives on behalf of all member states.

☐ *Steel.* The ECSC Treaty is essentially based on a liberal economic philosophy in the sense that it is principally concerned with the removal of barriers to trade. So, for the products falling within its jurisdiction – of which, of course, steel is one – it provides for the removal of internal tariffs, quantitative restrictions and most state aids. It also forbids, subject to certain exemptions, price discrimination and cartels. However, some direct intervention is also permitted and powers are given to the ECSC authorities to grant loans for capital investment, to finance research and development and, above all, to set mandatory minimum prices and production quotas when a 'manifest crisis' is deemed to exist. These policy instruments, developed and clarified by secondary legislation, do not add up to a comprehensive legal framework for steel – key decisions on individual enterprises, for example, are still taken primarily at national levels – but they do constitute a very important part of the sectoral law. The EU authorities have, indeed, potentially greater powers of intervention on steel than in any other sector apart from agriculture and fishing, and they have used these powers to try and deal with the problems of falling demand which gave rise to crises in the steel industry in the late 1970s/early 1980s and again in the 1990s. The way in which the powers have been used are described in Chapter 11.

☐ *External policies*

The nature of the EU's external policies are examined at length in Chapter 14. Suffice it, therefore, to make just two key points here. First, there are many aspects to the external policies, but they can be grouped broadly under three headings: external trade policies, foreign and security policy, and development cooperation policy. Second, external policies constitute an extremely important part of the overall EU policy agenda, and they are likely to loom even larger in the future as, within the framework of the TEU's provisions for a Common Foreign and Security Policy (CFSP), foreign policy is more fully developed and defence policy is tackled.

■ Characteristics of EU policies

Three features of EU policies are particularly striking.

☐ *The range and diversity of EU policies*

The EU is still sometimes referred to as 'The Common Market'. It is so because many of its policies and its laws centre on the promotion and defence of an internally free and externally protected market. So, there are the policies that are designed to encourage the free movement of goods, persons, services, and capital; there is the competition policy that seeks to facilitate fair and open competition within and across the borders of the member states; there is the common external tariff (CET); and there is the common commercial policy (CCP). In practice, however, not all of these policies are complete or are wholly successful. There are, for example, still barriers related to company law and company taxation which can make it difficult for firms in different member states to be able to engage in joint commercial activities, and, despite strenuous activity on harmonisation and approximation, many non-tariff barriers to internal trade still exist. In consequence, the EU is, in some respects, less than the common market it is commonly supposed to be.

But in other respects it is more than a common market, in that many of its policy concerns range far beyond matters that are part and parcel of a common market's requirements. The policy concerns of the EU are not, in other words, just concerned with dismantling internal barriers and providing conditions for fair trade on the one hand, and presenting a common external front on the other. There are two main aspects to this.

First, as regards the EU's economic policies, many of these are not based solely on the non-interventionist/*laissez faire* principles that are often thought of as providing the ethos, the ideology even, of the EU. In some spheres the EU tends very much to interventionism/managerialism/regulation, and in so doing it does not always restrict itself to 'market efficiency' policies. This is most obviously seen in the way in which the regional, the social, and the consumer protection policies, plus much of the

CAP, have as their precise purpose the counteracting and softening of nationally unacceptable or socially inequitable market consequences. On a broader front, those policies which are designed to promote economic and financial cooperation at the macro level are part of a drive to take the EU beyond being 'just' a common market: they have as their ultimate purpose making it an economic and monetary union.

Second, the EU has developed many policies which are not only non-market policies but are non-economic policies. Of these the most obvious are those falling within the CFSP framework, where the states consult and attempt to coordinate their positions on key foreign policy questions. In addition to the CFSP, there are many other policy areas – such as the environment, broadcasting, and combating crime – which were long thought of as not being the EU's concern, but where important developments have occurred.

☐ *The differing degrees of EU policy involvement*

The EU's responsibility for policy-making and for policy management varies enormously across its range of policy interests. In those spheres where significant responsibilities are exercised, arrangements are usually well established, and effective policy instruments – legal and financial – are usually available. Where, however, EU involvement is marginal, policy processes may be confined to little more than occasional exchanges of ideas and information between interested parties, whilst policy instruments may merely be of the exhortive and persuasive kind such as are common in many international organisations. Figure 10.1 gives an indication of the varying extent of EU involvement in different policy areas, and Figure 10.2 gives an indication of the varying nature of EU policy involvement.

Examples of extensive EU involvement are the CCP, the CAP, and the CFP. Here, most major policy decisions, such as on external tariffs, agricultural prices, and fishing quotas, are taken at the EU level, whilst their detailed and supposed uniform implementation is left to the states acting as agents of the EU. In areas where these so-called common policies are not, in reality, totally common – and both the CAP and the CFP allow room for governments to provide national aids and assistance – decisions of any significance normally require at least clearance from Brussels.

Moving along the spectrum of EU policy involvement, there are many spheres in which the EU's interests and competence, though less comprehensive than in the examples just given, remain very significant, and complement and supplement the activities of the states in important ways. Competition policy is an example. It seeks to encourage free and open competition throughout the EU by, for instance, setting out

Figure 10.1 *The extent of EU policy involvement*

Extensive EU policy involvement	Policy responsibility shared between the EU and the member states	Limited EU policy involvement	Virtually no EU policy involvement
Trade	Regional	Energy	Housing
Agriculture	Competition	Transport	Civil liberties
Fishing	Industrial	Macroeconomic	Domestic crime
Market regulation	Foreign	Combatting terrorism and drugs	
	Monetary	Pensions	
	Environmental	Health	
	Equal opportunities	Education	
	Working conditions	Defence	
	Consumer protection	International crime	
	Movement across external borders	Social welfare	

Figure 10.2 *The nature of EU policy involvement*

Heavy reliance on legal regulation	A mixture of legal regulation and inter-state cooperation	Monetary	Largely based on inter-state cooperation
Trade	Industrial	Monetary	Macroeconomic
Agriculture	Environmental		Health
Fishing	Transport		Education
Regional	Movement across external borders		Foreign
Competition			Defence
Consumer protection			Energy
Working conditions			Law and order
Equal opportunities			Combatting terrorism and drugs
Market regulation			Social welfare

conditions under which firms can make and sell their products, by laying down conditions under which national authorities may assist firms, and by imposing restrictions on certain types of company merger. Social policy provides another example, with much of the concern in this sphere being with job training and re-training, labour mobility, working conditions, and the general promotion of employment.

Turning, finally, to policy spheres where the EU's involvement is, at best, limited, examples include education, health, housing, pensions, and social welfare payments. As these examples make clear, many of the policies which fall into this category of low EU involvement are 'merit goods' (as opposed to 'public goods') and are also policies which have major budgetary implications.

Interestingly, if one looks back to, say, 1970, many issues which would have been listed then as being in the category of limited policy involvement – such as environment and foreign policy – are now no longer so marginal. As has already been indicated, environment has spawned policy programmes and legislation, foreign policy has evolved its own machinery and has seen increasingly coordinated policy development, whilst both have been awarded constitutional recognition via the SEA and TEU. At the same time, some policy spheres in which, in 1970, the Community would not have been thought of as having any competence at all, have crept onto the agenda. Examples include defence policy, which is to be developed under the CFSP pillar of the TEU, and the various policies which are included under the JHA pillar of the TEU.

The patchy and somewhat uncoordinated nature of EU policies

The EU's overall policy framework can hardly be said to display a clear pattern or overall coherence. Some effort is now being made to give it a pattern, a coherence, and a rationale, with the so-called subsidiarity principle, via which only those policies which it is agreed are best dealt with at EU level rather than national level do become the EU's concern. The problem with this principle, however, both as a description of the present reality and as a prescription for future action, is that it is vague and question-begging. Descriptions of the present and evolving policy framework as being centred on 'managed and tempered capitalism' or 'a controlled open market' are of more use in capturing the essence of the EU's policy interests, but they too are still far from wholly satisfactory in that they do not – especially since the TEU – embrace the full flavour of the array and varying depths of EU policy interests, nor do they draw attention to the conflicting principles that underlie different parts of the policy network.

The fact is that the considerable national and political differences which exist in the EU make coordinated and coherent policy development that is based on shared principles and agreed objectives very difficult. This is so because *any* policy development is usually only possible if searching questions are answered to the satisfaction of a large number of EU actors. From the viewpoint of the member states these questions include: is the national (or at least government) interest being served?; is the cooperation and integration that the policy development involves politically acceptable?; and, if the policy sphere does require closer relations with other states, is the EU the most desirable arena in which it should occur? As the EU's extensive range of policies demonstrates, these questions have often been answered in the affirmative, though normally only after being subject to caveats and reservations which sit uneasily beside, and sometimes clash with, one another. But often, too, the responses have been in the negative, or at least have been so on the part of a sufficient number to prevent progress.

Policy development has consequently been as much about what is possible as what is desirable. In the absence of a centre of power with the authority and internal coherence to take an overall view of EU requirements and impose an ordered pattern, policies have tended to be the outcome of complex and laboured interactions, where different, and often contrasting, requirements, preferences, reservations, and fears have all played a part. As a result, the EU's overall policy picture is inevitably patchy and rather ragged. A few spheres – such as the CAP and, increasingly, the operation of the SEM – are well developed. Other spheres, however, which it might have been expected would be developed, are either developed only in uncoordinated and partial ways, or are barely developed at all.

Industrial policy is a prime example of just such an uncoordinated and underdeveloped policy. With industry employing 35 per cent of the EU's active population and accounting for 40 per cent of the gross value added of the EU's economy, and with industrial growth in the EU lagging behind competitors, it might be expected that an industrial policy would be at the very centre of EU policy concerns. In practice, a fully developed, comprehensive, and coherent industrial policy does not exist. What do exist are a large number of policies, themselves usually only partially developed, which affect industry, but which do not in any sense constitute an integrated industrial framework with clear and consistent goals. The most obvious of these policies are those which are designed to promote the free movement of goods, persons, services and capital throughout the EU. Others include the competition policy, the research policy, aspects of the regional and social policies, and specific policies for some expanding and some contracting sectors.

■ Concluding comments

A central theme of this chapter has been the range and diversity of the EU's policy responsibilities and interests. There are now few policy areas with which the EU does not have at least some sort of involvement.

But another theme has been that there are many deficiencies in EU policies. Economic and monetary policy, industrial policy, energy policy, and regional policy are but four examples of key policy areas where there are not, if EU effectiveness is to be maximised, sufficiently strong or integrated policy frameworks with clear and consistent goals. They are too partial and too fragmented. They are also, in general, underfunded.

Of course, similar critical comments about underdevelopment and lack of cohesion can also be levelled against most national policy frameworks. But not to the same extent. For, at individual state level there is, even when the political system is weak and decentralised, usually more opportunity than there is in the EU for direction from the centre. This is partly because national decision-makers have access to more policy instruments than do EU decision-makers. It is mainly, however, because at state level there is normally some focus of political authority capable of offering leadership and imposing a degree of order: a Head of Government perhaps, a Cabinet or Council of Ministers, a Ministry of Economics or Finance, or a dominant party group. In the EU, the Commission, the Council of Ministers and the European Council are the main foci of political authority and leadership, but none is constituted or organised in such a way as to enable it to forge an overall policy coherence or to enforce a clear and consistent policy direction.

However, as Chapter 11 will attempt to show, the situation is improving.

■ *Chapter 11* ■

Policy Processes

■ Variations in EU processes

There can hardly be said to be a 'standard' or a 'typical' EU policy-making or decision-making process. A multiplicity of actors interact with one another via a myriad of channels.

□ *The actors*

There are three main sets of actors: those associated with the EU institutions, with the governments of the member states, and with Euro and national interests. As has been shown in previous chapters, each of these has responsibilities to fulfil and roles to perform. But so variable and fluid are EU policy processes that the nature of the responsibilities and roles may differ considerably according to circumstances. For instance, in one set of circumstances an actor may be anxious to play an active role and may have the power – legal and/or political – to do so. In a second set of circumstances it may not wish to be actively involved, perhaps because it has no particular interests at stake or because prominence may be politically damaging. And, in a third set of circumstances, it may wish for a leading part but not be able to attain it because of a lack of appropriate power resources.

□ *The channels*

The channels vary in four principal respects.

297

□ *In their complexity and exhaustiveness.* Some types of decisions are made fairly quickly by a relatively small number of people using procedures that are easy to operate. By contrast, others are the subject of complex and exhaustive processes in which many different sorts of actors attempt to determine and shape outcomes.

□ *In the relative importance of EU-level processes and member state-level processes and in the links between the two levels.* One of the EU's major structural difficulties is that it is multi-layered and there are often no clear lines of authority or of hierarchy between the different layers or levels.

□ *In their levels of seniority.* This is seen in the many different forums in which the member states meet: Heads of Government in the European Council; Ministers in the Council of Ministers; Permanent Representatives and their deputies in COREPER; senior officials and national experts in working parties, management and regulatory committees, and expert groups.

□ *In their degrees of formality and structure.* By their very nature the fixed and set piece occasions of EU policy processes – such as meetings of the Council of Ministers, plenary sessions of the EP, Council of Ministers/EP delegation meetings called to resolve legislative and budgetary differences – tend to be formal and structured. Partly because of this, they are often, in themselves, not very well equipped to produce the trading, the concessions, and the compromises that are so often necessary to build majorities, create agreements, and further progress. As a result they have come to be supported by a vast network of informal and unstructured channels between EU actors. Examples of such channels are everywhere and range from the after dinner discussions that are sometimes held at European Council meetings to the continuous rounds of soundings, telephone calls, lunches, lobbying opportunities, and pre-meetings that are such a part of EU life in Brussels, Strasbourg, Luxembourg and national capitals.

■ Factors determining EU policy processes

The central point made in the previous section – that EU policy-making and decision-making processes are multi-faceted in nature – is illustrated in some detail in Chapters 12, 13 and 14 on the budget, agricultural policy, and external relations. Taken together, these chapters demonstrate how difficult it is to generalise about how the EU functions.

It would, of course, be expected that, as in individual states, there would be some differences between EU processes in different policy arenas. What is distinctive about the EU, however, is the sheer range and complexity of its processes: a host of actors, operating within the context of numerous EU and national-level institutions, interact with one another on the basis of an array of different decision-making rules and procedures.

In trying to bring an overall perspective to the complexity of EU processes a number of factors can be identified as being especially important in determining the particular mix of actors and channels which are to be found in any particular context.

☐ *The Treaty base*

In treaty terms, the EU is based on the Treaty on European Union. As was shown in Chapter 3, the TEU is made up of several components – Common Provisions, the Treaties of the three European Communities, Provisions on a Common Foreign and Security Policy (CFSP), Provisions on Cooperation in the Fields of Justice and Home Affairs (JHA), and a series of protocols and declarations.

One of the most important things these component parts of the TEU do is to set out several different decision-making procedures and to specify the circumstances in which they are to be used. As a result, the TEU is of fundamental importance in shaping the nature of the EU's policy processes and in determining the powers exercised by institutions and actors within the processes. To give just a few examples of the variety of policy-making and decision-making procedures set down in the TEU (these are all explained at length elsewhere in the book – either below or in other chapters):

● There are four 'standard' procedures for 'non-administrative' legislation: the consultation, cooperation, co-decision, and assent procedures. Key points of difference between these procedures include: (1) the EP can exercise veto powers under the co-decision and assent procedures but cannot do so under the consultation and cooperation procedures; and (2) there are single readings in the Council and the EP under the consultation and assent procedures, two readings under the cooperation procedure, and potentially three readings – or, perhaps more accurately, two readings and a third voting stage – under the co-decision procedure.

● External trade agreements negotiated under Article 113 of the EC Treaty have their own special procedure, under which the Commission and the Council decide and the EP, at best, is able only to offer advice.

- The annual budget has its own arrangements, under which the Council and the EP are joint budgetary authorities.
- Under the Agreement on Social Policy concluded between the member states with the exception of the United Kingdom, there are provisions for legislative decisions to be taken – via the consultation or cooperation procedures – by eleven member states.
- The CFSP and JHA pillars set out largely, though not wholly, intergovernmental frameworks which enable non-legislative decisions of various sorts to be taken. Under both pillars the Council is given considerable room for manoeuvre to decide whether or not it needs to consult the EP. In broad terms, major decisions under both pillars require unanimity in the Council and consultation with the EP, whilst operational and procedural decisions can usually be taken by qualified majority vote if the Council so decides and without consultation with the EP. Whether or not the EP is consulted, the Council must keep it regularly informed of developments under the two pillars.

☐ *The proposed status of the matter under consideration*

As a general rule, procedures tend to be more fixed when EU law is envisaged than when it is not. They are fixed most obviously by the Treaties (see above), but also by Court interpretations (for example, the obligation that the Council must wait upon EP opinions before giving Commission proposals legislative status) and by conventions (for example, the understanding in the Council that when a member state has genuine difficulties the matter will not normally be rushed and an effort will be made to reach a compromise even when majority voting is permissible).

Where law is being made, Commission legislation is usually subject to much less review and discussion than Council legislation. The reason for this is that Commission legislation is normally of an administrative kind, more technical than political. Much of it, indeed, consists of updates, applications or amendments to already existing legislation – usually in the sphere of external trade or the CAP. As a result, Commission legislation, prior to being introduced, is often only fully discussed by appropriate officials in the Commission, and perhaps by national officials in a management or regulatory committee. Council legislation, on the other hand, because of its normally broader scope, is usually subject to one of the legislative procedures identified above and, as such, becomes the subject of representations and pressures from many interests, is assessed by the EP and the ESC, and is scrutinised in detail in national capitals and in Council forums in Brussels.

Where policy activity does not involve law making, considerable discretion is available to key decision-makers, especially governments, as to what policy processes will be used and who will be permitted to participate. A common procedure when states wish the EU to do something, but do not wish for it necessarily to involve making new law (which may be because there is no agreement on what the law should be or because, as with foreign policy pronouncements, law is inappropriate), is to issue Council resolutions, declarations, or agreements. These can be as vague or as precise as the Council wishes them to be. Often, resolutions and the like can have a very useful policy impact, even if it is just to keep dialogue going but, because they are not legal instruments, they are not normally as subject as most Council legislation to examination and challenge by other EU institutions and actors.

☐ *The degree of generality or specificity of the policy issue*

At the generality end of the scale, EU policy-making may consist of little more than exchanges of ideas between interested parties to see whether there is common ground for policy coordination, for the setting of priorities, or for possible legislation. Such exchanges and discussions take place at many different levels on an almost continuous basis, but the most important, in the sense that their initiatives are the ones most likely to be followed up, are those which involve *les grands messieurs* of the Commission and the member states.

Far removed from *grands tours d'horizon* by *les grands messieurs* is the daily grind of preparing and drafting the mass of highly detailed and technical regulations that make up the great bulk of the EU's legislative output. Senior EU figures, especially ministers, are not normally directly involved in the processes which lead to such legislation. There may be a requirement that they give the legislation their formal approval, but it is Commission officials, aided in appropriate cases by national officials, who do the basic work.

☐ *The newness, importance, controversiality or political sensitivity of the issue in question*

The more these characteristics apply, and the perception of the extent to which they do may vary – what may be a technical question for one may be politically charged for another – the more complex policy processes are likely to be. If, for example, it seems likely that a proposal for a Council directive on some aspect of animal welfare will cause significant difficulties for farmers, it is probable that the accompanying decision-making process will display all or most of the following features: particularly extensive pre-proposal consultations by the Commission; the raising of voices from many sectional and promotional interest groups; very careful examination of the proposal by the EP and the ESC; long and exhaustive negotiations in the Council; considerable activity and manoeuvring on the fringes of formal meetings, and in between the meetings; and, overall, much delay and many alterations en route to the (possible) eventual adoption of the proposal.

The balance of policy responsibilities between EU and national levels

Where there has been a significant transfer of responsibilities to the EU – as, for example, with agricultural, commercial, and competition policies – EU-level processes are naturally very important. In such policy spheres, EU institutions – and the Commission in particular – have many tasks to perform: monitoring developments, making adjustments, ensuring existing policies and programmes are replaced when necessary, and so on. On the other hand, where the EU's policy role is at best supplementary to that of the member states – education policy and health policy are examples – most significant policy and decision-making activity continues to be channelled through the customary national procedures, and policy activity at EU level may be very limited in scope.

Circumstances and the perceptions of circumstances

This is seemingly rather vague, but it refers to the crucially important fact that policy development and decision-making processes in the EU are closely related to prevailing political and economic circumstances, to the perceptions by key actors – especially states – of their needs in the circumstances, and to perceptions of the potential of the EU to act as a problem solving organisation in regard to the circumstances. Do the advantages of acting at EU level, as opposed to national levels, and of acting in the EU in a particular way as opposed to another way, outweigh the disadvantages?

It is best to explain this point about circumstances with a specific example. Steel will be taken because it shows in a particularly clear manner how changing circumstances may bring about related changes in EU processes.

As was explained in Chapter 2, the Treaty of Paris gave considerable powers to the High Authority (later Commission). Until the mid-1970s these powers were used primarily to liberalise the market, with the High Authority/Commission expending much of its time and energy attempting to ensure that internal barriers were removed and cartels were eliminated. From 1974, however, market conditions began to deteriorate as a result of falling internal and external demand, reduced profit margins, and cost increases. This led the Commission to look more towards its hitherto largely neglected interventionist powers. Initially an essentially voluntarist path was preferred, but when this proved to be ineffective a stronger approach was taken. By the end of 1980 an assortment of highly *dirigiste* policy instruments, some of which were mandatory, were in place. These included common external positions in the form of price agreements and export restraint agreements, strict controls on national subsidies, restrictions on the investment decisions of individual firms, and compulsory quotas (which became possible following the declaration by the Council of a 'manifest crisis' in October 1980).

The emphasis of EU steel policy thus switched between 1974 and 1980, from promoting the freedom and efficiency of the market, to managing the market. This switch had very important implications for decision-making processes. Four of these implications are particularly worth noting. First, there was now more policy responsibility and activity at ECSC level than previously. As a result of this, the overall policy picture as regards steel became a complicated mixture of Community and national processes, with not all of them pulling in the same direction. Second, the assumption by the Community of new and important policy powers, many of which had direct distributional consequences, inevitably created tensions in the Council. At the same time, it also resulted in the Council, as a collective body, taking greater care to ensure that, on key decisions, the Commission acted under its direction. (Although this did not stop governments from using the Commission as a useful device for deflecting the blame for necessary, but unpopular, decisions away from themselves.) Third, the Commission, notwithstanding its obligation to work within a Council-approved framework, extended its roles and functions in several important respects: as an initiator and proposer of policy; as a mediator amongst national and corporate interests (by, for example, putting together complicated production quota packages for the different types of steel product); as the Community's external negotiator (the Treaty of Paris did not establish a customs union and it was not until the late 1970s that the states began to adopt common external positions); and as a decision-maker (the Commission assumed more powers to act directly – for example, on investment aids subsidies). Fourth, non-institutional and non-governmental interests inevitably sought to become much more involved in decision-making as the Community developed policies with a very obvious and very direct impact on output, prices, profits, and employment. A striking illustration of this was the way in which EUROFER – the European Confederation of Iron and Steel Industries, which represents about 60 per cent of Community steel capacity – negotiated with the Commission on production quotas.

The steel crisis of the late 1970s/early 1980s thus significantly altered the nature of the Community's decision-making processes as regards steel. A consequence of this was that when, in the 1990s, the European steel industry faced another major crisis – characterised by falling demand, depressed prices, and many plants working below capacity – these processes again came into play: with the Commission bringing forth a package of restructuring measures which the Council, after long drawn-out negotiations – in which the Italian, Spanish, and German governments were especially prominent in seeking to build in protections for their steel industries – eventually agreed to in December 1993. An important aspect of the 1993 restructuring package was that it was not imposed in the manner of the 'manifest crisis' measures of the late 1970s/early 1980s, but was based more on a dialogue between the Commission and steel producers: a dialogue in which the steel industry played a central part in identifying capacity productions – though not as many as the Commission wanted – and in which the Commission offered 'compensations' in the form of financial aid, temporary subsidies, and increased tariffs and tight quotas on steel imports from Eastern and Central Europe. In an attempt to ensure that the scheme was effective – which was problematical given its semi-voluntaristic nature – the Council increased the monitoring and implementing powers of the Commission.

■ The making of EU legislation

Having established that there are considerable variations in EU policy-making and decision-making processes, it is necessary now to look at common, shared, and recurring features. For, except in the narrowest of senses, not every policy is formulated nor every decision taken, in a manner that is unique to it alone.

This is no more clearly seen than in relation to the making of EU legislation. Most legislation takes one of three 'set routes':

(1)   Administrative/management/regulatory/implementing legislation is issued mainly in the form of Commission regulations and decisions. The basic work on this type of legislation is undertaken by officials in the

relevant Directorate General. Commissioners themselves are only involved in the making of such legislation when it is not straightforward or someone requests they take a look.

National officials usually have the opportunity to voice their comments in a committee, but whether they have the power to stop legislation to which they object depends on which committee procedure applies. As was explained in Chapter 4, the Commission is in a much stronger position when it works through advisory committees than it is when it works through management, and even more so regulatory, committees.

When this type of legislation is issued as Council legislation, it naturally results in national officials playing a more active role, and formal ministerial approval is required.

(2)   Much of the legislation that is enacted in connection with the EU's external trade policies is based on agreements with third countries and is, therefore, subject to special decision-making procedures. These procedures are described in Chapter 14. Amongst their distinctive features are: the Commission usually acts as the EU's main negotiator in economic negotiations with third countries; the Council seeks to control and monitor what the Commission does during negotiations; the EP does not normally exercise much influence – except where cooperation and association agreements are proposed; most legislation produced as a result of negotiations, including virtually all legislation which is intended to establish the principles of a legal framework, is enacted in the form of Council regulations and decisions and therefore requires formal ministerial approval.

(3)   Most of what remains consists of legislation that is deemed to require examination via one of the EU's full legislative procedures. There are no hard and fast rules for deciding when proposals fall into this category but, in general, they are those that are thought to be significant or concerned with establishing principles. The broader in scope they are, the more likely they are to be in the form of directives.

Because of their obvious importance, these full legislative procedures need to be examined here. However, since much of the detail of how the EU institutions exercise their particular legislative responsibilities has already been set out in Part 2, a comprehensive account is not attempted in what follows. Attention is restricted to highlighting the principal features of the legislative procedures.

Since the TEU entered into force there have been four different legislative procedures: the consultation, cooperation, co-decision, and assent procedures. There are also two major internal variations to these procedures: (1) Under the consultation, co-decision, and assent procedures, qualified majority voting rules apply in the Council when legislation is being made under certain Treaty articles, whereas unanimity is required under other articles. (2) Under the consultation and cooperation procedures, legislation is made by, and for, only eleven member states (the United Kingdom being excluded) when the TEU Protocol and Agreement on Social Policy is being used (see Chapter 3).

Descriptions of the EU's legislative procedures now follow. Diagrammatic representations of the consultation and cooperation procedures are given in Figure 11.1 (p. 313) and of the co-decision procedures in Figure 11.2 (p. 316). A listing of the Treaty articles under which the procedures apply, and of the policy spheres which they cover, is given in Table 11.1 (pp. 318–22).

☐ *The consultation procedure*

☐ *Initiation.* The starting point of a legislative proposal is when somebody somewhere suggests that the EU should act on a matter. Most likely this will be the Commission, the Council, or the EP: the Commission because it is the only body with the authority formally to table a legislative proposal, and because, too, of its special expertise in, and responsibility for, EU affairs; the Council because of its political weight, its position as the natural conduit for national claims and interests, and its power under Article 152 (EC) to request the Commission 'to undertake any studies the Council considers desirable for the attainment of the common objectives, and to submit to it any appropriate proposals'; and the EP because of the desire of MEPs to be active and because under Article 138b of the EC Treaty (which was newly created by the TEU) 'The European Parliament may, acting by a majority of its members, request the Commission to submit any appropriate proposals on matters on which it considers that a Community act is required for the purpose of implementing this Treaty'.

Beyond the Commission, the Council, and the EP there are many other possible sources of EU legislation, but little progress can be made unless the Commission decides to take an issue up and draft proposals. Many circumstances may result in it deciding to do so, but often it is very difficult, in looking at specific proposals, to discover just why the Commission decided to act and to identify precisely from where the initiative originated. For example, a Commission proposal that may seem to be a response to a Council request may, on inspection, be traced back beyond the Council to a national pressure group influencing a minister, who then gradually and informally introduced the issue into the Council as an option to be considered. Similarly, a Commission proposal may seem to be a response to an EP request or to representations from European-wide interests, but in fact the Commission may itself have dropped hints to the EP or to interests that they should look at the matter (thus reinforcing the Commission's own position *vis-à-vis* the Council).

☐ *Preparation of a text.* Once it has been decided to produce a proposal (a decision that is usually taken at a fairly senior level within the most relevant Directorate General), a text is prepared. The standard way in which this is done is as follows: officials in the appropriate DG write an initial draft; the draft is passed upwards through superiors; as it is passed upwards the draft is discussed with all DGs and specialised Commission services which have an interest; when all directly involved Commission interests have given their approval, the draft is sent to the *cabinet* of the Commissioner responsible for the subject; the *cabinet*, which may or may not have been involved in informal discussions with Commission officials as the proposal was being drafted, may or may not attempt to persuade Commission officials to re-work the draft before submitting it to the Commissioner for approval; when the Commissioner is satisfied, he asks the Secretariat General to submit the draft to the College of Commissioners; the draft is scrutinised, and possibly amended, by the *chefs de cabinet* at their weekly meeting; if the draft is judged to be uncontroversial the Commissioners may adopt it by written procedure; if it is controversial the Commissioners may, after debate, accept it, reject it, amend it, or refer it back to the relevant DG for further consideration.

In preparing a text officials usually find themselves the focus of attention from many directions. Knowing that the Commission's thinking is probably at its most flexible at this preliminary stage, and knowing, too, that once a proposal is formalised it is more difficult to change, interested parties use whatever means they can to press their views. Four factors most affect the extent to which the Commission is prepared to listen to outside interests at this pre-proposal stage. First, what contacts and channels have already been regularised in the sector and what ways of proceeding have proved to be effective in the past? Second, what political considerations arise and how important is it to incorporate different sectional and national views from the outset? Third, what degree of technical knowledge and outside expertise is called for? Fourth, how do the relevant Commission officials prefer to work?

Assuming, as it is normally reasonable to do, Commission receptivity, there are several ways in which 'external' views may be brought to the attention of those drafting a proposal. The Commission itself may request a report, perhaps from a university or a research institute. Interest groups may submit briefing documents. Professional lobbyists, politicians, and officials from the Permanent Representations may press preferences in informal meetings. EP committees and ESC sections may be sounded out. And use may be made of the extensive advisory committee system that clusters around the Commission (see Chapter 4).

There is, therefore, no standard consultative pattern or procedure. An important consequence of this is that governmental involvement in the preparation of Commission texts varies considerably. Indeed, not only is there a variation in involvement, but there is a variation in knowledge of Commission intentions. Sometimes, governments are fully aware of Commission thinking, because national officials have been formally consulted in committees of experts. Sometimes, sectional interests represented on consultative committees will let their governments know what is going on. Sometimes, governments will be abreast of developments as a result of having tapped sources within the Commission, most probably through officials in their Permanent Representations. But, sometimes, governments are not aware of proposals until they are published.

The time that elapses between the decision to initiate a proposal and the publication by the Commission of its text naturally depends on a number of factors: (1) is there any urgency? (2) how keen is the Commission to press ahead? (3) how widespread are the consultations? (4) does the Commission want the prior support of all key actors? (5) is there a consensus within the Commission itself? Not surprisingly periods of over a year are common.

☐ *The opinions of the European Parliament and the Economic and Social Committee.* On publication, the Commission's text is submitted to the Council of Ministers, which in turn refers it to the EP and, where appropriate, to the ESC, for their opinions.

The EP is by far the more influential of the two bodies. Though it does not have the full legislative powers of national parliaments it has enough weaponry in its arsenal to ensure that its views are at least taken into consideration, particularly by the Commission. Its representational claims are one source of its influence. The quality of its arguments and its suggestions are another. And it has the power of delay, by virtue of the requirement that Parliament's opinion must be known before the proposal can be formally adopted by the Council.

As was shown in Chapter 7, most of the detailed work undertaken by the EP on proposed legislation is handled by its specialised committees and, to a lesser extent, by its political groups. Both the committees and the groups advise MEPs how to vote in plenary.

The usual way in which plenaries act to bring influence to bear is to vote on amendments to the Commission's proposal, but not to vote on the draft legislative resolution – which constitutes the EP's opinion – until the Commission states, as it is obliged to do, whether or not it will change its text to incorporate the amendments that have been approved by the EP. If the amendments are accepted by the Commission a favourable opinion is issued, and the amended text becomes the text that the Council considers. If all or some of the amendments are not accepted, the EP can attempt to exert pressure by not issuing an opinion and referring the proposal back to the committee responsible. A reference back can also be made if the whole proposal is judged to be unacceptable. Withholding of an opinion does not, it should be emphasised, give the EP the power of veto, because it is legally obliged to issue opinions, and the Court of Justice, in several judgements, has referred to the duty of loyal cooperation between the Community institutions. What the withholding of opinions does do, however, is to give the EP the often useful bargaining and pressurising tool of the power of delay.

For the reasons which were outlined in Chapter 7, and which are considered further below, it is difficult to estimate with any precision the impact the EP has on EU legislation. In general terms, however, it can be said that the record in the context of the consultation procedure is mixed:

- On the 'positive' side, the Commission is normally sympathetic to the EP's views and accepts about three-quarters of its amendments. The Council is less sympathetic and accepts considerably less than half of the amendments, but that still means that many EP amendments, on many different policy matters, find their way into the final legislative texts.
- On the 'negative' side, there are three main points to be made. First, there is not much the EP can do if the Council rejects its opinion. The best it can normally hope for is a conciliation meeting with the Council (not to be confused with a Conciliation Committee meeting under the co-decision procedure), but such meetings do not usually achieve much – mainly because the Council has no wish to re-open questions which may put at risk its own, often exhaustively negotiated, agreements. Second, the Council sometimes takes a decision 'in principle' or 'subject to Parliament's opinion', before the opinion has even been delivered. In such circumstances the EP's views, once known, are unlikely to result in the Council having second thoughts. Third, it is quite possible for the text of proposals to be changed after the EP has issued its opinion. There is some safeguard against the potential implications of this insofar as the Court of Justice has indicated that the Council should refer a legislative proposal back to the EP if it (the Council) substantially amends the proposal after the EP has issued its opinion. In practice, however, the question of what constitutes a substantial amendment is open to interpretation, and references back do not always occur.

❖   ❖   ❖   ❖

The ESC is, generally, not so well placed as the EP to examine legislative proposals. As was explained in Chapter 9, a major reason for this is that its formal powers are not as great: while it must be consulted on draft legislation in many policy spheres, consultation is only optional in some. Furthermore, when it is consulted, the Council or the Commission may lay down a very tight timetable, can go ahead if no opinion is issued by a specified date, and cannot be frustrated by delays if the ESC wants changes to the text. Other sources of weakness include the part-time capacity of its members, the personal rather than representational nature of much of its membership, and the perception by many interests that advisory committees and direct forms of lobbying are more effective channels of influence.

As a result of these weaknesses the ESC's influence over EU legislation is considerably less than that of the EP. Nonetheless, some note is taken of its opinions, though exactly how much is impossible to say, for even when ESC views do appear to have been taken into account, closer inspection often reveals that the really decisive influence has probably come from elsewhere. For example, a Council directive concerned with the implementation of the principle of equal treatment for men and women in occupational social security schemes, which was listed in the 1986 ESC Annual Report as being influenced 'to a large extent' by an ESC opinion, was also the subject of strong representations by sectional interests and member governments. In the 1987 Annual Report, a similar claim was made for a Council directive on the legal protection of original topographies of semi-conductor products, but on this very same proposal the EP made much the same claim and suggested that the Council had accepted eight of the twelve amendments it had adopted.

☐ *Decision-making in the Council.* As has just been noted, the Council does not necessarily wait on the EP or the ESC before proceeding with a proposal. Indeed, governments may begin preparing their positions for the Council, and informal discussions and deliberations may even take place within the Council itself, before the formal referral from the Commission.

The standard procedure in the Council is for the proposal to be referred initially to a working party of national representatives for detailed examination. The representatives have two principal tasks: on the one hand, to ensure that the interests of their country are safeguarded; on the other, to try to reach an agreement on a text. Inevitably these two responsibilities do not always coincide, with the consequence that working party deliberations can be protracted. Progress depends on many factors: the controversiality of the proposal; the extent to which it benefits or damages states differentially; the number of countries, especially large countries, pressing for progress; the enthusiasm and competence of the Presidency; the tactical skills of the national representatives and their capacity to trade disputed points (both of which are dependent on personal abilities and the sort of briefs laid down for representatives by their governments); and the flexibility of the Commission in agreeing to change its text.

Once a working party has gone as far as it can with a proposal – which can mean reaching a general agreement, agreeing on most points but with reservations entered by some countries on particular points, or very little agreement at all on the main issues – reference is made upwards to COREPER or, in the case of agriculture, to the Special Committee on Agriculture (SCA). At this level, the Permanent Representatives (in COREPER II), their deputies (in COREPER I), or senior agriculture officials (in the SCA) concern themselves not so much with the technical details of a proposal as with its policy and, to some extent its political, implications. So far as is possible differences left over from the working party are sorted out. Where this cannot be done, bases for possible agreement may be identified, and the proposal is then either referred back to the working party for further detailed consideration, or forwarded to the ministers for political resolution.

All proposals must be formally approved by the ministers. Those that have been agreed at a lower level of the Council machinery are placed on the ministers' agenda as 'A' points and are normally quickly ratified. Where, however, outstanding problems and differences have to be considered a number of things can happen. One is that the political authority that ministers carry, and the preparatory work undertaken by officials prior to ministerial meetings, may clear the way for an agreed settlement: perhaps reached quickly over lunch, perhaps hammered out in long and frequently adjourned Council sessions. A second, and increasingly utilised, possibility is that a vote is taken where the Treaty article(s) on which the proposal is based so allows. This does not mean that the traditional preference for proceeding by consensus no longer applies, but it does mean that it is not quite the obstacle it formerly was. A third possibility is that no agreement can be reached, a vote is not possible under the Treaties or is not judged to be appropriate, or if a vote is judged to be possible and appropriate no qualified majority exists. This may lead to the proposal being referred back down the Council machinery, being referred back to the Commission accompanied with a request for changes to the existing text, or being referred to a future meeting in the hope that shifts will take place in the meantime and the basis of a solution will be found.

As is shown in Figure 11.1, under the consultation procedure the decision-making process at EU level ends with the Council's adoption of a text.

☐ *The cooperation procedure*

The cooperation procedure was created by the SEA. There were two main reasons for establishing the procedure.

First, to increase the efficiency, and more especially the speed, of decision-making processes. This was achieved by permitting qualified majority voting in the Council of Ministers wherever decisions were subject to the procedure. Ten EEC Treaty articles were made subject to the procedure, the most important of which enabled the procedure to be used in respect of the Single European Market (SEM) programme. Under the TEU, most SEM legislation was 'transferred' from the cooperation procedure to the co-decision procedure.

Second, to respond to pressures for more powers to be given to the EP. This was achieved by introducing a two reading stage for legislation, and increasing the EP's leverage – though not to the point of giving it a veto – over the Council at second reading.

Under the EC Treaty as revised by the TEU, the cooperation procedure is not actually referred to as such in the Treaty, but rather as the Article 189c procedure. This is because the stages of the procedure are set out in Article 189c. Whatever name, however, is given to it, it is clear – as Figure 11.1 shows – that the route taken by legislative proposals which are subject to the procedure is much more complex than the route taken by proposals which are subject to the consultation procedure.

The main stages of the cooperation procedure are as follows:

☐ *EP first reading.* After the Commission has published its proposal, the EP examines the text and issues an opinion. The process by which the examination is conducted is broadly similar to the process of examination under the consultation procedure.

☐ *Council First Reading.* After obtaining the EP's opinion the Council does not, as in the consultation procedure, take a final decision on the proposal, but rather adopts, by a qualified majority vote if need be, what is known as its common position. As is the practice on single reading proposals, unanimity is required for any amendments with which the Commission does not agree. The Council and the Commission must inform the EP of the reasons for the common position and the Commission must explain its own position. (The Commission, of course, can alter its text at

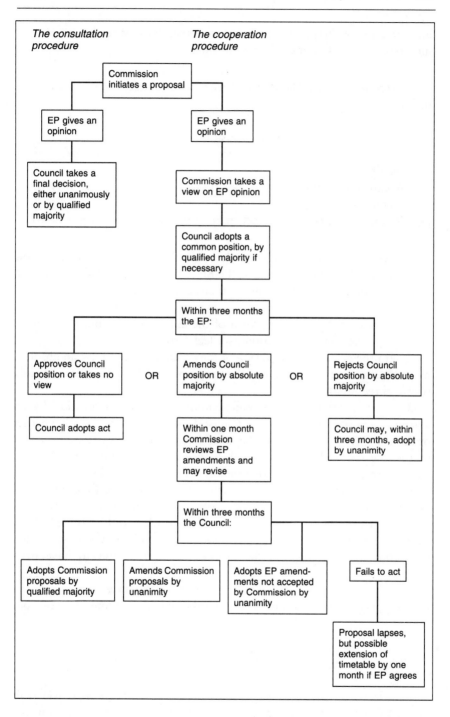

Figure 11.1 *The consultation and cooperation (Art. 189c) procedures*

any time, and is likely to have done so after the EP's first reading in order to incorporate at least some EP amendments.)

☐ *EP second reading*. The EP has three months to take one of four courses of action:

(1)   It can approve the common position.
(2)   It can reject the common position by an absolute majority of all members.
(3)   It can amend the common position by an absolute majority of all members.
(4)   It can choose (or fail) to act in none of the three ways just listed.

☐ *Council second reading*. What the Council does at its second reading depends on what has happened at the EP second reading. Taking, in turn, the four options available to the EP that have just been outlined:

(1)   In the event of EP approval of the common position, the Council may adopt the common position as a legislative act.

(2)   In the event of EP rejection of the common position by an absolute majority, the Council can adopt the proposal only by acting unanimously within three months.

(3)   In the event of EP amendment of the common position by an absolute majority, the Commission must decide within one month whether or not it wishes to incorporate the amendments into the version of the text that is referred back to the Council. If they are incorporated, the Council can approve them by a qualified majority or reject them by unanimity; if they are not incorporated the Council can only approve them by acting unanimously. Whether they are incorporated or not, all EP amendments not accepted by the Commission must be forwarded to the Council. If the Council does nothing within three months of receiving the re-examined text from the Commission, the proposal is deemed not to have been adopted.

(4)   In the event of the EP not acting in any of the three above ways, the Council may adopt the proposal in accordance with the common position.

☐ *The co-decision procedure*

The co-decision procedure was created by the TEU in a new Article 189b of the EC Treaty. Like the cooperation procedure, it is referred to in the Treaty by reference to the Article which sets out its provisions.

Just as the cooperation procedure extended the consultation procedure, so does the co-decision procedure extent the cooperation procedure. It does so, most crucially, by giving to the EP the right to veto proposals which are subject to the procedure. Before such a veto is exercised, however, there are ample opportunities under the procedure for the Council and the EP to resolve such differences as there are between them.

The various stages of the highly complex processes which constitute the co-decision making procedure are set out in Figure 11.2. The key features are as follows:

☐ *EP first reading*. This is as under the consultation and cooperation procedures.

☐ *Council first reading*. This is as under the cooperation procedure, except that in adopting its common position the Council must act by unanimity when taking decisions on cultural matters and on research and development multi-annual framework programmes (this unanimity requirement also applies to these two policy areas in respect of subsequent stages of the co-decision procedure).

☐ *EP second reading*. The EP has three months to do one of the following:
(1)   Approve the common position.
(2)   Take no action.
(3)   Indicate, by an absolute majority of its component members, that it intends to reject the common position.
(4)   Propose amendments to the common position by an absolute majority of its component members.

If either (1) or (2) applies, the Council adopts the proposal in accordance with the common position.

☐ *Council second reading*. In the event of the EP indicating that it intends to reject the common position, the Council may convene a meeting of the Conciliation Committee which is provided for under the co-decision procedure to explain further its position. The EP must then decide whether it wishes to confirm its rejection of the common position by an absolute majority of its members, in which case the proposal falls, or to propose amendments.

In the event of the EP proposing amendments to the common position – either directly at its second reading or following a meeting of the Conciliation Committee – the Council may decide, within three months, to accept them and adopt the proposal. In making its decisions on EP

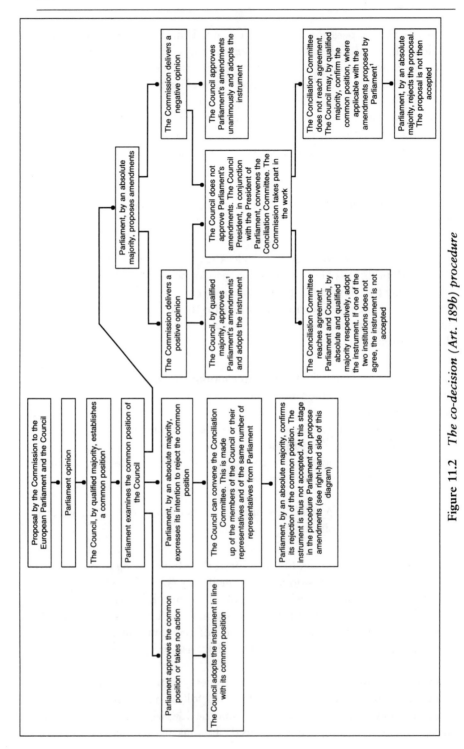

Figure 11.2 *The co-decision (Art. 189b) procedure*

Notes to Figure 11.2:
1 The Council acts unanimously if its recommendation differs from that made by the Commission.
   NB: (a) Each stage of the procedure is subject to time-limits which run from the moment a common position is adopted.
       (b) Proposals can be adopted very quickly under the procedure if the Commission, the EP, and the Council are in agreement. Where there is disagreement, the procedure lasts a maximum of 13 months, calculated from the date of the adoption of the Council's common position.

Source: adapted from European Documentation *European Union*, Office for Official Publications of the European Communities (1993).

amendments, the Council acts by qualified majority vote if the Commission gives them its approval, but by unanimity if it does not. If the Council does not accept the amendments, the President of the Council, in agreement with the President of the EP, convenes a meeting of the Conciliation Committee.

☐ *The Conciliation Committee.* The Committee is composed of an equal number of Council and EP representatives. (The exact composition of the Committee does, of course, vary between conciliation cases – although the EP's Rules of Procedures make provision for three MEPs to be appointed as permanent members of successive delegations for a period of twelve months). The Conciliation Committee has six weeks to try and approve a joint text.

☐ *Council and EP third readings.* These are not full readings in the sense that the details of proposals are examined again, but they are the third occasion on which proposals may be considered by the two institutions. Article 189b provides a succinct description of what happens at this stage:

If, within six weeks of its being convened, the Conciliation Committee approves a joint text, the European Parliament, acting by an absolute majority of the votes cast, and the Council, acting by a qualified majority, shall have a period of six weeks from that approval in which to adopt the act in question in accordance with the joint text. If one of the two institutions fails to approve the proposed act, it shall be deemed not to have been adopted.

Where the Conciliation Committee does not approve a joint text, the proposed act shall be deemed not to have been adopted unless the Council, acting by a qualified majority within six weeks of expiry of the period granted to the Conciliation Committee, confirms the common position to

Table 11.1   *The application of the EU's decision-making procedures*

(Qualified majority voting rules apply in the Council of Ministers except where an asterisk indicates that unanimity is required.)

The consultation procedure

Articles of EC Treaty	Policy sphere covered
8b*	Rights to stand and vote in municipal and European Parliament (EP) elections.
8e*	Citizenship of the Union – strengthen provisions of the Treaty. (Subject to ratification by the Member States.)
43	Agriculture.
54	Freedom of establishment – drawing up of a general programme.
56	Freedom of establishment – implementing measures during transitional period.
57*	Self-employed persons – law governing the professions.
75*	Transport. (Only where decisions 'would be liable to have a serious effect on the standard of living and on employment in certain areas and on the operation of transport facilities'.)
87	Implementation of competition principles.
94	Implementation of rules on state aids.
99*	Indirect taxation.
100*	Harmonisation legislation concerned with 'the establishment or functioning of the common market'. (Derogations from this article mean that, in practice, it mainly applies to provisions relating to fiscal matters, to the free movement of persons, and to the rights and interests of employed persons. See also the co-decision procedure, Article 100a.)
100c	Visas for nationals of non-Member States. (Unanimity required until 31 December 1995; qualified majority voting thereafter.)

104–109	Various aspects of EMU and the movement to EMU. (A mixture of unanimity and qualified majority voting rules.)
130*	Industry.
130b*	Economic and social cohesion outside the framework of the structural funds.
130i	Research and technological development – adoption of specific programmes.
130o*	Research and technological development – establishment of joint undertakings.
130s*	Environment – provisions of a fiscal nature, measures concerning town and country planning, measures concerned with energy sources and energy supply.
201*	Community's own resources. (Subject to ratification by the Member States.)
209*	Making of financial regulations.
228	Certain types of international agreements. (A mixture of unanimity and qualified majority voting rules apply.)
235*	This is the notorious 'catch-all' provision. It empowers the Council to take 'the appropriate measures' if 'action by the Community should prove necessary to attain, in the course of the operation of the common market, one of the objectives of the Community and this Treaty has not provided the necessary powers'.

Under the Agreement on Social Policy concluded between the member states with the exception of the United Kingdom, the consultation procedure (with unanimity in the Council) applies in the following areas:

- social security and social protection of workers;

- protection of workers who are made unemployed;

- representation and collective defence of the interests of workers and employers;

- conditions of employment for third-country nationals residing in the Community;

- financial contributions for promotion of employment and job creation.

The cooperation procedure (the Article 189c procedure)

Articles of EC Treaty	Policy sphere covered
6	Discrimination on the grounds of nationality.
75	Common transport policy.
103–105	Various aspects of EMU and the movement towards EMU.
118a	Health and safety of workers.
125	European Social Fund (ESF) – implementing decisions.
127	Vocational training – implementing decisions.
129d	Trans-European networks – implementing decisions.
130e	European Regional Development Fund (ERDF) – implementing decisions.
130o	Research and Technological development – implementation of programmes.
130s	Environment – action to achieve objectives set out in The Treaty on European Union, and implementation of general action programmes.
130w	Development Cooperation – adoption of measures to further the objectives set out in The Treaty on European Union.

Under the Agreement on Social Policy concluded between eleven member states, with the exception of the United Kingdom, the cooperation procedure applies in the following fields:

- improvement in particular of the working environment to protect workers' health and safety;
- working conditions;
- the information and consultation of workers;
- equality between men and women with regard to labour market opportunities and treatment at work;
- the integration of persons excluded from the labour market.

The co-decision procedure (the Article 189b procedure)

Articles of EC Treaty	Policy sphere covered
49	Free movement of workers.
54	Freedom of establishment – implementation of general programme.
56	Freedom of establishment – special treatment of foreign nationals.
57	Mutual recognition of formal qualifications.
57	Self-employed persons.
100a	Harmonisation for the purpose of completing the internal market.
100b	National laws affecting the operation of the internal market.
126	Education, vocational training and youth (incentive measures only).
128*	Culture.
129	Public health (incentive measures only).
129a	Consumer protection.
129d	Trans-European networks (guidelines).
130*	Research and technological development – adoption of multi-annual framework programme.
130s	Environment – adoption of general action programmes.

The assent procedure

Articles of EC Treaty	Policy sphere covered
8a*	Citizenship of the Union – adoption of provisions designed to promote the right to move and reside freely within the territory of the Member States.
105*	Supervisory tasks of the European Central Bank (ECB).
106	Amendment of the Statute of the European System of Central Banks (ESCB).

130d*	The Structural Funds – definition of the tasks, priority objectives, organisation, and general rules. Establishment of Cohesion Fund.
138*	Elections to EP in accordance with a uniform procedure in all Member States. (Without prejudice to national ratification procedures.)
228	Certain types of agreements with non-member states or groups of states – association agreements; cooperation agreements; agreements having important budgetary implications; and agreements amending an act adopted under Article 189b. (A mixture of unanimity and qualified majority voting rules apply.)

Under Article O of the TEU accessions to the Union require the assent of the EP acting by an absolute majority of its component members.

which it agreed before the conciliation procedure was initiated, possibly with amendments proposed by the European Parliament. In this case, the act in question shall be finally adopted unless the European Parliament, within six weeks of the date of confirmation by the Council, rejects the text by an absolute majority of its component members, in which case the proposed act shall be deemed not to have been adopted.

This third reading stage clearly allows for the possibility of unilateral action by the Council if the EP cannot muster an absolute majority to reject a Council decision to proceed with a proposal after a failure to agree on a joint text in the Conciliation Committee. In the Rules of Procedure which it adopted just before the TEU entered into force in late 1993, the EP sought to head off this possibility of unilateral Council action. It did so by providing: 1) in the event of no agreement being reached on a joint text within the Conciliation Committee, the EP President shall invite the Commission to withdraw its proposal and shall invite the Council not to adopt the proposal; 2) in the event of the Council deciding to proceed with the proposal, the President of the Council shall be invited to justify the Council's actions before the EP in plenary session, and the EP shall automatically vote on a motion to reject the proposal.

Periods of three months and six weeks referred to in the procedure may be prolonged for a limited period by common accord of the Council and the EP.

Legislation made under the co-decision procedure is made jointly under the names of the European Parliament and the Council of Ministers.

☐ *The assent procedure*

The assent procedure, which was first established by the SEA, is simple in form: it specifies that certain types of decisions must be approved by the EP – in some cases by a majority of the votes cast, in others by an absolute majority of the EP's component members. The assent procedure, which is a single reading procedure, does not allow for the EP to make amendments.

Under the TEU the scope of the assent procedure was widened considerably, from its SEA remit of accessions to the EC and association agreements with third countries, to matters as diverse as citizenship and EMU-related issues. The roles and powers of the EU institutions under the procedure, and particularly of the Commission and the Council, now vary considerably. So, for example, where decision-making under the procedure involves the preparation of detailed proposals (as in relation to the Structural Funds under Article 130d of the EC Treaty) or complex negotiations with third countries (as in relation to association and cooperation agreements under Article 228 of the EC Treaty) then the Commission is in a very strong position to influence and shape outcomes – especially if, as is the case in some instances, qualified majority voting rules apply in the Council. Where, however, unanimity is required in the Council and matters of political principle are of crucial importance – as, for example, in regard to citizenship issues (Article 8a, EC) and the devising of a uniform electoral procedure for EP elections (Article 138, EC) – then the Commission is much less favourably placed and the views of the national governments, and of the Council collectively, are critical.

As for the EP, it might be thought that, because under the assent procedure it can only pronounce on final proposals, and cannot table amendments, it would be confined to a rather limited confirmatory/withholding role. To some extent it indeed is, but not completely, because by having the power to say 'No' to proposals, the EP also has the power to indicate to what it would say 'Yes'. Almost as soon as the procedure first came into operation in 1987 this power was being used – to put pressure on the human rights records of third countries who had signed association and cooperation agreements with the EC, and to put pressure on the Commission and the Council to amend and change the terms of some of these agreements.

▌ Implications of the SEA and TEU reforms for the EU institutions

The procedures established by the SEA (cooperation and assent procedures) and TEU (co-decision procedure) have had many implications, in terms of both functioning and influence, for the institutions which have to operate them. The main implications are these:

• The institutions are now working much more closely with one another than they used to. At a broad level this is seen in increased numbers of inter-institutional meetings of various sorts, and in the practice – which began in 1988 – by which the Commission discusses and agrees its annual legislative programme and timetable with the EP. At more specific levels it is seen in conciliation meetings under the cooperation procedure and in meetings of the Conciliation Committee under the co-decision procedure.
• When presenting legislative proposals, the Commission has to ensure that it is using the correct legal base – that is to say, correct Treaty article – for this determines which procedure applies. Normally the matter is straightforward and there is no argument, but sometimes disputes do arise: is, for example, an internal market proposal with environmental aspects to be based on Article 100a of the EC Treaty (which covers most internal market matters and which provides for the co-decision procedure to apply) or Article 130s of the EC Treaty (which covers most environmental matters and which provides for the cooperation procedure to apply)? Where there is room for argument, the institutions frequently have different preferences: (1) The Commission – because it wishes to see its proposals adopted, if possible without being amended too much – usually prefers to use a procedure where qualified majority voting rules apply in the Council and where the EP does not have a veto. (2) The Council also usually prefers a procedure under which the EP does not have a veto, whilst national governments which are concerned about the implications of particular policy proposals are also likely to prefer a procedure where unanimity is required in the Council. (3) The EP, which is naturally anxious to maximise its position, prefers those procedures which give it a veto and which permit qualified majority voting in the Council. Knowing that many subjects where the legal base is open to possible dispute are politically sensitive, knowing that the Legal Services Departments of the Council and the EP will thoroughly examine each legal base, and knowing too that its decisions on the legal base are subject to challenge in the Court of Justice, the Commission necessarily acts with great care. The taking of care does not, however, always satisfy everyone: the Council, the EP, and individual

governments have all at times been aggrieved, the Council has changed some legal bases, and there have been references to the Court.

• The Commission has a more difficult task under the cooperation and co-decision procedures than it has under the consultation procedure, in exercising its judgement as to whether, and if so at what stage, it should amend its text so as to get proposals through in a reasonably acceptable form. At the second reading stage, in particular, a delicate balance may have to be struck: between, on the one hand, being sufficiently sympathetic to EP amendments so as not to upset MEPs too much, and, on the other hand, being aware that a revised text might break up a majority attained in the Council at first reading.

• Decision-making in the Council has been speeded up. This is partly accounted for by the provisions for Council qualified majority voting and partly by the timetable limitations which come into effect under the cooperation and co-decision procedures after the Council has agreed its common position. Decisions on particular proposals can still be delayed by the Council's preference – whatever the legal position – for decision-making by consensus but, overall, decision-making in policy areas now subject to the cooperation and co-decision procedures is much quicker than it was before the procedures applied.

• Under the cooperation procedure the Council has the problem of having to be unanimous not just at one legislative stage but at two, if it wishes to avoid incorporating Commission accepted EP amendments into the final text. Moreover, since amendments at the EP second reading require the support of an absolute majority of MEPs and are therefore hardly the reflection of minority interests, the EP – theoretically at least – has a reasonable chance of finding the only ally it needs when the Council holds its second reading. To try and get round this problem one thing the Council sometimes does at its first reading, on proposals where the EP appears likely to cause 'difficulties' at its second reading, is to take time to see if unanimity can be achieved: if it can – and that may be possible only after considerable horse-trading and compromising – the EP is very unlikely to be able to divide the Council and prevent unanimity at the second reading.

• The EP has had to adjust its working methods in several ways: (1) MEPs, and especially *rapporteurs* and committee chairmen, have had to develop a fuller grasp of the technical implications of Commission proposals. (2) The texts embodying Parliament's opinions have had to become more substantial and detailed documents. (3) There is pressure, especially on the group whips, to muster absolute majorities at second readings under the cooperation procedure and at second and third readings under the co-decision procedure, and – under the assent procedure –

sometimes to muster majorities and sometimes to prevent them from being mustered. (When such majorities are desired and are clearly not going to be achieved there are sometimes references back to committees. There have been instances of an absolute majority having been declared on a show of hands when there have been less than 260 in the Chamber – in such instances there has been little opposition to the proposal in question, or opponents have been too slow to call for a roll-call vote.) (4) As noted in previous paragraphs, there is much more liaising and negotiating to be done with the Commission and the Council.

• Regarding the distribution of power between the institutions, the EP is the most obvious beneficiary of the SEA and TEU reforms, for it is placed in a much more advantageous position to pressurise the Commission and the Council to accept its views. Even under the cooperation procedure, where it does not have veto powers, it is able to act in ways to adopt strategies which enable it to have significant policy inputs: EP committees prepare detailed and 'sensible' reports on Commission proposals; the increased channels of communication the EP has with the Commission and the Council are exploited; and legislative proposals are occasionally rejected and are frequently amended by an absolute majority vote at second reading.

■ EU legislation after adoption

What happens to proposals after they are adopted as EU legislation, what use is made of them, and how they are applied, varies considerably. Many of these variations are considered on an individual basis in other chapters – notably in Chapters 4, 8, and 15 – but it will be useful to briefly pull the more important variations together here so as to give an indication of the overall picture. The more significant of the variations are as follows:

• Whereas regulations and most decisions do not require any measures to be taken at national level before they apply, directives do not assume legislative force until after they have been incorporated into national law by the appropriate national authorities. The member states themselves determine which are the appropriate national authorities in their case, and by what process the incorporation is to be made. As a result the mechanisms by which directives are incorporated at national level varies between member states according to both differing national legislative procedures and differing perceptions of how important particular directives are judged to be. The general pattern, however, is for incorporation to be achieved either by attaching appropriate administrative measures to existing primary or secondary legislation, introducing new secondary legislation, or adding new clauses to already planned primary legislation. States are given anything from a few months to a few years to effect the incorporation – the final date being specified in the directives – and are obliged to notify the Commission of the national legislation, regulations, or administrative provisions they have adopted to give formal effect to each directive.

• Much Council and European Parliament and Council legislation needs to be supplemented by implementing legislation so as to fit it to particular circumstances and keep it up to date. Indeed, on a quantitative basis, the vast bulk of EU legislation is implementing legislation – issued usually in the form of Commission regulations.

• Some Council and European Parliament and Council legislation needs to be followed up not just with implementing legislation, but with further 'policy' legislation. This is most obviously the case in respect of 'framework' legislation, which is legislation that lays down general principles for an area of activity and basic rules which states have to follow, but which needs usually to be complemented by more narrowly focused legislation that covers in a reasonably detailed manner policies/issues/initiatives that fall within the remit of the framework. An example of framework legislation is the *Council Directive of 12 June 1989 on the introduction of measures to encourage improvements in the safety and health of workers at work* (89/391/EEC). That this legislation was intended to be a base and a focus for further legislation is seen in Article 16 of the Directive which states: 'The Council acting on a proposal from the Commission, based on 118a of the Treaty, shall adopt individual Directives, *inter alia*, in the areas listed in the Annex.'

• Legislation which also requires further measures, but measures which are very different in character from those that have just been outlined, is the 'new approach' legislation that constitutes an important part of the SEM programme. Under the 'new approach', the EU does not try to harmonise all the specifications and technical standards of marketed goods, as it formerly did, but confines itself to producing relatively short texts which lay down 'essential requirements' – in particular, requirements relating to health and safety matters, and consumer and environmental protection. As long as member states conform to the 'essential requirements' they can have their own national standards, which are subject to mutual recognition by other states, but the intention is that national standards are replaced as quickly as possible by European standards which are agreed by European standards bodies. The main such bodies are the European Committee for Standardisation (CEN) and the European Committee for Electrotechnical Standardisation (CENELEC). Both CEN and CENELEC include EFTA as well as EU countries amongst their membership, and both use weighted voting procedures for the taking of final decisions on standards. Once European standards are agreed EU states must adopt them within a fixed time limit, and within the same time limit must remove all conflicting national standards.

● Issues arising in connection with the implementation of EU legislation were well aired in Chapter 4 in the examination of the Commission's executive and legal guardianship functions. Attention here will, therefore, be restricted to just a few key points on the two main problem areas:

(1) Regarding the incorporation of directives into national law, the Commission has – as was noted above – to be informed of the measures member states take. It therefore has a reasonably good picture of what is happening. Notwithstanding this, however, some states have a considerably better record of incorporating directives than do others (the United Kingdom, Denmark, and Germany have the best records). In consequence, there are variations between the states in terms of the speed at which, and extent to which, directives are applied, and variations too in terms of the frequency with which states are subject to Commission and Court action for non/incomplete/incorrect incorporation of EU law (see Table 11.2 on pp. 330–1).

(2) Regarding the application of EU legislation, responsibilities are shared between EU authorities and national authorities. The main EU authorities are the various DGs that are responsible for particular policies, DGXX (Financial Control), the Commission's anti-fraud unit, the Court of Auditors, and the EP's Budgetary Control Committee. The national authorities are the numerous agencies and officials whose responsibility it is to collect excise duties, to read tachographs, to monitor fishing catches, to check that beef for which payments are made is of the quality that is claimed, etc.

In very broad terms the division of responsibilities between the two levels as regards day-to-day policy implementation is that the Commission oversees and the national authorities do most of the 'front line' work. This means that the Commission needs to move carefully and, assuming it does not wish to stoke up national resentments, must negotiate and discuss implementing problems with national authorities rather than rush them to Court. (An indication of the extent to which it does this is given in Table 11.2.)

Despite however (although in some respects it might be argued because of) the range of agencies which have some responsibility for policy implementation and implementation control, it is evident that all is not well with the application of some EU policies. The problem is partly one of fraud – the Commission's anti-fraud unit estimates that fraud accounts for 10–20 per cent of the EU budget. The problem is also, however, partly one of irregularities: that is to say, not of deliberate deception but of incorrect understanding and application of EU law. Doubtless the control mechanisms and administrative procedures could be improved – not least in respect of flows of information between the Commission and the national agencies. But the fact is that with the Commission being unable to do very much direct surveillance of its own because of limited powers and limited resources, and with much EU legislation being so complicated that it is barely comprehensible even to the expert, it will probably never be possible to ensure that all laws are fully, properly and uniformly implemented.

■ Characteristic features of EU policy processes

A number of general features are characteristic of much EU policy-making and decision-making. They include compromises and linkages, difficulties in effecting radical change, tactical manoeuvring, and variable speeds.

□ Compromises and linkages

The diversity of competing interests across the member states, coupled with the nature of the EU's decision-making system, means that successful policy development is frequently heavily dependent on key actors, especially governments, being prepared to compromise. If they are not so prepared, effective decision-making can be very difficult.

As part of the process wherein compromises provide the bases for agreements, deals are frequently formulated in which different, and sometimes seemingly unrelated, policy issues are linked. Linking issues together in 'package deals' can open the door to agreements by ensuring that there are prizes for everybody and not, as might be the case when only a specific issue is taken, for just a few.

The European Council has been instrumental in formulating some of the EU's grander compromises and linked deals. For example, in 1984, at the Fontainebleau summit, it put together the package that included increasing the EU's budget revenue, decreasing the UK's budgetary contribution, and establishing budgetary discipline guidelines. And at Edinburgh, in 1992, it pulled together an agreement on a range of matters that had been causing considerable difficulties, including the Delors II budgetary proposals, financial aid to the EU's poorer countries, the opening of enlargement negotiations, and the application of the subsidiarity principle.

One of the reasons the European Council has become involved in the construction of overarching deals of the kind just described is that other

Table 11.2 Infringement proceedings classified by member state, stage reached and legal basis

Member State	Stage of the infringement proceeding	1990 Directives: No measures notified	1990 Directives: Not properly incorporated	1990 Directives: Not properly applied	1990 Treaties, Regulations, Decisions	1991 Directives: No measures notified	1991 Directives: Not properly incorporated	1991 Directives: Not properly applied	1991 Treaties, Regulations, Decisions	1992 Directives: No measures notified	1992 Directives: Not properly incorporated	1992 Directives: Not properly applied	1992 Treaties, Regulations, Decisions
Belgium	FN	26	11	16	15	49	5	7	10	84	1	15	10
	RO	18	7	6	2	22		9	15	13	1	2	6
	RCJ	6	2	2	3	3	3	1	1	2		1	3
Denmark	FN	22	1	6	7	34	1	4	13	39		2	4
	RO			3	1	1		1	1	2			2
	RCJ	1		2	1			1					
Germany	FN	18	2	18	23	36	1	12	11	77	6	10	4
	RO	7	3	5	6	6		4	3	4	2	5	7
	RCJ		1	1	3			1		1	1	3	
Greece	FN	78	2	26	14	34	19	18	17	93	4	7	8
	RO	36	2	5	12	37	2	5	4	13		7	10
	RCJ	4	1	1	4	2		2	5	1	1	1	1
Spain	FN	73	7	19	15	41	9	12	17	89	2	16	20
	RO	1	3	7	4	18	3	5	4	20	3	4	12
	RCJ			3				2		1	1	2	1
France	FN	31	3	18	24	30	2	8	14	66	3	25	17
	RO	9	2	1	6	4	1	4	6	2			8
	RCJ		4		2	1	1	1	1			1	

Ireland	FN	36	6	3	7	46	1	8	4	79	3	5	1
	RO	12	2	1	2	22	2	2	1	12			1
	RCJ	2		1		2		1		8		1	
Italy	FN	55	12	28	16	56	3	31	25	87	4	26	20
	RO	35	5	16	6	40	5	23	8	10	1	13	16
	RCJ	16	1	5	3	15	3	6		5	1	4	1
Luxembourg	FN	38	1	2	2	35	19	4	6	90	1	5	1
	RO	8	1	4	2	29	2	2	2	13	1		7
	RCJ	3			1	3			1	10	1	1	2
Netherlands	FN	40	13	2	6	39	2	12	9	61	1	6	5
	RO	10	3	4	3	14	2	4	3	7	2	5	2
	RCJ		1		1	5	1		1	5			
Portugal	FN	147	7	16	8	64	1	11	10	88	6	14	8
	RO	3	1	3	5	79		3	2	18	1	2	1
	RCJ				2	2						1	
United Kingdom	FN	26	2	10	6	40	7	1	15	82	2	9	4
	RO	1	2	1	2	7		2	2	12		2	1
	RCJ		2	1	1								1

Notes: FN: Letter of Formal Notice.
RO: Reasoned Opinion. ⎫ These different stages are explained in Chapter 4.
RCJ: Reference to the Court of Justice. ⎭

Source: Adapted from the *Tenth Annual Report to the European Parliament on Commission Monitoring of the Application of Community Law – 1992. Official Journal of the European Communities*, C233 (30 August 1993)

EU institutions and actors, and EU processes as a whole, are ill-adapted to linking different policy areas and constructing complex package deals. The Foreign Ministers have a theoretical potential in this regard but, in practice, they tend not to have the political authority or status to impose global solutions on sectoral Councils. As for the sectoral Councils, they do not normally become involved in discussions beyond their immediate policy concern, and they certainly do not have the effective means – except perhaps occasionally in joint Councils – of linking difficulties in their own areas with difficulties being experienced by other ministers elsewhere.

Much EU policy-making and decision-making thus tends to be rather compartmentalised, and it is within, rather than across, policy compartments that the trading, bargaining, linkaging and compromising that is so characteristic of EU processes are mainly to be found. At Council working party level, trading may consist of little more than an official conceding a point on line 8 of a proposed legal instrument in exchange for support received on line 3. At ministerial level, it may result in a wide-ranging and interconnected package, such as is agreed annually between Agriculture Ministers to make up the farm price settlement.

☐ *Difficulties in effecting radical change*

Partly as a consequence of the prevalence of compromise, much EU policy-making and decision-making displays a deep gradualism and increment-alism. It is just not possible for the Commission, the Council Presidency, a national government, or anyone else, to initiate a clear and comprehensive policy proposal, incorporating bold new plans and significant departures from the status quo, and expect it to be accepted without being modified significantly – which usually means being watered down. Ambitious proposals customarily find themselves being smothered with modifica-tions, escape clauses, and long transitional periods before full implementation.

The obstacles to innovation and radical change are powerful, and stem from a range of different national and ideological positions and perspectives. Moreover, some of the obstacles have increased in force over the years. They have done so for four principal reasons. First, the way forward is not as clear as it was in the 1960s, when specific Treaty obligations were being honoured and 'negative integration' (that is, the dismantling of barriers and the encouragement of trade liberalisation) was generally accepted as the main policy priority. Second, international economic uncertainties have made states – some much more than others – cautious about ceding too many decision-making powers to the EU. The uncertainties have also exacerbated the pre-existing tension between an EU founded on an essentially liberal model of integration and states that have traditionally sought to regulate economic life by intervention. Third, the EU has become more politically and ideologically heterogeneous. This is partly because of enlargement and partly because the broad Keynesian consensus on social and economic policy that existed in most Western European countries until the mid-1970s has been called into question by high rates of inflation, high unemployment, and low economic growth. Finally, policy development has inevitably created and attracted interests which have a stake in the *status quo*. This is most obviously the case in agriculture, where Commission proposals for reform invariably produce protests from powerful sectional groups and from electorally sensitive governments.

All this is not to suggest that change and reform are not possible. On the contrary, there clearly have been major integrationist advances, of both an institutional and policy kind, since the mid-1980s. These changes have been driven by a range of external and internal factors, and have been guided and shaped by complex interactions between EU and national level political forces. (These factors and forces are discussed extensively elsewhere in this book, notably in Chapter 3.) The identification of obstacles to change does not, therefore, preclude it occurring, but what it does do is to suggest that since just about any policy innovation is likely to meet with at least some resistance from some quarter(s), bold initiatives are always likely to be weakened and/or checked.

☐ Tactical manoeuvring

Tactical manoeuvring and jockeying for positions are universal characteristics of policy-making and decision-making processes. However, they are especially apparent in the EU as a result of the multiplicity of its actors and channels and the diversity of its interests.

It is not possible to attempt a comprehensive catalogue of tactical options here, but a sample of the questions that often have to be considered by just one category of key EU actors – national representatives in the Council – will serve to give a flavour of the intricacies and potential importance of tactical considerations:

● Can a coalition be built to create a positive majority or a negative minority? If so, should it be done via bilateral meetings or in an EU forum?
● Is it necessary to make an intervention for domestic political purposes? (Although Council meetings are not open to the public or the media, most of what goes on, especially in ministerial meetings, gets reported back – either through unofficial channels or through formally minuted national objections to Council decisions.)

- Is it possible to disguise an opposition to a proposal by 'hiding' behind another state?
- Should concessions be made in a working party or in COREPER to ensure progress, or should they be held back until the ministers meet, in the hope that this will be seen as conciliatory and helpful – with the consequences that it might reap dividends on another occasion?
- How is the necessary balance to be struck between being seen to be tough in the defence of the national interest and being seen to be European minded and ready to compromise? (Often, on a particular issue, some states have a vested interest in an agreement being reached, whilst the interests of others are best served by the absence of any agreement and, as a result, the absence of EU obligations.)

☐ Variable speeds

EU processes are often criticised for being cumbersome and slow. Unquestionably they can be, but it should be recognised that they are not always so. Procedures exist that allow certain types of decisions to be made as and when they are necessary. So, farm price and budgetary decisions are made (more or less) according to a predetermined annual timetable; Commission legislation can be issued almost immediately; and Council regulations and decisions can be pushed through via urgent procedures if the circumstances require it.

As for 'standard EU legislation', the introduction of new legislative processes under the SEA and the TEU has greatly speeded up decision-making. The key element is usually whether qualified majority voting rules apply in the Council, for if they do ministers are not normally prepared to wait – as they must if unanimity is required – for everyone to agree to all aspects of a proposal. Rather is it customary to give a state which objects strongly to a proposal time to adjust to the majority view – perhaps with encouragement via compromises and derogations – and then proceed to a vote.

Decision-making is likely to be at its slowest when a proposal creates difficulties of principle for a state or states, and this is combined with a decision-making process which is not subject to the dictates of a timetable and in which qualifying majority voting cannot be used in the Council. In such circumstances the Council's decision-making capacity is weak and it can be very difficult for progress to be made. There may not even be much of a concerted attempt to force progress if it is felt that the minority state(s) genuinely has considerable difficulties with the proposal, for governments tend to be very sensitive to the needs of one another – not least because they are aware that they themselves may be in a minority one day.

■ The efficiency of EU policy processes

The EU lacks a fixed, central authoritative point where general priorities can be set out and choices between competing options can be made. In other words, there is no adequate framework or mechanism for determining and implementing an overall policy view in which the requirements of agriculture, industry, the environment and so on, are weighed and evaluated in relation to one another and in relation to resources. The Commission, it is true, attempts to set general priorities but it does not itself have the decision-making power to carry them through. In the Council of Ministers, the sectoral Councils do not link up with one another in a wholly satisfactory manner, and although incoming Presidencies do set priorities, these are essentially short-term in nature and in most policy sectors are not part of a properly integrated long-term programme. As for the European Council, it has had some limited success in coordinating policies, such as at the 1988 Brussels summit when a five year reference framework for expenditure was agreed, but it has never attempted to set out anything like a comprehensive EU policy programme.

Within individual policy sectors, there are, as has been shown, many obstacles to coherent and properly ordered policy development. For example, resistance by states to what they regard as an excessive transfer of powers to the EU has undoubtedly resulted in many policy spheres being less integrated and comprehensive in their approach than is – from a policy efficiency perspective – ideally desirable. Regional policy, industrial policy, and environmental policy are examples of policy areas where policy responsibilities are shared between the EU and the states, where frequently the activities of the two levels are not properly coordinated, and sometimes where they are not even mutually complementary.

EU policy thus tends not to be the outcome of a rational model of decision-making. That is to say, policy is not normally made via a procedure in which problems are identified, objectives are set, all possible alternatives for achieving the goals are carefully evaluated, and the best alternatives are then adopted and proceeded with. Rather other models of decision-making are often more useful for highlighting key features of EU processes. For example:

● The *political interests* model of decision-making draws attention to the interaction of competing interests in the EU, to the variable power exercised by these interests in different decision-making situations, and to the ways in which decisional outcomes are frequently a consequence of bargains and compromises between interests.

- *Political elite* models highlight the considerable concentrations of power, at official and political levels, that exist across the EU's decision-making processes. Concentrations are especially marked in areas such as monetary policy and foreign policy, where processes are more secret and more closed than they are, for example, in steel or agriculture. Political elite models also draw attention to the absence of mechanisms available to EU citizens for exercising direct accountability over EU decision-makers.

- The *organisational process* model of decision-making emphasises how the rules and understandings via which EU decisions are made do much to shape the nature of the decisions themselves. The organisational processes, that is to say, are not neutral. So where, to use Jacques Delors' phrase, policy can only 'make progress twelve abreast', and where every conceivable national, regional and sectional interest is entitled to be consulted before policy can be developed, progress is frequently slow and outcomes are often little more than lowest common denominators. Where, on the other hand, processes are more streamlined – and permit, for example, majority voting in the Council of Ministers, or the Commission to disburse funds directly – then decision-making is likely to be more decisive and, perhaps, more coherent.

Having identified weaknesses in the quality of EU policy and decision-making processes, some re-balancing is now in order lest the impression be left of a system that is wholly and uniquely disordered and undemocratic. There are three main points to be made.

The first point is that, in many respects, EU policy and decision-making processes are not so different from national processes. This is not to say that differences do not exist. The international nature of the EU, for example, makes for more diverse and more powerful opposition to its initiatives than customarily exists within states. It is also the case that EU decision-makers are less directly accountable than are national decision-makers to those who are subject to their decisions: the power of the European Council, the Council of Ministers, and the Commission, on the one hand, and the comparative weakness of the EP on the other, does make, as many have observed, for a 'democratic deficit' in the EU. Another difference is that the EU's institutions, taken collectively, are much weaker than their national counterparts. But recognition of these and other differences should not obscure similarities of type – if not perhaps intensity – between EU and national processes: political interest, political elite, and organisational process models of decision-making can, after all, throw light on features of the latter, as well as the former. So, for example, in all member states, especially those where there are coalition governments (which is the norm in most EU states), political accommodations are an everyday occurrence and policy trimming is common. Furthermore, in those countries where there is a considerable geographical decentralisation of power as, for example, there is in Germany, tensions between levels of government over who does what, and who pays for what, are by no means unusual. In short, many of the EU's decision-making 'problems' – such as the prevalance of incrementalism, and of policy slippages – are by no means unknown in national political systems.

The second point is that not all EU policy and decision-making processes are completely a matter of cobbling together deals which can satisfy the current complexion of political forces. These certainly are crucially important features, but they do not amount to the complete picture. In recent years, greater efforts have been made, especially by the Commission, to initiate rather than just to react, to look to the medium-term rather than just tomorrow, and to pull at least some of the pieces together into coordinated programmes.

At the level of overarching policy coordination, progress in the direction of more forward-looking and more coordinated policy planning has, it must be said, been only modest. But there have been some potentially significant developments. An important example of such a development is seen in the Commission's 1987 document *The Single Act: a new frontier*, which made recommendations for dealing with what it saw to be the central priorities over the period up to 1992. The programme outlined in the document became the subject of exhaustive Council and European Council negotiations. These negotiations led, at the 1988 Brussels summit, to a package deal which, though the outcome of the usual political trading, did at least address, in an interlinking five year financial programme some, though by no means all, of the Community's most pressing problems. Similar proceedings occurred in 1992 when the 1988 package needed to be renewed. On this second occasion the Commission's proposals were presented in its document *From the Single Act to Maastricht and Beyond: the Means to Match Our Ambitions*, and the final deal, on a new medium-term financial programme, was concluded at the December 1992 Edinburgh summit.

Below the level of overarching policy coordination, within certain policy sectors clear medium- to long-term policy objectives and rounded programmes are to be found. These are drawn up by the Commission, usually in consultation with appropriate consultative committees and committees of experts, and have to be approved by the Council. They appear in various forms. For example: White Papers (the best known of which is still the 1985 White Paper which contained detailed proposals for the completion of the internal market); communications (such as *The Development and Future of the CAP*, which was published in 1991, approved – with modifications – by the Council in 1992, and which set out proposals for major reforms of the financing of agriculture); framework legislation and programmes (for example, the major overhaul of the Structural Funds which was set out in Council Regulation (EEC) No.2052/ 88 of 24 June 1988); and action programmes.

It is worth saying a little about action programmes to illustrate how, within specified fields of activity, a measure of coordinated development over a planned medium-term period is possible. Action programmes vary in nature, from the broad and general to the highly specific. The broad and general typically include measures for improving the monitoring and supervision of existing legislation, ideas for new legislation, running a pilot scheme, and spending programmes. Such an action programme, aimed at improving 'equal opportunities for girls and boys in education' was approved by the Education Ministers in June 1985. The ten point programme was rather modest, as it had to be to attract the support of those governments which are not especially committed to such concerns and/or have little national legislation in the sphere themselves, but the provisions were not without significance. They included: educational and vocational guidance to be provided as a service to all pupils to encourage girls and boys to diversify their career choices; opening schools to working life and the outside world; eradicating persistent stereotypes from school textbooks, teaching materials in general, and guidance and assessment materials; and special measures to help the underprivileged. By contrast with the broad and general action programmes, the specific action programmes are naturally much more specialised in their areas of concern and tighter in their provisions. Examples are the ECSC social research programmes on such matters as safety in mines and industrial hygiene, which are given appropriations for a given period and which provide up to about 60 per cent of the costs of approved research projects.

The third, and final, 'rebalancing' point to be made about EU processes is that critical judgements about how the EU functions ought to be placed in the context of the very considerable degree of cooperation and integration that has been achieved. There is no comparable international development where individual states have voluntarily transferred so many policy responsibilities to a collective organisation of states and, in so doing, have surrendered so much of their national sovereignty. It is hardly surprising, given the enormity of the exercise, that pressures and desires for cooperation and integration should so often be challenged, and held in check, by caution, uncertainties, conflicts, and competition.

■ *Chapter 12* ■

The Budget

The EU raises and spends money in many different ways. Mostly it does so within the framework of the annual budget and it is with the budget that this chapter is primarily concerned.

However, so as to give a full picture of the EU's financial activities and instruments, an outline of the non-budgetary financial operations will be presented before examining the budget. The main non-budgetary operations are as follows:

● The EU borrows sums on capital markets which are then made available, in the form of loans, to both public and private undertakings for investment. The European Investment Bank (EIB), which is the principal source of EU investment finance, has already been discussed in this connection (see Chapter 9).

● The December 1992 Edinburgh summit decided to establish a European Investment Fund (EIF). The main objective of the Fund, which was scheduled to start functioning in 1994, is to stimulate investment and economic growth by providing guarantees for both publicly and privately funded projects. It is estimated that the Fund could support investment projects worth up to 20 billion Ecu, from a subscribed capital of 2 billion Ecu contributed by the EIB (40 per cent), other EU sources (30 per cent), and public and private banks (30 per cent).

● The December 1993 Brussels summit, responding to the Commission's White Paper on *Growth, Competitiveness and Employment*, decided that up to 20 billion Ecu should be made available annually for up to six years to enable the EU to act upon the recommendations made in the White Paper and, hopefully, to create up to 15 million new jobs. Of this 20 billion Ecu, some 5 billion Ecu is to come from existing headings of the EU's budget, another 7 billion Ecu from the EIB and the EIF, and a further 8 billion Ecu from sources to be determined.

● Borrowing and lending activities are undertaken to enable member states to cope with balance of payments difficulties. The Community Loan

Instrument was established for this purpose in 1975, and in 1979 standby arrangements between the Central Banks were created within the framework of the European Monetary System (EMS). An example of a loan being made to a member state for balance of payments purposes is the 8 billion Ecu which was approved by Ecofin Ministers for Italy in January 1993: the loan, which was to be disbursed in four tranches over two years, was conditional on Italy being able to reduce the country's debt to GDP ratio, limiting government borrowing, and implementing public expenditure reforms.

- The ECSC is resourced from its own funds, the principal component of which is a levy on coal and steel production.
- The EU provides loans and loan guarantees to certain non-member states. Particular beneficiaries in recent years have been countries of the former Soviet bloc and former Soviet Union. The Edinburgh summit decided that considerations of prudent budgetary management and financial discipline required that the increasing level and scope of loans and loan guarantees to non-member states called for a new financial framework. Accordingly, it set in motion procedures for the creation of a Guarantee Fund, to be financed by a reserve in the budget.
- The European Development Fund, which finances aid to the African, Caribbean and Pacific countries under the Lomé Convention (see Chapter 14), is not resourced from the budget but from direct contributions by the member states.

Turning now to the EU budget, one point needs to be emphasised at the outset: despite the considerable attention it has received over the years, and despite the enormous amount of political acrimony it has generated, the budget is, in fact, relatively small. In 1994 it totalled 73.4 billion Ecu in commitment appropriations: about £56 billion and $85 billion at January 1994 exchange rates. This represented only 1.2 per cent of the Gross Domestic Product (GDP) of the member states and about 2.4 per cent of their total public expenditure. The reason why the budget is so small is that most of the policy sectors which make up the bulk of public expenditure – defence, education, health, social welfare, etc. – remain primarily the responsibility of the member states. Many of the EU's policy activities, such as those designed to create the SEM, do not involve much in the way of operational costs. When EU policies do involve significant operational costs, for example where they impose obligations to introduce measures so as to conform with EU environmental legislation, the financial impact often falls not on the EU's budget but on private firms and public authorities in the member states.

The modesty of the size of the EU's budget should, therefore, be borne in mind when assessing its financial and policy impact. Clearly the budget cannot, and does not, serve to effect a major transfer of financial resources from national exchequers to the EU, or vice versa.

■ The composition of the budget

□ Revenue

Following a decision taken by the member states in 1970, the funding of the budget was changed between 1970 and 1975 from a system based on national contributions to one based on 'own resources'. A major reason for bringing about this change was that it would give to the Community an increased financial independence. The member states would determine the upper limit of the own resources, but the resources themselves would belong to the Community and not the states.

At the time of the introduction of the new arrangements the own resources consisted of customs duties, agricultural levies, and a proportion of Value Added Tax (VAT) up to a 1 per cent ceiling. At the beginning of the 1980s, however, it became apparent that these resources were not capable of generating enough income to meet the Community's increasing financial obligations. The member states could, in theory, have resolved this problem easily enough by raising the own resources limit, but some states – the United Kingdom in particular – were reluctant to do this. The consequence was that the Community experienced a series of budgetary crises in the early 1980s. These crises led, eventually, to the conclusion of a complicated deal at the 1984 Fontainebleau European Council. Key elements of the deal included new rules on budgetary discipline, a formula for reducing UK budgetary contributions (which were generally recognised as being excessive), and an expansion of own resources through the setting of a new 1.4 per cent ceiling for VAT from 1986. The Fontainebleau agreement was, however, too little too late, in that no sooner had the 1.4 per cent ceiling been introduced in 1986 than it was exhausted and the Commission was forced to open a new campaign for a further expansion of the revenue base.

That campaign culminated in the 1988 Brussels summit which saw a further, but as compared with Fontainebleau much more radical, reform designed to deal with the Community's recurring budgetary difficulties. The Brussels reform was given added force when, in June 1988, its key elements were incorporated in the *Interinstitutional Agreement on Budgetary Discipline and Improvement of the Budgetary Procedure*, which was signed by the Presidents of the Council of Ministers, the Commission, and the European Parliament. The importance of the

Interinstitutional Agreement was that it contained a formal commitment by all three institutions to the framework of a financial perspective for the years 1988 to 1992. Included in the perspective were provisions for expanding certain categories of expenditure, a continuation of special abatement arrangements for the UK, a much tighter framework for ensuring budgetary discipline, and a significant expansion of own resources through the creation of a new budgetary resource based on the Gross National Product (GNP) of each state. An increase in own resources was thus linked to an expanding spending programme, subject to the limitation that the total amount of own resources for any one year could not exceed the following percentages of the total GNP of the Community for the year in question – 1988: 1.15; 1989: 1.17; 1990: 1.18; 1991: 1.19; 1992: 1.20.

In 1992 the Commission put forward proposals for a new financial perspective under the title *From the Single Act to Maastricht and Beyond: the Means to Match our Ambitions.* After discussions and negotiations between the member states in the Council of Ministers and the European Council which took up much of 1992, a financial perspective for the years 1993–9 was agreed at the December 1992 Edinburgh summit. The core elements of this new financial perspective, which are outlined in Document 12.1, p. 346, were based on the principles of the 1988 financial perspective: a further planned increase in certain categories of expenditure; a parallel increase in own resources, up to a ceiling of 1.27 per cent of GNP in 1999; a continuation of the existing four revenue resources, though with some modifications to make them weigh less heavily on the poorer states; continuing tight budgetary discipline; and no changes in the abatement arrangements for the United Kingdom.

The EU's own resources thus currently consist of the following:

- *Common Customs Tariff duties and other duties* which are collected in respect of trade with non-member countries.
- *Agricultural levies, premiums and other duties* which are collected in respect of trade with non-member countries within the framework of the CAP. These differ from customs duties in that they are not fixed import taxes, but are fluctuating charges designed to have the effect of raising import prices to EU levels. There are also certain internal agricultural levies and duties, notably connected with the framework of the common organisation of the market in sugar, which have as their purpose limiting surplus production.

● *The application of a uniform percentage rate to the VAT assessment base* which is determined in a standardised manner for member states. So as to protect countries whose VAT base was high, under the 1988–92 financial perspective the assessment base for VAT could not exceed 55 per cent of the Gross National Product at market prices. To further reduce the regressive aspect of this element of budgetary resources, it was decided at the 1992 Edinburgh summit to lower the uniform rate of VAT from 1.4 per cent to 1 per cent between 1995 and 1999, and also to cut the assessment base for the VAT resource from 55 per cent to 50 per cent of GNP – this latter change to take effect immediately for the four poorer countries (Greece, Ireland, Portugal and Spain) and to be phased in between 1995 and 1999 for the other countries. (It should be emphasised that these VAT rules still allow countries to vary their national VAT rates, subject to EU limitations on minimum rates and on exemptions.)

● *The application of a rate to a base representing the sum of member states' Gross National Product at market prices.* This is the fourth own resource which was created at the 1988 Brussels summit. The rate is determined under the budgetary procedure in the light of the total of all other revenue and the total expenditure agreed. Since this resource is very much like a national contribution, it has been suggested by many observers that it does not have quite the own resource character of the other resources. Key features of this resource are that it introduces into the EU's revenue system a link with ability to pay, and it also creates a resource which can be easily adjusted to bring budgetary revenue into balance with budgetary expenditure. The agreement at Edinburgh to reduce the VAT component of budgetary resources was matched by an agreement to increase this GNP element.

Precisely what proportion of total budgetary revenue comes from each resource naturally varies a little from year to year according to such factors as trade flows, world agricultural prices, and national growth rates. In 1993 the proportions were as follows – VAT: 53.8 per cent; GNP resource: 22.4 per cent; customs duties: 19.8 per cent; agricultural levies: 3.4 per cent; miscellaneous: 0.7 per cent. The decisions taken at Edinburgh will see the VAT element of budgetary resources decrease and the GNP element increase – with the former scheduled to constitute 34 per cent of total revenue by 1999 and the latter 48 per cent.

As regards national contributions to EU budgetary resources: Germany, the United Kingdom, and France are net contributors; Italy and the Netherlands are broadly in balance; all other countries are net recipients. EFTA countries which join the EU will be net contributors.

☐ *Expenditure*

The EU makes a distinction between expenditure which is a direct result of Treaty application or acts adopted on the basis of the Treaties – called compulsory (or obligatory) expenditure – and that which is not – called non-compulsory (or non-obligatory) expenditure. The former accounts for around 55 per cent of the total budget. Of this 55 per cent most is used for the purpose of farm price guarantees. Two main factors account for this dominant role of agriculture in EU expenditure. First, agriculture has seen a greater transfer of financial responsibility from national budgets to the EU budget than any other major policy area. Second, as is explained in Chapter 13, an agricultural price guarantee policy has been pursued that has kept EU prices well above world prices, and in a number of product sectors this has resulted in production levels well in excess of the capacity of the market. In consequence, the EU has had to pay for agricultural produce it does not require: by buying up surplus production; by storing it; by selling it at subsidised rates on domestic and world markets; and by converting it into animal feed.

On a 'rational' and 'commonsense' basis this can hardly be justified. Agriculture is clearly overfunded, whilst policy areas drawing on non-compulsory expenditure – such as regional policy, research policy and energy policy – are (most would argue) underfunded. However, budgetary expenditure, like budgetary income, is not determined by 'objective' criteria but by political interplay. And in that interplay there are many powerful forces which wish to maintain high levels of spending on agriculture: governments anxious to receive farmers' votes do not normally wish to upset this often volatile section of the electorate, and net beneficiaries of the CAP (both states and sectional interests) are not inclined voluntarily to surrender their gains.

However, notwithstanding these obstacles to reform, the pressures for radical change became intense by the mid- to late-1980s: previous schemes for reducing agricultural expenditure were having only a marginal effect; ever-larger surpluses for some products were being predicted; and some states were becoming increasingly anxious to increase non-agricultural spending. As a result, measures designed to bring about a gradual shift in the EU's pattern of expenditure were central to the 1988–92 financial perspective: the proportion of the budget devoted to agriculture was planned to be reduced to around 60 per cent by 1992, and the proportion devoted to structural operations (mainly the Regional Fund and the Social Fund) was planned to be doubled to around 25 per cent.

As was noted above, an agreement on a second financial perspective, covering the years 1993–9, was reached at the Edinburgh European Council meeting in December 1992. After protracted discussions which went on for most of 1993, during which the EP complained long and bitterly about not having been properly consulted about the contents of the perspective, the Edinburgh agreement was – subject to a few minor alterations to the figures – converted in November 1993 into a new *Interinstitutional Agreement on Budgetary Discipline and Improvement of the Budgetary Procedure.*

In the 1993–9 financial perspective, EU budgetary expenditure is grouped under six headings (see Document 12.1 for details):

● *Agriculture.* As under the 1988–92 financial perspective, agriculture is subject to tight budgetary discipline and is projected to fall to 46 per cent of total budgetary expenditure by 1999.
● *Structural operations.* These are again planned to rise: this time by 41 per cent, to bring them to 35 per cent of total budgetary expenditure. The poorer states are to be the principal beneficiaries following the creation at Edinburgh of a new Cohesion Fund designed exclusively for the benefit of the four less prosperous member states, and following also changes in the rules of the existing Structural Funds which will result in the Funds being targeted more towards the poorer regions.
● *Internal policies.* This heading includes all internal policies, of which research is the most important, and it is scheduled to rise only slightly, to around 5 per cent of the total.
● *External policies.* This heading too is not subject to major changes, although it is projected to rise appreciably above internal policies in the last period of the perspective.
● *Administrative expenditure.* This is scheduled to rise by 16 per cent in real terms, to take it to 4.6 per cent of total expenditure.
● *Reserves.* The size of reserves was not significantly changed, but new provisions were made for emergency aid and for guarantees against loan default.

A detailed picture of particular budget allocations is presented in Table 12.1, which looks at the 1994 budget. The most striking feature of Table 12.1 is the relatively modest sums available in all categories other than for agricultural price guarantees. So, to take three key areas of non-compulsory expenditure: the European Regional Development Fund (ERDF), which has as its principal aim the correction of serious disparities in levels of development and prosperity in different regions of the EU, is allocated 12 per cent; the European Social Fund (ESF), which is primarily concerned with vocational training and employment promotion activities, especially amongst youth, is allocated 9 per cent; and research activities are allocated just over 3 per cent. As is explained above, and is apparent from Document 12.1, these potentially very important areas are

Document 12.1   Financial Perspective 1993-9
Appropriations for commitments (million Ecu – 1992 prices)

	1993	1994	1995	1996	1997	1998	1999
1. Agricultural guideline	35230	35095	35722	36364	37023	37697	38389
2. Structural actions	21277	21885	23480	24990	26526	28240	30000
– Cohesion Fund	1500	1750	2000	2250	2500	2550	2600
– Structural Funds and other operations	19777	20135	21480	22740	24026	25690	27400
3. Internal policies	3940	4084	4323	4520	4710	4910	5100
4. External action	3950	4000	4280	4560	4830	5180	5600
5. Administrative expenditure	3280	3380	3580	3690	3800	3850	3900
6. Reserves	1500	1500	1100	1100	1100	1100	1100
– Monetary Reserve	1000	1000	500	500	500	500	500
– External Action							
emergency aid	200	200	300	300	300	300	300
loan guarantees	300	300	300	300	300	300	300
Total appropriations for commitments	69177	69944	72485	75224	77989	80977	84089
Appropriations for payments required	65908	67036	69150	71290	74491	77249	80114
Appropriations for payments (% GNP)	1.20	1.19	1.20	1.21	1.23	1.25	1.26
Margin for unforeseen expenditure (% GNP)		0.01	0.01	0.01	0.01	0.01	0.01
Own Resources Ceiling (% GNP)	1.20	1.20	1.21	1.22	1.24	1.26	1.27

Source: European Parliament Briefing (October 1993).

all being expanded under the second financial perspective, but even when they have reached their limits in 1999 the EU's financial capability to effectively act as an agent for tackling pressing problems such as under-investment, technological change, unemployment, and regional imbalances will remain very limited.

■ Budgetary decision-making

☐ *The budgetary process*

A timetable and set of procedures for drawing up and approving the annual budget is laid down in Article 203 of the EC Treaty. However, in practice, Article 203 gives only an approximate and rather formal guide to what actually happens. It provides a framework which has been fleshed out and adapted over time in response to pressures, necessities, and convenience.

In broad terms, and assuming no major problems exist or arise to severely disrupt the process, the pattern of budgetary decision-making is as follows.

☐ *Preparation of the Preliminary Draft Budget.* The Commission gets down to work on the budget in the late winter/early spring of the year before which it is due to come into effect. In attempting to look this far ahead – almost twelve months to the beginning of the financial year (in January) and twenty-four months to its close – the Commission is necessarily faced with many uncertainties on both the revenue and expenditure sides. Agriculture causes particular difficulties. For example, crop yields cannot be foreseen: a small change in weather conditions might raise production in a particular product from 101 per cent of consumer demand to 102 per cent, thus resulting in a considerable underestimate of the amount of budget support required for that product. Another problem is that agriculture expenditure is highly dependent on world agricultural prices and currency movements which cannot be controlled: a falling dollar can have a drastic effect on EU finances because export subsidies for farm products are linked to dollar-denominated international market prices. (The fall of the dollar in December 1986–January 1987 alone added more than 1 billion Ecu to spending commitments.)

The Commission has, therefore, to make many assumptions, some of which, in the event, may not be realised. If changed situations become apparent during the course of the budgetary cycle corrections can be made fairly easily, by sending rectifying or amending letters to the Council and the Parliament. If, however, the financial situation changes for the worse during the budgetary year itself, that is more serious. In the past, 'temporary' solutions, such as postponement of payments, delays in the introduction of new programmes, and supplementary budgets were used. Since the 1988 Brussels agreement, however, the Commission has had available, and has used, a range of stronger management powers to enable it to take appropriate action at an early stage if agricultural expenditure – the main problem – gets out of hand: it can, for example, impose levies and price support cuts on certain products if designated production ceilings are exceeded.

The prime responsibility within the Commission for drawing up what is known as the Preliminary Draft Budget (PDB) falls to the Directorate General for Budgets (DGXIX). Inevitably it is subject to pressures from many sides: from other DGs which forward their own estimates and bids; from national representatives – both through the Council and on a direct lobbying basis; from the EP, especially leading figures of its Committee on Budgets; and from sectional interests. The Budget Commissioner and officials from DGXIX have many meetings, of both a formal and informal kind, to enable many of these interested parties to have their say. Naturally, those that have the most chance of achieving some satisfaction are those that carry political weight and/or are already in tune with the Commission's thinking.

Under the terms of the 1993 *Interinstitutional Agreement* it was decided, as part of an attempt to improve relations and understandings between the Commission, the Council, and the EP during the budgetary procedure, that at some point before the Commission takes a final decision on the PDB there should be a meeting of the trialogue (delegations from the three institutions). The purpose of the meeting is 'to discuss the possible priorities for the budget of that year, with due account being taken of the institutions' powers'.

Once DGXIX has its proposals ready they must be presented by the Commissioner to his fellow Commissioners and all must agree on the package. When they do, the proposals officially become the Preliminary Draft Budget.

Prior to the 1988 reform, the PDB usually disappointed those who wanted to see the budget used as the motor for change in Community priorities. The Commission did make several attempts to use the PDB to effect at least modest shifts in policy emphases – notably by proposing the containment of agricultural expenditure and the expansion of the Structural Funds – but its manoeuvrability was always severely restricted by existing expenditure commitments, and also by the knowledge that any significant change that it might propose from the *status quo* would be fiercely resisted in the Council. The existence since 1988 of financial perspectives has changed this situation by setting out a framework and a programme for using the budget to effect change.

The financial perspective is particularly important in three interrelated ways. First, the budget must conform with the principles of the agricultural guideline – which means that the rate of increase in agriculture guarantee expenditure in any one year must not exceed 74 per cent of the annual rate of increase in EU GNP (see Chapter 13 for further details). Second, the budget must be set within the framework of the financial perspective. As Document 12.1 (p. 346) shows, the perspective contains a financial programme for altering the balance of EU expenditure. Third, the Commission, the Council, and the EP, are strictly bound to respect the ceilings set out in the financial perspective. Apart from technical adjustments the financial perspective can only be revised by a joint decision of the Council and the EP, acting on a proposal from the Commission – as, for example, the 1988–92 perspective was revised in June 1990 when new funding (200 million Ecu in 1990, 1225 million Ecu in 1991, and 1478 million Ecu in 1992) was made available for a number of purposes, notably assistance to Eastern Europe.

The financial perspective does not, it should be emphasised, totally constrain the Commission when it draws up the PDB. It does have manoeuvrability below the ceilings, and it does have options within expenditure headings. The financial perspective, in other words, is not a straightjacket. But it does place very clear limits on what the Commission can do.

The Commission presents the PDB in two forms: payment appropriations, which cover actual expenditure during the financial year; and commitment appropriations, which cover expenditure during the financial year plus liabilities extending beyond the year. Commitment appropriations are naturally always a little higher than payment appropriations – usually by a total of 2–3 billion Ecu.

☐ *Council first reading.* Assuming there are no major or special problems, the PDB is referred to the Council in late April or during May.

Most of the Council's detailed examination of the budget is undertaken by the Budget Committee, a working group of national officials who, in what are frequently long and exhaustive sessions, examine the PDB chapter by chapter, line by line. As the date of the Ministers' meeting in the Budget Council approaches, the Committee is likely to meet with increasing frequency in order to resolve as many issues as possible. The negotiators are in almost constant contact with their national capitals about what transpires in the Committee, and so they mostly have a prepared view when items come up for discussion. When this produces a rigidity in negotiating positions, much responsibility is thrown on the chairman to find a solution. The Commission can assist him in this task.

From the Committee the draft proceeds to COREPER. The number of unresolved items put before the Permanent Representatives naturally depends on what has happened in the Committee. Normally, much remains to be done, and COREPER attempts, like the Committee, to clear as many items as possible before the Ministers meet. It is usually most successful with those issues which do not have a potentially conflictual political aspect attached to them.

If it becomes apparent at some point prior to the meeting of the Ministers that a disagreement may arise with the EP over the categorisation of expenditure between compulsory and non-compulsory, then the 1993 *Interinstitutional Agreement* provides for a conciliation procedure. (Because, as was explained in Chapter 7, the EP's powers are stronger over non-compulsory expenditure than they are over compulsory expenditure, it always wants as much expenditure as possible to be classified as non-compulsory.) The conciliation procedure begins with a trialogue meeting which is convened in time to enable the institutions to seek an agreement by no later than the date set by the Council for establishing its first draft. At this trialogue meeting the institutions' delegations are led by the President of the Council (Budgets), the Chairman of the EP's Committee on Budgets, and the Commissioner with responsibility for the budget. Following the trialogue meeting a conciliation meeting is held between the Council and an EP delegation, with the Commission also taking part.

The Ministers customarily meet in mid-July, although there have been occasions when they have not gathered until September. Prior to the establishment of financial perspectives, the Budget Council normally lasted for a couple days and involved 15 to 20 hours of negotiations in formal sessions, plus extensive informal discussions and manoeuvrings in the wings. Qualified majority voting usually allowed a draft to be eventually agreed, but on controversial proposals a blocking minority sometimes existed. On two occasions the divisions between the member states were such that the July meeting was unable to approve a draft, which meant that there had to be a reference back to officials. The officials then produced a new package for the Ministers to consider when they returned in September – by which time the timetable was pressing and an agreement had to be reached.

The reason why the July meeting was often so difficult was that the states differed, both in their views about the balance to be struck between restraint and expansion, and in their perceptions of problems and priorities. What emerged, therefore, was a draft reflecting accommodations and compromises. Almost invariably, however, the general thrust of the draft was, on the one hand, to propose a tighter overall budget than that envisaged in the PDB and, on the other hand, to propose some shift from non-compulsory expenditure to compulsory expenditure – that is, from items such as regional, social and research expenditure (which were relatively 'soft' because of their non-compulsory character) to agriculture (which was difficult to touch given existing commitments).

Financial perspectives have constrained the Council, as they have the Commission, in what it can do. This has had two effects on the Council's first reading stage. First, the decision-making process is less divisive and troublesome than in the past. Second, though the Council still customarily cuts the PDB, its hands are largely tied and it is obliged to produce a draft that is very similar to the PDB.

☐ *Parliament first reading.* On being approved, the Council's first draft is referred to the Parliament. If the timing is suitable the President of the Budget Council may formally present the draft himself: to the Budget Committee and/or in an address to the plenary.

Although this presentation of the Council's draft marks the first public point at which the EP becomes involved in the budgetary process, it always, in practice, has been attempting to exert influence for some time: before the PDB is agreed the EP – normally at its March plenary meeting – approves guidelines which it hopes will be followed by the Commission; a trialogue meeting will have been held with the Commission and the Council to discuss budgetary plans for the year (see above); the PDB is sent by the Commission to the EP at the same time as it is referred to the Council, and the Committee on Budgets begins its considerations almost immediately; and, as was indicated above, conciliation procedures may have been held to try and resolve differences over whether appropriations should have been categorised as compulsory or non-compulsory expenditure.

Now, with the Council's draft available, the pace is stepped up. There is a brief debate in plenary session, but the detailed work is given over to committees. The Committee on Budgets naturally has most responsibility. It examines the budget in detail itself, and it also acts as a coordinating agency for reports submitted to it by other EP committees which look at the budget to see how their sectors are affected. The Committee on Budgets does not, however, have the power completely to control what goes forward to the plenary: it cannot, for example, stop an amendment that has support elsewhere, especially if it is backed by any of the larger political groups. Partly in consequence of this, hundreds of proposed changes are usually put forward (600 for the 1994 budget), many of which conflict with one another, or are even mutually exclusive. Much, therefore, rests on the liaising, organising, and leadership skills of the chairman of the Committee on Budgets and the appointed *rapporteur*.

The intention is normally to hold the plenary session dealing with the budget in October, but if the submission of the Council's draft is delayed it may have to be put off until November. At the plenary MEPs can do three things with the contents of the Council's draft: accept them; propose amendments to non-compulsory expenditure (which requires majority support of members); propose modifications to compulsory expenditure (which requires majority support of votes cast).

As with both the drafting of the PDB and the Council's first reading, the EP's first reading has been affected by the establishment of financial perspectives. Prior to the 1988 reforms the customary pattern at this stage was for the EP to propose increases in non-compulsory expenditure and often, also, to raise general points of principle. So, for instance, in 1984 – re the 1985 budget – the Parliament complained about the lack of provision for a projected budget deficit; in 1985 – re the 1986 budget – it criticised the inadequate provision for the accession of Spain and Portugal and for the 'weight of the past'; and in 1986 – re the 1987 budget – it stressed the urgent need to tackle agricultural over-expenditure. The position since 1988 has been that there has not been such a gap between the Council and the EP. This has been because of the obligations and constraints of the financial perspectives which, in addition to partly satisfying some of the EP's policy ambitions – through changes in expenditure patterns – have also reduced, though by no means eliminated, the significance of the distinction between compulsory and non-compulsory expenditure.

Prior to 1988 there was frequently a disagreement during the budgetary process between the Council and the EP over the 'maximum rate of increase'. This was a figure calculated annually by the Commission according to a complex formula based on inflation, growth of national budgets, and the overall level of economic growth, and it applied to non-compulsory expenditure. After the 1988 Brussels agreement the Council attempted to continue to apply the maximum rate of increase to what it called the 'non-privileged' element of non-compulsory expenditure. (This non-privileged element was to include transport, energy and fisheries; the privileged element was to include the structural funds, research, and the Integrated Mediterranean Programmes or IMPs.) The EP resisted the Council's attempts to make this distinction between types of non-compulsory expenditure and insisted that it was the ceilings set out in the financial perspective that counted. The resistance was successful, with the consequence that the maximum rate of increase lost most of its former significance. The 1993 *Interinstitutional Agreement* ended the maximum rate of increase altogether in its previous form, by declaring that 'The two arms of the budgetary authority [the Council and the EP] agree to accept for each of the financial years from 1993-1999, the maximum rate of increase for non-compulsory expenditure from the budgets established within the ceilings set by the financial perspective'.

Since 1988 disagreements between the Council and the EP in the budgetary process have mainly focused on EP efforts to ensure: (1) that funds are allocated up to the level of the ceilings set out in the financial perspective (as noted, the EP is in a stronger position to ensure this for non-compulsory expenditure than it is for compulsory); (2) that unforeseen and emergency expenditure (such as to help meet the cost of German unification) is met by revisions of the financial perspective and not by diverting funds from existing allocations.

After the EP has debated the draft budget in plenary session, and after all amendments and modifications have been voted upon, a resolution on the budget is adopted by the Parliament.

□ *Council second reading.* From Parliament the draft goes back to the Council where officials prepare for the ministerial second reading which is usually held in mid- to late November. If issues remain to be settled activity can be feverish, and many meetings – including trialogue meetings – may be held to try and achieve progress.

In looking at the EP's proposed changes, the Budget Council can, within the financial perspective, take three sorts of decisions:

● Acting by a qualified majority, it can modify amendments to non-compulsory expenditure.
● Acting by a qualified majority, it can reject modifications to compulsory expenditure that do not have the effect of increasing total expenditure. In the absence of decisions to reject them, proposed modifications stand as accepted.
● Acting by a qualified majority, it can accept modifications to compulsory expenditure that have the effect of increasing total expenditure. In the absence of decisions to accept them, proposed modifications are rejected.

Where it is clear that Parliament's views have not been fully met, and particularly where significant funds are involved or possible points of principle are at stake, then the Council has to decide whether it wishes to close the door on the matter (and hope for the best at the EP's second reading) or leave it ajar for a possible compromise. Before 1988 this frequently produced sharp divisions in the Council, because it raised the possibility of budgetary rejection.

☐ *Parliament second reading.* The EP holds its second reading on the budget in December. What happens before, at, and after the plenary depends very much on the extent to which contentious issues remain unresolved.

If the situation is relatively straightforward and most problems have been sorted out, then the normal procedure is for the Committee on Budgets to meet, to reinsert such non-compulsory expenditure as it legally can and, on this basis, to recommend adoption. The plenary then votes, and if the budget is approved the President formally signs it and declares it to be adopted.

But where, as prior to the Brussels summit was frequently the case, major differences between the Council and the EP remain, the two sides are obliged to get down to negotiations. Various procedures can come into play: the President of the Budget Council, accompanied by the Budget Commissioner, may meet with the Committee on Budgets; the President of the Budget Council may make an appeal to the plenary; a trialogue meeting may be held; or a special Budget Council may be hurriedly called, perhaps to meet again with an EP delegation, perhaps to give the budget what is, in effect, a third reading. If all efforts to reach a Council–EP agreement fail, the latter can reject the budget by a majority of its members, including two-thirds of the votes cast.

☐ *Non-approval of the budget.* In five of the first nine years following the introduction of direct elections in 1979, budgets were not approved in time to be implemented at the beginning of the financial year on 1 January. These were the budgets of 1980 and of 1984–8.

If a legal budget is not approved by the EP before 1 January a fall back position applies. This allows for funding to continue, but only on the basis of what are known as 'provisional twelfths', which means that spending is limited to the monthly average expenditure of the previous year. Policies do not therefore collapse, but some payments may have to be suspended, and programmes, especially those that are new, may have to be delayed. A speedy agreement on the budget of what is, by this stage, the current financial year, is thus desirable.

There is no formal procedure or set pattern regarding what happens in the event of non-adoption. The expectation and assumption is that the process is resumed at the point at which it broke down, but practice has shown matters not to be so simple. Developments following non-adoptions have varied considerably, depending principally on the reasons for the non-adoption. So, for example, the 1986 budget was, like those for 1985 and 1988, not approved until halfway through the financial year. The problem with the 1986 budget was not that a budget was not approved by the EP in December 1985, but rather that the Council judged the budget that had been adopted by the EP to be illegal on the grounds that it included more non-compulsory expenditure than was legally permissible. The Council, therefore, asked the Court of Justice for a ruling. On 3 July 1986 the Court eventually delivered its judgement and, in essence, upheld the Council's claim that the budget was illegal. The next week then saw hectic activity, a truncated budgetary procedure and, on 10 July, the adoption of a budget in which creative accountancy and financial ingenuity played prominent parts.

The adoption of medium-term financial perspectives and interinstitutional agreements has removed, or at least blunted the sharpness of, many of the problems that occasioned non-adoption of budgets in the 1980s. In particular, agricultural expenditure has been made subject to stronger budgetary discipline, the size of the Structural Funds has been increased, mechanisms have been established to improve the match between income and expenditure, and decision-making procedures have been made less confrontational. Of course, not all differences or potential problems have been totally erased. But the prospect of budgets normally being adopted at December plenaries has been considerably enhanced, and up to the time of writing (early 1994), all budgets to have come forward since 1988 have indeed been so adopted.

☐ *The making of a specific budget – 1994*

The processes described in the previous section can be illustrated by looking at the making of a specific budget – that for 1994 (see Table 12.1).

As has been customary since the establishment of the first financial perspective in 1988, the procedures which led to the making of the 1994 budget ran relatively smoothly, on schedule, and – as the figures in Table 12.1 show – within relatively narrow financial margins. The principal developments at the main stages were as follows:

● The Commission agreed on the 1994 PDB in late April 1993. In presenting the PDB the Budget Commissioner stressed that it incorporated the need for budgetary discipline and was placed firmly within the framework of the 1993–9 financial perspective. The PDB amounted to 73.2 billion Ecu in commitments (only the figures for commitments will be given in this account) which constituted an increase of 5.9 per cent over the 1993 budget. Agricultural spending was planned to rise by 7.1 per cent, much of this being accounted for by costs associated with CAP reforms, structural operations by 4.5 per cent, internal policies by 3.3 per cent, and external policies by 1.5 per cent. The Budget Commissioner emphasised

Table 12.1 The EU Budget 1994: different stages

	Budget 1993	Financial perspective 1994	Preliminary draft budget	Council first reading	EP first reading	Council second reading	Budget 1994
Common Agricultural Policy (apart from EAGGF – Guidance)	35.4	36.5	36.5	36.5	36.5	36.5	36.5
Structural operations, of which:	22.2	23.2	23.2	23.2	23.2	23.2	23.2
ERDF	8.0		9.0	9.0	9.0	9.0	9.0
ESF	5.8		6.5	6.5	6.5	6.5	6.5
Internal policies, of which:	4.1	4.4	4.3	3.6	4.4	4.2	4.4
research	2.7		2.7	2.5	2.8	2.7	2.8
education, etc.	0.3		0.3	0.2	0.3	0.3	0.3
trans-European networks	0.2		0.3	0.2	0.3	0.3	0.3
External action, of which:	4.1	4.3	4.2	4.0	4.3	4.2	4.3
cooperation – Latin American countries	0.6		0.6	0.6	0.6	0.6	0.7
cooperation – Mediterranean countries	0.4		0.5	0.4	0.5	0.5	0.5

cooperation – Central and Eastern European countries and independent states of former USSR	1.6		1.6	1.6	1.5	1.6	1.5
Administration	3.4	3.6	3.7	3.6	3.6	3.6	3.6
Reserves	1.2	1.5	1.5	1.5	1.5	1.5	1.5
Total, of which: compulsory expenditure	70.4	73.5	73.4	72.4	73.4	73.2	73.4
compulsory expenditure	37.4		39.0	39.0	39.0	39.0	39.0
non-compulsory expenditure	33.0		34.5	33.5	34.5	34.2	34.5

Notes:
1. Figures in billion Ecu.
2. All figures are appropriations for commitments
3. Figures have been rounded up where appropriate – hence some seemingly minor discrepancies
4. The reduction of figures to one decimal point, does, of course, mask some variations within these margins

Source: Adapted from XXVIIth General Report on the Activities of the European Communities 1993.

that recent currency changes meant the 7.1 per cent for agriculture might not be enough.

● Budget ministers gave their first reading to the PDB in July. Before embarking on their examination they met an EP delegation which was headed by the EP's President and which consisted mainly of members of the Committee on Budgets. The Council established a first draft budget of 72.4 billion Ecu in commitments, which trimmed 760 million Ecu off the PDB, and involved an increase of 4.3 per cent over the 1993 budget. The PDB appropriations for agriculture and for regional and social expenditure were largely untouched. Cuts fell mainly in the areas of research, Third World aid, and various internal policies including the trans-European network programme, consumer protection, and the environment.

● Prior to the EP first reading at the October plenary, the EP's Committee on Budgets met for two days to consider some 600 amendments. After the customary exhaustive, and exhausting, voting process in the plenary was completed, the EP had voted to increase the Council's first draft by 1 billion Ecu in commitments, from 72.4 billion Ecu to 73.4 billion Ecu. The increases included both internal policies (such as audiovisual, energy, transport, and research) and external policies (such as aid to the Third World and to Non-Governmental Organisations).

● At its second reading, in mid-November, the Council decided on a budget of 73.1 billion Ecu in commitments, and in so doing accepted around 700 million Ecu of the extra 1 billion Ecu voted by the EP at its first reading.

● At their second reading, during the December plenary session, MEPs increased the Council's second reading budget by some 330 million Ecu and voted through a budget of 73.4 billion Ecu in commitments. Amongst the principal changes made by the EP were increases in overseas aid, research, the LIFE environmental programme, and funds to combat unemployment. In the debate the Commission, and more especially the Council, indicated reservations about some of Parliament's decisions. After the budget had been approved by MEPs, the President of the EP formally signed and released it.

☐ *Characteristic features of the budgetary process*

Some features of the budgetary process merit particular comment.

First, the budget, like the annual agriculture price review, is unusual in the EU decision-making context in the sense that it is supposed to operate according to a clear timetable. Legislative proposals can be pushed along if they are strongly supported, and the SEM momentum and the greater use of majority voting have greatly quickened the pace of much legislative decision-making, but it is only in the later stages of the cooperation and co-decision procedures that a timetable applies. It is still the case that legislative proposals can drag on in the Council until some sort of agreement is reached, and if this proves not to be possible they may be indefinitely postponed or even dropped altogether. With the budget such a relaxed and open-ended approach is not possible, since expenditure and resource decisions have to be made each year. The existence and exigencies of the timetable thus introduce an urgency into budgetary decision-making that is not always found in other spheres of EU decision-making.

Second, the power balance between the institutions is not the same on the budget as it is elsewhere, for the Council and the EP jointly constitute the budgetary authority and are co-decision-makers. The Commission remains important, but after the presentation of the PDB it is cast in an essentially servicing capacity: responding to what happens in the Council and the Parliament and doing what it can to bring the two sides together. As for the particular nature of the balance between the Council and the EP, the former is unquestionably the stronger, but the changes which have been made since 1988 have improved the position of the EP. They have done so in three ways: by binding the institutions into a financial framework which can only be revised by common agreement; by significantly increasing the proportion of the budget over which the EP has most control – non-compulsory expenditure; and by giving the EP a glimpse of shared control over compulsory expenditure – a glimpse which may become reality in the future, since a condition of the EP's agreeing to the 1993–9 financial perspective was that it would have the right to scrutinise the compulsory expenditure part of the budget, with a view to forcing the Commission to justify the legal base of compulsory budget lines.

Third, many of the arguments and confrontations that have occurred during the budgetary process have been occasioned not so much by the financial sums involved – which have usually been relatively small – but more by a broader institutional struggle, especially between the Council and the EP. With the EP dissatisfied with its overall position in the EU system, it is only natural that it should have sought to use the budget to maximum advantage. There are a number of ways in which it has gone about this. One was its willingness in the 1980s to reject the budget. Another has been interpreting the Treaties, along with agreements and understandings about budgetary decision-making, in ways which are advantageous to itself – as on matters such as the bases for budgetary calculations, and the classification of expenditure in terms of compulsory and non-compulsory. And a third way has been by attempting to exploit differences within the Council – by, for example, seeking to exert pressure in a particular direction through the indication of preferences in plenary votes or, less formally, in interinstitutional exchanges such as conciliation meetings.

Fourth, certain fundamental budgetary decisions are not taken via the annual budgetary process. As has been shown, decisions on resource ceilings, on patterns of expenditure growth, on 'rebates' for countries making excessive budgetary contributions, and on budgetary discipline, have all been taken, essentially, by European Council meetings.

Fifth, and finally, the effectiveness of the budgetary process has, like virtually all EU decision-making, tended to be weakened by the absence of a consensus amongst decision-makers as to how the EU should develop. Until the 1988 *Interinstitutional Agreement* this resulted in budgetary outcomes being highly incremental in nature with, in terms of the Community's policy balance, only marginal adjustments being effected to the *status quo*. The use of financial perspectives since 1988 has allowed for some modest changes in this situation. The perspectives have not established 'cohesive' or 'objective' budgetary planning, but they have at least enabled the budget to become the instrument for important, though not fundamental, reform.

■ Chapter 13 ■

Agricultural Policy and Policy Processes

Despite the fact that it accounts for only 2.4 per cent of EU GDP and 6.5 per cent of EU employment, agriculture looms large in the life of the EU. It does so in three main ways. First, the EU carries, via the Common Agricultural Policy (CAP), major policy-making and decision-making responsibilities for agriculture. Second, as the major recipient of EU funds, agriculture is central to EU financial deliberations and serves to restrict policy development in non-agricultural spheres. And third, there is a greater institutional presence and activity in the agricultural field than in any other: the Agriculture Ministers meet more frequently than all other Councils except for the Foreign Ministers; uniquely, Agriculture Council meetings are prepared not by COREPER but by a special body, the Special Committee on Agriculture (SCA); DGVI (Agriculture) is the second largest of the Commission's twenty-three Directorates General (only DGIX is larger and that deals not with a policy sector but with Personnel and Administration); and there are far more Council working parties and Commission management and advisory groups in the sphere of agriculture than in any other single policy area.

For its supporters, the CAP is important both in itself – the benefits accruing from joint policy-making and common management are seen as far outweighing the disadvantages – and important, too, as a symbol and indicator that real policy integration is possible at EU level. Those who criticise the CAP are thus liable to be attacked, both on technical and efficiency grounds (with the claim that national solutions would be much less satisfactory), and more broadly for being *non communautaire* (with the assertion that this most integrated of EU policies should not be undermined). For opponents of the CAP, economic efficiency is the key issue. Subsidisation of wealthy farmers, high prices for consumers, and production of farm surpluses which nobody wants are the most frequently heard criticisms.

Yet even amongst those who are most critical of the CAP, few seriously challenge the view that there should be an EU agriculture policy of some kind. Certainly no member state believes that the agricultural edifice should be uprooted and policy returned to national capitals. The view that there is something special about agriculture, something that distinguishes it from other sectoral activities and merits it receiving advantageous treatment, whilst not commanding such strong support as in the early days of the EC, still strikes a chord with EU decision-makers.

■ What is special about agriculture?

The attention given to agriculture in the EEC Treaty, and the subsequent creation of the CAP through long and often tortuous negotiations, is often seen as being part of a trade-off between France and Germany. There is something in this view. In exchange for the creation of a common market in industrial goods, which the French feared would be greatly to Germany's advantage, France – with her large, but uneconomic, agricultural sector – would benefit from an agricultural system which, though also in the form of a common market, would be based not on free and open market principles, but on foundations which would protect farmers from too much competition.

Important though it was, however, the Franco–German 'deal' provides only part of the explanation for why agriculture, from the earliest days of the Community, was given an elevated policy status. For the fact is that when the CAP was being created in the late 1950s and early 1960s, none of the then six member states seriously objected to it in principle – the Netherlands, for example, was a strong supporter – though there were differences on the pace of its construction and the precise nature of its policy instruments. This consensus on the general principle was a result of a shared recognition that agriculture required special treatment.

Today, despite the original EC having greatly increased in size, despite the circumstances and conditions of agriculture having dramatically changed, and despite the CAP having caused major difficulties and disruptions to the whole EU system, agriculture is still generally regarded by the national governments as requiring special treatment. Many of the reasons for this are much the same as they were in the EC's early days. Others are more recent. The reasons can be grouped under two general headings: the distinctive nature of agriculture, and political factors.

☐ *The distinctive nature of agriculture*

For many years, but especially since the Second World War, most governments of the industrialised world have taken the view that agriculture is not like other areas of economic activity. It is special and merits special treatment to encourage, to assist and to protect it. In the EU four main arguments have been, and still are, advanced in support of this view.

(1)   If they are not controlled by governmental authorities agricultural prices are more subject to fluctuation than are the prices of most other goods. Agricultural price instability is undesirable for two reasons. First, if prices suddenly go up, inflation is immediately fuelled (given that food constitutes around 21 per cent of the budget of the average EU citizen). Second, if prices fall too low, farmers may not be able to make an adequate living and may be forced off the land; even those who are able to stay in farming may experience severe difficulties as a result of high debt loads carried on land and capital purchases.

(2)   Reliance on imports for vital foodstuffs creates a potential vulnerability to outside pressures. This is a particular source of weakness during periods of strained international relations.

   In the relatively calm trading climate of the 1990s, and with many foodstuffs which are produced in the EU in surplus – including cereals, dairy produce, and meat – this argument is perhaps less weighty than it used to be. However, in the early years of the EC, when memories of wartime shortages and of the vulnerability and misery this occasioned were fresh, it played an important part in encouraging a drive for greater self-sufficiency.

(3)   Because people must have food, insufficient domestic production means that the gap between output and demand has to be met by imports, with potentially damaging consequences for the balance of payments. Moreover, since the demand for food is fairly inelastic up to necessity levels – as long as income allows it, food will still be bought even if prices go up – the economic vulnerability of an importing state is high.

   This balance of payments argument has not been so forceful since the early to mid-1970s, when Community prices became significantly higher than world prices and Community production began to move significantly into surplus. High domestic prices mean that EU processors cannot maximise the exports of their value added goods by buying at the cheapest possible prices, and surpluses mean that national treasuries have to pay – via the EU budget – for their disposal.

(4)   Social and environmental reasons for keeping farmers on the land have been increasingly heard in recent years. Sometimes these have an idealistic tone to them, with pleas that a populated countryside is part of

the natural fabric, or the suggestion that management of the land is a desirable end in itself. Rather more hard-headed perhaps is the argument that, with relatively high levels of unemployment in the EU – the overall average was 10.1 per cent in 1993 – it is both undesirable and potentially dangerous to allow farm incomes to deteriorate to the point that poor farmers and agricultural workers are forced to move to the towns in search of employment that often does not exist.

☐ *Political factors*

Farmers enjoy political assets that they have been able to translate into influence on EU policy. Three of these assets are especially important.

(1)   At the national decision-making level, Ministries of Agriculture have tended traditionally to be slightly apart from mainstream policy processes, and since 1958 this has been reproduced at the EU level with the position of DGVI in the Commission. All policy areas, of course, attempt to use their own expertise, knowledge and information to provide themselves with some insulation from the rest of the decision-making system, but agriculture is particularly well placed to be able to do this. Its supposed distinctive nature, the complexity of much of its subject matter, and the customary close relations between agricultural decision-makers and producers, all combine to make it difficult for 'outside' decision-makers to offer an effective challenge or alternative to what is presented to them.

(2)   Farmers enjoy considerable electoral weight. Even though their relative numerical importance has declined sharply over the years – in 1958 around 25 per cent of total EC employment was in agriculture, by 1994 it was around 6.5 per cent – the agricultural vote is still very significant. The significance varies from state to state. The size of the domestic population engaged in agriculture is one important factor in determining this significance: proportions range from around 25 per cent in Greece and 17 per cent in Portugal to 2.7 per cent in Belgium and 2.2 per cent in the United Kingdom. Another consideration is the direction of the agricultural vote. On the whole, farmers, especially richer farmers, incline to Centre-Right and Right parties, with the consequence that it is they, rather than parties of the Left, who are usually the strongest defenders of agricultural interests in EU forums. But this inclination to the Right does not, in most countries, amount to an exclusive loyalty, so few parties can afford to ignore the farmers: at a minimum, parties must give the impression of being concerned and solicitous.

(3)   In most EU countries farmers have long had very strong domestic organisations to represent and articulate their interests. When it became clear in the late 1950s and early 1960s that much agricultural policy and

decision-making was to be transferred to Brussels, similar organisations were quickly established at Community level. As early as 1963, approaching 100 Community-wide agriculture groups had been formed. By the 1990s this number had grown to around 130. The most important of these groups is COPA, which is an umbrella or peak organisation representing all types of farmers on the basis of affiliation through national farming groups. Beyond COPA and a few other overarching organisations, specialist bodies exist to represent virtually every product that is produced and consumed in the EU, and every participant in the agricultural process – farmers most obviously, but also processors, traders, retailers, etc.

There can be no doubt that this agricultural lobby has been, and remains, a very powerful force in the EU. It is worth setting out the reasons why.

□ *The sheer size of the lobby is formidable.* It operates at two levels, the national and the EU.

At the national level there are considerable variations in the pattern and strength of agricultural representation. But, in all member states, there are groups of some kind which have as part of their purpose the utilisation of whatever devices and channels are available to them to influence both national agricultural policy (within the general principles of the CAP, states still enjoy a considerable policy discretion) and EU agricultural policy. Thus, the National Farmers' Union for England and Wales employs a full-time professional staff of around 240 at its London headquarters and 600 or so in the regions. Additionally it funds, in conjunction with the NFU of Scotland and the Ulster Farmers' Union, a Brussels office, known as the British Office of Agriculture, which has a regular staff of between five and ten who are topped up as required.

At the EU level the large number of Euro-agric groups means that lobbying activities across the agricultural sector are almost continuous. COPA moves on the broadest front and, with some 49 full-time officials (in early 1994), is by far the best resourced and staffed organisation. (See Chapter 9 for further information on COPA.) The more specialised groups – the mustard makers (CIMCEE) for example, or the butchers (COBCCEE) – are much more modestly provided for and may have, at best, one full-time member of staff working in an office made available by a national affiliate. But since the interests of these small groups are usually narrowly drawn this may be enough to allow basic lobbying requirements to be fulfilled – meetings and consultations with decision-makers, feeding information through to the EU institutions, preparing policy and briefing documents. If circumstances require it, reinforcements are usually available from national and Euro-umbrella associations.

☐   *Agricultural interests generally enjoy good contacts with, and access to, decision-makers.* Again, this factor operates at both national and EU levels.

At the national level, influence with governments is vital, not only because of their control over nationally determined policies but also because they are the route to the Council of Ministers. Most governments are at least prepared to listen to representations from national agricultural interests, and some engage in a virtual automatic consultation on important issues. There are a number of reasons why governments are generally approachable in this way: there may be a pre-existing sympathy for the interests' views; a fuller picture of what is going on in the agricultural world is made possible; policy implementation may be made easier; and political support may be generated by being supportive, or at least by giving the impression that the government and the interest are as one. If, despite being sympathetically listened to by its government, a national agricultural interest is dissatisfied with what is agreed in the Council of Ministers, the government can always try to blame 'the awkward Italians', 'the impossible Greeks', or 'the immovable Germans'.

At the EU level, the Commission is the prime target for agricultural interests. For the most part it is only too willing to listen. Indeed, it has encouraged the establishment of Euro-agric groups and readily makes itself available to them. Close Commission–group relations are viewed by the Commission as being as useful to it as to the groups: the groups can contribute their knowledge and their experience which may improve policy; the Commission can explain to the groups why it is engaging in certain actions and thus seek to sensitise them to Commission concerns and aims; face-to-face meetings can help break down barriers and resistance arising from suspicions that 'the Eurocrats' do not really understand farming practicalities; and if Euro-groups can do something to aggregate the conflicting national interests and demands that arise in relation to most proposals, they can considerably simplify the Commission's task of developing policies that are acceptable and can help to legitimise the Commission as a decision-maker in the eyes of the Council and the EP.

☐   *The agricultural organisations are not counterbalanced by strong and vigorous groups advancing contrary attitudes and claims.* 'Natural opponents' do exist – consumers and environmentalists most notably – but they are relatively weak by contrast. A major reason for their weakness is that whereas farmers constitute a clear section of the population with a readily identifiable common sectoral interest, consumers and environmentalists do not have such a group consciousness, are dispersed and, in consequence, are just not so easy to mobilise or organise. So, though there are many more consumers than there are farmers in the EU, the largest of the Euro-consumer groups – the European Bureau of Consumers' Associations (BEUC) – carries a staff of only seven or eight. This is respectable enough when compared with most Euro-groups, but it pales when compared with the massed ranks of the agriculture associations. Moreover, the BEUC has to cover the whole spectrum of relevant EU policies; agriculture takes up only part of its time.

In terms of access to decision-makers, the farmers' 'rivals' do not, as a rule, enjoy the 'insider status' granted to much of the agriculture lobby. They rarely have a 'sponsoring' ministry in the way that agricultural interests do. Nor are they necessarily consulted by the Commission on agricultural matters as a matter of routine, or automatically called in for discussions when something of importance or potential interest arises. The fact is that they do not have the political and economic power of farmers, they cannot offer trade-offs in the way of cooperation on policy implementation, they are – in some instances – relative latecomers, and a few – notably the more radical 'Greens' – are seen as not quite conforming with established values and the rules of the game. Some of the more respectable of these 'oppositional' agriculture groups have their foot in the EU door, but none has quite entered the room in the manner of the agricultural lobby.

☐ *Agriculture has powerful friends.* While farmers and those directly engaged in the agricultural industries have been the most obvious beneficiaries of the CAP, others have gained too, notably the owners of land. Huge profits have been made by investment institutions, financiers, banks, industrial corporations and private landlords from the rising value of land that has been associated with the CAP. Many of these interests have direct access to decision-makers, indeed are themselves numbered amongst the decision-makers in some governments, and have sought to use their influence accordingly.

☐ *Unity has been a considerable source of strength.* Despite the great range of interests represented, the agriculture lobby was, until the mid-1980s, more or less united in its aims: it pressed for comprehensive market regimes for as much produce as possible, and it sought the largest price increases it could get. In recent years, however, as significant steps to bring agriculture spending under proper control have been taken, the unity of the lobby has been subject to increasing strains and its effectiveness has accordingly been weakened a little. Sectors have vied with one another as careful attention has had to be paid not only to the size of the cake, but also to the way in which it is cut.

☐ *Farmers sometimes resort to direct action.* In some EU countries, most notably France, farmers sometimes take matters into their own hands if they are dissatisfied with policies and decisions affecting their sector. Whilst decision-makers never care to admit that they have been swayed by direct action, there is no doubt that farmers' militancy has affected at least some of those who are responsible for running EU agriculture. Certainly, for example, the tough stances adopted by the French Government in the Council of Ministers in respect of the reform of the CAP in 1991–2 and in respect of the agricultural aspects of the GATT Uruguay Round in 1992–3, were at least partially influenced by the knowledge that angry farmers had already signalled their fears of possible 'sell-outs' by holding large demonstrations and by creating widespread disruption of French transport networks.

■ How the Common Agricultural Policy works

Title II of the EC Treaty (Articles 38–47) – which, post the TEU, is still as it was written in 1957 in the EEC Treaty – sets out the general rationale and framework of the Common Agricultural Policy. The objectives are laid down in Article 39:

(a)   to increase agricultural productivity by promoting technical progress and by ensuring the rational development of agricultural production and the optimum utilisation of the factors of production, in particular labour;
(b)   thus to ensure a fair standard of living for the agricultural community, in particular by increasing the individual earnings of persons engaged in agriculture;
(c)   to stabilise markets;
(d)   to assure the availability of supplies;
(e)   to ensure that supplies reach consumers at reasonable prices.

Many matters are barely touched on in Title II because, in 1957, they were deliberately left aside for later consideration by representatives of the states. Amongst the first fruits of these deliberations was the adoption by the Council of Ministers in December 1960 of the three major operating principles of the CAP. These still apply today.

☐ *A single internal market with common prices*

Agricultural goods are supposed to be able to flow freely across EU borders, unhindered by barriers to trade and unhampered by devices such as subsidies or administrative regulations which might distort or limit competition. However, it is not a free trade system based on pure market principles because common prices are set by the Council for most important agricultural products. These prices include: a target price, which is the price it is hoped farmers will be able to obtain on the open market; a threshold price, which is the price to which Community imports are raised when world prices are lower than EU prices; and a guaranteed or intervention price, which is the price at which the Commission will take produce off the market by stepping in and buying it up (see Figure 13.1). The amount of support a product is given is a consequence of how high these prices are set, the size of the gap between the prices, and the ways in which price and currency mechanisms and intervention practices function.

The price support system dominates the CAP. It does so mainly because it is so costly to finance. There are three principal reasons why it is expensive. First, many goods are produced in amounts that are surplus to

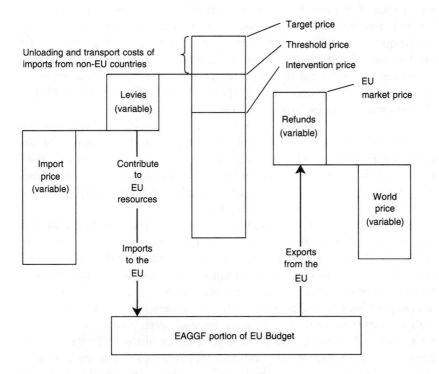

Source: Adapted from *The Common Agricultural Policy and its Reform*, European Documentation (1987).

Figure 13.1 *Outline of the different price levels and the levy and refund system for a full market regime product*

EU requirements. To cite some staple products, by the early 1990s the EU's level of self-sufficiency was 127 per cent in wheat, 120 per cent in other cereals, 106 per cent in vegetables, 105 per cent in dairy products, 104 per cent in poultrymeat, and 104 per cent in beef and veal. High guaranteed prices are the main reason for these surpluses, but improved farming techniques and the concentrated use of fertilisers and additives have also played a part. Second, the range of products protected by a market regime has been extended over the years so that now 94 per cent of all EU produce is covered in some way. Different regimes provide different forms of protection – so that in practice there are several agricultural policies rather than just one – but most products (around 70 per cent) are the beneficiaries of support prices. For some products the support prices are available on an unconditional and open-ended basis, but more commonly, following a series of Council decisions since the mid-1980s designed to tackle the problem of surpluses and reduce CAP expenditure, they are subject to restrictions. The precise nature of the restrictions varies from product to product, but they usually take one, or some combination, of three main forms: quotas; co-responsibility levies; and stabilisers – which consist of a mechanism in which production thresholds (maximum guaranteed quantities) are set, and if these are exceeded the guaranteed payments are automatically reduced. Third, apart from a brief interlude in 1974–5, EU agricultural prices have consistently been above world prices, which has meant that it has not been possible to export surpluses without suffering a financial loss. Several devices are used to dispose of the surpluses: exporting and providing a refund (a 'restitution' in EU jargon) to the exporter to ensure he incurs no loss on the transaction; storing until EU prices rise; food aid; converting to animal foodstuffs. All these devices, however, have to be financed from the EU budget.

To try and deal with the problem of surpluses, and therefore also with the problem of heavy demands on the budget, decisions were taken in the 1980s which were designed not only to stop the system of open-ended guarantees at the level of intervention prices – by the establishment of quotas, co-responsibility levies, and stabilisers – but which were also designed to bear down more directly and generally on prices. From the 1985–6 marketing year, annual price reviews were very tight, and from 1988 – as part of the budgetary discipline ethos of the 1988–92 financial perspective (see Chapter 12) – agricultural expenditure was not permitted to increase by more than 74 per cent of the rate of growth of Community GNP.

By the early 1990s, however, it was evident that the reforms of the 1980s were having only a limited effect. Large structural surpluses still existed, and the Community was coming under increasingly strong external pressure – notably from the United States in the context of the GATT

Uruguay Round – to cut back its domestic and its export subsidies and to open up its market. In consequence, in 1991 the Commission produced a radical package of reforms under the title *The Development and Future of the CAP*. Months of negotiations then followed in Council forums, during which the Commission's proposals were weakened in some respects. Eventually, however, in May 1992, following a marathon four day meeting of Agriculture Ministers, a political agreement was reached. The agreement was formally confirmed in June 1992 when the Council adopted the various regulations which were necessary to give the reforms legal effect.

The main features of the 1992 reforms, which started coming into effect in 1993, are:

● A substantial reduction in support prices to bring them more into line with market demand: cereal prices to be reduced by 29 per cent over three years starting in 1993–4, beef prices to be reduced by 15 per cent, and the price of butter to be reduced by 5 per cent over two years.
● The introduction of a system of compensatory aid or premiums to soften the effect of lower prices on farmers' incomes. This measure has the effect of shifting support from farm prices to direct income support. So as to ensure it does not encourage increases in production, this aid is dependent not on output but on land area and past practices.
● The establishment in the arable crop sector of a set-aside scheme, in which farmers are paid to take some of their land out of production.
● A range of flanking measures designed to encourage the restructuring of farms by providing schemes and incentives for early retirement, for the afforestation of agricultural land, for the proper management of land taken out of production, and for the use of environmentally friendly methods.

In addition to its cost, another major problem with the agricultural price system is that it is not truly based, as was originally intended, on common prices: the prices that are agreed annually by the Agriculture Ministers for the products that are covered by a market regime are set in agricultural units of account – 'green' European Currency Units (Ecus) – which are linked to the Deutschmark; for payments purposes green Ecus are converted into national currencies. Green currencies were created when currency market rates in the late 1960s and early 1970s became subject to sharp and rapid fluctuations, and this had implications for agriculture which governments were not prepared to accept: farmers' incomes and food prices were affected and trade patterns became distorted. As a result, it was decided to try and stabilise agricultural incomes, prices, and markets by the use of 'green' rates of exchange which would be periodically set by the Agriculture Ministers and which would remain fixed whatever happened to the market rates of exchange. To ensure that differences between market rates and green rates would not distort intra-Community flows in agricultural products, a system of border levies and subsidies, known as Monetary Compensation Amounts (MCAs) was also introduced.

Because MCAs involved extensive border controls, they were eliminated from 1 January 1993 as part of the Single European Market (SEM) programme. Green rates, however, were not abolished, which meant there was still the problem of ensuring that the gap between market rates and green rates did not become too wide and so lead to artificial trade flows. The original hope was that mechanisms which were created to oblige green rates to shadow their market rates would guarantee order in the market: under the mechanisms various adjustments are used to ensure that the monetary gaps between market rates and green rates are pegged within specified limits. However the exchange rate crises of 1992 and 1993 (see Chapters 3 and 10) upset these hopes and, indeed, seemingly upset the hopes of the Commission that green currencies and special protective currency mechanisms can eventually be abolished.

As a result of agrimonetary complications the setting of agriculture prices cannot be viewed in isolation from exchange rates. Indeed, governments have tended to look at the price–exchange rate linkage as a useful and necessary device both for protecting their farmers or consumers and for giving themselves a greater flexibility in Council negotiations. Trade-offs in the Council have been common with, for example, a government that has felt pressurised by its farmers, agreeing to low price increases only on the condition of being allowed to devalue its green rate on specified products. (Green rate devaluations raise the national currency value of common Ecu prices.) Convenient though it has sometimes been to governments, however, the agrimonetary system has undermined common prices, has been a major stumbling block in the way of a unified agricultural market, has weakened the attractions of product specialisation, and has been a drain on the EU budget.

☐ *Community preference*

A necessary consequence of the guaranteed price system is that the EU market should be protected from the international market. Since world prices are normally lower than EU prices, free access onto the EU market would clearly destroy the whole CAP system. Community preference (the term 'EU preference' is rarely heard as yet) is, therefore, required.

Whether, however, it is required at quite such preferential levels as in practice apply is a matter of dispute.

The mechanics of the preference system vary according to the market regime for the product concerned. For the 21 per cent of produce which has a market regime but not one based on guaranteed prices (wines other than table wines, some fruit and vegetables, some cereals, eggs and poultry), external protection takes the form of levies, customs duties, and a combination of the two. For the 70 per cent of produce which does enjoy guaranteed prices (most cereals, dairy produce, milk, beef, lamb) the system is such as to prevent imports entering the EU at prices below the agreed target prices. This exclusion is, as is shown in Figure 13.1 (p. 369), achieved by the threshold price which is calculated at a level to bring the world price up to the EU's target price, minus an allowance for unloading and transport costs. The gap between world prices and the threshold price is bridged by the imposition of a levy, which is adjusted according to variations in EU and world prices. The levies become part of the EU's own resources.

The exclusion procedures just described do not apply to all the imports into the EU from all states. As is explained in Chapter 14, the EU has negotiated arrangements by which a large number of countries, most of them underdeveloped, are given special access to EU markets for at least some of their products, including agricultural products. So, the EU grants 'generalised preferences' to more than 120 developing countries and one effect of this has been the abolition or reduction of levies on about 300 agricultural products intended for processing. Under the Lomé Convention, virtually all of the exports of the 69 ACP countries have free access to the EU. (It should perhaps be pointed out here that these 'concessions' do not stem simply from generosity and goodwill. Much of the produce falling under the generalised preferences and Lomé agreements is tropical in nature and not in competition with EU produce.)

□ *Joint financing*

The cost of the CAP is financed jointly by the member states through the European Agricultural Guidance and Guarantee Fund (EAGGF) of the EU budget. This is divided into two sections: the Guarantee section which finances markets and prices, and the Guidance section which finances structural policy. The early intention was that the Guarantee section would be larger than the Guidance section by a ratio of two or three to one, but, in practice, this has never been even remotely approached, and the Guidance section hovers somewhere in the region of only 8 per cent of total EAGGF expenditure. The demands on the Guarantee section occasioned by high EU prices is the main reason for this imbalance. A second reason is that, unlike expenditure on price support, expenditure on structural measures is not wholly financed by the EAGGF but is co-financed – usually by the EU in partnership with either member states or regions. And a third reason is that member states have not always been enthusiastic supporters of EU agricultural structural policy – mainly because it usually involves contraction of the sector and/or bringing about changes to which agricultural interests are opposed.

But notwithstanding the limited size of the EAGGF Guidance section, there is still a very considerable amount of non-price-related agricultural expenditure in the EU. Some of this comes from other EU sources – in particular the Regional Fund and the European Investment Bank (EIB). By far the most of it, however, comes from national exchequers: member states are allowed to assist their farmers in almost whatever way they like as long as they do not – in the judgement of the Commission – distort competition or infringe the principles of the market. In some states national subsidies to agriculture far outstrip those of the EU.

■ The impact and effects of the Common Agricultural Policy

Whether the CAP is to be regarded as a success or not obviously depends on the priorities and interests of those making the judgement. Since, however, the issue raises so much controversy it is worth examining some of the major developments under the CAP system. This will be done initially via the five aims that were set out in Article 39 of the EC Treaty and which were listed above.

● *Agricultural efficiency has increased enormously as a result of modernisation and rationalisation.* Furthermore, despite the popular impression in some places that the CAP is little more than a device to cushion farmers, agriculture, both as a proportion of GNP and as a source of employment, has more than halved amongst the original six since 1958. That said, it may still be asked whether the overproduction of certain products at great cost, and the encouragement that high prices have given to many who would otherwise have left the land to stay on their farms, is wholly consistent with 'ensuring the rational development of agricultural production'.

- Under the CAP *agricultural incomes have grown roughly in parallel with incomes in other sectors.* However, this overall average masks enormous variations, both between large farmers (who have done very well for the most part) and small farmers, and also between producers of northern temperate products (notably dairy produce, cereals, and beef which are the main product beneficiaries of the price support system) and producers of other – mainly Mediterranean – products.
- *Markets have been stabilised,* in the sense that there have been no major food shortages and EU prices have escaped the fluctuations that have occurred in world market prices on some products.
- The EU *is now self-sufficient in virtually all of those foodstuffs its climate allows it to raise and grow.* In 1958 the six member states produced about 85 per cent of their food requirements; in 1993 the twelve produced about 125 per cent. This movement beyond self-sufficiency to the production of surpluses has been expensive in that it has only been possible to dispose of the surpluses at considerable cost.
- The exclusion of cheaper (and often much cheaper) produce from outside the EU means that the *aim of 'reasonable prices' to the consumer has had a low priority.* The undeniable fact is that, within the EU, the principal beneficiaries of CAP's pricing system have been rich farmers, whilst the main losers have been poor consumers.

Beyond an assessment of the CAP through its five Treaty aims, three other significant consequences of the policy are also worth noting. First, the CAP's dominance of the budget has unquestionably made it more difficult for other policies to be developed. The financial perspectives which have been in operation since 1988 (see Chapter 12), coupled with the series of reforms to the CAP since the mid-1980s, are gradually bringing agriculture under some sort of financial control, but even at the end of the 1993–9 financial perspective it is still scheduled to take 46 per cent of the total budget. Second, the CAP has been the source of many disagreements and tensions both within the EU and between the EU and non-EU states. So, for example, within the EU, France's generally protectionist attitude to the CAP – which is explained by France accounting for almost a quarter of the EU's food production – has frequently led to it being at loggerheads with other member states over aspects of agricultural policy. As for impacting on relations between the EU and non-EU states, the CAP has fuelled many trading disputes, and was the principal reason for the prolongation of the Uruguay Round negotiations. Thirdly, the protection of the EU market from cheaper world produce, and the release onto the world market of heavily subsidised EU produce, has distorted the international division of labour and the rational utilisation of resources.

■ Policy processes

In many respects, policy and decision-making processes for agriculture are much the same as in other policy sectors. However, the importance, the range, and the complexity of the CAP, plus the ever-changing nature of the world's agricultural markets, means that there are significant variations from the 'standard' EU model. The principal variations are as follows.

☐ *Commission initiation and formulation*

Whereas the policy initiation and formulation responsibilities of the Commission in most sectors are much concerned with creating a policy framework, in agriculture they are inevitably directed more towards improving the efficiency of one that already exists.

But, as has been indicated above, there are formidable obstacles in the way of the Commission if it is to come forward with proposals that both go to the heart of the agricultural problem and are also acceptable to the Council. As long ago as 1968, the then Commissioner for Agriculture, Sicco Mansholt, launched a major plan to reduce the size of the agriculture sector and improve the efficiency of what remained, but his proposals had little effect and were not followed up by enough Council legislation. As a result, the Commission in the 1970s approached its policy initiation and formulation responsibilities in a very cautious way. It became reluctant to advance wide-ranging schemes aimed at fundamental reform and concentrated more on short-term measures of an essentially reactive nature: reacting, that is, to specific problems in particular market sectors.

In the 1980s circumstances changed in such a way that they enabled, even obliged, the Commission to bring a longer-term view back onto the agenda and force real and properly integrated reform to be at least seriously discussed. The most important of these circumstances were deteriorating market conditions and increasing surpluses, recurring budgetary problems, international pressures against the EC's high levels of protectionism and subsidisation, and the enlargement of the Community to states which would not do especially well out of the CAP as constituted. It was against this background that in 1985 the Commission launched a consultative Green Paper – *Perspectives for the Common Agricultural Policy* – which outlined policy options for the future of agriculture until the end of the century. After wide-ranging discussions with interested parties the Green Paper was followed up with more detailed guidelines in the form of a communication to the Council and the EP entitled *A future for European agriculture*. At the heart of the

Commission's proposals lay an ambitious long-term strategy for a movement to a more market-based and restrictive pricing policy, more flexibility in guarantees and intervention mechanisms, and a much greater degree of producer co-responsibility for surpluses. These objectives were restated in the Commission's influential 1987 document *The Single Act: A New Frontier for Europe*, and constituted the basis for important agricultural reforms that the Agriculture Ministers agreed to in December 1986 and the Heads of Government agreed to at their special summit at Brussels in February 1988.

Some of the pressures which obliged the Commission to bring forward measures for reform in the 1980s – notably surpluses and the hostile views of trading partners – were behind the even more radical reforms that the Commission proposed in 1991. As in 1985 the reforms were launched in two stages, with a consultation document – entitled *Communication . . . The Development and Future of the CAP. Reflections Paper of the Commission* – followed six months later by specific proposals under the title *Communication . . . The Development and Future of the Common Agricultural Policy. Follow-up to the Reflections Paper. Proposals of the Commission*. Although subsequently watered down, these proposals provided the general framework for the still significant reforms of the CAP to which the Agriculture Ministers agreed in May 1992 (see above).

☐ *Council decision-making*

Of all the Councils, the Agriculture Council is perhaps the one which is most reliant on issue linkages and package deals for conducting its business (see Exhibit 5.1, on pp. 138–41, for an indication of the range of business which is covered by Agriculture Ministers).

One reason it *has* to be so reliant is that whereas in some sectors issues can be allowed to drift, in agriculture certain decisions, most obviously those taken as part of the annual price review, cannot be continually postponed. They must be resolved, but a resolution is normally possible only if it is based on a recognition of the different interests and priorities of the states: most states, for example, are net exporters of agricultural produce, but a minority are net importers; some have temperate climates, some Mediterranean; some have mainly large and efficient farms, others still carry many small and inefficient family-based units; and some have vast tracts of 'less favoured' land, whilst others have very little.

A major reason the Council is *able* to make use of linkages and packages is that it has available to it a variety of possible policy instruments. By bringing these together in carefully weighted combinations the way can often be opened to agreements in which there is something for everyone.

An example of extensive political wheeling and dealing in the Council of Ministers being necessary before an agreement on agriculture matters could be reached occurred in the autumn of 1990. This was in connection with the negotiating mandate to be given to the Commission in the Uruguay Round of GATT negotiations. Agriculture had proved to be the major problem in the Uruguay Round because of an insistence by most of the Community's major trading partners, notably the United States and the Cairns group of fourteen farm exporting countries, that the Community's system of subsidising agriculture should be virtually dismantled: the United States wanted the internal farm subsidies to be cut by 75 per cent, and the export subsidies to be cut by 90 per cent, over a ten year period. The Council of Ministers was quite unable to accept this, but France and Germany, with some support from Ireland, were instrumental in temporarily blocking the Council from even agreeing to a compromise negotiating formula put forward by the Commission whereby Community farm subsidies as a whole would be cut by 30 per cent over a ten year period backdated to 1986 – which, since the post-1986 reforms had already had some effect in cutting subsidies, meant a real cut of only about 15 per cent between 1990 and 1995. As a result, the Community was unable to meet the mid-October 1990 deadline, by which time it had been agreed that all the participating parties in GATT should formally table their negotiating positions. It was not until early November – after extensive negotiations on the matter in seven different Council of Ministers meetings involving Agriculture, Foreign, and Trade Ministers – that a marathon joint session of Agriculture and Trade Ministers was eventually able to agree a negotiating brief for the Commission. Almost inevitably the agreement bore all the hallmarks of both a fudge and a compromise, combining a commitment to cut subsidies by 30 per cent with other commitments to cushion farmers from loss of incomes, to protect them against any sudden increase in cheap food imports, and to introduce import levies on some products hitherto allowed free access to the Community.

In the event, the Community's stance on agriculture within GATT was still seen as being too protectionist by the agricultural exporting nations, with the consequence that negotiations became extremely protracted. A breakthrough was eventually achieved with the so-called Blair House agreement in November 1992, when the Commission, in its capacity of EC external trade representative, agreed in bilateral negotiations with the United States to reduce EC agricultural exports by 36 per cent and subsidies by 21 per cent. Further delays, however, then followed when the French Government claimed the Commission had exceeded its powers and had offered the United States terms which would require greater cuts in subsidies than were implied by the May 1992 reforms. As a result, disputes rumbled on in the Council of Ministers during 1993 over the agricultural aspects of the Uruguay Round, the Commission was obliged to expend much time and energy attempting to demonstrate that the Blair House agreement was in conformity with the May 1992 agreement and, as the December 1993 deadline for the completion of the Uruguay Round loomed, the Foreign Ministers – who as well as nominally being the most senior Council also look after external trade – became increasingly involved in agriculture matters. It was they – the Foreign Ministers – who, on the very day before the negotiating deadline expired, gave final approval to all parts – including the agricultural parts – of the Uruguay Round settlement.

Management and implementation of the Common Agricultural Policy

Because of the nature of the CAP, the EU is much more involved in the management and implementation of agricultural policy than it is in other policy spheres. The Commission, and particularly DGVI, are central in this regard. They oversee the general operation of the whole system, they adjust it as necessary and, insofar as it is possible, they try to ensure that the national agencies which undertake the front line implementation of policy – Ministries of Agriculture, intervention agencies, customs and excise authorities, etc. – fulfil their obligations in a proper manner.

In exercising these duties the Commission must operate within EU law and Council guidelines. This means that much of what it does in managing the CAP is of an essentially technical nature: making adjustments to match ever-changing market conditions. But in some spheres it can do this in ways which amount to rather more than simply applying tightly drawn rules. Many of its decisions – for example on the operation of the intervention and support systems, on refunds, on storage – are taken within margins of manoeuvre that give it at least some flexibility. It is a flexibility that can result in the Commission's choices having important financial implications for producers, traders, processors, and the EU budget.

Where payments and charges have to be adjusted almost daily, and in other instances where quick management decisions have to be taken, the Commission is authorised to act without reference to any other body. However, as was explained in Chapter 4, the Commission's general agricultural management responsibilities are not exercised by Commission officials alone but via management committees made up of civil servants from the member states. There are around twenty such committees, including one for each product that has a market regime, and the

Commission would not normally go ahead with anything important – in relation to export refunds, for example – without referring to the appropriate committee, and to the Council if necessary. It is generally accepted that the Commission determines the direction and sets the pace in the committees, but the existence of the committees does mean that the member states have a direct input to, and ultimately a control over, all but the fine details of agricultural policy and the management of that policy.

■ The annual price review

A distinguishing feature of agriculture decision-making is that many of the key decisions are made as part of a regular annual process: in the price review. Contrary to what the name suggests, prices are not the only element of the reviews. Many non-price elements get swept up and become components of what is usually a highly complex and interconnected package by the time the final agreement is made. The core of the package usually consists of a range of different price increases, adjustments to product regimes, agrimonetary adjustments (though less than there were before the dismantlement of MCAs), and statements of intent about future action.

The date of the beginning of the marketing year varies between products, but as some begin on 1 April the intention of the Commission is always to have a settlement before this date. To achieve this a timetable exists that is supposed to culminate with the Agriculture Council making decisions in March. In practice, it has not usually been possible to keep to the later parts of the timetable in recent years and agreements have been delayed into April, May, and even later. This has obliged the Council to prolong the previous year's allocations in order to permit payments still to be made.

There is an important sense in which price reviews are a constant part of the work of DGVI, since market situations are subject to constant monitoring, whilst medium- to long-term schemes for agricultural reform have to be implemented, to some extent at least, via reviews. The systematic work on particular reviews, however, is concentrated into the six to seven month period before they are due to come into effect. The main stages are as follows:

(1)   In September the directorates and divisions of DGVI, working with the management committees, begin to analyse and draw up reports on such matters as quantities, state of stocks, prices, and exports in their market sectors. This is essentially a technical exercise.

(2)   During October and November consultations occur between the Commission and interested parties. Some of these are in the structured settings of management and advisory committees and working groups of national experts, others are more informal exchanges between DGVI officials and representatives of governments and sectional interests. Amongst the sectional interests which feed their views into the Commission are farmers' organisations (notably COPA), consumers' organisations (notably BEUC), trade organisations (such as COCERAL – which represents the grain trade), and food industry organisations (such as ASSILEC – which represents the dairy industry).

(3)   The first drafts from the various sectors should be ready by mid-November. The process of integrating them necessitates several rounds of meetings involving the Commissioner for Agriculture, members of his *cabinet,* the director general, assistant directors general, directors, and senior officials representing the three main product areas of the review – livestock, crops, and wine. In attempting to bring everything together the Commissioner and his advisers have to bear in mind a number of considerations, of which the most important are:

● The limitations imposed by the agricultural reference framework. Recognising that previous attempts to control agricultural expenditure via budgetary discipline guidelines had not been successful, and faced with growing agricultural surpluses and (another) impending budgetary crisis, the Heads of Government, as part of their February 1988 Brussels 'package deal' which established a five year financial perspective, agreed to a reference framework for agricultural expenditure which had as its aim a significant decrease in the proportion of the Community budget devoted to agriculture. The agreement at Brussels specified that from a reference base of 27.5 billion Ecu EAGGF Guarantee expenditure for 1988, annual growth rates in the years up to 1992 should not exceed 74 per cent of the annual rate of increase in Community GNP. The successor to the 1988–92 financial perspective, covering the years 1993–9, confirmed the 74 per cent restriction and anticipated total spending on agriculture moving from 35.2 billion Ecu in 1993 to 38.4 billion Ecu in 1999, at 1992 prices. (See Chapter 12 and Document 12.1, p. 346, for more on the significance and nature of the financial perspectives.)

● Commission and Council preferences drawn from both rolling programmes and continuing commitments. Several such programmes and commitments were, for example, contained in the reform measures which were agreed by the Council in May 1992.

● Political factors and the implications proposals may have for those who are affected by them. The Commission has no interest in making 'enemies' in the Council, or indeed amongst sectional interests, so it may wish to soften the effect of proposals which are likely to arouse opposition.

(4)   On being agreed in DGVI and by the Commissioner for Agriculture, a draft is submitted to the College of Commissioners for their approval. Ideally this submission is made by mid-December, although usually the timetable slips and it is later.

The Commissioners' deliberations are preceded by meetings of the relevant members of their *cabinets*, including *chefs de cabinet*, assisted by senior officials from DGVI. An important function of these inter-*cabinets* meetings is to ensure that the interests of the Commissioners dealing with the likes of external trade, environment, and development cooperation are considered. If all goes well a general agreement on most key points can be reached at this stage. The Commissioners themselves, however, have to approve the final proposals. Whether this is largely a formality or involves difficult negotiations depends on what has happened at the pre-meetings.

(5)   As soon as they are agreed – which should be by mid-January – the Commission's proposals are sent to the Council, and also to the ESC and the EP for their opinions.

The influence of the ESC is very marginal. This reflects its limited role in the EU as a whole, though such potential for exerting influence on the review as it does have is not helped by its customary inability to take a united view on agricultural questions. Its opinion – which in recent years has been issued by its March or April plenary session – frequently incorporates a mixture of agreements, disagreements, and agreements subject to conditions, and is sometimes adopted on the basis of a vote in which not much more than half of the ESC's members support the opinion.

The EP, by virtue of its greater power and authority, is listened to rather more seriously – or, at least, the Commission and the Council strive harder to give the impression that they are listening. Most MEPs, however, fully realise that they are hardly central actors in the price review exercise. Indeed, largely because of this, the EP has long since abandoned its former practice of holding a special session on the review and now incorporates its debate and the delivery of its opinion into the earliest practicable plenary session – which should be March if the timetable is on schedule, but because of slippages usually means April or May. The proceedings are conducted on the basis of reports drawn up by the Committee on Agriculture in consultation with other interested committees – most notably the Committee on Budgets, the Committee on External Economic Relations, and the Committee on the Environment. In the plenary, as many as 300–400 amendments to the Commission's proposals may be voted upon, with MEPs usually following the recommendations which are made to them by the Agriculture Committee's *rapporteur*.

In the Council, ministers are likely to have an early meeting, probably in February, to give their first reactions to the Commission proposals. All arrive well armed with briefs and analyses as to how the proposals would, if agreed, affect their farmers, their consumers, their budgetary contributions, their balance of payments and so on. Most usually say that the proposals are too restrictive in some respects, and all twelve usually put down markers for future meetings by identifying particular points that are unacceptable as they stand. Subsequent ministerial meetings are arranged as necessary, by which time new points may have arisen and others may have been resolved as a result of meetings at lower Council levels: most of the agricultural working parties – of which there are around 25, including one for each of the principal commodity regimes – will meet at least twice to consider the Commission's proposals as they affect their areas; the Agrifin working group deals with many of the financial aspects of the proposals; and the SCA (see Chapter 5) tries to pull the working parties' reports together and give them an overall coherence.

(6)   In the light of views expressed – and quite apart from formal pronouncements by the ESC, the EP, and the Council, intense lobbying campaigns are conducted by national and sectional interests – the Commission makes adjustments to its proposals. These are designed to improve the prospects of a settlement in the Council, whilst clinging to as much of the original proposals as possible.

(7)   Towards the end of March, or later if proceedings have fallen behind schedule, the Agriculture Council meets to try and agree a settlement. Marathon sessions are common, and meetings may have to be reconvened if solutions cannot be found at the first time of asking.

Each minister naturally tries to get the best terms he can and wishes also to be seen to be putting up a vigorous defence of national interests. This can make for extremely difficult negotiations, with much posturing and striking of attitudes sitting alongside genuine differences on such matters as price preferences, EU budgetary implications, elimination of surpluses, and commitments to farmers and consumers. Complicated package deals, with many non-price factors being dragged in to increase flexibility, are usually the only means by which a solution can be found. Voting is common, and ministers may well make their vote of approval on one issue dependent on guarantees of support on another. Frequently those who are dissatisfied with the proposed settlement on a matter – say rice prices, or the premium for producers of potato starch – seek 'compensation' elsewhere – perhaps in the form of permission to offer national subsidies of some kind. Wheeling and dealing and the trading of points can thus usually give to all participants something to identify in the way of national benefits when they leave the negotiating table.

Looking at the overall nature of the annual agricultural price review, it is worth emphasising that it has been considerably affected in recent years by the use of financial perspectives since 1988, by the incorporation into the perspectives of agricultural guidelines, and by the adoption – most notably in May 1992 – of measures to reduce surpluses and to restructure agriculture. One effect has been to enhance a development that began to get underway in the mid-1980s – namely for price settlements to be restrictive and tight. Another, and closely related, effect has been to ensure that there are close alignments between the original Commission proposals and the final settlement. And a third effect has been to make the deliberations in the Council just a little less acrimonious – because there are now greater limits on what it can do.

■ Concluding remarks

The CAP is not quite as common or as integrated as it is often thought to be. This is most obviously seen in the way that national governments still have the option of making various forms of special assistance available to their farmers. Some of the richer states, especially Germany, have, in response to the restrictive measures of recent years, considerably extended the assistance they give. This has happened on such a scale that some observers have even spoken of there having been a movement towards a 'renationalisation' of agricultural policy.

Nonetheless, the CAP is, in many respects, still the most important and most integrated of the EU's sectoral policies. It is a policy which, despite all the obstacles and hurdles that litter the decision-making process, has been the subject of considerable reform in recent years. Important changes are under way, with EU prices scheduled to move more closely to world prices, and with support measures becoming less focused on farm prices and more focused on farmers' incomes.

The reforms have not, however, it must be stressed, solved all of the CAP's problems. Within the EU sharp differences still exist over the balance to be struck between market efficiency on the one hand, and the granting of support – and what sort of support – on the other. Outside the EU many countries continue to be dissatisfied with what they regard as an overprotected EU market and oversubsidised EU produce on world markets.

There are thus still important issues concerning the CAP which continue to attract considerable controversy. They are, moreover, issues which cannot be easily resolved. Agriculture will therefore continue to loom large in the life of the EU.

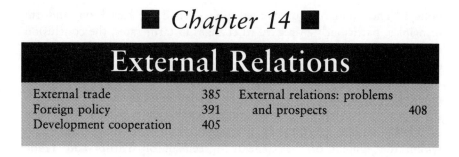

Chapter 14

External Relations

The EU is an extremely important, and an increasingly important, actor on the world stage. It is so partly because of its size and resources, and partly because of its ability to act in a united, or at least coordinated, manner in many international contexts and settings.

There are three broad aspects to the EU's external relations: trade, foreign and security policy, and development cooperation. Each of these will be examined in this chapter.

■ External trade

☐ Trade agreements and trade policies

The member states of the EU present a united front to the world in respect of international trade, and they act as one in contracting the terms of trade agreements. If they did not do so the unified internal market would not be possible.

The main foundations of the united front are the Common External Tariff (CET) – or Common Customs Tariff (CCT) as it is also known – and the Common Commercial Policy (CCP). Together, the CET and the CCP enable, indeed oblige, the member states to act in common on matters such as the fixing and adjusting of external customs tariffs, the negotiation of customs and trade agreements with non-member countries, and the taking of action to impede imports – this being most likely where unfair trading practices, such as dumping and subsidies, are suspected.

The EU – strictly speaking, the EC in the context of external trade – has trade agreements, or agreements in which a substantial part of the content is concerned with trade, with just about every country in the world. These agreements take three main forms:

• *Trade agreements.* These are negotiated on the basis of Article 113 of the EC Treaty which obliges the EC to operate a common commercial policy: 'The common commercial policy shall be based on uniform principles, particularly in regard to changes in tariff rates, the conclusion of tariff and trade agreements, the achievement of uniformity in measures of liberalization, export policy and measures to protect trade such as those to be taken in the event of dumping or subsidies.' Article 113 agreements may be preferential or non-preferential in kind, but they are all subject to the general framework of international trading rules which have been established (and to which the EC is a signatory on the basis of Article 113) within the context of the General Agreement on Tariffs and Trade (GATT).

• *Trade and economic cooperation agreements.* These are negotiated on the basis of Article 228 of the EC Treaty and used to be used for the purpose of establishing some sort of privileged or special relationship between the EC and third countries or groups of countries. Increasing numbers of such agreements over the years have meant that they are now not so privileged or special, but they usually do still involve some trade preferences and some forms of assistance from the EC to the other signatory(ies). Since the 1980s, political conditions – usually concerning human rights and democratic processes – have increasingly been attached to cooperation agreements.

• *Association agreements.* These are based on Article 238 of the EC Treaty which states that 'The Community may conclude with one or more states or international organizations agreements establishing an association involving reciprocal rights and obligations, common action and reciprocal procedure'. Typically, association agreements include highly preferential access to EC markets, the prospect of a free trade area eventually being formed between the signatories, economic and technical cooperation of various sorts, financial aid from the EC, political dialogue, and – in some, though not all, cases – the prospect of the associated countries eventually becoming members of the EU. Association agreements, which have been developed out of earlier cooperation agreements, have been used in the 1990s as a central mechanism in the forging of closer relationships between the EU and the countries of the 'new' Eastern and Central Europe. Known as Europe Agreements, these association agreements have been seen by the EU as a means of encouraging economic liberalisation and political democratisation in countries such as Poland, Hungary, the Czech Republic and Romania, without causing too many disruptions to the SEM and without imposing major budgetary burdens on the EU.

The EU presents itself as being committed to a liberal trade policy and as having, as its main priority in external trade negotiations, the opening up of markets. The most important international trade negotiations of recent years – the multilateral GATT Uruguay Round, which ran from 1986 to the end of 1993 – are seen as providing evidence in support of this view of the nature of the EU's trading stance. Priorities for the EU during the negotiations included: lowering international customs duties (as a result of the Uruguay Round average EU duties will gradually fall from around 5 per cent to 2.5 per cent); removing non-tariff barriers to trade; and opening up hitherto restricted spheres of trading activity – especially those, such as services, in which the EU, or at least some of its member states, are strong.

It is a liberal trading policy, however, which is not always pursued with complete consistency or uniformity. Protectionism is never far from the surface as the governments of the member states seek to cope with 'special' national economic circumstances and accompanying political pressures. EU trade policy is thus concerned not only with promoting the general liberalisation of trade, but also with ensuring that the consequences of this are not damaging. This results in trade policy being much taken up with matters such as the seeking of special exemptions from general trade agreements, the negotiation of 'orderly marketing' agreements and voluntary export restrictions with more competitive countries, and the imposition of anti-dumping duties.

The most obvious sectoral sphere of EU protectionism is agriculture which, as a result of mainly, though not exclusively, French pressure, has long been sheltered from the full rigours of external competition. EU negotiators in the Uruguay Round ensured that shelter will continue to be provided as the agreements which were concluded under the Round gradually enter into force, even though there is to be a progressive reduction in the extent of protection which is provided to EU farmers. Other sectors which attract EU special protection include: the motor vehicle industry, which is assisted by export restraint agreements with Japan; textiles, which are helped by the Multifibre Arrangement – an international agreement incorporating export quota restrictions and export restraint agreements with Far Eastern countries; and steel, which is given protection under the terms of the association agreements with Eastern and Central European countries.

□ *Policy processes*

The EU conducts trade negotiations in many forums: with single states; with other regional groupings, such as EFTA and the Association of South-East Asian Nations (ASEAN); and in international frameworks, such as GATT and the United Nations Conference on Trade and Development (UNCTAD). The single most important feature of the way in which the EU conducts itself in such forums is that it always acts as a single bloc. This means that it is able to bring very considerable economic and trading strength to bear:

- The combined Gross Domestic Product (GDP) of the EU countries accounts for around 25.8 per cent of world GDP. This places it very slightly ahead of the United States, which accounts for around 24.1 per cent, and well ahead of Japan which accounts for around 16.1 per cent.
- EU exports to the rest of the world account for about 15 per cent of world exports, whilst imports account for about 16 per cent of world imports. The comparable figures for the USA are 12 per cent and 15 per cent, and for Japan 9 per cent and 7 per cent. The EU is, thus, the world's largest external trading bloc.
- In terms of population, the EU market, with over 340 million people, is much larger than both the US market, which numbers just over 250 million people, and the Japanese market, which numbers around 125 million.
- Many of the countries and groupings with which the EU negotiates on trade matters are heavily reliant on the EU market for their exports – either for reasons of geography (most obviously non-EU European countries, including those of Eastern and Central Europe) or for reasons of historical linkage (most notably former French and UK colonies).

Trade agreements which are made on the basis of Article 113 and in the context of the CCP are essentially the responsibility of the Commission and the Council. The normal procedure for contracting agreements is as follows:

- The Commission makes a recommendation to the Council (Foreign Ministers) that the EU should seek to conclude a trade agreement with a third country or organisation.
- The Committee of Permanent Representatives (COREPER) discusses the recommendation and places it on the agenda of the Council. The Council takes a decision as to whether negotiations should proceed. In making its decision the Council may, on the basis of proposals which have been drawn up by the Commission and which have been discussed, and perhaps modified, by COREPER, give to the Commission negotiating directives, guidelines, or – to use the most commonly used, but not most accurate, term – mandates. If necessary, the Council may act, as it may act on any decisions taken in connection with Article 113 agreements, by qualified majority vote.
- Working within the framework of directives it has been given by the Council, the Commission negotiates on behalf of all twelve EU states. DGI (External Economic Relations) normally takes the lead role on behalf of

the Commission, but other DGs, such as DGIV (Competition) and DGVI (Agriculture), are also involved if they have a direct interest. How much room for manoeuvre the Commission has in conducting negotiations varies according to circumstances. Usually, differences of both principle and special interest between the member states result in negotiating directives being fairly tightly drawn – reflecting, often, a compromise between those countries which tend towards protectionism and those which favour free trade. While Commission officials acknowledge privately that Council directives are usually less of a dead weight than is often supposed, there is no doubt that the Commission's flexibility in negotiations is often constrained by the necessity of not disturbing compromises that have been agreed only with difficulty in the Council. (Although it should also be said that it is not unknown for the Commission to use Council reins to the EU's advantage: during negotiations it can be helpful to say, in response to an unwanted proposal, 'the Council would never agree to that'.)

• Throughout the period during which negotiations are being conducted, the Commission is in touch with the Article 113 Committee. This is a Council committee that normally meets weekly to review, discuss, and make decisions on trade agreements which come within the scope of Article 113. The Committee meets at two levels: full members, who are normally senior officials from the national ministries responsible for trade, gather once a month to consider general policy issues; deputies, who may be from either national ministries or the Permanent Representations in Brussels, usually meet three times a month to deal with detailed policy matters.

• During particularly difficult or important negotiations the Commission may return to the Council for clarification of the negotiating directive, or for an amended directive which might break a deadlock. (In the closing stages of the Uruguay Round negotiations in November and December 1993, the chief Commission negotiator – External Economic Relations Commissioner, Sir Leon Brittan – presented written and verbal reports, and made requests, to several Foreign Ministers' meetings.)

• At the (apparent) conclusion of negotiations, the Commission can initial negotiated settlements, but Council approval is necessary for agreements to be formally authorised and signed.

The powers of, and relations between and within, the EU's institutions in connection with the CCP are such that tensions of different sorts are by no means uncommon. Four areas cause particular difficulties.

First, the power balance between the Council and the Commission can be very delicate, with the Council wishing to ensure that the Commission remains under its control, and the Commission wanting and needing enough manoeuvrability to enable it to be an effective negotiator.

Second, the different national interests and preferences of the member states can create difficulties in the Council. A graphic instance of this was seen in the high profile campaign of resistance conducted by France in 1992–3 to the settlement terms proposed by the Commission in respect of agriculture under the Uruguay Round. (This episode is examined in Chapter 13.)

Third, problems can arise within the Commission when DGs other than DGI (External Economic Relations) believe they have an interest in particular external trade policies and agreements. Thus, in June 1990, the Farm Commissioner – Raymond MacSharry – stressing that he was determined to defend the Community position on farm reform in the GATT Uruguay Round talks, felt obliged to state publicly that he, not the Trade Commissioner – Frans Andriessen – was 'in charge of agricultural negotiations'. In November 1992, when the much troubled bilateral negotiations with the United States on the agricultural aspects of the Uruguay Round were at their most difficult, MacSharry temporarily resigned from his position in the Commission negotiating team because of the alleged excessive interference by the Commission President, Jacques Delors.

Fourth, MEPs are dissatisfied that the EP has no automatic right to be consulted, let alone to insist that its views be considered, in connection with Article 113 agreements. In practice, the EP is notified about agreements, and the Commission, and to a lesser extent the Council, do discuss external trade matters with the EP – primarily in the forum of the Parliament's External Economic Relations Committee – but it is clear that Parliament's influence is usually limited. Or at least it has been so in the past, but it does seem to be increasing. One reason why it is so is that the EP has constantly pressed its dissatisfaction and has done what it can to maximise its influence, not least by incorporating into its Rules of Procedure (8th edition, 1993, Rule 90) a range of measures which request the Council to take note of the EP as regards the opening, the negotiating, and the concluding of trade agreements. Interestingly, and potentially very significantly, in early 1994, Sir Leon Brittan recommended to the Commission that the EP be given assent power over the GATT Uruguay Round agreement. The basis of his recommendation was Article 228 of the EC Treaty which states that the assent procedure applies in respect of international agreements 'having important budgetary implications for the Community'.

Turning to procedures in respect of cooperation and association agreements, the powers of, and relationships between, the Council and the Commission are similar to those which apply in respect of Article 113 agreements – except that unanimity, rather than a qualified majority, is required for Council decisions on association agreements. (Unanimity tends to reduce the position of the Commission, since it cannot afford to sideline the wishes of any member state.) The powers of the EP, however, are much greater in regard to cooperation and association agreements than they are in regard to Article 113 trade agreements, for its assent is required. That is to say, agreements can only be finally authorised once the EP, on a single reading and with no amendments permitted, has given its approval. This power, which was first granted to the EP under the SEA, albeit on a more restricted basis than that which now applies under the TEU, gives to the Parliament a lever to try and influence the course of negotiations, and a block on the outcome of negotiations if it finds them to be unsatisfactory. The EP's assent has been withheld on a number of occasions since the assent procedure was first used in 1987 – the reason for the withholding sometimes being a protest against the lack of democracy or the abuse of human rights in the state(s) with which the agreement(s) is being contracted.

■ Foreign policy

□ *Evolution*

There are many obstacles in the way of a developed, let alone a common, EU foreign policy. Amongst the obstacles are the following:

● The EU is not a state and, therefore, does not have the (usually) long established 'givens' which help to make up and focus national foreign policies. There is, most notably, no national territory to protect, and no national political, economic, social and cultural interests to promote.
● Following on from the point just made, many member states, especially those larger ones which have long histories of being influential on the world stage in their own right, are reluctant to lose control of their foreign policies.
● Some member states have traditional and special relationships with particular parts of the world which they are anxious to maintain.
● Differences between EU states on foreign policy questions sometimes arise from conflicting ideological orientations of national governments – differences, for example, towards 'liberation'/'revolutionary' movements in South America, and over relations with the United States.
● Defence, which of course is inextricably linked with foreign policy, is extremely problematical for a number of reasons, not least: (1) its close association with national sovereignty; (2) the varying defence capabilities

of the member states; and (3) the differing degrees of willingness to use armed force that the member states display when pressed.

Notwithstanding these difficulties and obstacles, however, important developments have occurred since foreign policy cooperation was first launched, under the name European Political Cooperation (EPC), in 1970. Initially on a tentative basis, and quite outside the framework of the Community Treaties, the EC member states in the 1970s and 1980s increasingly cooperated with one another on foreign policy matters – to such an extent that by the mid-1980s there were few major international issues on which the EC did not pronounce. This developing importance of foreign policy cooperation was recognised when EPC was accorded its own section – Title III – in the SEA. Amongst other things Title III stated 'The High Contracting Parties [the member states], being members of the European Communities, shall endeavour jointly to formulate and implement a European foreign policy'. However, unlike certain other policy areas which were also recognised in the SEA, such as environment, Title III was not incorporated into the Treaties. This was mainly because the member states were unwilling to allow the normal Community decision-making processes to apply to foreign policy. As a result, EPC continued to be much looser, more voluntaristic in nature, than most other policy areas with which the Community concerned itself. No laws were made within EPC, most decisions were arrived at by consensus, and no state could be prevented from engaging in independent action if it so chose.

But though the SEA signalled the increasing important of EU foreign policy, and facilitated its further development, the EU's standing until the early 1990s continued to be very much that of economic giant on the one hand and political pygmy on the other. That is to say, it was exercising considerable international influence in respect of economic, and more particularly trade matters, but its voice was not counting for a great deal in respect of political, and more particularly defence and security, matters. Since the early 1990s, however, this situation has been changing and it has come to be increasingly accepted by the member states that the EU ought to be doing rather more than issuing general – and often anodyne – declarations, and – very occasionally – imposing mild economic sanctions. Five factors have been especially important in bringing about change.

First, the ending of the Cold War and the collapse of Communism in the Soviet bloc and the Soviet Union have transformed the nature of international power relationships. In particular: the international political context in which Europe finds itself has changed dramatically, with a shift of focus from the global East–West dimension to regional issues and conflicts; strategically, Western Europe no longer finds itself squeezed between two superpowers, with little chance but to ally itself to one – the

United States – in a more-or-less subservient manner; and the bases of power relationships have altered, with nuclear and military capacity becoming less important and economic strength and geographical position (especially in relation to the rapidly changing Central and Eastern Europe and the troubled Middle East) becoming more important. In this 'new' world, in which international relations are much more fluid, and in which the nature and future development of the European continent is far from clear, Western Europe naturally wishes to play a leading part in guiding and managing events. In so doing it is being given encouragement by the United States, which is anxious to lighten some of its international, and more especially some of its European, commitments.

Second, German unification has increased pressures on the foreign and security policy front, as it has too on the economic and monetary union front, to create an EU framework in which Germany is firmly located and to which it is firmly attached. The much quoted determination of EU leaders, not least German leaders themselves, to ensure there is a European Germany rather than a German Europe, has been seen by many as needing to apply particularly to foreign and security policy given the sensitivities associated with Germany's past and given, too, the actual and potential political turbulence to Germany's east and south. That Germany must be 'tied in' more tightly was confirmed for many by the way in which, in late 1991, Germany successfully pressurised other EU states to grant diplomatic recognition to Croatia and Slovenia much earlier than most would have preferred.

Third, the 1990–1 Gulf crisis and war demonstrated that EPC would always be restricted in its effectiveness if defence and security policy were to continue to be kept apart from foreign policy. The Community's response to Iraq's invasion of Kuwait was to coordinate diplomatic action and to jointly impose economic sanctions, but on the key issues of the appropriate military response and of contributions to that response, the member states reacted in a piecemeal and uncoordinated fashion.

Fourth (and the impact of this is still unfolding at the time of writing), the EU's response to the post-1991 break-up of Yugoslavia has been seen as being, in several respects, inadequately prepared, inadequately coordinated, and inadequately mobilised. Deficiencies which have been identified include the following:

● The under-resourced nature of EPC decision-making mechanisms was perhaps partly responsible for why the EC was slow in 1991 to recognise that the break-up of Yugoslavia was unavoidable.
● The loose and intergovernmental nature of EPC enabled Germany to exercise excessive influence on the other EC states regarding the 'premature' diplomatic recognition of Croatia and Slovenia.

- After the outbreak of the civil war in 1992 the EC just about managed to pursue a common policy stance – centred on a belief that a long-term solution would need to be based on the independence of former Yugoslav republics, and that in the particularly troubled state of Bosnia some form of cantonisation would be required – but national contributions to practical action were, as in the Gulf, very unevenly spread. Moreover that practical action was not, as many thought it should have been, coordinated and controlled by the EC/EU but was rather distributed around several international organisations: (1) At an early stage of the conflict the Community despatched observers in a European Community Monitoring Mission (ECMM). The observers were not acting directly on a Community mandate but were carrying out a mission decided by the Conference on Security and Cooperation in Europe (CSCE) and were working alongside observers from such non-EC countries as Canada, Poland, and Sweden. (2) The EC co-sponsored the international peace conference on Bosnia with the United Nations (UN). (3) The Western European Union (WEU), in conjunction with NATO, enforced the blockade of Serbia in the Adriatic, and played a part in assisting the blockade on the Danube. (4) The UN, using mainly West European (but not exclusively EC) troops, took a lead role in peace monitoring and humanitarian relief efforts. (5) NATO was involved in various aspects of the implementation of UN declarations, including the enforcement of the air exclusion zone over Bosnia.

Fifth, the TEU provides for significant advances to be made in foreign and security policy cooperation, albeit on a basis which maintains their essentially intergovernmental nature and non-EC status. The means by which the TEU does this is via its provisions for a Common Foreign and Security Policy (CFSP). Like so much of the TEU, the CFSP provisions are essentially a compromise – in this case between those who would have liked to move ahead quickly to developing common foreign and defence policies within the framework of the EC and those who wished to move much more cautiously. The contents of the CFSP pillar of the TEU were specified in Chapter 3, so only a brief reminder of the most salient points is necessary here: general objectives of the CFSP are identified (see below as well as Chapter 3); systematic cooperation is to be established between the EU states on any matter of foreign and security policy that is of general interest; where it is deemed to be necessary the Council of Ministers shall, on the basis of unanimity, define common positions to which the member states should conform; on the basis of general guidelines from the European Council, the Council of Ministers may decide that a matter should be the subject of a joint action; the CFSP is to include security issues 'including the eventual framing of a common defence policy, which might in time lead to a common defence'; and the WEU is to be 'an integral part of the development of the Union'.

☐ *Policy content and policy action*

Two main criticisms were traditionally made of EPC. First, it was essentially reactive. Apart from a very small number of initiatives – such as pressing from 1980 for the Palestine Liberation Organisation (PLO) to be included in Middle East peace talks – the EC was seen as following events rather than making and shaping them. Second, it was too declaratory: policy positions were not followed up with the use of effective policy instruments; at best, as in protesting against the then apartheid regime in South Africa, weak, and essentially symbolic, economic sanctions were employed against states engaging in activities of which the EC disapproved.

The CFSP pillar of the TEU is designed, in large part, to enable the EU to tackle these weaknesses. The principal means to be used are the more conscious pursuit of common policies, and the development of properly coordinated policy actions and policy instruments.

Regarding common policies, Article J.1 of the TEU states the following:

(1) The Union and its Member States shall define and implement a common foreign and security policy, governed by the provisions of this Title and covering all areas of foreign and security policy.
(2) The objectives of the common foreign and security policy shall be:
  – to safeguard the common values, fundamental interests and independence of the Union;
  – to strengthen the security of the Union and its Member States in all ways;
  – to preserve peace and strengthen international security, in accordance with the principles of the United Nations Charter as well as the principles of the Helsinki Final Act and the objectives of the Paris Charter;
  – to promote international cooperation;
  – to develop and consolidate democracy and the rule of law, and respect for human rights and fundamental freedoms.

These objectives are to be achieved by two principal means: (1) establishing systematic cooperation between the member states in the conduct of policy – this to include the defining of common positions where necessary and the coordination of actions in international organisations and at international conferences; and (2) gradually implementing joint action in areas where the member states have important interests in common (see Exhibits 14.1 and 14.2 for examples of a common position and a joint action).

Since the Maastricht summit, the general objectives set out in the TEU have been given greater precision and the sort of circumstances in which joint actions might be deemed to be appropriate have become clearer. The June 1992 Lisbon summit was particularly important in setting out ground rules. It was agreed, for example, that in assessing whether important common interests were at stake, and in defining the issues and areas for joint action, account should be taken of the following factors:

- the geographical proximity of a given region or country (to the EU);
- an important (EU) interest in the political and economic stability of a region or country;

Exhibit 14.1
A common position under the CFSP

(*Common position defined by the Council of the European Union*)

COUNCIL DECISION
of 22 November 1993
on the common position defined on the basis of Article J.2 of the Treaty on European Union with regard to the reduction of economic relations with Libya
(93/614/CFSP)

THE COUNCIL OF THE EUROPEAN UNION,
Having regard to the Treaty on European Union, and in particular Article J.2 thereof,
Having regard to Resolution 883(93) adopted by the United Nations Security Council on 11 November 1993,

HAS DECIDED AS FOLLOWS:

1. Economic relations with Libya shall be reduced in accordance with the relevant provisions of Resolution 883(83) adopted by the Security Council on 11 November 1993.
2. This Decision shall be published in the Official Journal.

Done at Luxembourg, 22 November 1993.

For the Council
The President
W. CLAES

Source: *Official Journal of the European Communities*, Vol. 36, L295 (30 November 1993)

Exhibit 14.2
A joint action under the CFSP

(Joint actions adopted by the Council of the European Union)

COUNCIL DECISION
of 20 December 1993
concerning the joint action adopted by the Council on the basis of Artcle J.3 of the
Treaty on European Union on the inaugural conference on the stability pact
(93/728/CFSP)

THE COUNCIL OF THE EUROPEAN UNION,

Having regard to the Treaty on European Union, and in particular Articles J.3 and J.11 thereof,

Having regard to the conclusions of the European Council on 21 and 22 June 1993 on a pact on stability in Europe and the general approach of the European Council on 29 October 1993 whereby a stability pact to resolve the problem of minorities and to strengthen the inviolability of frontiers will be a staple component of joint action aimed at promoting stability, reinforcing the democratic process and developing regional cooperation in Central and Eastern Europe.

Having regard to the conclusions of the European Council on 10 and 11 December calling upon the Community to implement the initiative on a pact on stability in Europe as a joint action in accordance with the Treaty on European Union.

HAS DECIDED AS FOLLOWS:

Article 1

The European Union will convene an inaugural conference on a pact on stability in Europe, to be held in Paris around April 1994, to which the countries principally concerned, States likely to make a particular contribution to the initiative, countries with an interest in stability in Europe by virtue of their defence commitments and countries which have association agreements with the Union (Albania, Austria, Belarus, Bulgaria, Canada, Cyprus, the Czech Republic, Estonia, Finland, the Holy See, Hungary, Iceland, Latvia, Lithuania, Malta, Moldova,

Norway, Poland, Romania, Russia, Slovakia, Slovenia, Sweden, Switzerland, Turkey, Ukraine and the United States) will be invited as participants, and representatives of international organizations concerned by the initiative (CSCE, Council of Europe, WEU, NATO and the United Nations). Those countries and organizations would be prepared to endorse the idea of and arrangements for the conference adopted by the Union at the end of the formal consultations which it is to hold. Any other States participating in the CSCE which accepted that idea and those arrangements would also be invited as observers.

Article 2

The inaugural conference will put into effect preventive diplomacy aimed at fostering good neighbourly relations and encouraging countries, in particular through the conclusion of appropriate agreements, to consolidate their borders and to resolve the problems of national minorities which arise. Those agreements, and the complementary arrangements that accompany them, should constitute the basis for a stability pact which would be intended to be forwarded to the CSCE, which would act as its guardian.

Article 3

The inaugural conference will be preceded by a round of formal consultations held by the Union with all the countries and organizations in the project, with a view to preparing for it.

Article 4

The detailed arrangements which will have to govern the holding of this conference, the negotiation process to be conducted and the stability pact to be concluded are laid down in the reports on the stability pact approved by the European Council on 10 and 11 December 1993.

Article 5

The inaugural conference will be organized by the host country in close coordination with the Presidency. This Decision entails no operational expenditure.

Article 6

This Decision shall enter into force on this day. It covers the first stage of the joint action, which will end with the meeting of the inaugural conference. In due course the Council will take the necessary measures for continuation of the joint action.

Article 7

This Decision shall be published in the Official Journal.

Done at Brussels, 20 December 1993.

For the Council
The President
W. CLAES

Source: Official Journal of the European Communities, Vol. 36, L339 (31 December 1993).

● the existence of threats to the security interests of the Union.

The Lisbon summit also identified a preliminary listing of areas in which EU joint action might be particularly beneficial for the attainment of the objectives of the Union, and gave illustrations of what such joint actions might consist of. The listing, with some examples of possible joint actions, was as follows:

● *Russia and the former Soviet Republics*: support for the setting up of a framework of harmonious relations between the EU and the new states; reinforcing existing patterns of cooperation and trade between the new states themselves; encouraging full compliance with all the treaties on disarmament and arms control to which the states are parties; opening joint facilities and missions.
● *Other countries in Central and Eastern Europe, including the Balkans*: establishing political frameworks to foster these countries' relations with each other, with the EU, and with other European organisations.
● *The former Yugoslavia*: reinforcing the EU's efforts to promote peace through the Peace Conference and the peace monitoring missions; contributing to the strengthening of democracy, the rule of law and human and minority rights, by means of legal and technical cooperation.

- *The Maghreb*: promoting a constructive dialogue aimed at creating an area of peace, security, and prosperity in which respect for the principles of international law is assumed; strengthening the existing cooperation measures on the foreign policy aspects of the fight against terrorism and illicit traffic in drugs.
- *The Middle East*: ensuring the EU's active involvement in the peace process; making efforts to persuade Israel to change its policy regarding settlements in the Occupied Territories and to persuade Arab countries to renounce their trade boycott.
- *Domains within the security dimension* – but not (a fine and difficult distinction which seems to mean, in practice, military actions) 'issues having defence implications': the CSCE process; the policy of disarmament and arms control in Europe; nuclear non-proliferation issues; the economic aspects of security.

It is clear from this listing, and from what else is known, that the main policy instruments of the CFSP are not to be so different from those which are commonly employed by the EU's own member states: diplomacy, political pressure, trade sanctions, economic and financial assistance, and technical, scientific, cultural and other forms of cooperation. But what of that most sensitive, and in many respects most important, of all policy instruments: defensive manpower and hardwear?

That the EU might have defence resources available to it in certain circumstances is hardly implied by the relevant TEU article on defence policy for, as noted above, it refers to 'the *eventual* framing of a common defence policy, which might *in time* lead to a common defence' (my italics). Notwithstanding this implied gradualism, however, the WEU – which, as was seen in Chapter 2, is a long-established defence organisation – is identified in the Treaty as 'an integral part of the development of the Union' and is requested 'to elaborate and *implement* decisions and actions of the Union which have defence implications' (my italics). In a Declaration attached to the TEU the potential role of the WEU is described in even more forceful terms: 'WEU will be developed as the defence component of the European Union and as a means to strengthen the European pillar of the Atlantic Alliance. To this end it will formulate a common European defence policy and carry forward its concrete implementation through the further development of its operational role.'

To help give effect to the WEU's new role in the framework of the EU, various changes have been made since the TEU was agreed to bring the operation of the WEU more closely into line with the operation of the EU. These changes have included the synchronisation of relevant WEU and EU meetings, and the moving of the WEU Council and Secretariat from London to Brussels. The membership of the two organisations has also been more closely aligned, with the three EU states which were not members of the WEU when the TEU was signed changing their status: in November 1992 Greece became a member of the WEU and Denmark and Ireland became observers.

This increasingly close relationship between the WEU and the EU does not, of course, mean that the EU can now be said to have a clear defence capability. Quite apart from the fact that the EU and the WEU are still separate organisations, the defence resources of the EU states still essentially remain under national control – even if they do frequently operate within the framework of, or are 'lent out' to, international organisations such as the UN, NATO, and the WEU. Nonetheless, the developments that have been noted here in relation to the WEU, plus developments of an integrating nature which are occurring elsewhere – such as the creation in 1993 by France, Germany and Belgium of a Eurocorps – suggest that when the CFSP arrangements come up for review in 1996 there will be very strong pressures for a defence capability of some kind to be made directly available to the EU.

☐ *Policy processes*

The functioning of the CFSP is centred on a network of cooperative and consultative activities between the member states, with regular rounds of meetings at political and official level at their heart. The aim of all the activity is to try and ensure maximum information flow and cooperative effort between the member states, to enable the EU to issue joint statements on important foreign policy issues wherever possible, and – following the TEU – to enable the EU to develop common positions and to engage in joint actions when it is deemed to be necessary and appropriate.

The CFSP is based primarily on intergovernmental, and in large part on inter-Foreign Ministry, arrangements. There are a number of interlinking and overlapping reasons for this, but they basically boil down to the fact that because of the politically sensitive nature of much of the content of foreign and security policy, EPC, and now the CFSP, have been kept outside of the framework of the EEC/EC Treaty and system.

Notwithstanding, however, this exclusion from the 'mainstream' EC system, EPC and CFSP have over the years gradually assumed many of the characteristics of 'normal' Community decision-making. This increasing approximation to the functioning of the EC has been assisted by three formally authorised 'advances':

● In 1981 the EC Foreign Ministers, in what became known as the London Report, first established a role for the Commission by stating that it should have 'full association' with EPC.

- The SEA confirmed that the Commission should be 'fully associated' with EPC but, in addition, stated that the EP should be 'closely associated' with it. The SEA also established a small, permanent EPC Secretariat based in the Council of Ministers building in Brussels.
- The TEU set out five particularly important changes to how the CFSP (as EPC was renamed by the Treaty) should operate. (1) The European Council (which though itself remaining outside the EC is now very important in setting the EC policy agenda) was given a formal role in outlining the principles of the CFSP. (2) The Council of Ministers was given the responsibility of defining common positions 'wherever it deems it necessary', and was also empowered to decide that some matters be the subject of joint actions – with implementing decisions in the context of joint actions being potentially subject to qualified majority voting. (3) The role of the Council Presidency in relation to the CFSP was enhanced. (4) The Commission was, for the first time, given the right to initiate proposals – though not the exclusive right it enjoys in respect of other policy areas under the EC Treaty. (5) The EP's standing was strengthened – it now has to be 'consulted' rather than 'closely associated', though its role is still essentially advisory.

The decision-making structure and processes of the CFSP, and the powers of the EU institutions, are as follows:

□ *The European Council*. Under Article J.8 of the CFSP pillar of the TEU 'The European Council shall define the principles of and general guidelines for the common foreign and security policy'. Communiqués from European Council meetings have long contained declarations on a range of foreign policy issues, but since the Maastricht summit they have also concerned themselves with establishing frameworks in which the CFSP should operate and be developed. The role of the 1992 Lisbon summit in this respect has already been noted above. The two Brussels summits in the second half of 1993 might also be cited, for they were used to launch an initiative for a Pact on Stability in Europe. In the words of the Presidency Conclusions of the December summit 'The aim of the initiative is to contribute to stability by averting tension and potential conflicts in Europe, fostering neighbourly relations and encouraging countries to consolidate their borders and to resolve problems of national minorities'.

□ *The Council of Ministers*. The Council is at the very heart of CFSP processes. It functions at several levels:

- *The General Council*. The Foreign Ministers, with the Commission in attendance, normally meet about once a month, with additional special meetings convened when necessary. In addition to General Affairs Council meetings, Foreign Ministers also meet in other forums – notably at European Councils and at twice yearly informal weekend gatherings.

The General Council is the main decision-making body of the CFSP. Operating within the context of such general policy guidelines as have been issued by the European Council, it makes, or for routine matters formalises, most CFSP decisions – including those on defining common positions and adopting joint actions.

The Council Presidency has a particular responsibility to 'represent the Union in matters coming within the common foreign and security policy' and to be 'responsible for the implementation of common measures' (Article J.5, TEU).

The Presidency works closely with the previous and successive Presidencies in the so-called 'troika'. The purpose of the troika is to ensure smoothness of transition between Presidencies, to assist in promoting policy consistency and stability, and to facilitate some work sharing (which is of particular value to small countries).

• *The Committee of Permanent Representatives* (COREPER). Composed of the Permanent Representatives of the member states to the EU, and meeting weekly, COREPER acts on CFSP matters primarily as a filtering agency between the Political Committee and the General Affairs Council.

• *The Political Committee*. This is made up of the Political Directors of the member states (who are senior civil servants from Foreign Ministries). The Commission is represented by its Political Director – who is the Director General for External Political Relations – but it is not technically a member of the Committee in the sense that its approval is not required for a consensus to be reached.

The Political Committee meets at least once a month, and in total about twenty times a year. It serves very much as the lynchpin of the CFSP in that it prepares all CFSP work for COREPER and for the General Council, and it deals itself with routine matters such as non-controversial foreign policy declarations and the direction of the working groups. As compared to how it functioned under EPC, the Political Committee has, necessarily, become more operational in focus under the CFSP.

• *The Correspondents' Group*. Composed of those officials who are responsible for the coordination of CFSP inside Foreign Ministries, and with the Commission in attendance, the Correspondents' Group meets at least once a month. As well as acting as a key liaising mechanism between Foreign Ministries, it regularly deals with business coming up from the working groups which the Political Committee does not have the time, or the inclination, to deal with.

• *Working groups*. There are usually around twenty or so working groups in existence, most of which are permanent but a few of which are *ad hoc.* A total of about 120 working group meetings are held each year, with permanent working groups meeting at least once during each Presidency. The groups are composed of senior diplomats – who are often departmental heads – from the member states, plus a Commission representative. Some working groups deal with regions, e.g. the Middle East, Central and South America, Africa; some deal with themes, e.g. the CSCE, disarmament, human rights; and some deal with operational matters, e.g. EU representation in third countries, the CFSP telecommunication system, and joint actions.

• *The General Secretariat.* Following the transmution of EPC into the CFSP, the previously separate EPC Secretariat became a part of the General Secretariat of the Council. The principal job of the dozen or so officials, plus support services, who deal with CFSP aspects of the Council's work is, essentially, to provide administrative support. How this task is interpreted and applied depends partly on the preferences of the Presidency and on the administrative capacities of the Presidency's own country.

☐ *The Commission.* Under the TEU the Commission is, as it has been since the 1981 London Report, 'fully associated' with the work carried out in the CFSP. The most important innovation of the CFSP pillar of the TEU from the Commission's viewpoint is that it gained the right, albeit the non-exclusive right, of initiation. In practice, it had been initiating for some time but, necessarily, only by stealth and by the informal circulation of papers. Now that it can formally and openly initiate proposals, a more assertive Commission role can be anticipated in respect of seeking to shape the agenda and direction of foreign and security policy.

Quite how this will work out in practice remains to be seen, though doubtless, as in the past, the influence exercised by the Commission will vary according to circumstances. It is, for example, in a strong position when CFSP actions involve the use of economic sanctions as a policy instrument, for then the Council can only act, under Article 228a of the EC Treaty, on the basis of Commission proposals. The Commission is, however, less favourably placed in regard to 'purely political' matters – especially if the incumbent Presidency is a large member state with a big and effective Foreign Ministry and/or is a member state with a preference for foreign policy to be conducted mainly on an intergovernmental basis.

In response to its potentially greater foreign policy role under the TEU, the Commission made two important organisational changes in 1993. For the first time a Commissioner was appointed with the portfolio of External Political Relations. Significantly, the person appointed – Hans van den Broek – was a former Dutch Foreign Minister. The second change involved the creation of a new Directorate General to handle the CFSP – DGIA (External Political Relations).

☐   *The European Parliament.* Under Article J.7 of the TEU 'The Presidency shall consult the European Parliament on the main aspects and the basic choices of the common foreign and security policy and shall ensure that the views of the European Parliament are duly taken into consideration. The European Parliament shall be kept regularly informed by the Presidency and the Commission of the development of the Union's foreign and security policy'.

This would appear to mark some advance on the SEA, which provided for the EP to be 'associated with' EPC rather than to be consulted. However, the fact is that unless special circumstances apply – as, for example, when a foreign policy issue becomes linked to a cooperation agreement and the assent procedure thus needs to be used – the EP is still confined to an advisory role on foreign policy under the TEU.

All the EP can thus do is make maximum use of such mechanisms as it has at its disposal to try and ensure that the Commission, and more importantly the Council, really do consult and really do listen. The main mechanisms are: exchanging views with the Council Presidency in the Committee on Foreign Affairs and Security; asking questions – written and oral – of the Council; holding debates in plenary sessions; and making recommendations, passing resolutions, and tendering opinions.

☐   *Embassies, delegations and missions.* The development since the Second World War of rapid international travel and of instantaneous electronic communications has undermined much of the role and value of diplomatic representations as a means for countries to communicate with one another. Nonetheless, embassies, delegations and missions are still used to promote and defend interests abroad.

Because it is not a state the EU is not able to maintain overseas embassies, but it does have an extensive network of external delegations – delegations which are, technically, delegations of the Commission. In early 1994 there were just over 100 such delegations in third countries, and five delegations to international organisations. (It might also be added – and this exemplifies how important the EU appears to the outside world – that in early 1994 152 countries had diplomatic missions officially accredited to the EU/EC.)

Overseas representations are, of course, concerned with many issues other than foreign policy – most notably, the promotion of trade and, in the case of national representations, the safeguarding of citizen's interests. The CFSP is, however, a matter which embassies of the member states and

Commission delegations need very much to be aware of and to promote. In this context Article J.6 of the CFSP pillar of the TEU states 'The diplomatic and consular missions of the Member States and the Commission Delegations in third countries and international conferences, and their representations to international organizations, shall cooperate in ensuring that the common positions and common measures adopted by the Council are complied with and implemented'.

This requirement of Article J.6 is likely to result in a continued development of processes which have been under way for some time, whereby embassies of EU member states in third countries and delegations attached to international organisations exchange information and coordinate activities.

■ Development cooperation

□ *Policies*

The EU is actively engaged in promoting development in the Third World. The general principles of the policy were laid down in the TEU, where a new Title XVII – entitled Development Cooperation – was incorporated in the EC Treaty. Article 130u of Title XVII states:

1.   Community policy in the sphere of development cooperation, which shall be complementary to the policies pursued by the Member States, shall foster:
   – the sustainable economic and social development of the developing countries, and more particularly the most disadvantaged among them;
   – the smooth and gradual integration of the developing countries into the world economy;
   – the campaign against poverty in the developing countries.
2.   Community policy in this area shall contribute to the general objective of developing and consolidating democracy and the rule of law, and to that of respecting human rights and fundamental freedoms.
3.   The Community and the Member States shall comply with the commitments and take account of the objectives they have approved in the context of the United Nations and other competent international organizations.

The reasons for the EU's active engagement in development policy are a mixture of the historical, the moral, and the economic: the historical – some EU countries, notably France and the UK, have long established ties with parts of the Third World as a result of their colonial past; the moral – EU governments believe, although with different degrees of enthusiasm, that something should be done about world poverty and hunger; the economic – Third World countries account for around 30 per cent of EU exports, and the EU is highly dependent on the Third World for products such as rubber, copper and uranium.

Some of the forms of assistance made available by the EU apply to the whole of the Third World. Amongst these are:

(1)   *Generalised preferences.* All developing countries can export their industrial products to the EU without paying tariffs (subject to volume limits for some products). Additionally, many agricultural products can also be exported free of duty.

(2)   *Food aid.* Foodstuffs are sent to countries with serious food shortages.

(3)   *Emergency aid.* Aid of an appropriate sort is made available to countries stricken by natural disasters and other crises.

(4)   *Aid to non-governmental organisations.* The EU makes available aid to projects sponsored by non-governmental organisations in a number of Third World countries.

In addition to these general forms of assistance, the EU makes additional assistance and aid available to countries with which it has entered into special relationships. Most of these special relationships take the form of economic, trade, industrial, technical, and financial cooperation agreements. The most important, and most wide-ranging, agreement is the Lomé Convention which links the EU with African, Caribbean and Pacific countries (the ACP countries) with which some member states have historical links. Lomé IV (covering the years 1990–2000) was signed in 1989 and now involves 69 ACP states. It contains amongst its main features: duty-free access to the EU market for virtually all ACP exports; stabilisation of export earnings schemes (Stabex and Sysmin); and the European Development Fund (EDF) which, with resources of 12,000 million Ecu for the period 1990–5, has as its main purpose financially assisting, on the basis of long-term concerted programmes, the development of ACP countries, especially as regards rural development, industrialisation, and economic infrastructure.

Development aid is financed in two different ways. (1) Non-EDF aid is funded by the EU budget. Accounting for around 5.5 per cent of the budget, about half of this aid is used to provide financial assistance to non-ACP countries and about half is used for food aid purposes. (2) EDF aid is funded by special contributions from the member states. Taking EDF and non-EDF aid together, the principal beneficiaries are sub-Saharan Africa (which receives approaching 60 per cent), southern Asia (about 10 per cent), and Latin America and the Caribbean (also about 10 per cent).

It should be stressed that these EU policies do not constitute the sum total of the EU's overall contribution to Third World development. This is because, unlike with trade policy, the EU itself does not enjoy exclusive policy competence in the development field but rather shares it with the member states. In some respects the EU takes the leading role, in other respects it aims to supplement, complement, and coordinate national development policies. So, the trade aspects of development policy are necessarily the EU's responsibility, but the states are much more prominent in respect of financial assistance – as is seen in the fact that the EU's own financial aid represents only about 15 per cent of the combined efforts of the member states.

Strains have sometimes arisen between the EU states regarding both their respective national development policies, and the relationship of these policies to EU policies. Particular problems have arisen where states have been using aid for the purpose of promoting national political and economic interests. In an attempt to ensure that there is consistency and convergence in the policies and activities of the EU and its member states, the Council of Ministers issued a series of guidelines in 1992–3 aimed at promoting maximum coordination in respect of policy content, policy operations, and policy positions in international forums.

☐ *Policy processes*

The EU makes all sorts of decisions in connection with its development policy. Just as in other policy areas, the actors who are involved, and the procedures which apply, vary enormously.

Regarding the actors, the most important players are: the Council of Ministers (Development Cooperation); the Commissioner for Cooperation and Development; DGVIII –' Development; the EP Committee on Development and Cooperation; and the numerous diplomatic missions of Third World countries in Brussels which are accredited to the EU.

Regarding the procedures, they are dependent on the sort of decisions which are envisaged. If, for example, the Council is simply intending to issue a declaration or a resolution on a matter, it is not obliged to consult the EP and it can move at its own pace – which may mean proceeding very cautiously and only after receiving proposals from the Commission and/or from a specially convened Council *ad hoc* working party. If a trade agreement is envisaged, Article 113 applies – which, as noted above, means the Commission and the Council are the key actors, qualified majority rules apply, and there is no formal role for the EP. If cooperation or association agreements are proposed, the assent procedure set out in Article 228 is used – which means qualified majority voting rules for cooperation agreements and unanimity for association agreements, and a veto power for the EP. If any other type of agreement is being sought the cooperation procedure set out in Article 189c is used – which involves two readings in the Council and the EP, and qualified majority voting rules applying but with Council unanimity required to overturn amendments or rejections carried by the EP at second reading with an overall majority.

As was shown above, the Lomé Convention is the most important of the numerous agreements to which the EU is party in connection with its policy on development cooperation. It is worth saying a little about how it functions, for the Convention has its own institutional structure. This structure is made up of three principal bodies. The first is the ACP–EC Council of Ministers, which is composed of the members of the EU Council of Ministers, a member of the Commission, and a member of the government of each ACP country. The Council meets at least once a year and takes the major political and policy decisions that are necessary during the life of a Convention. The second body is the Committee of Ambassadors, which is composed of a representative of each EU state, a representative of the Commission, and a representative of each ACP state. The Committee meets at least twice a year and is charged with assisting and advising the Council of Ministers, monitoring implementation of the Convention and progress towards achieving its objectives, and generally supervising and coordinating the work of the many committees and subsidiary bodies that exist under the general umbrella of the Convention. Finally, there is the Joint Assembly, which is made up of equal numbers of MEPs and ACP members of parliament or national representatives. It meets twice a year and acts as a general advisory and deliberating body.

■ External relations: problems and prospects

Article C of the Common Provisions of the TEU states 'The Union shall in particular ensure the consistency of its external activities as a whole in the context of its external relations, security, economic and development policies'. Ensuring such consistency clearly is something of a problem for the EU given the spread of its activities and interests in respect of external relations, and given too the diversity of actors and processes that are involved in external relations decision-making. To effect the consistency that is required to maximise effectiveness, more attention will have to be given in the future to linking the different aspects of external relations to one another. Indications that this is now being done include: (1) the increasing attachment to EU development programmes of requirements on

Third World states that they respect human rights and promote democratic principles; (2) the incorporation of political programmes and political dialogue in the association agreements which the EU has contracted with Central and Eastern European countries.

As part of effecting good coordination, it is necessary that the EU institutions work closely together. This is a matter to which greater attention also needs to be given, for the past has seen too many competitions for power: between, for example, different DGs in the Commission; between the Commission and the Council Presidency and between the Commission and individual member states over who – if anyone – should speak on behalf of the EU in international negotiations; and between the EP and the Council over what powers should be assigned to the former.

There are grounds for believing that as attempts are made to resolve the tensions that are associated with 'who does what', the roles of the Commission and the EP are likely to increase.

Regarding the Commission, its role in representing the EU in external trade relations is, of course, already firmly established. It is, however, gradually coming to establish an important position for itself in negotiations which have a more explicit political aspect to them. This is partly because of the increasing intermingling of economics and politics – seen no more clearly than in EU–Eastern Europe relations – but it is also partly because of the sheer range of Commission responsibilities and competences. An example of this developing role of the Commission – and its presence sometimes with the Council Presidency in a sort of EU dual representation – is seen in transatlantic relations where, under the 1990 Transatlantic Declaration, the US President meets once every six months with the Presidents of the Council and the Commission. It is probable that the creation of DGIA (External Political Relations) will see the Commission asserting with ever increased vigour its external political role.

Regarding the EP, the grievances of MEPs with their limited powers in respect of external relations are not going to disappear. Rather can MEPs be expected to continue badgering the Commission and the Council to listen to their views, and for the next IGC to concede real powers in respect of trade agreements. But even without the powers it would ideally like, the EP still has a range of devices and levers at its disposal which it can be expected to continue using to maximise its potential influence – most notably, assent power in regard to accessions and association and cooperation agreements, and ongoing dialogue with the Council Presidency in EP committees and plenary sessions.

But important though issues of coordination are, the greatest problems – and indeed uncertainties – surrounding the future development of the EU's external relations centre on the CFSP. Amongst the many (in practice overlapping) questions which will need to be resolved in the years ahead are the following: where is the balance to be struck between 'Atlanticism' and 'Europeanism'?; what is the nature of 'Europeanism', and to what extent does it incorporate East European interests as opposed to defining West European interests *vis à vis* East European interests?; what is to be the role of, and the CFSP's relationship to, NATO and the CSCE?; to what extent should the CFSP's decision-making processes be intergovernmental or supranational in character?; how far and how quickly should the EU act upon the TEU declarations concerning the construction of a common defence policy and, perhaps, a common defence?; how precisely should the WEU be aligned with the EU given that the membership of the two organisations is not quite the same, and given too that the WEU's Charter runs out in 1997?; and what are the implications for the CFSP of EU enlargement to, in the short term EFTA states (which include previously neutral and non-aligned countries), and in the longer term Eastern and Central European states (which clearly raise numerous security issues – not least relations with Russia)?

Such questions are not necessarily insoluble. After all, a whole series of what were hitherto seen as almost insurmountable barriers in the way of the development of what is becoming the CFSP have been removed in recent years. For example: the special relationships of some EU countries with particular parts of the world have become less problematical as historical ties have been loosened; the difficulties created by the neutrality of Ireland and the non-participation of France in the military command of NATO have largely been overcome in the wake of the ending of the Cold War; and, for a host of reasons, EU member states – including those which are most concerned with the preservation of national sovereignty – have increasingly come to regard both foreign and security issues as wholly proper and legitimate matters for the EU agenda.

Whilst the turbulence and fluidity of the international system dictates extreme caution in looking to the future evolution of the CFSP, it can be anticipated with some confidence that it will loom increasingly large on the EU policy agenda, and that its special role in the EU system – as a separate pillar – will be much debated in the period leading up to, and during, the next round of constitutional (IGC) negotiations.

Chapter 15

National Influences and Controls on European Union Processes

It is generally agreed that the highest price states have to pay for their membership of the EU is a substantial loss of their own law making powers. In some policy spheres – agriculture and external trade in particular – autonomous national powers have been very largely removed. The reason the states are prepared to countenance this loss of sovereignty and are willing to participate in collective decision-making is that their national decision-makers, supported by large sections of their populations, believe it to be in their national interest to do so. The particular balance of advantages and disadvantages varies from state to state, but each judges that there is more to be gained from being in the EU than being out.

But belonging to the EU is seen to require care and vigilance so as to ensure that national interests are fully articulated and properly defended. Since, however, there are competing views within the member states about what these interests are, and since too there are a variety of domestic institutions, agencies, movements, and parties which wish to be heard, there are many inputs from each of the states into EU policy-making and decision-making processes.

The precise nature of these inputs varies from state to state – reflecting such factors as different national political systems, traditions, and cultures – but they can all, in broad terms, be seen as being directed through seven principal channels: governments, parliaments, courts, sub-national levels of government, public opinion, political parties, and interests.

■ Governments

Governments are naturally in the strongest position to exercise national controls and influence on EU processes. This is most obviously seen in their relationships with the Commission and the Council of Ministers.

There are many opportunities for governments to seek to persuade, to influence, and to bring pressure to bear on, the Commission. Formal opportunities include the groups of experts which advise the Commission on all sorts of matters, the management and regulatory committees through which the Commission exercises many of its executive functions, and the numerous meetings which take place within the Council system from working party level upwards – meetings which the Commission always attends. Informal opportunities can range from a minister ringing up a Commissioner, to a working party representative meeting a Commission official for lunch.

Appointments to the Commission, which all governments watch closely so as to ensure that fellow nationals are well represented and well placed, can also be used to advantage. At the level of the Commissioners themselves, the practice of appointment by national nomination institutionalises national inputs. Below the Commissioners, a similar function is performed by the informal national quota system that exists for senior grades. (The decision of the Court of First Instance in March 1993 to annul the appointment of two directors to DG XIV (Fisheries) on the grounds that they were chosen not because of their qualifications but because their member states – Spain and Italy – were 'owed' the jobs, may temper the quota system, but it will not end it.)

This potential for Council influence on the Commission is not to suggest that Commissioners or Commission officials act as governmental representatives. As was shown in Chapter 4, they do, for the most part, look to the EU-wide interest and are not open to instructions from national capitals. But they may, quite naturally, be inclined to take a particular interest in the impact of proposals on their own country. And governments looking for sympathetic ears in the Commission may well make fellow nationals their first port of call. (Though not necessarily: competent national officials, especially from the Permanent Representations, cultivate a broad range of contacts in the Commission.)

It should also be recognised that governmental influence on Commission thinking is not necessarily a bad thing. On the contrary, it can be positively helpful by, for example, improving the prospects for the eventual adoption of proposals for legislation. Where, however, it can become unhealthy is when governments try to lean too heavily on their fellow nationals in the

Commission, and when clusters of nationals have a disproportionate influence on policy development in a key sector (as, for example, is frequently alleged of the French in respect of agriculture).

The potential for any single government to exercise control over what happens in the Council depends on a number of factors:

☐ *The size of the state it represents.* No matter what is being discussed the larger countries, especially France and Germany, are always likely to carry more weight than the smaller countries, such as Portugal and Luxembourg.

☐ *The importance of the state to particular negotiations.* On the Common Fisheries Policy (CFP), for example, the Spanish government represents many more interests and is likely to be a much more central actor than Belgium.

☐ *The desire of the government to play an active role.* An illustration of the importance of this factor is seen in the way German governments, until the late 1960s, acted very much as political lightweights, even though their country was clearly an economic heavyweight. This was partly because of Germany's historical legacy and partly because of the delicacies involved in the 'normalisation' of her relations with Eastern Europe and especially the German Democratic Republic (GDR). In more recent years, as Germany's position has come to be seen as not so unique or so special, her governments have increasingly asserted themselves across the EU's policy spectrum, and have not been unwilling to adopt 'awkward' and even isolated positions.

☐ *The capacity of the government to play an active role.* A government may have clear views on an EU initiative, and may wish to play an active role in supporting or opposing it, but be restrained from doing so by domestic political considerations such as a finely balanced coalition government, opposition from key interest groups, or possible electoral damage.

☐ *Relations with other governments.* Cohesive and fixed alliances within the EU between particular governments do not exist. Rather, governments tend to divide and join in different combinations on different issues. However, some governments do make more conscious efforts than others to seek general understandings and cooperation with EU partners, and where they are successful they do appear often to increase their influence as a consequence. The best example of this is the close relationship that has been consciously fostered between most French and German governments since the early 1960s. The so-called Franco–German axis is not so commanding now as it was when there were only six Community members, or when Chancellor Schmidt and President Giscard d'Estaing worked closely together in the 1970s, but it still plays an important part in helping to shape and set the pace of EU developments.

☐ *The procedures applying.* Of particular importance is whether majority voting is constitutionally permissible and politically acceptable. If it is, concessions and compromises might be preferable to being outvoted. If it is not, any government can cause indefinite delay, though by so doing it may weaken goodwill towards it and so damage its long-term interests.

☐ *The competence of governmental negotiators.* Given the extensive tactical manoeuvrings involved in EU processes, and given too that many negotiations are not about the broad sweep of policy but are about highly technical matters, the competence of individual negotiators can be crucial. Are they well briefed and able to master details? Can they judge how far their negotiating partners can be pushed? Can they avoid being isolated? Can they build coalitions? Can they time their interventions so as to clinch points? The evidence suggests that variations in such competencies are not so much between states as between individual negotiators.

☐ *The arrangements for linking representatives in the Council with national capitals.* This point is worth developing in a little detail because there are significant variations in the ways in which governments attempt, and are able, to control their inputs into the Council via their representatives. Two aspects of the control are particularly worth mentioning:

First, some countries – including Belgium, Italy, Luxembourg and the Netherlands – appear generally to allow their representatives to work within a relatively loose framework. That is to say, representatives are often able to negotiate on important policy matters not just at ministerial level but also in working parties and in COREPER. As well as assisting the functioning of the Council as a whole – by reducing the need for awkward issues to be referred upwards – manoeuvrability and flexibility of this kind can be used to the national advantage by competent negotiators. At the same time, however, too much independence for representatives can lead to the necessity for awkward backtracking at a later negotiating stage if a misjudgement is made. By contrast, representatives from other states – including France, Greece, Ireland and the United Kingdom – tend to have less room for manoeuvre in working parties and in COREPER and are generally reluctant to negotiate on policy issues below ministerial level. Whether, as is sometimes claimed, this greater rigidity improves the consistency and effectiveness of a country's negotiating position is doubtful. Undoubtedly, the more that countries lean in this direction, and all do at times, the more negotiations at the Council's lower levels are limited to technical matters and the more the overall Council process is protracted.

At the most senior Council level – ministerial meetings – there is, of course, not such a problem of control from national capitals. It is important to ensure that the minister is fully briefed on the national implications of proposals, and is accompanied by national officials who fully understand all aspects of agenda items, but the political weight of the participants usually means that, if the will is there, commitments can be entered into without having to refer back to the relevant ministry for clearance. This is not to say that those in attendance at ministerial meetings can do as they like. At a minimum they are obliged to operate within the general guidelines of their government's policies. They may also be subject to special national constraints: perhaps occasioned by an inability of the minister himself to attend; perhaps linked to domestic political difficulties caused by the existence of a coalition government; or perhaps a consequence of a particular national interest having resulted in the establishment of a rigid governmental position in advance.

Second, the ability of governments to coordinate their national position across different sectoral Councils is important. Unless there is some particular advantage, no government wishes its representatives in one policy sphere to be contradicting or undermining the efforts of its representatives in another. All member states have, therefore, established internal coordinating mechanisms of some kind. These work with varying degrees of efficiency, depending largely on the nature of the domestic political and governmental system and the sophistication of the mechanisms that are established.

In the United Kingdom, the centralised governmental system and the majority party political system provide a favourable base for effective coordinating mechanisms. The mechanisms themselves are formalised, structured, and seemingly well integrated. At the general policy level, the Foreign and Commonwealth Office (FCO), the Cabinet Office, and the UK Permanent Representation to the European Communities (UKREP), are the key bodies: the FCO has two European Community Departments – Internal and External; the Cabinet Office contains a European Secretariat which, amongst other things, convenes each year around 200 interdepartmental meetings of civil servants attended by representatives from appropriate ministries, including one regular weekly meeting which is attended by the Permanent Representative; and UKREP – which is formally an FCO overseas post – acts as the eyes and ears of the United Kingdom in Brussels. Together these three attempt to monitor, coordinate and control overall EU developments: by giving general consideration to important matters due to come up at forthcoming meetings; by looking at whether a broadly consistent line is being pursued across different policy areas; by trying to ensure that ministries have issued sufficiently clear guidelines for representatives in Council meetings; and, in the cases of the FCO and the UKREP, giving briefings themselves to representatives where appropriate. 'Above' these three bodies, but not involved in such a continuous manner, there is a Cabinet Committee on the European Community, the Cabinet itself, and the Prime Minister. 'Below' them, each ministry has its own arrangements for examining proposals that fall within its competence and for ensuring that specialist negotiators are well briefed and fully aware of departmental thinking. Where EU matters loom large in a ministry's work, special divisions or units exist for coordination purposes.

In Germany, by contrast, all sorts of factors make effective coordination very difficult: the usual existence of a coalition government and the need to satisfy – though not on a consistent basis across policy areas – the different elements of the coalition; the relative autonomy of ministers and ministries within the federal government (seen, most notably, in the long-running disagreement between the Finance Ministry and the Agriculture Ministry over the cost of the CAP); the lack of an authoritative coordinating centre – the Foreign Ministry has a rather imprecise responsibility for general integration policy, and the Economics Ministry has responsibility for routine matters; the relative independence from government of the Bundesbank (which has resulted in open differences between the government – or at least parts of the government – and the Bank, on EMU); the strong powers of the federal states – the Länder – in certain policy areas; and strong sectoral specialisation, allied with loyalties to different federal ministries, amongst the staff of the German Permanent Representation in Brussels. As a result, Germany's European policies are sometimes less than consistent. Fortunately for Germany, its position as the strongest single EU state seemingly enables it to avoid being too seriously damaged by this internal weakness.

Whatever the particulars of their arrangements for controlling and influencing EU activities all governments have found the task becoming increasingly difficult in recent years. Three factors are especially important in accounting for this:

• Many more decisions are now being taken by the EU. This applies to both major and long-term decisions – on EMU, on institutional reform, on the social dimension, etc. – and to more specific and technical decisions – such as much of the SEM-related legislation.

• Not only are more decisions being made, but many are being made much more quickly. The much greater use of majority voting means that governments cannot now always delay progress on a proposal until they are ready and satisfied.

• The increased scope of EU policy interests means that there are now no longer just a few domestic ministries – agriculture, trade, finance and so forth – which are directly involved with the EU. The 'Europeanisation' of domestic politics and administration has resulted in most ministries in most states being affected by, and becoming actively involved in, EU affairs.

■ Parliaments

Parliaments are much less influential than governments in influencing EU developments. Of course, governments normally reflect the political composition of their national legislatures and must retain their confidence; so, in an indirect sense, governmental activity in relation to the EU could be said to be reflective of parliamentary will. But that is a quite different matter from direct parliamentary control.

One of the major reasons for the lack of much direct parliamentary control is that national parliaments have no formal EU Treaty powers, so governments can choose what to consult their parliaments about. All governments do consult their parliaments on fundamental matters where the Treaties refer to ratification in accordance with 'respective constitutional requirements' (enlargements, Treaty amendments, and the EU's budgetary base carry this provision), but otherwise there are variations between the states. Another reason for weakness is the particular difficulties that arise in relation to what might be expected to be the major sphere of influence of national parliaments: advising on EU legislation. The difficulties here are legion: a high proportion of EU legislation is, or is regarded by governments as being, 'administrative' legislation and not, therefore, within parliamentary competences; much EU legislation is so technical that it is almost incomprehensible to the average legislator; there is little opportunity for considering even the most important legislation at the formative and crucial pre-proposal stage; proposed legislation that is considered is often well advanced in, and may even be through, the Council system before it is examined by parliaments; and majority voting in the Council means that a parliament whose government has been outvoted has no way at all of calling the real decision-makers to any sort of account.

But notwithstanding these problems and difficulties all national parliaments have established some sort of specialised arrangements for attempting to deal with EU affairs. They are arrangements which, in different ways and with different degrees of effectiveness, are focused on examining proposed EU legislation, scrutinising ministerial positions and performances, producing reports on EU-related matters, and generally monitoring EU developments. Amongst the many differences that exist between the national arrangements three are particularly worth noting:

(1)   Virtually all parliaments have established European committees of some sort, but whereas in some cases these serve as the main forum for dealing with EU matters, in others they serve more as coordinating committees and the detailed work is undertaken by appropriate 'domestic' committees.

(2)   The appearance of ministers before the appropriate parliamentary bodies varies considerably.

(3)   In a few parliaments – including the Belgian, German, and Greek – the specialised parliamentary organs include MEPs, and in a growing number of parliaments use is being made of MEPs as experts when appropriate.

Despite the changes and adjustments made by parliaments in recognition of the importance of the EU, it is still the case, however, that parliaments are mostly confined to a relatively minor role.

The position of the Irish Parliament is fairly typical. Following Irish accession to the Community in 1973, arrangements were made which were supposed to give Parliament monitoring, advisory, and deliberating responsibilities in respect of Irish participation in the Community. These arrangements were to consist, in particular, of an obligation on the part of the Government to present a six-monthly report to Parliament on developments in the Community, and the creation of a new committee – the Joint Committee on Secondary Legislation comprising 25 Dail Deputies and Senators – with the brief of examining Community proposals and advising the Government on their implications and suitability for Ireland. The evidence indicates that these arrangements had but a marginal effect and in the spring of 1993 the Committee was subsumed within a new Joint Committee on Foreign Affairs. The fact is that in Ireland, as in many member states, EU policy tends to be in the hands of a small, government-dominated, network of politicians and officials who listen to Parliament only as they see fit. So, in the case of agriculture for example, the Minister of Agriculture, senior officials in the Department of Agriculture, and leaders of appropriate organisations – particularly the Irish Farmers' Association – hold the key to decision-making and decision implementation, and they are not unduly incon-venienced by parliamentary probing.

The major exception to the general pattern of legislative weakness is the Danish Folketing. Two principal factors combine to put the Folketing in a rather special position. First, there has been a powerful anti-Community movement and a strong anti-Community popular sentiment in Denmark since accession in 1973. No Danish government has been able to ignore this – especially since all governments have been coalitions or minorities. Second, the Folketing has a very strong Market Relations Committee comprised of senior politicians which meets weekly to review the forthcoming business in the Council of Ministers and to hear reports from ministers on their proposed negotiating positions. The Committee does not vote or formally grant negotiating mandates, but it does tender advice, and it is necessary that a 'negative' clearance is given to the minister's position in the sense that there is no majority against it. The principal advantage of the Market Relations Committee procedure is that it helps to ensure that agreements reached by Danish ministers in the Council are not subsequently queried or endangered at home. The principal disadvantage is that it can make it difficult for Danish representatives to be flexible in the Council and can result in them being isolated if new solutions to problems are advanced during the course of negotiations.

■ Courts

National courts might be thought to have a significant role to play as the guarantors and defenders of national rights against EU encroachment. In practice, they do not.

The reason for this, as was explained in Chapter 8, is that the principle of the primacy of EU law is accepted by national courts. There were some initial teething problems in this regard, but it is now extremely rare for national courts to question the legality of EU proceedings and decisions. The Treaties, EU legislation, and the case law of the Court of Justice are seen as taking precedence when they clash with national law. The frequent practice of national courts to seek preliminary rulings from the Court of Justice in cases where there is uncertainty over an aspect of EU law is testimony to the general desire of national courts not to be out of step with EU law.

That said, national courts have occasionally sought to assert national rights and interests against the EU. For example, there have been a few instances where national courts have refused to acknowledge the legality of directives that have not been incorporated into national law by the due date, even though the Court of Justice has increasingly ruled that in such circumstances they may be deemed as having direct effect. Constitutional law, especially as applied to individual rights, has been another area where some assertion of national independence has been attempted by national courts, though not so much since the principle of the precedence of EU law over national constitutional law was confirmed in Court of Justice rulings in the early 1970s.

In recent years the most important instances of national court interventions have been in connection with Irish ratification of the SEA and German ratification of the TEU. The Irish intervention occurred in December 1986 when the Irish Supreme Court, by a vote of three to two, found in favour of a Raymond Crotty who challenged the constitutional validity of the SEA. The judges ruled that Title III of the Act, which put foreign policy cooperation on a legal basis, could restrict Ireland's sovereignty and might inhibit it from pursuing its traditionally neutral foreign policy. The Act must therefore, they indicated, be endorsed by a referendum. As a result, the SEA was unable to come into effect in any of the twelve Community states on 1 January 1987, as had been intended, and was delayed until the Irish gave their approval in the duly held referendum. The SEA eventually entered into force on 1 July 1987. The German intervention occurred when several people – including four Green MEPs – appealed to the country's Constitutional Court to declare that the TEU was in breach of Germany's constitution, the Basic Law. The appeal was made only shortly after the Bundestag and the Bundesrat had ratified the TEU by huge majorities in December 1992, with the consequence that from being one of the first countries to seemingly ratify the Treaty, Germany became the very last – the Court not issuing its judgement until October 1993. In the judgement, the Court declared that the TEU did not infringe Germany's constitution, but it was made clear that certain conditions would have to be satisfied in respect of further integration – most notably, it would need to be accompanied by a parallel increase in the democratic control of the EU.

■ Sub-national levels of government

The parts played, and the influence exercised, by sub-national levels of government in the EU were considered in Chapter 9 in the sections on the Committee of the Regions and on Interests. Suffice it here, therefore, to make only a few observations on key points.

Sub-national levels of government have grown in importance within the EU system in recent years, with the consequence that national authorities – especially governments – have lost some of their powers in regard to the articulation and advancement of 'the national position' in EU decision-making forums. The extent to which national authorities have seen their gatekeeping role undermined naturally varies according to a number of factors, not least the national constitutional status of sub-national levels of government, but even where central powers remain strong – as, for example in Ireland, Denmark, and the UK – by no means all EU-national official communications are channelled through the central authorities.

Channels of communication between the EU and sub-national levels of government include the following:

- Most EU states have sub-national levels of government of some kind which have offices and representations in Brussels. So, for example, all of Germany's Länder have offices, as do most of France's and Spain's regions, and as do around 15 UK regions, counties and cities (the largest UK offices being those of Scotland Europa and the Wales European Centre). The tasks of these offices include lobbying, information gathering, generally establishing contacts and 'keeping in touch' with appropriate officials and decision-makers, and acting as intermediaries between the EU and the regions/localities.
- Many sub-national levels of governments which do no have their own offices in Brussels make use of Brussels-based consultancies and/or have domestically-based EU offices and officers.
- The Committee of the Regions, which began functioning in March 1994, exists for the precise purpose of enabling EU decision-makers to seek the views of regional representatives on regional issues.
- Two governments – the Belgian and German – are sometimes represented in the Council of Ministers by regional ministers when agenda items are the responsibility of regional governments.

The EU may be a long way from the Europe of the Regions that some people advocate and others claim to detect, but clearly the national dimension of EU affairs has an increasingly powerful sub-national element attached to it.

■ Public opinion

National public opinion exercises both a direct and an indirect influence on EU decision-making.

The most direct means by which the populace can have their say is in referenda. Several of these have been held on EC/EU-related matters. However, it is hard to sustain a case that they have added very much to the democratic base of either the Community or the EU: partly because of their infrequency, and partly because at least four of them were not genuine attempts to consult the citizenry but were the consequences of internal politicking. Those to have been held are:

• In 1972 France held a referendum to ratify the enlargement of the Community. In reality it was designed to boost the legitimacy and status of President Pompidou and produce a public split in the Socialist-Communist opposition. The enlargement was approved.
• In 1972 Denmark, Ireland, and Norway held referenda on Community membership after their governments signed Treaties of Accession. The Danes and Irish gave their approval but a majority of Norwegians voted against membership and Norway withdrew its application.
• In 1975 a referendum was held in the United Kingdom on continued Community membership following the renegotiation of UK membership terms at the Heads of Government meeting in Dublin. The real purpose of the referendum was to settle a split in the Labour Cabinet on the principle of EC membership. Continued membership was approved.
• In 1986 Denmark held a referendum on the ratification of the SEA. This was brought about after the Folketing had rejected the Act, nominally on the grounds that it undermined national sovereignty, but partly too because the Left thought rejection would force an election they might win. The Conservative Prime Minister, Poul Schlüter, outmanoeuvred them by calling a referendum rather than an election. The SEA was ratified.
• In 1987, in circumstances described above, Ireland held, and approved, a referendum on the ratification of the SEA.
• In 1989, on the same day as the EP elections, a referendum was held in Italy on whether the European Community 'should be transformed into an effective Union'. The referendum, which resulted in a large 'yes' vote, was initiated by senators and deputies in the European Federalist Movement and was designed to reinforce the authority of Italian ministers and MEPs in giving the process of European integration a push.
• In 1992–3 there were four referenda on the ratification of the TEU: in June 1992 the Danes narrowly voted, by 50.7 per cent to 49.3 per cent, to reject the Treaty; also in June 1992 the Irish voted by a large majority, 69 per cent to 31 per cent, to endorse the Treaty; in September 1992 – in a referendum which had been called by President Mitterrand in the immediate aftermath of the Danish vote and which he had anticipated would boost his authority by giving a ringing endorsement to the TEU – the Treaty was only just approved, by 51 per cent to 49 per cent; and in a second Danish referendum, in May 1993, the Danes voted to approve the Treaty by 56.8 per cent to 43.2 per cent.

As was shown in Chapter 3, the Danish and French referenda of 1992 had, and continue to have, a very considerable impact. At a general level they have drawn attention to how European integration is essentially an elite driven process and have emphasised that it is important that decision-makers should not get too far in advance of public opinion. In recognition of this, the rhetoric of supporters of European integration has tended to be more tempered since mid-1992, decision-makers have moved more cautiously, and much has been made by all concerned of the merits of the 'buzz' concepts of subsidiarity, transparency, and decentralisation. At a more specific level, at the 1992 Edinburgh summit, Denmark was given, as an inducement to approve the TEU, clear opt-outs from EMU and from the projected common defence policy.

By contrast with the only occasional and localised opportunities for participation offered by referenda, the elections to the EP are regular and European-wide (see Chapter 7 for details). For some observers, these elections provide the EU with a democratic base and, through the involvement of political parties and the election of MEPs, serve to link the peoples of the EU with EU processes. This view, however, must be counterbalanced by a recognition of the fact that since the elections are not, in practice, contested by European parties standing on European issues, but are more second-order national elections, they can hardly be regarded as occasions when the populace indicate their European policy preferences. That voter turnout is, in most cases, low by national standards, and that those who are elected to be MEPs have only limited powers, raises further doubts about the participatory and democratic impact of the elections.

Another way in which public opinion exercises an influence on EU affairs is via national elections, since most important EU decisions are taken by the elected representatives of the member states in the Council of Ministers. It is an influence, however, that is indirect, in the sense that it is exercised at two or three stages removed, with voters in national elections electing legislatures, from which governments are formed, which send representatives to Council meetings. It is an influence too that is somewhat tangential, in the sense that in national elections voters are not much concerned with 'European issues' or with the competence of candidates in dealing with European matters: beyond some limited support for far right and nationalist parties because of their generally 'anti-Europe' stance, there is not much evidence of 'Europe' as such being an issue, or of it swaying many votes.

As for the extent to which governments respond to public opinion – as measured by public opinion polls and as interpreted by politicians – that depends very much on their own ideological and policy preferences, their perceptions of the importance and durability of issues, and the time remaining until the next election. The existence of, for example, less than enthusiastic support for European integration amongst sizeable proportions of national electorates (see Table 15.1) may both restrain and encourage politicians depending on their viewpoint, but there certainly is no automatic relationship between what the people think about EU matters and what governments do. The UK Conservative Government, for example, made no move to withdraw from the Community in the early 1980s even though a majority of the British population thought it should, and it did not weaken its opposition in the 1990s to the Social Charter even though polls suggested the Charter was supported by about two-thirds of the British people.

That said, where an issue is generally accepted as constituting a national interest, or at least commands strong domestic support, then governments of whatever political persuasion are likely to pursue it in the Council. Even if they themselves do not wish to be too rigid, they may well be forced, by electoral considerations and domestic pressures, to strike postures and make public displays of not being pushed around. So, for example, Irish and French governments invariably favour generous settlements for farmers, Danish and German governments press for strict environmental controls, and Greek and Portuguese governments argue for increased structural operations to enable them to modernise their economies.

Where no very clear national interest is at stake, or national opinion is unformed or divided, then the positions adopted by governments in the Council may be more reflective of domestic partisan divisions. So, for example, from 1974 to 1979 the attitude of the UK Government to the Community budget was largely conditioned by Labour objections to the resources devoted to the CAP. Since 1979, however, the attitude has mirrored the Conservatives' general ideological distaste for high public expenditure.

■ Political parties

Political parties normally wish to exercise power which, in liberal democratic states, means they must be able to command popular support. This, in turn, means they must be able to articulate and aggregate national opinions and interests. At the same time, parties are not normally content simply to act as mirror images of the popular will.

Table 15.1 Typology of European attitudes

	Belgium	Denmark	France	Germany West	Germany East	Greece	European Union 12
Positive	60	52	52	54	49	63	54
Ambivalent	36	34	39	39	47	31	39
Negative	4	14	7	7	5	6	7
Total	100	100	100	100	100	100	100

	Ireland	Italy	Luxembourg	Netherlands	Portugal	Spain	United Kingdom	European Union 12
Positive	62	67	62	68	55	51	40	54
Ambivalent	35	30	36	30	42	43	45	39
Negative	3	3	2	2	3	6	15	7
Total	100	100	100	100	100	100	100	100

Notes: 1. All figures are percentages.
2. The typology is based on the answers to two questions:

Generally speaking, do you think your country's membership of the EC is a good thing?
In general, are you for or against efforts being made to unify Western Europe?

3. The survey was undertaken between 13 March and 16 April 1993.

Source: Adapted from *Eurobarometer*, 39 (June 1993).

Drawing on their traditions, and guided by leaders and activists, they also seek to direct society by mobilising support behind preferred ideological/ policy positions. Judgements thus have to be made about the balance to be struck between 'reflecting' society and 'leading' it. Those parties which lean too much towards the latter have little chance of winning elections, although in multi-party systems they may well still find themselves with strong negotiating hands.

Of course, the precise extent to which parties are, on the one hand, reflecting and channelling opinions on particular issues and are, on the other, shaping and determining them, is very difficult to judge since, in most instances, the processes are two-way and interrelated. But whatever the exact balance may be between the processes, both are very much in operation in relation to the EU. The experiences of Denmark, Greece and the United Kingdom in the 1980s and early 1990s illustrate this. In each of these countries there was widespread popular scepticism in the early to mid-1980s about Community membership and this found both expression and encouragement at the party political level, with some parties advocating a complete withdrawal from Community membership, and others expressing a considerable concern about aspects of the implications of membership – especially in relation to sovereignty. As the 'realities' of Community membership began to seep through, however, both public opinion and party attitudes began to change. So much so that by the beginning of the 1990s Greece had become one of the more enthusiastic Community states in terms of public opinion, and a 'typical' one in terms of the attitudes of its political parties, whilst Denmark and the United Kingdom were not lagging too far behind the Community 'average' on either count.

Apart from their interactive relationship with the attitudinal climate in which EU processes work, political parties feed also directly into EU decision-making. First, by providing much of the ideological base of the ideas of governments, and by providing most – if not all – of the leading personnel of governments, they do much to determine and shape the attitudes, priorities and stances of the member states in the Council. While it is true that many policy positions are barely altered by changes of government, shifts of emphasis do occur and these can be significant. Second, even when they are in domestic opposition, political parties can influence government behaviour in the Council because governments do not wish to be accused of being weak or not strongly defending national interests. Third, national political parties are the main contestants of the European elections and their successful candidates become the national representatives in the EP.

■ Interests

Acting either by themselves or through an appropriate Euro-group, national sectional and promotional interest groupings have a number of possible avenues available to them to try and influence EU policies and decisions. Some avenues are at the domestic level – such as approaches through fellow national MEPs, government officials, and ministers. Others are at the EU level – such as contacts with the Commission, EP officials, or taking a case to the Court of Justice. These avenues were discussed in some detail in Chapter 9.

In very general terms, the most successful national interest groups tend to fulfil at least one of two conditions. Either they are able to persuade their government that there is little distinction between the group's interests and the national interest. Or, they have power and information resources that persuade at least some EU decision-makers that they ought to be listened to. A major reason why farmers have been so influential is that both of these conditions have applied to them in some countries. In France, Germany, Ireland, and elsewhere, this has resulted in Ministries of Agriculture perceiving a major part of their responsibility in the Council being to act virtually as a spokesman for the farmers.

■ Concluding remarks

The existence of different and frequently conflicting inputs from member states is the major obstacle in the way of the creation of a smooth, efficient and decisive EU policy- and decision-making machinery. But that national views and requirements should be able to be articulated, and incorporated into decisions, is vital if the EU is to work at all. For, ultimately, the EU exists to further the interests of those who live in its member states. If the citizens of the states and, more particularly, the political elites in governments and in parliaments, were to feel that the EU was no longer serving that purpose, then there would be no reason for continued membership. The EU must, therefore, be responsive to its constituent parts.

■ *Chapter 16* ■

Conclusion: Present Realities and Future Prospects

▌ The European Union and the changing nature of the international system

The European Union should not be viewed in too narrow a context. Whilst many of the factors which have influenced its development have applied to it alone, many have not. This is most clearly seen in the ways in which modernisation and interdependence, which have been crucial in the creation of many of the central features of the EU, have produced similar effects elsewhere in the international system – albeit usually to a more modest degree. There has, for example, been a steady increase in the number and variety of international actors, and some corresponding weakening in the dominance of states. An increasing range of methods and channels are used by international actors to pursue their goals. Relationships between governments are no longer so controlled as they used to be by Foreign Offices and Ministries of External Affairs. The range of issues on international agendas has grown with, in particular, traditional 'high' policy issues – those concerned with security and the defence of the state – being joined by an array of 'low' policy issues – those concerned with the wealth and welfare of citizens. And there has been a decline, in the Western industrialised world at least, in the use of physical force as a policy instrument – conflicts over trade imbalances and currency exchange rates are not solved by armed conflict but by bargaining, adjusting, and compromising.

The EU must, therefore, be set within the context of the rapid changes that are occurring throughout the international system. It is a system that is becoming, like the EU system itself, increasingly multi-layered and interconnected. Whether the purpose is to regulate international trade, to promote the efficient functioning of the international monetary system, to set international standards on packaging for the transportation of hazardous material, or to control the hunting and killing of whales, states now come together in many different ways, in many different combinations, for many different purposes.

The most obvious, and in many respects the most important, way in which states come together is via the creation of international organisations. Countless such organisations – each with their different memberships, their different functions, their different powers, and their different structures – have been constituted since the Second World War. To cite, by way of illustration, just a few of the more important international organisations which have been, and still are, used by Western European states: global organisations include the United Nations (UN), the International Monetary Fund (IMF), and the General Agreement on Tariffs and Trade (GATT); Western organisations include the Organisation for Economic Cooperation and Development (OECD), the North Atlantic Treaty Organisation (NATO), and Group of Seven (G7) meetings (not perhaps quite officially an organisation, but increasingly structured and increasingly meeting not just at summit level, but also at sub-summit levels); and Western European organisations include the Council of Europe, (though this is becoming increasingly European-wide in its composition), the Western European Union (WEU), the European Free Trade Association (EFTA), and more specialised organisations such as the European Space Agency and the European Patent Organisation.

Amongst this array of organisations with which Western European states have been, and are, associated, the EU stands out as being particularly important and distinct. It is, indeed, in many respects, unique amongst international organisations.

■ The uniqueness of the European Union

□ *Three unique characteristics*

Three aspects of the EU's uniqueness are particularly worth emphasising.

First, the EU has a much more developed and complex institutional structure than is found in other international bodies. The standard pattern of international organisations – permanent secretariats and attached delegations – is perhaps, in a much grander and more elaborated form, replicated in the EU with the Commission and the Permanent Representations, but to these are added many other features. Among the more obvious of such features are: the regular and frequent meetings between member governments at the very highest political levels; the constant and many varied forms of contact between national officials; the Court of Justice; and the EP – the only directly elected multi-state assembly in the world.

Second, no other international organisation has anything like the policy responsibilities of the EU. In terms of width, there are now few significant policy areas which have completely escaped the EU's attentions. In terms of depth the pattern varies, but in many important areas, such as external trade, agriculture, and competition policy, key initiating and decision-making powers have been transferred from the member states to EU authorities.

Third, the EU has progressed far beyond the essentially intergovernmental nature of most international organisations and has incorporated many supranational characteristics into its structure and operation. Since the nature of the balance between intergovernmentalism and supranationalism in the EU has not been directly examined in any of the previous chapters, and since also hostility to too much supranationalism – and the loss of sovereignty it is perceived as entailing – is a major reason why governments, especially those of Denmark and the United Kingdom, are sometimes reluctant to accept integrationist initiatives, it is appropriate at this point to give some consideration to intergovernmentalism and supranationalism in the EU.

☐ *Intergovernmentalism and supranationalism*

In the 1960s, the governments of five of the Community's then six member states were willing to permit, even to encourage, some movement in the direction of supranationalism. President de Gaulle, however, who wished to preserve 'the indivisible sovereignty of the nation state', was not. In order to emphasise this point, and more particularly to prevent certain supranational developments which were due to be introduced, he withdrew France in 1965 from most of the Community's key decision-making forums. The outcome of the crisis which this occasioned was the 1966 Luxembourg Compromise (see Chapter 5) which, though it had no legal force, had as its effect the general imposition of intergovernmentalism on Community decision-making processes: the powers of the Commission and of the EP were contained, and decisions in the Council came customarily to be made – even where the Treaties allowed for majority voting – by unanimous agreements.

The first enlargement of the Community in 1973 reinforced intergovernmentalism, bringing in as it did two countries – Denmark and the United Kingdom – where there was strong domestic opposition to

Community membership and where supranationalism was viewed with suspicion. The Greek accession in 1981 had a similar effect. International economic uncertainties and recession also encouraged intergovernmentalism, since they made states look rather more critically at the distributive consequences of Community policies, produced a temptation to look for national solutions to pressing problems, and resulted in a greater caution with regard to the transfer of powers to Community institutions.

However, intergovernmental attachments and pressures were never able, and have never been able, completely to stop the development of supranationalism. The Treaties, increasing interdependence, and the logic of the EU itself, have all ensured that in terms of both decision-making processes and decision-making outcomes national sovereignties have been progressively undermined. Indeed, not only has supranationalism become more embedded, but since the mid-1980s it has been given a considerable boost as most of the states have adopted a much more positive attitude towards its development. They have done so partly because the effects of the delays and the inaction that intergovernmentalism sponsors have become more obvious and more damaging, and partly because it has been recognised that as the number of member states has grown, over-rigid intergovernmentalism is a greater recipe than ever before for stagnation and sclerosis.

The EU thus displays both intergovernmental and supranational characteristics.

The principal intergovernmental characteristics are as follows:

● In most of the major areas of public policy – including foreign affairs, defence, macroeconomic policy, financial and monetary policy, education, health, and justice and home affairs – decisions are still mainly taken at the national level. Each state consults and coordinates with its EU partners on aspects of these policies, and is increasingly subject to constraints as a result of EU membership, but usually, in the last analysis, a state can decide for itself what is to be done.

● Virtually all major decisions on the general direction and policy priorities of the EU are taken by Heads of Government in the European Council: that is, in the forum of most senior national representatives. Only rarely does the European Council take decisions by majority vote.

● Most important decisions on EU legislation are taken by national ministers in the Council of Ministers. Under the EC Treaty some key decisions – including those of a constitutional or a fiscal nature – can only be taken by unanimity. Where qualified majority voting is permissible, attempts are always made to reach a consensus if a state makes it clear that it believes it has important national interests at stake.

• The Commission and the EP, the two most obvious 'supranational political rivals' to the European Council and the Council of Ministers, are restricted in their decision-making powers and cannot impose policies which the representatives of the member states do not want.

Of the supranational characteristics of the EU, the following are particularly important:

• The Commission may have to defer to the European Council and the Council of Ministers with respect to the taking of major decisions, but it is an extremely important decision-maker in its own right when it comes to secondary and regulatory decision-making. Indeed in quantitative terms most EU legislation is issued in the name of the Commission.

• In the Council of Ministers, qualified majority voting is now common. This is partly a result of changing norms and expectations, and partly a result of the SEA and TEU extensions of the policy spheres in which majority voting is constitutionally permissible.

• The EP may not enjoy the constitutional status and authority of national parliaments, but its influence in EU decision-making should not be underestimated. This influence has been greatly enhanced by the cooperation and assent procedures which were both created by the SEA and by the co-decision procedure which was created by the TEU.

• The force and status of decision-making outcomes is crucial to EU supranationalism for, clearly, the EU could hardly be described as supranational at all if its decisions had no binding force. Some, indeed, do not and are merely advisory and exhortive. But many do, and constitute EU law. It is a law that constitutes an increasingly prominent part of the legal systems of all member states. It is a law, too, that takes precedence over national law should the two conflict, and a law that, in the event of a dispute, finds its final authority not in national courts, but in the interpretations of the EU's own Court of Justice.

□ *A pooling and sharing of sovereignty?*

The three aspects of EU uniqueness which are referred to above – the complex institutional structure, the range of policy responsibilities, and the combination of intergovernmental and supranational characteristics – have combined, and are combining, to produce a system which is quite unique in the extent to which it involves states engaging in *joint* action to formulate *common* policies and to make *binding* decisions. As the words 'joint', 'common', and 'binding' imply, the process of working together is resulting in the EU states becoming ever more intermeshed and interdependent. This is no more clearly seen than in the ratchet-like effect of many aspects of their relationships and their shared activities: ratchet-like in the sense that it will not be possible for them to be reversed without creating major constitutional, legal, political and economic difficulties at both EU and national levels.

Clearly a central aspect of the intermeshing and the interdependence, and one of the principal distinguishing characteristics of the EU, is the way in which the member states have voluntarily surrendered some of their national sovereignty and independence to collective institutions. Indeed, in a few policy sectors, such as agriculture and external commercial policy, the requirements of the EU system have resulted in the role of the states being relegated almost to that of intermediaries. However, viewed from a broader perspective, the EU is not only the cause of a decline in national powers, but is also a response to decline. This is so because much of the rationale of the EU lies in an attempt – an attempt for which there is no international parallel – on the part of the member states to increase their control of, and their strength and influence in, a rapidly changing world. Although all of the states have reservations, and some have fundamental criticisms, about aspects of the EU, each has made the judgement that membership enhances its ability to achieve certain objectives. The precise nature of these objectives varies from state to state but, in virtually all cases, the main priorities are the promotion of economic growth and prosperity, the control of economic and financial forces which are not confined to national boundaries, and the strengthening of political influence. Insofar as these objectives are being attained, it can be argued that the diminution in the role of the state and the loss of sovereignty that arises from supranationalism is counterbalanced by the collective strength of the EU as a whole.

Indeed, since international change has resulted in all of the member states experiencing a considerable *de facto*, if not *de jure*, loss of national sovereignty quite irrespective of the loss which is attributable to EU membership, it can be argued that discussions of national sovereignty, in the classic sense of the term at least, are no longer very meaningful. Rather should it be recognised that the only way in which medium-sized and small states, such as those which make up the membership of the EU, can retain control of their operating environments is by pooling and sharing their power and their sovereignty.

It is a pooling and a sharing, however, which needs to be seen in the context not solely of decision-making at the EU and the national levels. The role of the sub-national level of decision-making needs to be recognised too. For national decentralisation of power is not just confined to one or two EU countries – Germany is most frequently quoted in this context – but is quite common: Belgium, France, Italy and Spain, for example, all have significant regional structures. The exercise of power in the EU is thus layered and tiered, with some powers 'transferred up' from national-level decision-makers to EU decision-makers, and some 'transferred down' to sub-national decision-makers. It is, therefore, quite appropriate to think of the EU as being characterised by a multi-level system of governance in which power is exercised, and is competed for, not only by EU-level and national-level decision-makers, but also – to different degrees in different countries – by sub-national decision-makers. Recognition of the existence of this multi-level governance system naturally makes the concept of sovereignty even more diffuse and even more difficult to apply.

■ The future of the European Union

☐ *Factors affecting prospects*

Integration in Europe has not evolved in quite the way, or as quickly, as was envisaged by many of its early founders. The expectation that policy interests and responsibilities would grow, with achievements in initially selected sectors leading to developments in other sectors, has been partly borne out, but only up to a point, and certainly not consistently – in the 1970s and early 1980s policy development was extremely sluggish. The anticipation that national institutions and political and economic actors would become progressively entwined with one another has been similarly partially realised, but it has also been partially frustrated – not least because of the persisting reluctance of some governments to transfer responsibilities and powers to European institutions. The assumption that the focus of political activities and attentions would switch from national capitals to Europe has happened to an extent – but in most policy areas the national level is still more important than the EU level. And, finally, the belief that a European spirit would emerge, based on shared perceptions of a common interest, has proved to be over-optimistic.

There has, in short, been no semi-automatic movement in an integrationist direction. But if integration has not inevitably, and of itself, led to more integration, it has certainly stimulated pressures for more integration. It has done so, for example, by creating 'client groups' – of which, in the EU context, Eurocrats are not the least prominent – that have strong vested interests in sustaining and extending integration. Integration has also provided an institutional framework into which integrationist pressures, of many different sorts, have been channelled.

Among such pressures on the EU today are: the international trade challenge of the United States, Japan, and the newly-industrialising countries; the increasingly perceived need for monetary stability; the transnational character of problem areas such as the environment and terrorism; and the need to respond to the integration that is occurring outside formal EU processes through developments as diverse as industrial mergers, closer cross-border banking and other financial arrangements, and population movements.

How, in the future, the EU will respond to these and other pressures will depend on a number of factors, the most important of which are perceptions, support and opposition, and leadership.

The importance of *perceptions* is seen in the way prospects for progress are considerably enhanced when all of the member states perceive an initiative to be broadly desirable, or at least regard the costs of not proceeding as being too high. Very frequently, of course, there is no such common perception, especially where new types of development are envisaged and/or when initiatives have sovereignty or clear distributional implications.

The extent to which key actors are motivated to *support* or oppose an initiative is dependent on many things. Perception of merit is obviously central, but this can be offset by other considerations. A government, for example, may fiercely resist a proposal in the Council of Ministers not because it regards it as being innately unsound, but because acceptance would be electorally damaging or would lead to problems with an important domestic pressure group.

Leadership has long been a weakness of the EU in that there is no strong and central focus of decision-making authority. The Commission, the European Council, and the Council of Ministers are in many ways the key decision-making bodies, but their ability to get things done is subject to limitations. When attempts are made to provide forceful leadership – by, perhaps, an informal coalition of states, by an ambitious Council Presidency, or by a forceful Commission President – there is usually resistance from some quarter.

Perceptions, support, and leadership are, of course, not static, but rather are in constant transition. Since the early to mid-1980s they have undergone significant changes, in ways which have facilitated integrationist developments. Factors accounting for the changes are many and varied, and range from the specific – such as the appointment of the highly dynamic Jacques Delors to the Commission Presidency in 1985 – to the general – such as the opening up of the SEM and the related increasing interdependence of international economic and political life. The changes have helped to produce a climate wherein, for example, the European Council and the Commission are both offering bolder policy leadership than formerly they did, and in government circles there is now an increased perception of the need of, and also increased support for, further integration.

But if the SEM and other developments are resulting in a new sense of dynamism being inserted into integration processes, they have not removed all of the obstacles. This is no more clearly seen than in the different public positions taken by governments on the future shape of the EU. On the one hand, there are the 'maximalists', such as the Italians and the Belgians, who are enthusiastic about economic, monetary and political union, and who do not automatically recoil at the prospect of a federal Europe. On the other hand there are the 'minimalists', with the United Kingdom and Denmark in the vanguard, who talk more of cooperation than they do of integration and who still make much of the importance of preserving national independence and sovereignty.

Of course, rhetoric is one thing and actual deeds are another. The statements of national politicians may do something to capture the many different ideas which exist about the future of the EU, but they sometimes also serve to mask as well as to reveal. So, UK governments have done much to facilitate integration through such acts as approval of the SEA and the TEU, acceptance of the 1988 Brussels and 1992 Edinburgh summit packages, and strong support for the dismantling of barriers which prevent the free movement of goods, services, capital and labour. At the same time, those governments which are highly vocal in their support for integration processes are often quite prepared to drag their feet and create difficulties when specific proposals do not accord with their own preferences or national interests – as, for example, does France when the case for political integration is pressed too hard and as does the Netherlands when proposals for security integration look as though they may threaten the position of NATO.

☐ *Deepening and widening*

Of critical importance in determining the future evolution of the EU will be how the many pressures for expansion are handled. These pressures for expansion take the form of both pressures for further integration – which are designed to bring about a deepening of the EU – and pressures for further enlargements – which are designed to bring about a widening of the EU.

☐ *Deepening the EU.* The TEU significantly advanced the deepening of the EU by making provision for further policy and institutional integration. It did not, however, for most participants or observers, mark the end of the deepening process. Rather was it generally seen as a step, albeit an extremely important step, in a process which would continue. Indeed, that it would continue was virtually ensured with the provision in Article N of the TEU for another IGC in 1996 'to examine those provisions of this Treaty for which revision is provided, in accordance with the objectives set out in Articles A and B'. (See Document 3.2, p. 66, for Articles A and B).

What aspects of EU deepening are most likely to receive attention in the foreseeable future?

Regarding *policy* deepening, the following matters are likely to figure prominently in debates and negotiations:

• The SEM is still not wholly completed and is still not wholly governed by a common legal framework. Not all barriers to free movement have been removed and there is still far from complete accord between the member states over what needs to be harmonised and approximated for genuinely free, open and fair competition to exist.

• The procedures and the timetable for moving towards EMU were brought into question by the 1992–3 crises in the ERM. Do these need to be adjusted, or at least made to be more flexible, so as to allow a significant number of states to be able to enter the projected third stage of EMU which includes the establishment of the single currency?

• In addition to EMU, several other policy areas given an enhanced status by the TEU – notably the social dimension, and the CFSP and JHA pillars – are likely to attract controversy as they are developed. This is partly because of their natural sensitivity, partly because of the known differences between existing member states on aspects of these policies, and partly because states which seem likely to join the EU will bring with them their own preferences and concerns in these policy areas – on security policy for example (the neutrality or near neutrality of several EFTA states and Finland's 700 mile border with Russia are possible problems) and on social and environmental protection (EFTA states have generally higher standards than those which are prevalent in the EU).

• Prior to the TEU the Community had allowed, in response to the different requirements and propensities of member states, for a limited flexibility and diversity in the bases of its policies. When the 'standard' Community method was judged to be inappropriate or over-rigid, interstate relations took other forms. This was seen, for example, in the development of European Political Cooperation (EPC) alongside, but outside, the formal Community structure, and in the creation of the EMS on a partial membership basis. The TEU, however, saw departures from the 'standard' method given virtual constitutional status with the creation of the three pillar structure and with the projection of three key policies being developed without a full complement of member states participating: EMU, the social dimension, and defence (a Danish opt-out from the latter being formally guaranteed at the 1992 Edinburgh summit). Doubtless there will be pressures to ensure that this fragmentation does not grow, but there will also be pressures from countries for opt-outs when policies are judged to be unacceptable or undesirable.

It is, of course, not possible to predict the EU's future policy evolution with precision, for whatever the mix of pressures for development and action prove to be, it is quite certain that many of them will be strongly resisted. The reasons for the resistance will be found in the familiar barrage of barriers which explain why so much policy activity is slow, uneven, and uncertain: differences over the merits of proposals, over the costs of proposals, over the distributional consequences of proposals, over whether proposals are appropriate EU business, and over whether or not loss of national controls and sovereignty are acceptable. Conceivably such obstacles to progress may have the effect of causing the states to divide in certain respects into fast and slow integration streams. Certainly they will ensure that many initiatives which command a fair measure of support among the states and in EU institutions will nonetheless be put on indefinite hold, will be watered down, or will be diverted away from the making of legislation into relatively harmless liaising and coordinating channels.

Regarding *institutional* deepening, the EU continues to be criticised for persisting with a policy- and decision-making institutional framework that is seen by many to be slow, inefficient, and insufficiently subject to democratic controls. Schemes and proposals for reform usually focus on two main themes. First, the need for a stronger executive – among specific measures advocated are a merging of the Commission and the Council of Ministers, a more independent Commission, and majority voting in the Council of Ministers on everything other than constitutional matters. Second, the need for a stronger Parliament – measures advocated range from further modest extensions of the EP's existing rights, to making the EP the real and effective legislature of the EU.

Clearly the adoption of almost any of these proposed measures would extend political integration in the EU. It is for this very reason that national governments, or at least a sufficient number of them, have been inclined in the past to resist calls for fundamental institutional reforms and have preferred to cede to EU institutions only such powers as have seemed to be necessary. But what has seemed to be necessary has changed over the years, and this has brought about integrationist developments in the Community's institutional structures and decision-making processes. Some of these developments, such as the increasing use of majority voting in the Council of Ministers in the early 1980s, were not a consequence of formal political agreements or constitutional amendments but came about gradually, almost imperceptibly, as the Community adjusted to evolving circumstances and requirements. Other developments, such as the budgetary reforms of the 1970s, the SEA, and the TEU, involved formally contracted and ratified Treaty amendments. Doubtless further integrationist institutional developments will continue via both of these means.

Whether, however, they can continue to be essentially incremental in character must be doubted. At some stage it seems likely that the EU is going to have to respond to the increasing size of its membership by engaging in rather more root and branch reform than it has in the past. The size of institutions cannot be indefinitely expanded, and changes to the working structure and practices of institutions cannot be forever restricted to adjustments and trimming. Amongst the questions which will have to be addressed at some point are these:

● Should a more powerful and more accountable executive be created? This could be done in various ways – starting, perhaps, with greater appointing powers for the President of the Commission and leading on to greater decision-making powers for the Commission which are linked to a more regularised accountability to the EP.
● Does every member state need a Commissioner, and do the big states need two? After all, one of the first things Commissioners do after being appointed is swear an oath that they will be independent in the performance of their duties.
● For how much longer can the Presidency of the Council keep rotating between the member states on a six monthly basis? If the EU grows to 20 members there would be a ten year gap between each national Presidency. Should there perhaps be a move towards a 'troika' system – in which two small states and one larger state share a Presidency?
● If the EU is to become more democratic as its powers increase, should national representations in the Council, the EP and other bodies not be made more proportional to size of population?
● Should the nettle of the language problem not be grasped by establishing, say, three 'working languages'? With 12 member states there are 72 possible language combinations. If the four EFTA states which agreed accession terms in 1994 become members there will be 132 combinations. The proliferation of languages cannot be allowed to expand indefinitely.

❊   ❊   ❊   ❊

Tackling these and related problems does, of course, require political will. It must be doubted whether the will is present to act in the radical manner that would seem to be required if efficiency, and indeed democracy, are to be maximised.

☐ *Widening the EU*. Since the late 1980s several countries have either applied for EU membership or have indicated that they would like to become members in the medium term. These applicants and potential applicants have come from three directions. First, from EFTA member states: Austria applied for membership in 1989, Sweden in 1991, and Finland, Switzerland and Norway in 1992. Second, from the EU's southern or Mediterranean flank: in 1987 Turkey applied for membership and in 1990 Cyprus and Malta did so. Third, from former Soviet satellite countries in Central and Eastern Europe: the first applications from this group of countries arrived in the spring of 1994 with applications from Hungary and Poland.

This interest in EU membership stems from three main factors. First, there is the economic strength of the EU. There are obvious attractions for medium- and small-sized states to be members of a powerful international bloc. Second, there is the increasingly integrated EU market. For states which conduct a large part of their trade with the EU, there are considerable disadvantages in having to meet EU rules and regulations without having a direct say in determining what those rules and regulations are. Third, there are the processes of democratisation and economic liberalisation in Eastern Europe, which have not only made the previously Communist countries theoretically eligible for membership, but have encouraged them to look to the EU for markets, for economic assistance, and – in some cases – for possible bolstering of their fledgling democracies. The changes in Eastern Europe have also – by removing the East–West division that existed in Europe from the late 1940s – made it possible for the neutralism of countries such as Austria and Sweden to no longer be a barrier to EU membership.

The EU has not encouraged applications. On the contrary, indeed, it has sought to head them off by offering to potential applicants privileged and special relationships – but relationships which stop short of membership. Notable examples of privileged and special relationships are those contained in the European Economic Area (EEA) with the EFTA states (see Chapter 1) and the Europe Agreements with Central and Eastern European states (see Chapter 14). In the event, these relationships have been viewed by non-EU states as very much 'second best' and have, if anything, encouraged them to make applications for EU membership by drawing attention to what is not available to non-members.

As was explained in Chapter 1, four EFTA states – Austria, Finland, Norway and Sweden – agreed accession terms in early 1994 and are expected to join the EU in 1995 subject to ratifications proceeding on schedule. Beyond these four states, however, further accessions are unlikely much before the end of the decade because countries which are interested in becoming members all have problems – or perceived problems – of one sort or another attached to them. They are not in the situation of the EFTA countries which are all economically advanced, which will all be net contributors to the EU budget on accession, and which all have well established liberal democratic systems and political cultures. Obstacles in the way of non-EFTA applicants include: most need considerable economic development before they can hope to compete on an open and equal basis in the SEM; all would be costs on the EU budget – not an enticing prospect for existing EU states given the difficulties of reaching an agreement on the relatively narrow margins of the 1993–9 financial perspective; all need to develop more sophisticated political and administrative structures if they are to convince EU decision-makers that they are psychologically ready to play by EU rules and understandings and if they are not to exacerbate problems of ensuring that EU policies are implemented in a common and uniform manner; and the EU itself would, as noted above, almost certainly have to engage in major structural reform if its membership was to go much beyond 16.

■ The re-shaping of Europe

The pressures for EU enlargement reflect the wider re-shaping of Europe that has been under way since the late 1980s. As part of this re-shaping, the identities and boundaries of Europe, which have always been somewhat imprecise, and indeed shifting, are being re-thought. The countries of Western Europe, which for almost half a century regarded themselves as virtually *being* Europe, have seen their assumptions about the nature of Europe, and about likely scenarios for the future, brought fundamentally into question.

The most obvious and most important aspect of this wider re-shaping of Europe is the progressive incorporation of Central and Eastern European countries into what were previously Western and Western European settings and arrangements. In organisational terms this is seen, for example, in the opening up of the Council of Europe to Central and Eastern European countries and in the creation of new pan European and predominantly European organisations – for example, the European Bank for Reconstruction and Development (EBRD) (which is a primarily

Western financed bank that has as its purpose helping Central and Eastern European countries to establish market economies), and the Conference on Security and Cooperation in Europe (CSCE) (which is emerging as a useful pillar of a new European order).

The impartial and detached observer, noting the many organisational changes which are taking place across Europe, might conclude that what is required is a new European-wide organisation bringing together all those states which wish to cooperate and integrate with one another. In the long term such an organisation may indeed emerge. It is hardly likely, however, in the foreseeable future. Amongst the obstacles in the way of such a fundamental restructuring are uncertainties in Western Europe about the future development of what is now a very heterogeneous Central and Eastern Europe, differences between West European states regarding what organisational developments are desirable, and a reluctance in some quarters – not least EU quarters – to disentangle established, and in many respects successful, structures and relationships.

For some years yet the organisational shape of Europe is thus likely to continue to be based on a number of different organisations, each with their own – often overlapping – memberships and functions. Doubtless the EU will continue to be, in many respects, the most important and most dominant of these organisations.

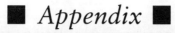

■ *Appendix* ■

Composition of the European Union Institutions Following the Accession of New Member States

The European Council at its meeting in Brussels in December 1993 decided that the composition of EU institutions would be as follows should any or all of the four countries negotiating to become members of the EU accede:

■ The Commission

Number of members

– Belgium	1	– Luxembourg	1
– Denmark	1	– Netherlands	1
– Germany	2	– Norway	1
– Greece	1	– Austria	1
– Spain	2	– Portugal	1
– France	2	– Finland	1
– Ireland	1	– Sweden	1
– Italy	2	– United Kingdom	2
		TOTAL	21

■ The European Parliament

Number of members

– Belgium	25	– Luxembourg	6
– Denmark	16	– Netherlands	31
– Germany	99	– Norway	15
– Greece	25	– Austria	20
– Spain	64	– Portugal	25
– France	87	– Finland	16
– Ireland	15	– Sweden	21
– Italy	87	– United Kingdom	87
		TOTAL	639

■ Court of Justice

- Each Member State will propose one Judge for appointment. In addition, should an even number of States accede, Germany, France, Italy, Spain and the United Kingdom will take part in a system involving the rotation of an additional Judge,
- Germany, France, Italy, Spain and the United Kingdom will each propose one Advocate-General for appointment,
- the other Member States will take part in a system involving the rotation of three Advocates-General.

■ The Court of First Instance

Each Member State will propose one member for appointment.

■ The Court of Auditors

Each Member State will propose one member for appointment.

■ The Economic and Social Committee

Number of Members

– Belgium	12	– Luxembourg	6
– Denmark	9	– Netherlands	12
– Germany	24	– Norway	9
– Greece	12	– Austria	11
– Spain	21	– Portugal	12
– France	24	– Finland	9
– Ireland	9	– Sweden	11
– Italy	24	– United Kingdom	24
		TOTAL	229

■ The Committee of the Regions

Number of members

– Belgium	12	– Luxembourg	6
– Denmark	9	– Netherlands	12
– Germany	24	– Norway	9
– Greece	12	– Austria	11
– Spain	21	– Portugal	12
– France	24	– Finland	9
– Ireland	9	– Sweden	11
– Italy	24	– United Kingdom	24
		TOTAL	229

■ The Council

(a) *Rotation of the Presidency*
    (i) Article 146 of the Treaty will be amended as follows:

        The Council shall consist of a representative of each Member State at ministerial level, authorized to commit the Government of that Member State.

        The office of President shall be held in turn by each Member State in the Council for a term of six months in the order decided by the Council acting unanimously.

    (ii) When the Accession Treaty enters into force the Council will adopt the following Decision:[1]

        The office of President shall be held:
- for the first six months of 1995 by France;
- for the second six months of 1995 by Spain;
- for the subsequent periods of six months by the following countries in turn in the following order:

        - Italy
        - Ireland
        - Netherlands
        - Luxembourg
        - United Kingdom
        - Austria
        - Norway
        - Germany
        - Finland
        - Portugal
        - France
        - Sweden
        - Belgium
        - Spain
        - Denmark
        - Greece.

    The Council, acting unanimously on a proposal from the Member States concerned, may decide that a Member State may hold the Presidency during a period other than that resulting from the above order.

(b) *Weighting of votes within the Council**

– Present Member States	current weighting maintained
– Austria, Sweden	4 votes per country
– Norway, Finland	3 votes per country

---

[1] This Decision will be adjusted if enlargement involves fewer than four countries.

Source: General Secretariat of the Council, *European Council in Brussels, 10 and 11 December 1993: Presidency Conclusions*

*This allocation raises the total number of votes in the Council from 76 to 90. In March 1994 it was agreed by the Council of Ministers (General Affairs) that if all four applicant states became members, the blocking minority would be raised from 23 votes to 27. In deference to the United Kingdom, which wished to retain the blocking minority at 23 votes, it was conceded that if 'members of the Council representing a total of 23 to 26 votes indicate their intention to oppose the adoption by the Council of a decision by qualified majority', then 'a reasonable time' would be allowed to elapse to see if an agreement could be found before the new blocking minority figure was used.

■ Official languages

The official languages of the Union after enlargement will be the nine existing official languages, to which will be added on accession Finnish, Norwegian and Swedish.

Chronology of Main Events in the Development of the European Union

1947 March   Belgium, Luxembourg and the Netherlands agree to establish a customs union. Subsequently an economic union is established in October 1947 and a common customs tariff is introduced in January 1948.

        March   France and the United Kingdom sign a military alliance, the Treaty of Dunkirk.

        June   General George Marshall, United States Secretary of State, offers American aid for the economic recovery of Europe.

        September   Sixteen nations join the European Recovery Programme.

1948 March   Brussels Treaty concluded between France, the UK and the Benelux states. Aim is to promote collective defence and to improve cooperation in the economic, social and cultural fields.

        April   Founding of the Organisation for European Economic Cooperation (OEEC) by sixteen states.

        May   A Congress is held in the Hague attended by many leading supporters of European cooperation and integration. It issues a resolution asserting 'that it is the urgent duty of the nations of Europe to create an economic and political union in order to assure security and social progress'.

1949 April   Treaty establishing North Atlantic Treaty Organisation (NATO) signed in Washington by twelve states.

        May   Statute of Council of Europe signed in Strasbourg by ten states.

1950 May   Robert Schuman, the French Foreign Minister, puts forward his proposals to place French and German coal and steel under a common authority. He declares 'it is no longer the moment for vain words, but for a bold act – a constructive act'.

        October   René Pleven, the French Prime Minister, proposes a European Defence Community (EDC).

1951 April   European Coal and Steel Community (ECSC) Treaty signed in Paris by six states: Belgium, France, Germany, Italy, Luxembourg and the Netherlands.

1952	May	EDC Treaty signed in Paris by the six ECSC states.
	July	ECSC comes into operation.
1954	August	French National Assembly rejects EDC Treaty.
	October	WEU Treaty signed by the six ECSC states plus the UK.

1955 June   Messina Conference of the Foreign Ministers of the six ECSC states to discuss further European integration. The Spaak Committee established to study ways in which a fresh advance towards the building of Europe could be achieved.

1956 June   Negotiations formally open between the six with a view to creating an Economic Community and an Atomic Energy Community.

1957 March   The Treaties of Rome signed establishing the European Economic Community (EEC) and the European Atomic Energy Community (Euratom).

1958 January   EEC and Euratom come into operation.

1959 January   First EEC tariff cuts and increases in quotas.

1960 January   European Free Trade Association (EFTA) Convention signed at Stockholm by Austria, Denmark, Norway, Portugal, Sweden, Switzerland and United Kingdom. EFTA comes into force in May 1960.

      December   Organisation for Economic Cooperation and Development (OECD) Treaty signed in Paris. OECD replaces OEEC and includes Canada and United States.

1961 July   Signing of Association Agreement between Greece and EEC. Comes into effect November 1962.

      July–August   Ireland, Denmark and United Kingdom request membership negotiations with the Community.

1962 January   Basic features of Common Agricultural Policy (CAP) agreed.

      July   Norway requests negotiations on Community membership.

1963 January   General de Gaulle announces his veto on UK membership.

      January   Signing of Franco–German Treaty of Friendship and Cooperation.

      July   A wide-ranging association agreement is signed between the Community and 18 underdeveloped countries in Africa – the Yaoundé Convention. The Convention enters into force in June 1964.

1964 May   The GATT Kennedy Round of international tariff negotiations opens in Geneva. The Community states participate as a single delegation.

1965	April	Signing of *Treaty establishing a Single Council and a Single Commission of the European Communities* (The Merger Treaty).
	July	France begins a boycott of Community institutions to register its opposition to various proposed supranational developments.
1966	January	Foreign Ministers agree to the Luxembourg Compromise. Normal Community processes are resumed.
1967	May	Denmark, Ireland and UK re-apply for Community membership.
	July	1965 Merger Treaty takes effect.
	July	Norway re-applies for Community membership.
	December	The Council of Ministers fails to reach agreement on the re-opening of membership negotiations with the applicant states because of continued French opposition to UK membership.
1968	July	The Customs Union is completed. All internal customs duties and quotas are removed and the common external tariff is established.
1969	July	President Pompidou (who succeeded de Gaulle after his resignation in April) announces he does not oppose UK membership in principle.
	July	Signing of the second Yaoundé Convention. Enters into force in January 1971.
	December	Hague summit agrees on a number of important matters: strengthening the Community institutions; enlargement; establishing an 'economic and monetary union' by 1980; and developing political cooperation (i.e. foreign policy).
1970	April	The financial base of the Community is changed by the *Decision of 21 April 1970 on the replacement of financial contributions from Member States by the Communities' own resources*. The Community's budgetary procedures are regularised and the European Parliament's (EP's) budgetary powers are increased by the *Treaty amending Certain Budgetary Provisions of the Treaties*.
	June	Preferential trade agreement signed between Community and Spain. Comes into effect in October 1970.
	June	Community opens membership negotiations with Denmark, Ireland, Norway and United Kingdom.
	October	The six accept the Davignon report on political cooperation. This provides the basis for cooperation on foreign policy matters.

1972	January	Negotiations between Community and the four applicant countries concluded. Signing of Treaties of Accession.
	May	Irish approve Community accession in a referendum.
	July	Conclusion of Special Relations Agreement between Community and EFTA countries.
	September	Majority vote against Community accession in a referendum in Norway.
	October	Danes approve Community accession in a referendum.
	October	Paris summit. Heads of Government set guidelines for the future, including a reaffirmation of the goal of achieving an economic and monetary union by 1980.

| 1973 | January | Accession of Denmark, Ireland and United Kingdom to the Community. |
| | January | Preferential trade agreement between Community and most EFTA countries comes into effect. Agreements with other EFTA countries come into force later. |

| 1974 | December | Paris summit agrees to the principle of direct elections to the EP and to the details of a European Regional Development Fund (ERDF) (the establishment of which had been agreed at the 1972 Paris and 1973 Copenhagen summits). In addition it is agreed to institutionalise summit meetings by establishing the European Council. |

1975	February	Signing of the first Lomé Convention between the Community and 46 underdeveloped countries in Africa, the Caribbean and the Pacific (the ACP states). The Convention replaces and extends the Yaoundé Convention.
	March	First meeting of the European Council at Dublin.
	June	A majority vote in favour of continued Community membership in UK referendum.
	June	Greece applies for Community membership.
	July	Signing of the *Treaty amending Certain Financial Provisions of the Treaties*. This strengthens the European Parliament's budgetary powers and also establishes the Court of Auditors.

| 1976 | July | Opening of negotiations on Greek accession to the Community. |

| 1977 | March | Portugal applies for Community membership. |
| | July | Spain applies for Community membership. |

| 1978 | October | Community opens accession negotiations with Portugal. |

| 1979 | February | Community opens accession negotiations with Spain. |
| | March | European Monetary System (EMS) (which had been the subject of high-level negotiations for over a year) comes into operation. |

	May	Signing of Accession Treaty between Community and Greece.
	June	First direct elections to the EP.
	October	Signing of the second Lomé Convention between the Community and 58 ACP states.
	December	For the first time the EP does not approve the Community budget. As a result the Community has to operate on the basis of 'one twelfths' from 1 January 1980.
1981	January	Accession of Greece to Community.
	October	Community foreign ministers reach agreement on the 'London Report' which strengthens and extends European Political Cooperation (EPC).
1983	January	A Common Fisheries Policy (CFP) is agreed.
	June	At the Stuttgart European Council meeting approval is given to a 'Solemn Declaration on European Union'.
1984	January	Free trade area between Community and EFTA established.
	February	The EP approves *The Draft Treaty establishing the European Union*.
	June	Second set of direct elections to the EP.
	June	Fontainebleau European Council meeting. Agreement to reduce UK budgetary contributions (which Mrs Thatcher had been demanding since 1979) and agreement also to increase Community resources by raising the VAT percentage from 1 per cent to 1.4 per cent.
	December	Signing of the third Lomé Convention between the Community and 66 ACP countries.
	December	Dublin European Council meeting agrees budgetary discipline measures.
1985	June	Signing of Accession Treaties between the Community and Spain and Portugal.
	June	The Commission publishes its White Paper *Completing the Internal Market*.
	June	Milan European Council meeting approves the Commission's White Paper. It also establishes an Intergovernmental Conference to examine various matters including Treaty reform. The decision to establish the Conference is the first time at a summit meeting a decision is taken by a majority vote.
	December	Luxembourg European Council meeting agrees the principles of the Single European Act (SEA). Amongst other things the Act incorporates various Treaty revisions – including confirming the objective of completing the internal market by 1992.
1986	January	Accession of Spain and Portugal to Community.

1987	June	Turkey applies for Community membership.
	July	After several months delay caused by ratification problems in Ireland the SEA comes into force.
1988	February	A special European Council meeting at Brussels agrees to increase and widen the Community's budgetary base. Measures are also agreed to significantly reduce expenditure on the CAP and to double expenditure on the regional and social funds.
	June	The Community and Comecon (the East European trading bloc) sign an agreement enabling the two organisations to recognise each other. As part of the agreement the Comecon states officially recognise, for the first time, the authority of the Community to negotiate on behalf of its member states.
	June	Hanover European Council meeting entrusts to a committee chaired by Jacques Delors the task of studying how the Community might progress to Economic and Monetary Union (EMU).
1989	April	The 'Delors Committee' presents its report (the 'Delors Report'). It outlines a scheme for a three stage progression to EMU.
	June	Third set of direct elections to the EP.
	June	Madrid European Council meeting agrees that Stage 1 of the programme to bring about EMU will begin on 1 July 1990.
	July	Austria applies for Community membership.
	September–December	The collapse of Communist governments in Eastern Europe. The process 'begins' with the appointment of a non-Communist Prime Minister in Poland in September and 'ends' with the overthrow of the Ceausescu regime in Romania in December.
	December	Signing of the fourth Lomé Convention between the Community and 68 ACP countries.
	December	Community and USSR sign a ten year trade and economic cooperation agreement.
	December	Commission advises Council of Ministers to reject Turkey's application for Community membership.
	December	Strasbourg European Council meeting accepts Social Charter and agrees to establish an Intergovernmental Conference (IGC) on EMU at the end of 1990. Both decisions taken by eleven votes to one, with the United Kingdom dissenting in each case.
1990	April	Special Dublin European Council meeting confirms the Community's commitment to Political Union.
	June	Dublin European Council meeting formally agrees that an IGC on Political Union will be convened.
	July	Cyprus and Malta apply for Community membership.

	October	Unification of Germany. Territory of former East Germany becomes part of the Community.
	October	Special Rome European Council meeting agrees that Stage 2 of EMU will begin on 1 January 1994.
	December	The two IGCs on EMU and on Political Union are opened at the Rome summit.
1991	July	Sweden applies for Community membership.
	August–December	Break-up of the USSR
	December	Maastricht European Council meeting agrees to The Treaty on European Union. The Treaty is based on three pillars: the European Communities, a Common Foreign and Security Policy (CFSP), and Cooperation in the Fields of Justice and Home Affairs (JHA). The European Communities pillar includes the strengthening of Community institutions, the extension of the Community's legal policy competence, and a timetable leading to EMU and a single currency.
	December	Association ('Europe') Agreements signed with Czechoslovakia, Hungary, and Poland.
1992	February	Treaty on European Union is formally signed at Maastricht by EC Foreign and Finance Ministers.
	March	Finland applies to join the EU.
	May	After several months delay caused by a Court of Justice ruling, the EEA agreement between the EC and EFTA is signed.
	May	Switzerland applies to join the EC.
	June	In a referendum the Danish people reject the TEU by 50.7 per cent to 49.3 per cent.
	September	Crisis in the ERM. Sterling and the lira suspend their membership.
	September	In a referendum the French people endorse the TEU by 51 per cent to 49 per cent.
	November	Norway applies to join the EU.
	December	In a referendum the Swiss people vote not to ratify the EEA by 50.3 per cent to 49.7 per cent. Amongst other implications this means that Switzerland's application to join the EU is suspended.
	December	Edinburgh European Council meeting agrees on several key issues, notably: (1) Danish opt-outs from the TEU and any future common defence policy; (2) a financial perspective for 1993–9; (3) the opening of accession negotiations in early 1993 with Austria, Finland, Sweden and Norway.
1993	February	Accession negotiations open with Austria, Finland, and Sweden.
	April	Accession negotiations open with Norway.

	May	In a second referendum the Danish people vote by 56.8 per cent to 43.2 per cent to ratify the TEU.
	August	Following great turbulence in the currency markets, the bands for all currencies in the ERM, apart from the deutschmark and the guilder, are increased to 15 per cent.
	October	German Constitutional Court ruling enables Germany to become the last member state to ratify the TEU.
	November	TEU enters into force.
	December	Settlement of the GATT Uruguay Round.
1994	January	Second stage of EMU comes into effect.
	January	EEA enters into force.
	March	Committee of the Regions meets for the first time.
	March	Austria, Finland, Sweden, and Norway agree accession terms with the EU.
	April	Hungary and Poland apply for membership of the EU.
	June	Fourth set of direct elections to the EP.
	June	In a referendum on accession to the EU, Austrian people vote in favour by 66.4 per cent to 33.6 per cent.

Selected Further Reading

■ Reference sources and information guides

A wide variety of reference and information material is available on the European Union. Leaving aside specialist works, the following are among the most useful:

Budd, S.A. and Jones, A.(1991) *The EEC: A Guide to the Maze,* 4th edn (Kogan Page).

Directory of Community Legislation in Force and Other Acts of the Community Institutions (Office for Official Publications of the European Communities, twice yearly).

Documents (Office for Official Publications of the European Communities, monthly plus cumulated and annual catalogues). Lists Commission Documents, EP Reports and ESC Opinions. *Publications of the European Communities* (issued quarterly and annually) is a companion catalogue listing monographs, serials and periodicals issued by the EU institutions. The name of both of these publications has been changed from time to time.

European Access (Chadwyck-Healey, bimonthly). Contains: (a) updating articles; (b) information developments; (c) listings of recent references from a wide range of EU and non-EU documentation.

Europe (Croner, updated monthly). A looseleaf handbook mainly covering EU law – especially as it applies to business.

European Communities Encyclopaedia and Directory (European Publications Ltd, updated annually).

Fallik, A. (ed.) *The European Public Affairs Directory* (Landmarks, updated annually). A comprehensive listing of EU institutions and decision-makers.

Index to Documents of the Commission of the European Communities (Eurofi, annual). A guide to Commission proposals for Council legislation and to reports presented by the Commission to the Council and the EP.

International Organisations Catalogue (HMSO, annual).

Martens, H. (1992) *EC Direct: A Comprehensive Directory of EC Contacts* (Blackwell).

Moussis, N. *Access to Europe* (Euroconfidential, revised annually). A detailed and up-to-date guide to EU policies, laws and programmes.

Myles, G. *EEC Brief* (Locksley Press, updated annually). A handbook, in looseleaf form, covering EU institutions, policies and laws.

Recent Publications on the European Communities (Office for Official Publications of the European Communities, monthly). Compiled by Commis-

457

sion library. Covers EU publications and documents, books from the commercial and academic presses, and articles from certain periodicals.

SCAD Bulletin (Office for Official Publications of the European Communities, weekly). Catalogues principal EU publications and documents, and presents summaries of articles on the EU taken from a wide range of journals and periodicals.

Schraepler, H.A. (1993) *European Handbook of Organisations* (Whurr). Short descriptions of the structure, purposes and activities of most important European organisations and organisations which influence European affairs.

Thomson, I. (1989) *The Documentation of the European Communities* (Mansell). An extensive guide to EC documentation.

Yearbook of the European Communities and of other European Organizations (Editions Delta, annual). Gives an account of the role and structure of EU institutions and of other European organisations. Also gives detailed listings of personnel in these institutions and organisations.

In addition to printed documentation, reference information about the EU is also available on several databases. The best known of these is CELEX, which is the official database of EU law. CELEX is organised into sectors which deal, for example, with the Treaties, secondary legislation, preparatory documentation, and case law of the Court of Justice.

■ Official European Union sources

The EU issues a vast amount of material, from brief information leaflets to weighty reports. Most of this material is available from the Office for Official Publications of the European Communities and/or directly from the appropriate EU institution. A good way of attaining a direct acquaintance of what is available is to browse at a European Documentation Centre (EDC). EDCs receive copies of most of the EU's published documents and are located throughout the member states. Usually they are attached to academic libraries.

Clearly a detailed review of EU publications is not possible here. For that, readers should refer to the various guides and catalogues that were itemised in the previous section. What follows is an outline guide to major publications.

The Treaties establishing the European Union, and especially the *Treaty on European Union* together with the *Treaty Establishing the European Community*, should naturally be consulted by all those who wish to understand the nature and functioning of the EU. They have been published in several editions by, amongst others, the Office for Official Publications of the European Communities and Sweet & Maxwell. The TEU and the EC Treaty can also be found in the *Official Journal of the European Communities*, C224, 31 August 1992.

The *Official Journal of the European Communities* (*OJ*) is issued on most weekdays and provides the authoritative record of decisions and activities of various kinds. It is divided into three series. The 'L' (Legislation) series is the vehicle for the publication of EU legislation. The 'C' (Information and Notices) series contains a range of information, including appointments to advisory committees, minutes of EP plenary proceedings and resolutions adopted by plenaries, ESC opinions, Court of Auditors reports, cases referred to the Court of

Justice and Court judgements, Commission communications and notices, and Commission proposals for Council legislation. The 'S' (Supplement) series is mainly concerned with public contract and tendering announcements. Debates of the EP are published in *Annex. Debates of the European Parliament*. An Index to the 'L' and 'C' series of the *OJ* is available in monthly and annual editions.

The monthly *Bulletin of the European Communities* provides a general account of most significant developments. Some of the information contained amounts to a summary of material included in the *OJ* (with appropriate references). Much else is additional: there are, for example, reports – albeit rather brief ones – of Council of Ministers meetings; there are updates on policy developments; there is a monitoring of progress in the annual budgetary cycle; and there is information on initiatives, meetings and agreements in the sphere of external relations.

The *General Report on the Activities of the European Communities* is published annually and provides an excellent summary of both institutional and policy developments. Where necessary it can be supplemented by the annual reports that are also published by most of the institutions.

Information about the annual budget is available in the *Bulletin* and in the *General Report*. The full budget, which runs to about 1800 pages of text, is published in the *OJ* (L series) about one month after it has been approved by the EP. A useful publication is *The Community Budget: the Facts in Figures*, which usually appears on an annual basis.

The most detailed analysis and information about EU policies is usually to be found in documentation produced by the Commission. Leaving aside one-off publications, this appears in three main forms. First, in serialised reports which are issued on a regular basis and which cover just about every aspect of EU affairs. As an indication of the sort of reports that are produced four might be mentioned: *European Economy* covers economic trends and proposals and is issued quarterly, with monthly supplements; *Social Europe* provides information on the many facets of social and employment policy and is issued three times a year; *Eurobarometer* reports on public opinion in the EU and appears twice a year; and the *Agricultural Situation in the Community* is an annual report. Second, an enormous volume of information is issued by the Statistical Office: on matters ranging from energy consumption patterns to agricultural prices. *Europe in Figures*, which appears every couple of years or so, is a useful general publication. All Statistical Office publications carry the *Eurostat* logo imprint. Third, there are Commission Documents (COMDOCS) which are made up principally of monitoring reports, policy reviews, and – most importantly – proposals for Council and EP and Council legislation.

Useful material stemming from other institutions on a regular basis includes: *Reports, Dossiers,* and *Research Documents* of the EP; the monthly *Bulletin of the ESC*; and *Reports of Cases Before the Court*.

Finally, it is worth mentioning that a number of EU publications are available without charge. Most of these are rather slight and are intended primarily for those who know very little about the EU, but some do go beyond basics and can be used to build up a useful collection. All of the institutions, for example, produce pamphlets or booklets describing how they are organised and what they do. The *European File* series – which is available from the Office for Official Publications of the European Communities – consists of around twenty pamphlets per year covering a variety of topics. The *European Documentation* series – which is also available from the Office for Official Publications – consists of four or five quite substantial booklets per year on a range of EU matters.

■ Other useful sources

The governments of the member states produce a considerable volume of documentation on the EU. The precise nature of this material varies from state to state, but mostly it consists of a mixture of 'state of play' reports, reports from relevant parliamentary committees, and information pamphlets/booklets/packs. Because many of the latter are intended to stimulate a greater public awareness about the EU, or are designed to encourage business to take advantage of EU policies, they are often available free of charge.

Several sources contain detailed and regular updating and monitoring of information about the work of the EU. A daily bulletin of events is provided by *Europe* – commonly known as *Agence Europe* – which is published by Agence Internationale D'Information Pour La Presse. *European Report*, which is published by Europe Information Service, also provides a detailed monitoring of events, in its case on a twice-weekly basis.

In most member states the 'quality' press provides a reasonable review of EU affairs. In the United Kingdom the most comprehensive coverage is to be found in the *Financial Times*.

Academic articles on the EU are to be found in a number of places. Particularly useful academic journals include the *Journal of Common Market Studies*, the *Journal of European Public Policy,* the *Journal of European Integration*, *Common Market Law Review*, and *European Law Review*.

Two annual reviews of the EU are: Nugent, N. (ed.) *The European Union: Annual Review of Activities* (Blackwell; this also appears as a fifth issue of the *Journal of Common Market Studies*); and Ludlow, P. *et al.*, (eds) *The Annual Review of European Community Affairs* (Brassey).

■ Books on the European Union

The number of books published on the EU is now voluminous. Since only a brief indication of what is available can be attempted here, references have been confined to texts in English and preference has tended to be given to recent publications. The titles listed are grouped into broad sections but it must be emphasised that the boundaries between the sections are far from watertight. Comments on books are entered only where particularly distinctive features apply.

☐ *Historical development and the dynamics of the integration process*

Archer, C. (1994) *Organizing Europe: The Institutions of Integration* (Edward Arnold). Looks at the development and functioning not just of the EU but also of the other main European organisations.

Arter, D. (1993) *The Politics of European Integration in the Twentieth Century* (Dartmouth).

Burgess, M. (1989) *Federalism and European Union* (Routledge).

Corbett, R. (1993) *The Treaty of Maastricht: From Conception to Ratification* (Longman).

Hallstein, W. (1972) *Europe in the Making* (Allen & Unwin). Now largely outdated, but useful in capturing the idealism that characterised many of the Community's founders.

Joll, J. (1990) *Europe Since 1870*, 4th edn (Penguin).

Milward, A.S. (1984) *The Reconstruction of Western Europe 1945–51* (Methuen).

Milward, A.S. (1992) *The European Rescue of the Nation-State* (Routledge). Both of these books by Milward contain detailed analyses of the post-war years that challenge some aspects of the interpretations of the 'standard' accounts.

Monnet, J. (1978) *Memoirs* (Collins). The memoirs of the 'father' of West European integration.

Nicholson, F. and East, R. (1987) *From the Six to the Twelve: the Enlargement of the European Communities* (Longman).

Pollard, S. (1981) *The Integration of the European Economy since 1815* (Allen & Unwin).

Pryce, R. (1987) *The Dynamics of European Union* (Croom Helm).

Urwin, D.W. (1989) *Western Europe Since 1945*, 4th edn (Longman).

Urwin, D.W. (1991) *The Community of Europe: A History of European Integration Since 1945* (Longman).

Wallace, W. (1992) *The Dynamics of European Integration* (Pinter).

Weigall, D. and Stirk, P. (1992) *The Origins and Development of the European Community* (Leicester University Press). A useful collection of extracts from primary sources.

☐ *General books on the government and politics of the European Union*

Archer, C. and Butler, F. (1992) *The European Community: Structure and Process* (Pinter Publishers).

Butler, M. (1986) *Europe: More Than a Continent* (Heinemann). An 'insider' account, by the former UK Permanent Representative.

Dinan, D. (1994) *Ever Closer Union? An Introduction to the European Community* (Macmillan).

George, S. (1991) *Politics and Policy in the European Community*, 2nd edn (Oxford University Press).

Holland, M. (1993) *European Community Integration* (Pinter Publishers).

Keohane, R.O. and Hoffman, S. (1991) *The New European Community* (Westview Press).

Laffan, B. (1992) *Integration and Co-operation in Europe* (Routledge).

Nicoll, W. and Salmon, T.C. (1994) *Understanding the New European Community* 2nd edn (Harvester Wheatsheaf).

Sbragia, A. (ed.) (1993) *Euro-Politics: Institutions and Policymaking in the 'New' European Community* (The Brookings Institution).

Taylor, P. (1983) *The Limits of European Integration* (Croom Helm).

Tugendhat, C. (1986) *Making Sense of Europe* (Viking). Another 'insider' account, this time by a former Budget Commissioner.

☐ *Institutions and actors*

Not many books focus exclusively on particular EU institutions and actors. Many of the sources listed in other sections of this bibliography do, however, contain relevant chapters and sections.

Bassompierre, G. de (1988) *Changing the Guard in Brussels: An Insider's View of the EC Presidency* (Praeger).
Bulmer, S. and Wessels, W. (1987) *The European Council* (Macmillan).
Greenwood, J. *et al.* (eds) (1992) *Organized Interests and the European Community* (Sage).
Jacobs, F. and Corbett, R. (1992) *The European Parliament*, 2nd edn (Longman).
Jenkins, R. (1981) *European Diary 1977–1981* (Collins). An 'insider' view by the former President of the Commission. Gives an excellent flavour of the many informal processes at work in Brussels.
Kirchner, E. (1992) *Decision-Making in the European Community: The Council Presidency and European Integration* (Manchester University Press).
Mazey, S. and Richardson, J. (1993) *Lobbying in the European Community* (Oxford University Press).
Siedentopf, H. and Ziller, J. (1988) *Making European Policies Work: The Implementation of Community Legislation in the Member States,* 2 vols (Sage).

☐ *The Court of Justice and European Union law*

Brown, L.N. (1989) *The Court of Justice of the European Communities*, 3rd edn (Sweet & Maxwell).
Hartley, T.C. (1989) *The Foundations of European Community Law,* 2nd edn (Clarendon Press).
Kapteyn, P.J.G. and Verloren van Themaat, P. (1989) *Introduction to the Law of the European Communities*, 2nd edn edited by L.W. Gormley, (Kluwer).
Lasok, D. and Bridge, J.W. (1991) *Law and Institutions of the European Communities*, 5th edn (Butterworths).
Mathijsen, P.S.M.F. (1990) *A Guide to European Community Law*, 5th edn (Sweet & Maxwell).
Millet, T. (1990) *The Court of First Instance of the European Communities* (Butterworths).
O'Keefe, D. and Twomey, P.M. (eds) (1994) *Legal Issues of the Maastricht Treaty* (Chancery).
Shaw, J. (1993) *European Community Law* (Macmillan).
Snyder, F. (1991) *New Directions in European Community Law* (Weidenfeld & Nicolson).
Tillotson, J. (1993) *European Community Law: Text, Cases and Materials* (Cavendish Publishing).

Weatherill, S. and Beaumont, P. (1993) *EC Law: The Essential Guide to the Legal Workings of the European Community*, (Penguin).

Wyatt, D. and Dashwood, A. (1993) *European Community Law* (Sweet & Maxwell).

☐ Policies and policy-making

Preference has been given in this section to books which examine not only policy content but also policy processes.

Andersen, S.S. and Eliassen, K.A. (1993) *Making Policy in Europe* (Sage).

El-Agraa, A.M. (1990) *The Economics of the European Community*, 3rd edn (Philip Allan).

Featherstone, K. and Ginberg, R. (1993) *The United States and the European Community in the 1990s: Partners in Transition* (Macmillan).

Gold, M. (1993) *The Social Dimension: Employment Policy in the European Community* (Macmillan).

Grilli, E. (1993) *The European Community and the Developing Countries* (Cambridge University Press).

Gros, D. and Thygesen, N. (1992) *European Monetary Integration* (Longman).

Harrop, J. (1992) *The Political Economy of Integration in the European Community*, 2nd edn (Elgar).

Holland, M. (1991) *The Future of European Political Cooperation* (Macmillan).

Ifestos, P. (1987) *European Political Co-operation* (Avebury).

Lefferink, J.D. (1993) (ed.) *European Integration and Environmental Policy* (Belhaven).

Lodge, J. (ed.) (1994) *The European Community and the Challenge of the Future*, 2nd edn (Pinter Publishers).

Meny, Y. and Wright, V. (1987) *The Politics of Steel* (Walter de Gruyter).

Moyer, H.W. and Josling, T.E. (1990) *Agricultural Policy Reform: Politics and Process in the EC and the USA* (Iowa State University Press).

Nuttall, S.J. (1992) *European Political Co-operation* (Clarendon Press).

Shackleton, M. (1990) *Financing the European Community* (Pinter).

Swann, D. (1992) *The Economics of the Common Market*, 7th edn (Penguin).

Tsoukalis, L. (1993) *The New European Economy: The Politics and Economics of Integration*, 2nd edn (Oxford University Press).

Wise, M. and Gibb, R. (1993) *Single Market to Social Europe: The European Community in the 1990s* (Longman).

☐ Member states and the European Union

Pinter Publishers have produced a useful series of books which examines the costs and benefits of EC membership on the member states. Amongst the books in the series are:

Bulmer, S. *et al.* (eds) (1992) *The United Kingdom and EC Membership Evaluated*.

Dreyfus, F. (ed.) (1993) *France and EC Membership Evaluated*.

Francioni, F. (ed.) (1992) *Italy and EC Membership Evaluated*.

Keatinge, P. (ed.) (1991) *Ireland and EC Membership Evaluated*.

Lyck, L. (ed.) (1992) *Denmark and EC Membership Evaluated*.

Meerhaeghe, M.A.G. van, (ed.) (1992) *Belgium and EC Membership Evaluated*.

Schweitzer, C.C. and Karsten, D. (eds) (1990) *Federal Republic of Germany and EC Membership Evaluated*.

Wolters, M. and Coffey, P. (1990) *The Netherlands and EC Membership Evaluated*.

Other useful books on the EU and its member states include:

Bulmer, S. and Paterson, W. (1987) *The Federal Republic of Germany and the European Community* (Allen & Unwin).

George, S. (1990) *An Awkward Partner: Britain in the European Community* (Oxford University Press).

George, S. (ed.) (1992) *Britain and the European Community: the Politics of Semi-Detachment* (Clarendon Press).

Kelstrup, M. (ed.) (1992) *European Integration and Denmark's Participation* (Copenhagen Political Studies Press).

Index